D1269977

· *Making the Empire Work* ·

ALISON GILBERT OLSON

Making the Empire Work

LONDON AND AMERICAN INTEREST GROUPS 1690–1790

·

HARVARD UNIVERSITY PRESS

CAMBRIDGE, MASSACHUSETTS

LONDON, ENGLAND

1992

This book is printed on acid-free paper, and its binding
materials have been chosen for strength and durability.

Library of Congress Cataloging-in-Publication Data

Olson, Alison Gilbert.
Making the empire work :
London and American interest groups, 1690–1790 /
Alison Gilbert Olson.
p.   cm.
Includes bibliographical references and index.
ISBN 0-674-54318-1
1. Pressure groups—United States—History.
2. United States—Politics and government—
Colonial period, ca. 1600–1775.
3. Pressure groups—Great Britain—History.   I. Title.
JK1118.O37   1992
322.4'3'0973—dc20   91-38360
CIP

FOR

ELLIKA, SEVERIN, AND SANDER

Acknowledgments

This book has been so long in the making that I am sure some of my friends wondered if it would ever see completion. For many of them, as for the institutions that gave me financial assistance and the library staffs who gave aid in the research, supporting this project was an act of faith, and for that faith I have many "thank you's" to offer.

My thanks first to several foundations that contributed financial help: the John Simon Guggenheim Foundation, the American Council of Learned Societies, and the General Research Board and the Research Center for Arts and Humanities at the University of Maryland.

I thank the friends who shared their time and research and made helpful comments. Horace Samuel Merrill and Nancy Struna read and commented invaluably on the whole manuscript. Jon Butler, Thomas Dorflinger, John Hemphill, Richard Johnson, Jon Kukla, Mary Lou Lustig, Jacob Price, George Rogers, Ian Steele, Pat Warren, Steve Webb, Renate Wilson, and Marianne Wokeck gave me the benefit of their advice, their information, or both. Participants in the Philadelphia Center for Early American Studies and the Washington Seminar on American History helpfully discussed sections of the manuscript, and members of the Maryland Seminar on Early American History kindly offered suggestions.

Librarians at Colonial Williamsburg, the Presbyterian Historical Society, the Haverford College Library, the Folger Library, the Library of Congress, and the Historical Societies of Virginia, New York, Massachusetts, Pennsylvania, and Maryland in the United States, and in London at the Friends Library, Lambeth Palace Library, Archives of the Society for the Propagation of the Gospel, Dr. Williams' Library, Public Record Office, House of Lords Record Office, Messrs. Coults and Company, the Bodleian Library, Oxford, and the Dartmouth Manuscripts at

Staffordshire certainly deserve my thanks for help given me in person and for providing microfilms.

Finally, Ellika, Severin, and Sander know, I hope, why they deserve a page in the book to themselves.

Contents

Preface

More than half a century ago Charles McLean Andrews published the first of his four great volumes, *The Colonial Period of American History.* The range of his interests was vast, and his Anglo-American vision awesome in its breadth, but his focus was on two subjects, the politics of imperial administration and the indigenous recreation of English customs and institutions in America. Andrews had no doubt at all that "the time must come when this duality of interest (England and America) will be regarded as a necessary part of the stock in trade of every serious writer on the subject who deals with it in a fair minded and comprehensive way";[1] he assumed that his interpretation was not simply a new synthesis of American history but *the* approach that all future historians would adopt.

Even in Andrews's lifetime, however, it was becoming clear that serious writers on the subject of American colonial history were not flocking to follow his interpretations; despite his genuinely wide-ranging approach he was being tagged a narrowly institutional historian. His own *Guides to the Sources for Colonial History in British Archives* emphasized governmental sources; his critics charged him with assuming that all changes in the colonies were imposed by British authority;[2] and even the *festschrift* prepared by his graduate students on his retirement was heavy on administrative history.[3]

Following his death Andrews's work came to be associated even more exclusively with imperial administration, after a number of scholars examined English institutions transplanted to the New World and found that they did not function the same way here as they did in England. As the scope of his work was being deflated to the study of imperial institutions, both "imperial" and "institutional" history themselves went into decline, with the increasing use of social history and the collapse of existing empires. Plagued by disinterest in empire and its institutions and by assumptions that English society was not recreated in the colonies as Andrews said it was, imperial studies languished in the 1940s, 1950s, and 1960s, not quite dead, but certainly comatose.

In the last few years, however, scholars have tried to revive such studies with increasing success. Some researchers who would never dream of calling themselves "imperial" students are discovering that some seventeenth-century American institutions—the family, the courts, the assemblies, for example—imitated their English counterparts fairly successfully. Other historians are finding that patterns of communication, trade, and cultural exchange indicate that there really was an English Atlantic World in the seventeenth and eighteenth centuries. Still others have taken up directly where Andrews left off, greatly broadening the imperial approach to allow the Americans some influence on imperial decisions in particular periods. Richard Johnson has described "a remarkable revival . . . of the Anglo American approach to the history of this period,"[4] and David Lovejoy has exulted, "the empire is back."[5]

It is back, indeed. But if it is to flourish, I think we must reorient ourselves and take off in a direction slightly different from the one pointed out by Andrews. We should be less concerned about how the empire was structured than about how it actually worked. I would even go so far as to suggest in retrospect that Andrews's institutional history ran into trouble because part of it didn't ring true. For all his masterly efforts to take his readers vicariously into the antechambers of the Board of Trade to share the worries of members and people who had business with them, Andrews failed to grasp fully the mindset of the seventeenth and eighteenth-century politician-administrator. He never really divested himself of his twentieth-century preconception about the ways administrators faced their problems and the ways in which they expected decisions to be carried out; he never quite conveyed that the stairways of seventeenth-century Whitehall were not the corridors of power in the twentieth century. Had he been as interested in function as he was in structure, he would have realized even more sharply than he did that by twentieth-century standards the number of British administrators in the American colonies was minuscule, their communication with their superiors minimal, and their resources for enforcing the law equally so. Any royal adviser worth his salt would have these points in mind when he made recommendations to the King. It was all very well to think of the ways in which the colonies should contribute to the mother country, but a policy that did not "work" in the colonies was useless.

My own book came out of a curiosity about just how the empire did work. Lacking most of the formal apparatus we now associate with empire, the first British Empire nevertheless did hold together for over a century and a half. How did it manage? I found part of the answer in the informal connections which supplemented the formal institutional ties Andrews described, and particularly in mercantile, ecclesiastical, and ethnic interest groups that had corresponding "branches" in London and the various colonies. They were what we now call "voluntary associations"; they were virtually nonexistent when colonial settlement began, flourished during the golden years of the empire, and suffered paralysis in the last fifteen years before the American Revolution. In their finest years the Londoners served as lobbyists for their colonial colleagues, arranging preferential treatment for their colonial associates in exchange for information about colonial conditions and assistance in winning colonial compliance with other decisions.

I uncovered, or at least I think I uncovered, something of a "rise and fall" story, though in telling the tale I had delicate choices to make and came up, inevitably, with a wish list that remains just that. I wanted to sketch the pattern so this remains a sketch, with some incidents and interests slighted—left, I hope, to the work of future researchers. In my eagerness to convey the remarkable development of the relations between interests in London and America, I have also had to limit the amount of attention I could pay to the rich political culture in which they functioned. In the interest of length I have even had to give short shrift to other interests and to the Boards of Treasury and Customs before which the interest groups did function, although I have worked in their papers. My wish list is extensive. I wish it were possible to assess with greater accuracy the numbers of cases that came before various branches of government. I wish it were possible to state with more precision what proportion of colonists—and what ranks—belonged to lobbies with transatlantic connections and were affected by their work. I wish that I had more case studies I could follow through all their stages, from the colonial churches, taverns, and coffee houses where requests for help were formulated, to the appropriate places in London where the requests were received and strategy mapped out, to the relevant government offices, and then back again as the Londoners explained to their colonial correspondents what they had done. All I can do is suggest how this probably happened and hope that future researchers might be inspired to draw up wish lists of their own—and see them fulfilled.

· *Making the Empire Work* ·

Introduction

For over a hundred and fifty years before they rebelled, American colonists were loyal subjects of the British monarch: they toasted the kings and queens at civic feasts, celebrated royal milestones with holiday salutes, and reiterated their obedience in public addresses and private correspondence. Such loyalty cannot be explained by coercion: throughout the colonial period the number of British officials in the colonies was pitifully small, and the military or police force to back them up was virtually nonexistent (the Revolution occurred only after the British began trying to put teeth into their colonial administration). Neither can American loyalty be explained away as purely ceremonial by arguing that the colonists enjoyed *de facto* autonomy within the empire and paid little attention to British authority. Quite to the contrary, Americans sent provincial laws to England for review, accepted governors and councillors appointed in England, paid customs duties, generally obeyed the Navigation Acts, and contributed men and money to imperial conflicts. By eighteenth-century standards theirs was not a bad record of compliance.

Why was it then that colonists numbering over two million by 1770 submitted with relatively little complaint to a government overseas and a handful of its local representatives? Does the answer lie in the weakness of local institutions and the absence of a "continental" orientation, which combined to make it unthinkable for the colonists to organize a rebellion and then exist as a separate government? Did the growing internal tensions make colonial elites reluctant to challenge British authority for fear of seeing their own position challenged by local groups? Were the colonists in thrall to custom, culture, emulation and habit—to the feeling of Englishness? One looks for all of these of course. But I find another explanation worth examining here: in the heyday of the empire substantial numbers of Americans identified with English interest groups and through them had an informal but effective voice in the making of English decisions that affected them; they cooperated with the British government because they were getting what they wanted out of it. Let me suggest briefly the contours of my argument.

.   .   .

The term "interest group" is so difficult of definition that scholars have not reached any agreement on its meaning. We will make do with this synthesis of various interpretations: "A group of individuals conscious of sharing a common concern, operating on the borders of power, and seeking to increase their own benefits through bargaining with a political system they accept and influence but do not attempt to control."[1]

Within this general definition fit several kinds of interest groups, classified very roughly through stages from traditional to modern. Between 1640 and 1790, the dates of this study, four different types of interests existed in London. The first two—"ascriptive" and "institutional"—were there when the period opened, only to become eclipsed by the third type, the associational (voluntary interests, the subject of this study) as the period went on. The last kind of interest to develop in the era, the public opinion lobby, appeared only toward the end of the eighteenth century.

The ascriptive type was composed of kinship groups whose negotiations with political authorities were handled primarily by patriarchal leaders. Ascriptive interests included especially the families of the nobility, which were becoming almost extinct and inoperative in London when the seventeenth century began.

Most of the other early interests were what we would now call institutional, that is, based on formally organized and legally chartered institutions—guilds, town corporations, universities, trading companies, and the like, and probably the Church of England. Their membership, with the exception of the Church of England, was deliberately restricted. The groups were accountable to local or national authorities for the politically responsible behavior of members, and they came up with financial gifts or loans when monarchs needed them, in trade for a monopoly of souls or markets.[2] In return for these services the interests' main demand was to be left alone to manage local affairs without interference. They were "semiautonomous collectivities [that] carried on their own public affairs relatively free from outside intrusion"[3] and expected to be left that way.

With the exception of the Church of England, London institutional interests shared one other characteristic: they were identified with a particular locality, in this case London itself.[4] This was clearly true of the City government; it was also true of the guilds, most of which had monopoly privileges which were legally limited to an area within a few miles of the City walls.[5] The emerging mercantile companies were London-based, for though they might have subscribers outside the City, the company organizations were solely in the City and their directors were by and large full-time London residents.[6] The one possible exception to this might be the Merchant Adventurers, who had branches in some of the outports, but there was continual strife among them, and most of the outport branches claimed local autonomy.

There was no place among institutional interests for American groups. The early colonists were not run by a trading company and they did not have ties with the established church. They did have their own embryonic institutional interests in the form of assemblies, but those legislatures were so bogged down with meeting the expenses of settlement and defense that they could not begin to consider the kind of gifts to the crown that English institutional interests could consider.

The third type of interest group, the associational, was identified by the purely voluntary character of its membership; it did have room for colonial participation. Associational interests included groups like Presbyterians, Jews, Lutherans, Quakers, Baptists, Huguenots, rudimentary labor organizations, and the merchant groups meeting at coffee houses. Almost nonexistent at the beginning of the period, this type developed quickly alongside the other two and by the end of the seventeenth century had largely, though not entirely, displaced them. In 1600, for example, virtually all hundred London churches were Anglican; in 1690 no churches, not even the Anglican—could claim a monopoly in any part of the City.[7] In 1600 one French church was adequate for Huguenot emigrants in the City; a century later something over 15,000 people, at least 3 percent of London's population, were non-English and required many churches.[8] In 1600 there was scarcely a coffee house for merchants in the city; in 1700 there were dozens.[9]

The voluntary nature of the associational interests shaped both their political needs and their political resources. Since it was relatively easy to join them and also easy to leave, these groups had less coercive power over their members than the older groups had. Lacking the coercive power to extract money from members, they could not expect to make financial contributions to the government; they relied instead primarily on their access to vital information and their growing electoral influence when bargaining with the government. They sought from government not a monopoly of particular political authority, trade, or souls, but rather a guarantee that they might safely participate in a competitive environment. All the groups—independent merchants competing for influence against mercantile companies, foreign minorities opposed by city corporations, dissenting churches opposed by the Church of England, craftsmen opposed by the guilds—needed in some way the protection of the national government against the hostility of local authorities. Mercantile groups, in addition, particularly needed government help on problems the large trading companies would have handled themselves, such as building lighthouses, sending convoys, and negotiating trade treaties. On the whole they were far more typical of modern interests than the more traditional interests of Elizabethan England.

At the end of the period yet another type of group emerged, one that would have been unthinkable a century and a half earlier. This was the public opinion lobby, begun with the somewhat disreputable Wilkeite movement and made respectable by later organizations like the anti-slavery society. Unlike the earlier interests, the public opinion lobby claimed to speak for large sections of the public; instead of protection and help for particular groups it sought major changes of policy, and it did not use information and local electoral influence to develop coop-erative relations with the government, but rather mobilized public opin-ion often hostile to the government. Indeed, there were considerable questions about whether it should be considered an interest group at all and whether its methods were legitimate models; it was over those very questions that the existing associational interests were to develop near-fatal divisions.

.   .   .

It was during the seventeenth century, well before the gathering of comparable groups in the English provinces, that a variety of voluntary interest groups took root in London, not all, of course, having anything to do with the American colonies. The City grew with unprecedented speed, and interest groups with potential American connections grew at the same time. From a handful at mid-century, they expanded to include about 2,000 overseas merchants, 15,000 non-English residents, and 20,000 dissenters by 1700. Since the death rate in the City was higher than the birth rate, the population increase must have come in good measure from European and provincial migration into the City.[10] The new interests were disproportionately drawn from the new immigrants: colonial trades, for example, fell largely to men who had migrated to London from elsewhere because established London merchants were not interested in going into those trades.[11] The same new merchants became leaders of the Independent churches, and, indeed, it is rational to assume that the rank-and-file members of the City's Puritan (later dissenting) churches came from groups of provincial villagers who found their local numbers too small to constitute a viable group and moved to the capital in search of numerical support. And certainly London's position as the stopping-off place for new immigrants planning to settle at various places in England would suggest, again, its strength as a focal point for non-English groups.

Members of similar interest groups appear to have begun collecting in London neighborhoods and to have been meeting very informally early in the century, but as late as the 1630s their meetings—probably in churches, counting houses, at lectures, and in private homes—were still scarcely visible. Small numbers account for part of their obscurity, but it also resulted from the efforts of hostile institutional interests in the City working hand in hand with Charles I to suppress them.[12] The King and the bishops controlled 80 percent of London's ecclesiastical patronage, for example, and Puritans there were strictly supervised before 1640. Similarly, London was the center of opposition to non-English (not "foreign": this category included emigrants from the English counties as well as immigrants from outside England[13]) immigration. It was the center of anti-immigration riots; London workers, tradesmen, and merchants regarded London as the natural place where foreigners would stop and not move on and felt particularly threatened by non-English competition.

In the same vein, the established London merchants were the most likely to oppose the new communities of independent merchants. This was most notable in the case of the Virginia Company. By the beginning of the seventeenth century merchants from the larger companies, especially the Merchant Adventurers, had worked their way into the various London companies and through the companies had come to dominate the City government. Some of the same men had participated in the original Virginia Company. When the old Virginia Company was dissolved in 1624, some of its members transferred their interests to other companies and some continued to try to win the Company's charter back. None was happy about encouraging the new men, from outside London, to carry on the Virginia trade as individuals. The members of the original Virginia Company continued to work in Parliament and the Privy Council to revive the Company's monopoly, while the interlopers' enemies denied them political influence in the City.

For the first decades of the seventeenth century London's voluntary interests were weak enough to be easily discouraged, not to say stifled, by a City government dominated by their opponents. During the Interregnum of 1640 to 1660, however, when first Parliament and then Oliver Cromwell virtually forced the City to allow them to function openly, they were given sufficient encouragement to withstand the restoration of royalist power in the City with Charles II's return to the throne in 1660. Thereafter the voluntary associations grew rapidly in numbers, wealth, and organization[14] as merchants gathered to share information about the rapidly expanding overseas trade, for example; as artisans organized for mutual aid and resistance to guild control; and as churches assembled to define doctrine, provide legal defense for fellow Englishmen, or allocate charity to refugees from continental persecution. The more active members began meeting at coffee houses (and merchants at the Royal Exchange); from these meetings in turn emerged core groups of recognized leaders, and some of the meetings even produced formal structures like the Yearly Meeting of Quakers or the French Committee of Huguenots. Gradually the independent dissenting (formerly Puritan) merchants were able to buy their way into City companies; this, along with declining royalist support for the old City fathers, allowed the newer merchants to insinuate themselves into City politics and by the end of the century to dominate them.

As the danger from City intermediaries subsided, the voluntary interests began cautiously to develop potential resources for approaching the national government directly. They discovered some electoral power, particularly in areas where their members could serve as swing voters; they were able to keep order among their own members and keep them away from popular tumults; and they could tap into information the government needed. The last resource was particularly important since both kings and Parliament were beginning to recognize the need for more systematic collection of information. As late as 1688, however, monarchs still continued to make important decisions during private conferences with individual courtiers who happened to catch their ear, so it was not yet possible for interests to develop regular, stable ways of exerting political influence. That was left for interests and politicians to achieve after the Glorious Revolution.

The Revolution settlement opened up government to the lobbying of associational interest groups. Competitive, cooperative, overlapping: a multitude of new interests came into English politics at the end of the seventeenth century, some domestic (the American colonists learned the strength of groups like the hatters and the ironmongers) some with foreign connections (the Society for the Propagation of Christian Knowledge, or S.P.C.K.) some representing other parts of the empire (the Irish and West Indians were strong), some active (the Virginia merchants met almost daily for political strategy) some relatively inactive (the Dutch community in London undertook surprisingly little political work at this time).

The interests lobbied with all parts of government, some more comfortably at one level than another. It is risky to generalize, but craft and agricultural interests seem to have preferred going to Parliament, while ethnic groups understandably did better with the monarchs. As government edged away from backstairs negotiations to more open decision-making, many of the new interests focused on burgeoning administrative boards and committees peopled by a new breed of bureaucrat. Government boards grew rapidly, staffed by men who realized—far more than had their Restoration predecessors—the need for system, openness, access to information in decision-making if the expanded government functions were to be both reasonable and palatable to British subjects. They were prepared to be responsive to interest group demands in exchange for cooperation.

The influence of a number of interest groups peaked in the years 1721 to 1754. A triumvirate of leaders—Sir Robert Walpole, Henry Pelham, and the Duke of Newcastle—was almost continuously in office during this time, and the interest group leaders were able to establish long-lasting and cordial relationships with them. The lobbyists' main resources continued to be information, electoral influence, and an ability to keep the lid on their more volatile members, and they made far more systematic use of these in the eighteenth than the seventeenth century. Aware that the country's stability, however prolonged, was always fragile, the ministers welcomed information and advice from spokesmen who could warn them away from popularly unacceptable decisions.

Londoners were willing to use the influence they had developed not only for themselves but on behalf of colleagues in the English and American provinces. Cooperation with English provincial interests began first: almost as soon as the London interests started to grow, they and the English provincials developed networks of cooperation. Sometimes the English provincial groups developed spontaneously, sometimes they were organized from other counties, sometimes they originated in a kind of diasporan movement of families from one town to others.

Whatever their origin, many of them found it natural to form voluntary connections with corresponding groups in other towns for the pursuit of shared objectives. The circulation of information was one such objective, indicated, for example, by the Quaker system of visitors who traveled from one meeting to another, Baptist "messengers" who held together a group of churches,[15] the Independents' "friendship networks,"[16] mercantile agents hired by merchants of one town to solicit opinions of merchants in other. Facilitation of migration was another shared objective: London Quakers helped Friends from the English provinces to migrate throughout the North Atlantic world, while London Huguenots helped coreligionists migrate into the English provinces from Europe.[17] The need for concerted political action, revealed by several widespread petitioning campaigns run by agricultural and craftsmen's associations, was on occasion the direct incentive for some kind of networking. The encouragement of mutual trade was another concern: Huguenots, Quakers, and Jews, to mention a few groups, all established trade networks linking the English provinces to London and the overseas world. All the groups, moreover, shared an awareness of the need for the government's protection against the established interests, whose authority they were often defying.

Rarely did these networks develop national organizations. They remained loose collections of local interests. But increasingly Londoners became the most important members; indeed, the London groups became focal points for the networks to which they belonged. London was certainly the best place through which the networks could exert political influence on the national government. It was where their organizational strength was forged in the battles with older interests over the course of the seventeenth century. Their position close to the government offices in Westminster enabled Londoners to find out about relevant issues faster than provincial groups did, handle day-to-day issues quickly, and deal comparatively easily with members of Parliament and officers of state. Londoners could call upon and entertain politicians more easily than their provincial fellows; Londoners could distribute published materials in Whitehall and in the galleries of Parliament. Londoners could also use—or control—mob action to greater effect: a politician might read about riots in Bristol or Whitehaven, but he might feel them in London. Conversely, the London interests' control over their members' behavior was more important to the national government than was the comparable control of provincial interests.

One of the main weapons of the new interest groups—possibly the main one—was information, and here the Londoners enjoyed decisive superiority over provincial groups. Over the second half of the seventeenth century London's population had to draw more and more on national suppliers of food and fuel to support itself; one of the corollaries of this was that roads had to be built between London and provincial supply centers so that all the merchants could travel them. There is considerable disagreement about just how much English transportation improved over the seventeenth century. But from the mid-century on, when turnpikes were being built, London became the hub from which the six great roads radiated. New roads, along with the new system of stagecoaches, made travel to London far easier than it had been before.[18] Improved transportation between London and the provinces made it easier for provincial representatives to attend meetings in London than in other parts of the country. It also made it easier for country couriers to bring messages from the provinces. London thus became a clearinghouse for information from provincial interests, giving them access to material that the government often needed.

If transportation improvements made London a convenient center for collecting information from the provinces, they also made London a natural source for disseminating information to the provinces. At least as early as 1643, some London religious groups other than the Church of England had their own printing press, or access to one, and some of the new mercantile leaders were getting pamphlets or news sheets printed. The same couriers or representatives who brought country news to the City could return to the provinces with printed tracts from City interests.[19]

Precisely because the English networks were loose, it was possible for London interests to extend their influence and connections beyond England and to include among their provincial associates the primitive interest groups that were beginning to emerge in the American colonies, but this happened very slowly. Since most colonial churches were offshoots of English denominations, since many colonial export merchants had to have English correspondents, and since a number of nonEnglish groups in the colonies had arrived via London where members stayed long enough to develop English friendships, one would have expected a close connection between Londoners and American provincial interests to have existed from the beginnings of colonial settlement. But it did not.

The American interests that were visible by 1690 were about a generation younger than their English counterparts, and they were, on the whole, too immature to cultivate English associations. They were too unstable, too divided, and too poor to concern themselves much with London politics. They were too preoccupied with getting organized and establishing a safe place for themselves in provincial politics to realize that London interests could help on both counts. Many of them did not at first see a natural affinity of interest with the relevant English groups. New England merchants would think twice before seeking political help from London merchants, whom they accused of supporting unpalatable trade regulations. New England Puritan leaders, left adrift after 1660, were not sure where among the mutable English dissenting interests they should seek help. On those few occasions when American interests had to appeal issues to London, they either appealed directly or sought help from highly placed individuals. The Americans' reluctance to send information, together with the Restoration monarchs' preference for discussing American affairs only when closeted with a few courtiers, meant that the newly forming English interests had little occasion to approach the government on American questions. Lacking their contribution, the governments of Charles II and James II undertook experiments in American regulation with inadequate information from the colonies themselves. The Americans, lacking consistent voices at Whitehall, could do little else than react, on their own and after the fact, acquiescing in or resisting decisions already made.

It was not until the quarter-century after the Glorious Revolution that

American interest groups developed the resources and the motivation to utilize the help of London interests. In the years after 1689 some of the American churches, ethnic communities, and mercantile associations grew in numbers, wealth, organization, and confidence enough to initiate correspondence with appropriate London groups and seek their political assistance. The London lobbies were now in a good position to give it: as his chief advisory body on imperial government William III in 1696 set up the Board of Trade whose members, caught up in the new bureaucratic enthusiasm for information-gathering, were eager to exchange favors for whatever intelligence on colonial conditions the lobbyists could provide.

The transatlantic cooperation was timely, for after the Glorious Revolution the English government pursued more vigorously than before its efforts to tighten control over the colonies, bringing more and more colonies directly under royal rule, regularly reviewing colonial laws, and making local appointments. It did so with very few administrators actually in the colonies—the central government's law enforcement machinery was growing relatively more slowly in the colonies than in England—and with virtually no backing from the Army sent to fight the French in North America. Yet its efforts produced far less turbulence in the American colonies than the sporadic attempts made in the Restoration had done. Why? Part of the explanation lies with the information interest groups could now provide. Despite the paucity of government servants who could send back reliable information from the colonies, William III's advisers, now including the Board of Trade, were far better informed through these groups about anticipated American responses than Restoration councils had been.

Thereafter, over the first half of the eighteenth century English interest groups lobbied with improved effectiveness on behalf of American colleagues, simultaneously filling a gap between the rapid growth of the colonial importance to the empire and the far more glacial growth of British knowledge about it. Ministers traded American favors, relatively costless to grant, for information, electoral support, and the London interests' ability to work with Americans on local disputes so the disputes did not spill over into English politics. The interests were careful to argue that particular policies would work to the benefit (or detriment) of groups of subjects; in all their lobbying they were at pains to eschew ideology. They found it useful to fit their demands into mercantile terms, to repeat the mercantile arguments about the need to provide manpower for the colonies and subordinate colonial trade to the benefit of the mother country. Ministers and bureaucrats too wanted to know what interests they advanced, not what causes they espoused, and it was to the advantage of the interests to keep their ideologies quiet. By the mid-eighteenth century English politicians and Anglo-American lobbyists had established comfortable working relationships with each other and English interest groups were serving as a lubricant that helped keep the British government stable and the empire running smoothly.

Then, shortly after the middle of the eighteenth century, while other interests continued to flourish in what Michael Kammen has called "an age of interests,"[20] the London lobbies with American connections fell into disarray. The reasons for this decline lie on both sides of the ocean and with interrelated changes in both the groups themselves and the government. Interests were hampered by their own disagreements with Americans on a series of issues relating to the Great Awakening, the Seven Years' War, and paper currency. Two decades of instability in the British government after Henry Pelham's death in 1754 made it impossible for Londoners to count on their political friends' continuing in office. Parliament's increasing assumption of responsibility for colonial government after 1760 and its concern to increase the number of officials and tighten up law enforcement there undercut the usefulness of transatlantic interests. By limiting the flexibility in colonial administration, Parliament severely restricted the opportunities for interests to seek favored treatment for American colleagues. Parliamentary legislation covering several colonies or several segments of the colonial population at once pointed up the inability of interests representing particular groups in particular colonies to respond to sweeping legislation.

The ineffectiveness of traditional lobbying against the new parliamentary measures raised in turn the question whether it was advisable, indeed, even ethical, to take up the methods of John Wilkes and the new public opinion lobbies, thus entangling interest with the ideology they had sought to avoid. Weakened and fragmented, the Londoners were helpless to advise the government on measures during the decade before the Revolution. Weakened and fragmented by demands of their own members for formal imperial representation to replace the informal representation they had lost, the American interests were equally helpless themselves to repair the transatlantic links.

We might conclude that there was a little bit of luck in the first British Empire's working as well as it did for as long as it did in America. For the hundred years after the Restoration of Charles II in 1660, colonial affairs were left largely to the "management" of the monarchs. In exactly the same time period a major influence upon the monarchs shifted from institutional interests that gave the crown money in return for being left alone, to voluntary interests that offered to facilitate the crown's administration in exchange for being allowed to participate in it. Associational interests with American connections were able to work the system well, forewarning against administrative missteps in return for the chance to bend administration from time to time in favor of their American cor-respondents. Without rushing to a *post hoc ergo propter hoc* argument, we can still suggest that the imperial crisis coincided in time with two related changes: the shift of colonial management away from the crown, and the temporary dislocation of London-American interest groups that had assisted in that management.

Did the appearance of influence at Whitehall, while it lasted, deceive the Americans into thinking they had broader influence throughout the government than they did? It may have. Did American willingness to appeal local issues to London obscure the fact that they complied with some imperial regulation because they were increasingly able to get other things done within the colonies? It may have. Did information the government got from lobbyists obscure the fact that the information they were receiving from the tiny force of colonial servants was not always adequate? It probably did. Perhaps the functions of transatlantic interest groups contributed to both English and American perceptions that the empire was running more smoothly than it actually was. But at the same time there seems little doubt that English politicians along with Americans in organized churches, mercantile networks, and non-English communities—certainly a goodly cross section of the colonial popula-tion—accepted for a while the way the empire worked.

CHAPTER I

The Civil Wars and Interregnum

Cooperation between London and American interest groups developed slowly. As late as the 1630s, when parts of the Chesapeake and New England colonies were already on the map, voluntary interest groups were scarcely visible on either side of the Atlantic. Having seen the last of the mercantile companies that had started them, the American colonists now supported a peculiar mixture of traditional interests: proprietary relatives and supporters in Maryland constituted an ascriptive group,local governments, particularly the colonial assemblies, were institutional ones. But the scattered settlers, still struggling with establishing their farms, lacked the time, the money, even the proximity to neighbors sharing similar extra-institutional interests to organize voluntary associations.

In London, an area with a population dense enough to support a variety of interests, such associations were beginning to form and some—the Puritan churches, the gatherings of merchants trading to North America, and the "stranger" (non-English) communities with Puritan leanings—had potential for developing common interests with the colonists. In the 1630s, however, they, too, were hardly visible. London's population was about 375,000; there were probably about seven thousand non-English, a few hundred North American merchants, and an unknown number of puritans or puritan sympathizers in overlapping interests. They and the members of other embryonic associations like artisanal organizations, which were of less concern to Americans, were made up of people fairly new to the City and its environs: merchants and artisans tended to be recent arrivals from the provinces, and while the Puritan and stranger communities dated back to Elizabethan days, their membership was constantly replenished from outside the City. Accordingly, the groups lacked stable membership; in addition their concerns were not focused, they lacked safe, open meeting places, and they faced the open hostility of established institutional interests—the guilds, mercantile companies, and church hierarchy in particular—whose authority they sought to bypass or undercut. From this it followed that they also faced the hostility of both the City government, representative of the institutional interests, and of the King, whose income depended upon gifts and loans from the City fathers.

In 1640, however, the King was forced to summon parliament for financial aid, and for two decades after that the ensuing turmoil in British politics allowed voluntary associations to develop unmolested by a strong government. The King and Parliament became embroiled in a Civil War which Parliament ultimately won; thereafter the government of England fell first to Parliament, then to a Commonwealth Council, and finally to the Lord Protector, Oliver Cromwell, before returning to the monarchy again in 1660. Parliament, the Council, and Cromwell supported the voluntary groups, accepted their petitions, facilitated their publicity by removing censorship, and even welcomed some of their members into positions of importance. The tiny interest groups began to surface and to experiment with political influence.

.   .   .

When we try to picture how the groups were coming together in the 1630s, much of our impression must be conjectural. Refugees from the continent, religious dissidents from the English provinces, men seeking work, or business entrepreneurs migrated to London seeking residence in congenial neighborhoods.

Private homes, taverns, Puritan lectures, parts of the Royal Exchange, the "stranger's" meetings at Austin Friars, all must have served as places to meet like-minded arrivals, but it is hard to come by details.[1] Almost certainly the London merchants trading to Virginia took part of the Exchange to themselves; almost certainly some of the merchants trading to New England met in the living room of Matthew Cradock, a leading Puritan merchant who later became M.P. for London. Many of the same merchants gathered on Sundays and lecture days at one of the fifteen or so London churches that had a Puritan minister. William Cokayne's "gathered church" was full of such merchants.[2] In addition, London residents who shared similar interests were almost certainly gathering in particular taverns: it is hard to imagine that the tavern clubs which became so active during the 1640s sprang up overnight.[3] But "almost certainlys" do not add up to a clear picture.

Beyond that we have only occasional scraps of information, suggesting informal meetings. Puritan ministers met in Edmund Calamy's living room:[4] Calamy does not say how many there were, but the fact that there were 80 to 100 signatures on ministerial petitions to Parliament in 1640 and again in 1641 suggests that the ministers who did meet were able to reach their colleagues throughout the City. Meanwhile communities of Huguenots were settling in Shoreditch and Spitalfields, and since these areas were a fair walk from the Huguenot Church on Threadneedle Street, it is possible that Huguenots were holding services in private homes. London's minuscule Jewish community held services *sub rosa* at the Portuguese embassy. We get brief glimpses of merchants, Puritans, and ethnic minorities meeting from time to time, and it is reasonable to assume they did so regularly, but there is very little evidence on the subject.[5]

Even if they did meet regularly, the emerging London interests had virtually no opportunity to develop political influence over the royal government; their concerns were too unfocused for them to concentrate their energies on particular issues, they could not legally approach the King except through the City government dominated by institutional interests who did not want to share power with the new groups, and it was hopeless to appeal to the King anyway, because he depended on the same institutional groups for loans and local law enforcement.

The groups, moreover, were too diffuse to concentrate their efforts on particular issues. The Huguenot community "covered a wide spectrum"; it was part Anglican, part Puritan. Puritans themselves represented a wide range of opinion, "a portmanteau of religious attitudes," everything from Presbyterianism to the more eccentric sects of the London religious underground.[6] The leading new colonial-trading merchants had interests all over the globe. The most prominent one, Maurice Thompson, was in the Canadian fur trade, sent provisions to New England, was recommended by the governor of Virginia as one of three merchants to be given a monopoly of the tobacco crop, and was an interloper in East Indian trade.[7] Another prominent merchant, Owen Rowe, was active in the Virginia trade, a leading merchant backer of Massachusetts Bay, and deputy governor of the Bermuda Company.[8] Indeed, the infant American colonies, to which many of the unincorporated merchants traded, were as yet so underdeveloped that an ambitious merchant would not limit his activities to any one of them. With such a variety of economic interests, it is hard to imagine merchants concentrating their efforts on the government's commercial policy in any one part of the world at this time; with such a spectrum of religious persuasions, it is hard to imagine any one of the religious or ethnic groups taking a stand in favor of a specifically focused set of demands.

Even if particular lobbyists had tried to present their concerns to the royal government, it is unlikely they would have got very far because they would have come up against opposition from the City of London, never very accommodating to "strangers" and now dominated by the Levant and East India Companies whose members, gradually replacing

the Merchant Adventurers on the Court of Aldermen, were hostile also
to both the Puritans and the merchants carrying on American trade
independently of Company organization.[9] Furthermore, by a tradition
dating back at least to the Tudors, petitions to the monarch or his
councillors could be presented only by formally recognized institutions—
for example, municipal or mercantile corporations, universities, or local
grand juries. So powerful was the City of London that even legally
recognized institutions within it, such as livery companies, had to have
their petitions to the monarch or Parliament approved by the City
government before they were presented; otherwise the City would not
back them and the petitions were likely to be thrown out. From 1630
to the beginning of 1642 there was really no chance for independent
merchants and religious or ethnic minorities to win support from a City
government whose members were reluctant to encourage rival associations, and Charles I himself made it clear that petitions from such groups
would be considered not merely inappropriate but seditious.[10]

Even had the new interests been able to approach the King, they
would have got nowhere: the King's personal sympathies were with their
enemies, and his political needs—for money and the performance of
imperial functions—were with them, too. The King's High Church in-
clination naturally gave him little sympathy for the Puritan lectures that
Archbishop Laud was trying to suppress. Charles's overt and covert
cooperation with Spain in the 1630s made him occasionally attempt to
discourage English trade with America, something he was inclined to do
anyway because of the Puritan connections of large numbers of American
merchants.

More generally important, Charles's desperate need for money drove
him to support whatever institutions could offer large loans or outright
gifts. He could not turn his back on the Church of England's Convocation—its annual gift was indispensable to the government. He could
often force gifts and loans from the reluctant City fathers; he therefore
dared not openly antagonize them. He supported large companies which
could sometimes be forced to lend him money, played them off against
wealthy interlopers who bribed generously for the privilege of breaking
the big companies' monopolies, then abandoned the interlopers for the
companies again.[11] The newer, lesser merchants could never offer anything like what the companies or courtiers produced; they were too poor
and too unorganized to capitalize upon the wealth of members whose
association was, after all, voluntary. Had the leaders of the Virginia
merchants, for example, attempted to bribe the King by the offer of a
gift, they would have failed; to begin with, they had no way of requiring
a contribution from merchants who met informally at the Exchange or
in someone's home.

Not only did the large commercial companies contribute directly to the King's finances, they also helped the King by performing functions he would otherwise have had to handle—and pay for—through the government, and these were functions the smaller merchant groups were not organized to carry out. Take employment, a terribly important service in an age of underemployment. The East India Company had 12,000 employees by 1630; North American merchants, even if one counts not only partners and tobacco growers but also the servants who worked for them, employed at most only fifteen or twenty men each. The large companies at least partially supplied their own shipping; smaller American merchants could not. Large companies, set up as quasi-state institutions, handled negotiations with foreign powers and overseas defense and were responsible for the conduct of their own employees toward the foreign powers with which they dealt.[12] Necessarily, none of these functions could be handled well by voluntary groups, but in addition, the failure of the Virginia Company to reach a stable arrangement with the Indians, guarantee the honorable behavior of its employees against the Indians, or protect its employees from the Indian massacre of 1622 raised unanswerable questions about whether a mercantile company could ever work effectively in North America.

If it was hopeless to work on the King, it was just as hopeless to appeal to his courtiers, for the new interests had neither bribes nor desirable memberships to offer. The East India Company and other large mercantile companies could offer courtiers substantial shares in return for their support in the Privy Council;[13] the City of London could offer the keys to the City; the Archbishop of Canterbury could offer jobs for ecclesiastical clients. The new interests had no such gifts. They had no jobs to offer, and since by definition their membership was voluntary, there was no point in giving it. The keys to the City were one thing; the keys to a meeting open to all interested parties were quite another.

. . .

The rather murky picture of new interest groups in the 1630s, diffuse, loosely organized, politically impotent, of questionable legitimacy, and scarcely even visible, began to alter in the early 1640s, as the political environment itself began to change. In 1640, beset with a Scottish Rebellion he could not put down, Charles was forced to call the Long Parliament in order to get money.

Over the next twenty years one crisis followed another in English politics, with each crisis actually proving a boon to the growth of the voluntary interests. In the first period of turmoil to 1649, when Parliament fought and then defeated the King, interests won legal recognition from both the municipal and the national government. In the second,

under the Commonwealth Council, 1649–1653, some of the interest group members actually had access to the highest political leaders, and under Oliver Cromwell, ruler until his death in 1658, the voluntary associations were allowed, even encouraged, to develop formal organizations. By the time monarchy was restored in 1660, voluntary interests had at least a foothold in English politics.

The very calling of Parliament in 1640 augured well for the voluntary interests. The Commons soon came to be dominated—or manipulated—by critics of the King eager to encourage associations that opposed him in City politics. Twenty-two merchants representing the new interests actually sat in the Long Parliament.[14] Together the parliamentary leaders proceeded almost at once to help the new interests undermine royalist power in City elections and at the same time weaken the City by broadening the government's source of revenue, so rulers would no longer be dependent upon loans from established institutional interests. They further encouraged the associations to organize for political participation by receiving their petitions directly, without demanding that they be funneled through the City government, and by effectively lifting government censorship of the groups' publications.

At the outset the Long Parliament was the inspiration for Puritans, Presbyterians (who were becoming the conservatives within the Puritan movement), and Independent merchants to challenge royalist forces for the domination of City government. Down to the beginning of 1642 the City's Common Council had consistently concurred with the royalist Court of Aldermen on general policies. But Puritans won the Common Council elections of December 21, 1641, and in separate aldermanic elections over the following year a majority of Presbyterians was elected. Under parliamentary direction the royalist Lord Mayor was impeached and deposed, and a parliamentary Puritan elected in his place.[15] From then until the end of 1647 the predominant sympathies of the City leaders were somewhere between Presbyterian and moderate Puritan, becoming more and more conservative as the years passed. When Cromwell's army defeated the alliance of King and Presbyterians in 1647, the Presbyterians were driven out of London politics and replaced by Independents who had supported the army; these men ruled the City, albeit with diminished powers under Cromwell, until Charles II's restoration in 1660.[16]

In addition to interfering in London's politics on their behalf, the Long Parliament also encouraged the growth of religious and mercantile interests by broadening the sources of national revenues, thereby diminishing the political influence of such traditional interests as the City Corporation, which had contributed heavily to the support of the government. By 1642 King and Parliament had gone to war against each

other. Once at war, parliamentary leaders faced far greater expenses than Charles's peacetime governments used to have, and disposed of fewer traditional resources than the King had had. The Convocation of the Church of England did not meet. The City and mercantile companies produced gifts and loans, but not enough to support parliamentary government. Parliament was forced to raise vastly increased sums by property and excise taxes, and given their difficulties they were remarkably successful.[17] The results of such success for new interests lay in the future; for the moment, it was clear to only the most astute observers that if taxes enacted by statute replaced traditional sources of revenue, then governments would be released from the very dependence upon convocation and companies that had helped keep the less organized interests from having any political influence.

No longer was the City leadership exclusively in alliance with company merchants hostile to the independent sects; no longer could the City fathers block petitions from Londoners to the national government, no longer could the City count on using gifts and loans to obtain national influence. At best, the new interests had won a power base in City government, but even at the worst they had, for the first time in twelve years, a nonthreatening local environment.

Indirectly, then, parliamentary leaders helped the new interests by helping them overthrow their royalist opponents in London. Directly, Parliament helped in other ways. For one thing, members made it clear from their earliest meetings that, unlike the King, they would accept petitions from groups of people not organized in legally recognized institutions. No longer did Londoners have to approach Parliament through City government; they could petition directly. Petitions were an important way of indicating the sentiments of people who were not yet highly organized—"divers merchants and citizens of London," "divers merchants of quality about London": the titles suggest a very loose grouping.[18] The very act of drafting, circulating, and presenting petitions constituted one step on the way to political organization.

Within three months of Charles's calling the Long Parliament, "merchants, owners of ships, planters, and adventurers to the several plantations in the parts of America" were complaining successfully against the "cruel exactions the customers demanded," and they went on to have the customs commissioners punished for their misdoings.[19] The tobacco merchants, overlapping several colonies, managed to get tobacco duties reduced from 4d to 1d a pound. "Planters in New England," "the merchants of New England" petitioned against Charles's restrictions on departures to New England in 1641.[20]

Once war broke out, parliamentary leaders became especially responsive to petitions from merchants trading to and informed about the

American colonies because they were concerned to keep the colonies from becoming potential bases for the King. In 1645 Governor Berkeley of Virginia wrote to leaders of Parliament suggesting direct parliamentary intervention in Virginia politics on behalf of these London merchants: "The like complyance required from us in affordinge of trade to the London merchant[s] and in givinge them free admission to our courts of justice hath been invioblie observed by us."[21]

Similarly, very loose groupings of Presbyterians and Puritans also found Parliament responsive to their petitions. Large numbers of ministers and laymen petitioned for the removal of Bishops "root and branch" from the church, and the Long Parliament received the petition almost as soon as it sat. In December 1641, and again a year later, eighty to a hundred ministers in and around London petitioned for reforms in the Anglican Church.[22]

Partly because the ecclesiastical petitions were more sweeping in their demands than the mercantile ones, partly for other reasons, Parliament's ecclesiastical reforms were of even greater importance than the concessions it made to merchant groups. In its first years Parliament began to break the power of the Church of England, making it legal for Puritans of various persuasions to hire their own lecturers if their parish agreed, removing the Bishops from the House of Lords, sending Archbishop Laud himself to the Tower, and summoning the Westminster Assembly to discuss ecclesiastical reform in 1643. By 1646 Parliament had legally established the Presbyterian Church, subsequently declaring that "All such persons as shall not conform to the said form of government and divine Service shall have liberty to meet for the service and worship of God."[23] The legalizing of religious toleration was undoubtedly Parliament's greatest contribution to the development of the various religious sects at mid-century.

Perhaps Parliament's second most important contribution to the growth of voluntary associations was the ordinance of 1643 shifting censorship of the press from the Archbishop of Canterbury and the Bishop of London to a parliamentary committee. On the face of it, this simply represented a shift of the locus of authority with no real change in intent. But the members of the committee could not agree which books to suppress, they could scarcely even punish authors or printers who published books in complete disregard of the committee's existence, and censorship of the press soon became futile.[24] Merchants were left free to publish uncensored tracts on trade, sectarians were left free to publish theological tracts or proposals for organization. In addition, the printing press made possible uniformity in worship, doctrine, and organization among geographically scattered groups and it gave them a wider audience than they had ever enjoyed before.

If the Long Parliament provided an opportunity for Englishmen of common interests to meet, proselytize, and make political appeals, the Commonwealth Council which followed it in 1649 gave new merchants and religious leaders access to the highest ranks of political power and a chance to shape legislation directly. Here we cannot separate the merchants from the Puritan leaders, for the men who made it to the top ranks of influence both in London and in the national government were often both Puritans and merchants. Certainly this was true of the men who dominated London politics as a result of the army's pressure on the City in 1647. It was also true of Parliament, where a number of M.P.s who were both Puritan and independent merchants sat regularly on the most important committees of the Rump Parliament and of the Commonwealth Council, which appointed new merchants to its committees for regulating customs and the navy.

The Puritan merchants, moreover, made their new positions pay off. In 1650 the Rump repealed the Elizabethan Act of Uniformity and the act for "punishing of persons obstinately refusing to come to church,"[25] and by the end of the Commonwealth English Christians, at least, were free to attend—and organize—whatever church they wanted. American merchants worked with Thomas Scot, head of the Admiralty, to build up the Commonwealth navy; they were also behind the Commonwealth government's sending a fleet to demand the surrender of royalist colonies. Just how much influence the "interloping free merchants" had on the Navigation Act of 1651 is unclear; what *is* clear is that this act was the first important government policy on which the lesser merchants had any influence at all. In fact, the merchants had succeeded in shaping, if they did not bring about, a major change in colonial policy, for in the Navigation Act's prohibition of colonial trade in any but English or colonial vessels, Parliament began transferring from the mercantile companies to itself the regulation of foreign trade.[26]

Under the rule of Oliver Cromwell, which followed that of the Commonwealth Council, the first signs of formal organization among the voluntary associations began to appear. Although the Civil War period had brought new mercantile and religious groups openly into politics and the Commonwealth government had welcomed their most important individuals to positions of importance, there was still little sign of organized group activity before the early 1650s. Only then did political influence and freedom from royal restraint make it possible for interests to organize, and Cromwell encouraged them to do so.

London coffee houses date from the 1650s and a Virginia-Maryland Coffee House seems to have existed from the middle of the decade,[27] a block or so away from the Exchange. Here merchants could gather year-round in considerably more comfort than at the Exchange, petitions could be left on the hall table for signatures, rooms could be sealed off for private discussion, and key leaders could try to politicize the lesser merchants who came to the coffee house for nonpolitical reasons. From the 1650s on, the opening of a coffee house marked the stage at which merchants first became organized for political purposes. At about the same time the Virginia-Maryland Coffee House was established, Chesapeake merchants came to exert considerable influence over Cromwell's parliaments, bringing tobacco duties down from 4d. a pound in early 1653 to 1d. a pound in 1656.[28] The correlation would suggest that the coffee house was already a center of political organization, but we do not know exactly how it functioned.

There is clearer evidence of ethnic and religious organization. It was Cromwell, for example, who first allowed the public organization of London's Jewish community in 1656, giving them rights to trade, residence, and private worship and (in 1657) allowing them to build their own cemetery.[29] More broadly, among Christian sects it is with Cromwell that we date both the "beginnings of denominational exclusiveness" and the beginnings of denominational organization. Cromwell's constitution, the Instrument of Government, went, if anything, further than earlier government pronouncements in protecting infant sects, "such as profess faith in God by Jesus Christ (though differing in judgement from the doctrine, worship or discipline publicly held forth) shall not be restrained from but shall be protected in, the profession of the faith, and exercise of their religion."[30]

The almost unlimited freedom for Christian sects not only allowed sectarian organization; it virtually required that sects among the Puritans organize or face fragmentation beyond their powers of survival. Existing groups themselves could be ruined by smaller groups splintering off if they did not establish order and discipline at once.[31] As far back as 1644 leaders of one of the sects, the London Particular Baptists, held a meeting to draw up a confession of faith.[32] In 1646 Presbyterians, briefly recognized as the national church by Parliament, had tried to set up a national organization. They managed to get eleven parishes organized into a London Classis, but this Classis and another in Lancaster were the only Presbyterian organizations that lasted.[33]

The most rapid organization of sects occurred between 1650 and 1658, years overlapping Cromwell and the last years of the Commonwealth. In 1650 the Particular Baptists had a meeting of representatives from several congregations in Wales. A Western Association was organized in 1653, a Midland Association in 1655, and a weekly meeting of London messengers began about the same time.[34] In 1651 the General Baptists of the Midlands organized, with two representatives from each of thirty churches meeting together. In 1654 General Baptists from seven counties met at London, and two years later the number of counties had grown to nine.[35] In 1654 the first of the Quaker monthly meetings was held. In 1657 or 1660—it is open to question—the first national meeting of Quakers was held.[36] In 1656 Richard Baxter organized the Worcester Association composed of Presbyterian and Congregational ministers.[37] Even the Congregationalists held a national meeting in 1658.[38]

Beyond the common desire to prevent further fragmentation there were other reasons for organization which varied from sect to sect. Quakers organized originally for mutual relief.[39] London Baptists gathered to propagate the faith in the provinces, and county meetings were brought together by London organizers.[40] Baptist and Quaker meetings were of laymen and Presbyterian meetings were composed of ministers, but all had the avowed purpose of agreeing upon discipline. All the groups came together at one point or another to agree upon responses to the rapidly changing national governments. The largest meeting of Baptists was in 1654, when they met to decide their official position in regard to Cromwell (they passed a statement supporting him and opposing his visionary "fifth monarchy" opponents).[41] When Cromwell died, Presbyterians met to discuss their approach toward his son Richard, who was opposed by the army leaders;[42] Quakers met on the same issues.[43] (Presbyterians came down on the side of Richard; Quakers, remarkably enough, on the side of the army.) In the attempts at sectarian organization, such as the merchants' petitions to Parliament or the occasional examples of mercantile influence on councils of the Commonwealth and Protectorate, there are suggestions of associational interest groups beginning to organize, to develop an interest in national politics, and to experiment with the means of exerting political influence.

There are also suggestions that London groups were communicating with the provinces: in the clearest cases, the London associations of General and Particular Baptists sent missionaries to organize provincial meetings, and London Quakers arranged for the publication and distribution of tracts written in the provinces. London Presbyterians and Congregationalists organized occasional conferences on doctrine to which provincials were invited. Less clearly, there was some kind of political correspondence between London and provincial tradesmen and merchants. Richard Baxter wrote vaguely of his county that the "tradesmen have a correspondency with London,"[44] and Valerie Pearl's recent studies of London during the Civil Wars show how taverns served as centers where information from London and the provinces was exchanged.[45]

Nevertheless, it is premature to speak of the "rise of modern interest groups" in this period if the expression implies that the groups had stable organization, sophisticated political techniques, and, above all, distinctive memberships. None of these seems to have been the case. Meetings of the religious groups were infrequent; merchants seemed as yet to have no organization beyond their informal meetings at private homes, the Virginia-Maryland coffee house, or the London Exchange. In the Commonwealth Parliament half a dozen London merchants sat together on important committees and developed increasing parliamentary sophistication as they learned to cooperate with merchant M.P.s from Sussex, Kent, and the West Country.[46] But the greatest power of both mercantile and religious groups derived from their identification with one member or another of the Commonwealth Council of State or one of Cromwell's top advisors, and the incessant personal feuding and frequent turnover of these men limited the ability of emerging interests to develop stable channels to political influence.

Even had their political influence been more steady, neither mercantile or religious groups could be considered full-blown interests. The investments of leading independent merchants continued to be scattered about the colonial world, and the walks on the Royal Exchange were not yet fully differentiated by the areas to which their merchants traded. The occasional parliamentary petitions submitted by men who appear to have been mainly Virginia or New England merchants were outnumbered by petitions from "divers merchants and citizens," "merchants trading to Virginia and other English plantations," "citizens as well merchants as others, inhabiting in the City of London and trading in the commodity of tobacco" (a combination of Chesapeake and Caribbean merchants).[47]

Similarly, there was so little differentiation among religious groups that we should probably speak of the "pre-history" of different denominations rather than of their early history.[48] Quakers and Baptists sent out visitors and ministers to compete with each other for the same groups of people, whose allegiances swayed from one to the other and were far from settled at the end of the period. At the time conservative Presbyterians and moderate Anglicans were closer to each other than to other wings of their own denominations. Independents (Congregationalists) became elders in the Presbyterian Church when it was established as the national church; that establishment itself was supported by many Anglicans, who thought political considerations of the moment were more important than settling fairly minor differences over ecclesiastical ceremony and organization. Richard Baxter, the Presbyterian leader, described his Worcester Association of ministers as "mere Catholicks, men of no faction, no siding with any party but owning that which was good in all as far as they could discern it."[49] The organization of "stranger churches" included Huguenots and Dutch sects.

Lacking stable memberships as well as strong organizations and techniques for maximizing political influence, the new interests were still quite vulnerable when there were major changes in the English government. But the experimental organization, the primitive systems of community organization, the tentative efforts at lobbying, and the enjoyment of a relatively unmolested existence were stronger than they might have appeared in 1659, and the new interests were sturdy enough to resist all efforts to drive them back to obscurity during the Restoration.

· CHAPTER 2 ·

Restoration England

Throughout England voluntary interest groups proliferated after the Restoration. Tanners, refiners, silversmiths, weavers, Irish merchants, cattlemen specializing in fattening Irish livestock—all acted in some way as voluntary associations in various localities, but it was in London that interest group growth was most noticeable. London grew at an unprecedented speed, from 400,000 in 1650 to 575,000 by the end of the century, its growth fueled in large part by migration from the provinces and the Continent. In the cosmopolitan London society interests organized, made their way into City government in numbers sufficient to undermine the initial royalist unity of the Restoration, and experimented with the systematic cultivation of political influence at the national level.

People flocked to London for a better life and, once there, congregated with other like-minded wanderers. Investors, sometimes men unable to buy shares in the restricted trading companies, were attracted to unregulated colonial trade; growing numbers of colonial traders began meeting in the London coffee houses. New workmen, producing goods for the expanding overseas and domestic markets, crowded into the London suburbs from the countryside and the Continent, creating rudimentary workingmen's associations and ethnic communities independent of the old guilds and companies. Puritans of various persuasions now found themselves at least for the moment defined as dissenters outside the established church; numbers of them moved to London to escape local persecution and join larger congregations of similar worshippers.

As the new groups took shape, their increasing electoral strength, their contributions to government through new forms of taxation, their ability to keep their members out of disturbances, and, most important, their access to information became particularly useful to government and suggested to both King and Parliament the importance of reaching accommodation with them. Since the King, some Parliamentarians, and some royal servants alike were beginning to realize the need to run government more systematically if its resources were to be maximized, they were responsive to groups that could offer order and information. The interests were hopeful, but they also remained cautious, even distrustful, aware that monarchs took counsel with courtiers they could not influence, and aware too that royal government had traditionally rested on institutional, not voluntary, interests and had earlier linked voluntary associations with riot and instability. The interests were growing, coalescing, experimenting, but their position was never stable.

.   .   .

Among the fastest growing were the interests with American connections—the ethno-religious communities and the associations of merchants trading to America. The commercial groups grew as a result of a dramatic increase in London's overseas trade encouraged by the Navigation Acts. Over the seventeenth century London shifted from the periphery of a predominantly intra-European system of commercial production in which wool and cloth were the chief English exports, to the center of a worldwide network based in good part on colonial staples required to be transported in English ships. Colonial trade, in other words, was heavily responsible for the growth of London trade and hence the London mercantile community. English exports and imports grew about 50 percent, especially in the boom decade of the 1680s, with the bulk of the increase going to London. Within this, colonial trade grew at a rate faster than trade with the rest of the world. Nearly a fifth of English commerce was with the colonies by the end of the period, with the fastest growth coming in the reexport of colonial products. London's mercantile community grew accordingly. There were about 2,000 overseas merchants in London in the 1680s, of whom several hundred were independent merchants trading with the American colonies.[1]

Trade in turn generated jobs for manufacturing in "fine goods." Lured to London by hope of jobs and a measure of religious toleration, English craftsmen (now mainly from the home counties) and foreign craftsmen (now mainly from France) set up in the suburbs, beyond the domination of established guilds and companies. By the end of the century continentals constituted about 3 percent of London's population, or about 15,000.

The new London groups with American connections seem to have developed at very different rates, though our knowledge of this is imprecise. The earliest evidence of mercantile organization concerns the London merchants trading to Virginia. In 1662 the Chesapeake produced more tobacco than the London merchants could profitably sell, and the merchants divided over the best way to handle the problem. One group, the Planters and Merchants of Virginia, urged the prohibition of further tobacco planting, but several groups of "Merchants, owners of ships, planters, traders to Virginia" and others petitioned the King not to limit it.[2] Merchants divided further over the best times for the Virginia convoys to sail, and the Committee for Trade and Plantations received several contradictory petitions on the subject between 1662 and 1666. Petitions and counterpetitions suggest a divided interest, but arguments within the lobby also taught each side the value of organization. When the lobby closed ranks in 1666, it was probably the stronger because of the experience.

The Virginia merchants went on to become the best organized and most effective of all the new mercantile lobbies in the Restoration, at once the giant and the grandfather of other mercantile groups. In 1670–71 "Virginia merchants [appeared] at the Door" of the House of Commons to argue against the current duties on tobacco. They also hired counsel who, incidentally, "said nothing every member of the House did not know before,"[3] an indication that the Virginia merchants had already been lobbying privately with Parliament. From then on the Virginia merchants appeared regularly before Parliament, the Treasury, the Customs Commissioners, and the various committees of trade.

Several factors account for the Virginia merchants' headstart over other mercantile groups. One was the opening of the Virginia-Maryland coffee house well before other merchants had their own coffee houses.[4] Another was simply the fact that more independent London merchants were trading to Virginia than to other areas; estimates ranged up to 400 Virginia merchants, whereas none of the other colonial areas commanded the attention of more than 100 merchants. There was also more wealth in the Virginia trade than in most other trades, and the Virginia merchants early produced a strong group of wealthy leaders. By 1690 they were led by a core group of nine such men, headed by Richard Perry, the elder Micajah Perry, and their partner, Thomas Lane.

Yet another reason for their success was that from the beginning of the Restoration the Virginia merchants were faced with a large number of issues coming before Parliament or the Lords of Trade that directly affected their interests and required sustained lobbying efforts. The very size of the tobacco trade meant that Parliament was far more concerned with tobacco duties than they were with duties on other American products: from 1670 to 1710 that subject came before Parliament on an average of once every two or three years. A prolonged slump in the tobacco trade beginning in the 1670s made the merchants press the government to negotiate favorable trade treaties affecting tobacco and to encourage tobacco sales on the Continent. They also opposed the monopoly on slave-dealing held by the Royal African Company. Finally, Virginia was the first mainland colony whose laws were reviewed in England; until 1685 it was the only one, and local laws on such subjects as the building of lighthouses, the establishment of towns, and the regulation of weights and measures were of recurring concern to London merchants.

Two other commercial groups, the merchants trading to New England and the West India merchants, also seem to have started organizing in this period, but the evidence about them is less clear. As early as February 12, 1661, some merchants trading to New England appealed to the Commissioners of Customs for permission to give bond to return the proceeds of the New England trade rather than actually bringing the goods to England. (The appeal was granted.)[5] The New England merchants did not reappear until 1675, when "Several merchants who Trade to Several Parts, and particularly to New England" complained to the Lords of Trade of "grat abuse in the Trade of the New England Men and the Subverting the Act of Navigation."[6] New England merchants testified before this Committee on February 4 on the same subject, and on April 13, 1676, "the most of them [spoke] plainly" about New England's trade directly with Europe.[7] After that the New England merchants went into political eclipse again; between 1676 and 1689 they never appeared before Parliament, and they appeared only once (in 1684) before the Lords of Trade, when they were asked to comment on the value of coins minted in New Hampshire.[8]

About West Indian merchants the evidence is even sparser: for a year, 1670–71, some kind of Committee for Concern of Barbados, formed of merchants and absentee planters, tried to meet weekly, but it failed to last. After that there are no records of West Indian merchants (or merchants trading to any one of the islands) appearing as a group before the Lords of Trade or Parliament, and their meetings seem to have been primarily social sendoffs for various royal governors and "token feasts" at which planters and merchants met socially to drink the health of friends in the islands.[9]

Sharply overlapping the commercial interests in London were the religious ones, and for these groups differentiation and organization also developed at varying speeds after 1660. The strongest were the Anglicans. Perhaps it is questionable whether they should be called an interest group at all because, as the established church, they were at the center of power. But in many ways they now behaved as other interest groups behaved. After the Restoration, as a result of an agreement between the Archbishop of Canterbury and the leading minister, representatives of the church no longer met in convocation to grant a voluntary gift to the sovereign.[10] Lacking the leverage that this had formerly brought, church leaders had to create a political lobby to substitute for it. Since the bishops' bench in the House of Lords was declining in influence (over the century the number of bishops dropped from a third of the House to an eighth),[11] Archbishop Sheldon had to turn his attention to the House of Commons, where he became a lobbyist par excellence. In 1668 the Bishop of Lichfield wrote of his "indefatigable industrie to prepare the votes of the commons against they met for so noble and happie a concurrence, to discourage non-conformists and sectaries."[12]

Weaker than the Anglicans were the various groups that dissented from the state church. When the Anglican Church was reestablished at the Restoration many Puritans expected to be comprehended within it, but the Clarendon Code, a series of acts passed in the first year of Charles's reign, made it difficult for many of them to conform and penalized those who did not do so. Ministers were required to conduct church services in conformity with the Book of Common Prayer, worshippers attending services not in Anglican forms were penalized, nonconformists were excluded from participation in borough governments. There are no reliable figures for the number of dissenters in Restoration England; we cannot even say whether they were growing, shrinking, or remaining constant. Probably they constituted about 5 percent of the population, or 250,000 at the end of the period; an estimated 20,000 lived in London. The number of congregations varied from one year to the next. Shortly after 1689 there were 89 dissenting churches in greater London; the number may even have been greater just before 1688, when French protestants were driven out of their country by Louis XIV's revocation of the Edict of Nantes.

Among the dissenters some groups held on to the hope that they would some day be comprehended in the Anglican Church, and others assumed they never would. Groups that assumed from an early date that comprehension was hopeless predictably developed the strongest organizations of their own, and these included the Baptists and the Quakers.

Representatives of some Quaker monthly meetings had gathered in London as early as 1660; in 1668 delegates from Quaker county meetings began meeting together regularly, and a London committee was established to correspond with each of them. Seven years later the London Meeting for Sufferings was established, primarily "to endeavour for relief by the law of the land to stop the destroyer," that is, to provide assistance to Quakers in legal trouble. Once organized, the Quakers quickly took up political activity. In 1670, just two years after their first meeting, Quakers were distributing broadsides in the lobby of the House of Commons,[13] and shortly after that the London Meeting for Sufferings sent instructions to Friends in the provinces to write to their representatives in Parliament seeking the redress of their sufferings. In 1678 they sent observers to the meeting of Parliament; a year later they were sophisticated enough in organization to hand the financial arrangements for lobbying over to a London committee.[14]

About the Baptists we know less, but it is clear they were close to the Quakers in their approach to lobbying. They began holding national meetings partly to arrange support for ministers turned out of their jobs by a government purge in 1663. General Baptists met again in 1672, 1678–1681, and regularly after 1686; Particular Baptists held their first national meeting in 1689. Along with Quakers, General Baptists sent observers to the 1678 Parliament; unlike the Quakers, however, they had not created any regular institutions for lobbying by 1690.[15]

The weakest groups—and again, one would expect this—were the Presbyterians and Congregationalists. They were neither clearly in nor clearly out of the permanent ecclesiastical establishment and hence were not at all sure about what organization they should best develop. Presbyterians were hopeful, at least until 1689, that they would be included in a comprehensive national church, and some Congregationalists may have held this hope until 1674, when representatives of dissenting groups were last summoned to meetings of Charles II and his bishops.[16] In addition, the very nature of Congregationalism made its practitioners reluctant to start a national organization. Neither Presbyterians nor Congregationalists developed any sustained organization with connections between London and the provinces. From time to time and place to place groups of dissenting churches organized charity drives or political committees, but they were generally small and short lived. Bristol, for example, had a committee of laymen dissenters to take over church services when ministers were jailed. Lichfield Presbyterians "laboured much with manie members of this countie, and have gained Mr. Dyot, our new Burgess unto them."[17] But these efforts were local and episodic, and in 1690, because of their peculiarly uncertain position vis-à-vis the national church, the Presbyterians and Congregationalists lagged far behind the other churches in organization.

Among the ethnic groups the Huguenots were the best organized; indeed, they were virtually the only ethnic interest with effective leadership. They were headed by the French Committee, elders of the proliferating French churches in London, whose main job was to administer monies collected in charity drives for recent Huguenot refugees. The original French community in London, dating back to the Middle Ages, had been swollen by vast numbers of Huguenot refugees fleeing persecution by Louis XIV. They had begun drifting over in Oliver Cromwell's time—and that was when the French Committee was established—but the numbers grew enormously after the Revocation of the Edict of Nantes in 1685, and by 1690 there were about 15,000 Huguenots in

London. They settled in two quite distinct neighborhoods. The rich gravitated to the Savoy, where some of them socialized comfortably with the English aristocracy: John Evelyn dined at Lady Arlington's with "divers French noblemen driven out of their country by the persecution," and on another occasion wrote of attending the French Church at the Savoy, which attracted London's fashionable society.[18] The poor tended more to settle in the Spitalfields area, and it was there, presumably, that the Committee had its greatest work to do.

In 1690, just after the Glorious Revolution, the French Committee was facing two problems that were to dog them throughout the eighteenth century. One was the need for money. Charity donations had dropped from £42,000 in 1686, when the English reaction to the Revocation was strongest, to £11,000 in 1689, and the extent of direct royal support to supplement the drives was as yet unclear. The other problem concerned the Committee's relationship with the Anglican Church. The government authorized the Committee to give charity only to those Frenchmen who took communion in the Anglican Church, and its work was examined by a committee of the church. For many of the immigrants, who considered themselves closer to the Presbyterian Church than to the Anglican, this was a bitter pill.[19]

Given these problems, the Committee still seems to have done extremely well, so well, in fact, that the philanthropist Thomas Firman proposed that Anglican parishes use their work as a model and appoint men "as it is now in the French and Dutch churches whose chief work and business it should be to visit such poor people and to inspect their wants and to have some part at least of the parish stock committed to them for the supply of their wants."[20] They were still primarily a private charity, but with money, organization, and an extensive constituency they had the makings of a strong interest group.

The French community in London had an effective organization, but the other two significant ethnic interests lagged far behind. Both of them—Jewish and German—were divided and leaderless. At Duke's Place the Sephardic community first recognized by Cromwell was now flourishing as a cultural and religious group, but their political leadership and institutions of political influence were still in the future; in 1690, moreover, they were beginning to be overwhelmed by an influx of Ashkenazim from northern Europe, who were attracted by the known tolerance of William III. Spread along the Thames, about a block or so from the quays, was the German community, fragmented along class (and educational) lines. There is evidence that both Germans and Jews were attempting with some success to emulate the French Committee in providing poor relief, and if they were, this suggests a high degree of organization. But they lacked connections to any part of the government.

As numbers of London merchants, laborers, dissenters, and foreign immigrants began collecting separately from the established institutional interests, they were also able to function more independently of the once threatening City Corporation. The combination of older taxes like the excise taxes, first begun during the 1640s, and new direct taxes like the Hearth tax, the more efficient collection of these after 1671 by government rather than corrupt tax farmers, and the increase in customs duties through the growth in trade expanded revenues so that the average net income of the government during Charles II's reign might have been adequate to the King's demand had not Charles squandered a good deal of it on unnecessary personal expenditures.[21] The collection of new revenues actually weakened the City Corporation by reducing the crown's dependence on it. The City gave Charles II and James II no substantial gifts, and the only mercantile company to give anything was the East India Company, which paid the relatively modest sum of £10,750 per annum from 1682 to 1686. It is harder to be certain about loans, because they were not itemized in the Exchequer accounts. City records indicate that the City gave the King a total of five loans, totalling £510,000, in the unsettled years 1660–1664, when Parliament was first voting, collecting, and adjusting its estimated receipts from taxes, but after that the City made only one other loan in the next quarter century. Since the City in Charles I's time had often depended on the livery companies for payments of its loans to the crown, the cessation of such loans also weakened the companies' influence on the City. By the end of Charles's reign loans from all sources were a less important source of royal income than customs duties from sugar and tobacco, suggesting a substantial shift in financial influence from older interests to new[22] and virtually eliminating what government influence the City had previously derived from offering gifts and loans.

What influence remained was further weakened by the fragmentation of City politics, as more and more colonial merchants bought into the livery companies and went into City politics themselves.[23] By the last decade of the century nearly 22 percent of merchants on the London livery were in the colonial trades. The City was no longer able to block the access of these merchants (and of the dissenting churches which many of them joined) to the centers of national power.[24]

In the increasingly safe environment of London the new groups organized; as they did, they came to develop a number of resources— electoral influence, ability to keep order among members in a period when there was widespread fear of renewed civil war, and, above all, their access to information at a time when a few political leaders were recognizing the mastery of information as essential to putting government on a systematic foundation.

Least developed at this point, but a potentially important resource, was the ability of some of the London groups and their provincial associates to bring electoral influence on members of Parliament. For many groups this power came only with the eighteenth century; for some, like the foreign groups whose members couldn't vote, it never came. But a few of the interests, particularly the ecclesiastical ones, already were able to run candidates for Parliament, throw their support selectively behind others, and put pressure on M.P.s once elected.

None of them had more than token parliamentary support by themselves. Jews, Catholics, and Quakers could not sit at all. Dissenters could, but there were not many of them in Parliament in the eighteenth century.[25] On the other hand, members of interests sometimes formed substantial "pockets" of voters in particular communities: they might be geographically concentrated so as to have electoral influence out of proportion to their small numbers throughout the country. When interest groups had pockets of voters in constituencies where ministers anticipated a contested election, they might have substantial bargaining power. The fact that in 1685 a bill to increase tobacco duties by 3 pence a pound was "much opposed by many members of the House who had either themselves or their friends an interest in the plantations"[26] suggests a mercantile representation in the Commons, though it does not tell much about how it worked. Between 1666 and 1678 Presbyterians ran a handful of their own members for Parliament and somewhat more successfully threw their electoral support to moderate Anglicans who in return supported the dissenters' interests.[27] In the parliamentary election of 1679 the greatest gain in numbers was made by moderate Anglicans vigorously backed by dissenters.[28] In the same election Quakers in York addressed their M.P.s: "we have at this time made our appearance with the rest of our neighbors at this city, in order to elect persons to sit in Parliament as the representatives of this County, and you now being elected, we look upon it to acquaint you with our grievances, desiring that you would endeavour to redress them."[29] Just how far these Quakers got in pressuring their M.P.s is unknown, but applying such pressure was in line with a directive to Quakers in 1675: "Friends in the several Counties [were to] seriously consider together and be unanimous about giving their voice in election of Parliament men to appear or not appear therein as in the wisdom of God they see convenient and safe."[30] Under Archbishop Sheldon, as has been mentioned, the Anglicans were also working hard to build parliamentary support. As the Bishop of Lichfield and Coventry wrote Sheldon after one vote, "by your Grace's dexteritie the house of Comons have past such a Godly vote, which makes the Presbyterians rather rage, then be humbled."[31]

Another resource of Restoration interests was the growing ability of their leaders to keep order among the rank and file and its associates, including some of the more volatile members of London's population. They did not do as well as traditional institutional interests, but well enough to make them potentially useful to the government. Ethnic groups like the French Committee and the Jewish Committee of Bevis Marks, for example, were beginning to provide almost cradle-to-grave support for destitute members and a discipline that kept them off the streets even in moments of desperation. The leading English churches provided much the same thing: financial assistance, education, adjudication of disputes within the group, procedures for disciplining wayward members.[32] The merchant walks and coffee houses were not set up to provide such services, but the leading merchants do seem to have exercised some discipline over clerks, apprentices, craftsmen, and lesser merchants. Presumably quarrels would ordinarily have been handled informally by the merchants themselves. The value to both crown and Parliament of the London groups' control over their members was to be demonstrated again and again in the century after 1660, but it was never more evident than in the turbulent years between 1679 and 1685, when London leaders, who had become hostile to Charles II and James II, nevertheless held their members back from several attempted plots and rebellions.[33] Their ability to keep members quiet was certainly one of the emerging interests' biggest assets.

A more consistently useful resource than direct parliamentary pressure was the interests' command of the information all sections of the government needed and could not get anywhere else. The Restoration saw the glimmerings of radical changes in the scope, organization, and management of public information.[34] Servants of the central government were seeking "the foundations of good government . . . in the practical arts of administrative efficiency rooted in political knowledge."[35] Such concern was most noticeable at the newly created Treasurer's Office, particularly under the Treasury Commission appointed in 1667, and later under Lords of Trade and Plantations. If the King or his servants wanted fresh advice on the best sailing date for a convoy, the best way to get it was to consult the appropriate merchants. If they wanted to know whether Huguenots in the provinces were having trouble getting jobs, the people to ask were the members of the French Committee; if they wanted to know how many Quakers in Norwich were in jail, the London Meeting for Sufferings could tell them. Such information was vital to a government trying to bring provincial centers under central control and having to rely on opinion rather than an army to do so. If the King or Parliament or both promulgated policy quite unacceptable to a large group of people in one of the provinces, particularly if the province was some distance from London, the policy would be openly opposed or ignored, and it was a moot point which response brought the government into greater disrepute. So it was essential to the King and his supporters (and also their opponents) to know what the local reaction to proposed policies would be. Often the best way to find this out was through the new interest groups, which, unlike the older institutional interests, had their network of connections in the counties.

In their command of information the government needed, their influence over provincial associates with electoral power, and their ability to keep order among volatile sections of the population, the emerging interests found means to influence Charles II, James II, and their parliaments. But this did not mean that they became effective lobbyists overnight, or even within a generation. Developing the techniques of lobbying was slow business for interests that still faced serious limitations. They were handicapped, for one thing, by having few presents to offer politicians in return for support. Since Tudor times the older interests had presented gifts to important M.P.s, had entertained sympathetic members at dinner before crucial votes were taken to make sure they showed up and voted in the City's interest, and had even entertained entire committees assigned to consider legislation affecting the City;[36] in Restoration England such entertaining was beyond the means of most new interests.[37] And there was no more point after 1660 than there had been thirty years earlier in offering honorary membership in groups whose membership was voluntary anyway.

It was also difficult for new interests to develop further the petitioning techniques they had begun with the Long Parliament, for both Restoration monarchs and their parliaments were reluctant to receive the groups' petitions. Petitioning was doubly important because similar petitions sent from London and the provinces indicated concerted effort on the part of various groups within the new networks, and pointed up to the government the strength and unity of the networks. But Charles II and many of his councillors shared his father's abhorrence of petitions from any sources other than legally recognized institutions. Why should they not? Petitions were associated in their minds with Civil War.

At the beginning of Charles's reign Parliament passed an Act Against Tumultuous Petitioning, clearly related to the Civil War, making illegal a petition with more than twenty signatures. Thereafter, for the rest of the Restoration, Parliament continued to debate vigorously the propriety of accepting various petitions. How many signatures did a petition need to have? Could petitions properly concern only part of a bill, not the whole? Could they be on bills currently under discussion? Again and again petitioning provided a bothersome, indeed a fundamentally disturbing issue to Restoration parliaments.

In 1662, when planters and merchants of Virginia petitioned the Privy Council's Committee on Plantations urging the prohibition of tobacco planting in Virginia and Maryland, the Lords first rejected the petition, then announced that henceforth they would not receive any petition of that nature, before deciding two weeks later that "it was not their intention to forbid or discourage the merchants and planters from making their addresses to them."[38] Parliament showed a similar hesitation about accepting petitions. It had long been the custom that Parliament did not accept petitions on money bills, but in 1661, when Quakers petitioned the House of Lords for exemption from oath-taking and from required attendance at the Church of England, the Lords took offense at the petition.[39] Ten years later a petition of London sugar refiners precipitated a long debate in the Commons. The petition was against an increase in sugar duties; it could certainly have been challenged on grounds that it concerned a money bill, but that was not the main ground of objection. Rather, it was that "The great reason why you have representatives is, because your people in numbers should not disturb the councils," as one M.P. remarked, and as another said, "No grievance but there is a person to represent the place."[40]

Daunted by the Lords' annoyance at their earlier petition, the Quakers turned to distributing handbills in the lobby of the Commons (this may possibly be the origin of the word "lobby"), upon which the House voted that "no printed briefs, papers, or breviates, of any matter, be brought to the doors or given or distributed amongst the members of this House."[41] Over the years Parliament did come increasingly to recognize the usefulness of petitions. The parliamentary diarist John Milward bothered to record petitions from only five interest groups in 1666–1668 (he devoted several pages to the Irish Cattle Bill, on which there were several petitions, but he never mentioned any), whereas Narcissus Luttrell, writing right after the Glorious Revolution, recorded at least a hundred in a similar time period.[42] But Parliament always resented pressure from "out of doors" which might either rival or discredit it. Whatever the reason, early lobbyists had to be careful in approaching Parliament.

They were handicapped also by the untrustworthiness of the kings: both Charles II and James II were prepared to be responsive to the new interests but they dared not abandon the traditional interests that had helped restore the monarchy. Charles II was genuinely aware that the stability of monarchy depended in some measure on his ability to placate interests; in this sense he may have been England's first "politician king." He was able also to be more flexible than his father because he did not share his father's desperate need for loans and gifts from established institutions; the combination of a rapidly growing overseas trade and a regularized system of customs duties assured him an income Charles I never had.

Charles II demonstrated his supposed responsiveness to new interests in several ways—through his willingness to consider the creation of a council of trade in which lesser merchants could be effectively represented,[43] his willingness to consider a general naturalization of foreign Protestants, and his appointment of London's leading French minister to be one of his royal chaplains.[44] He sought the support of various ecclesiastical interests by declaring even before his coronation that "no man should be disquieted or called in question for differences of Opinion on Matters of Religion which do not disturb the Peace of the Kingdom,"[45] and by declaring later, after Parliament had imposed penalties on worship outside the Anglican Church, that "the execution of all and all manner of penal laws in matters ecclesiastical against whatsoever sort of non-conformists or recusants be suspended."[46] In addition to issuing two general declarations of indulgence to dissenters from the Church of England, he personally intervened to release particular groups from jail (as he did with Quakers early in his reign) or to put a stop to proceedings at law against them (as he did with Jews in the same period).[47]

Still, it was never safe for an interest group to count on help from the King. Charles II was quite aware that he had come to the throne with the backing of a coalition of largely traditional interests, including the Anglican Church, and for much of his reign he vacillated between cooperating with the coalition and trying to build a rival one so he could become independent of his original supporters. Counterbalancing each other in the King's mind were, on the one hand, his reluctance to be trapped in the coils of the interests that had put him on the throne and, on the other, his reluctance to support rival interests because doing so often resulted in defining more narrowly the limits of royal power.[48]

Given the King's duplicity it was not at all clear what the best approach for London/provincial interests should be, especially in the 1680s. Some supported him, some went into opposition, and some cultivated friends among the King's allies and enemies alike, in order to be on the right side in an emergency, At one extreme some Quakers advocated full-scale cooperation with the monarch as the most viable approach; at the other extreme some West Country Baptists, Congregationalists, and Presbyterians rebelled and formed the core of the Duke of Monmouth's insurrection against James II. The moderates continued to circulate petitions at the Exchange an at taverns (1685), hoping the King or Parliament would accept them. These middle-of-the-road groups kept fair words for the monarch—"the king permits what God bids."[49] They also kept funds for legal defense against prosecution by the same monarchs and cultivated their friends in Holland, where enemies of the Stuart monarchy were gathering. A few Quakers did this: William Penn was negotiating for the charter of Pennsylvania in 1681; in the same year he was writing to the King's enemies on the Continent and contributing to the legal defenses of fellow Quakers. Six years later, while serving as on of James II's advisers, he was also corresponding with William of Orange's secret agent, who lamented that Penn "does good with one hand and harm with the other . . . He placates his majesty; he follows the plans of violent people," and makes plans to go to Pennsylvania, "his country in the Indies," if his other efforts fail.[50] Huguenot merchants were doing the same thing—flattering the kings for their kindness to refugees, maintaining a "state within a state" of Huguenots in London, who managed to their community with a minimum of interference from the King's government, and preparing to join the King's enemies in the event of an invasion.[51]

The Restoration thus began with merchants trading to the colonies still largely undifferentiated by the region with which they traded, a spectrum of churchgoers from Anglican to Puritan still hoping to be comprehended within the established church, most ethnic communities, except for the Jews, functioning passively as part of the Anglican Church, and with no vocational associations in sight. It ended with New England, West Indian, and Virginia merchants organized into separate lobbies, with Quakers, Baptists, Presbyterians, Congregationalists, and Anglicans also organized separately, with tanners, weavers, and cattlemen organized enough to petition Parliament, and with Huguenots, Germans, and Jewish groups all organized directly to handle charity to their own members and less directly to influence government on matters concerning their welfare. By 1690 the City itself was no longer the unified force in national politics that it had been earlier, and its opposition to the interests had been neutralized. Politics remained unstable after 1660, however; the political situation both complicated and was complicated by the existence of the new interests. Not until a new generation of politicians and interest group leaders came to power after 1690 did the new groups find a stable place in English politics.

CHAPTER 3

The Beginnings of Interest Groups in the American Colonies

About a generation after they first appeared in England, religious, mercantile, and even ethnic interests began to develop in the more populous seaboard towns of the American colonies. Since London interests beginning with the Interregnum often had loose ties with interests in the English provinces, it was certainly possible for them to develop connections in the American colonies; since during the Restoration London interests occasionally lobbied on behalf of some of their provincial colleagues, it was certainly possible for Americans to ask the Londoners for help. This rarely happened before 1690, however.

American interest groups through the 1690s generally held back from appealing to London counterparts for several reasons. On the whole the colonial interests were poor, unstable, confined to the larger towns, and often divided over local issues. Appealing to England cost money, appealing over the heads of local authorities could be politically damaging, and London correspondents did not see eye to eye with Americans on particular issues. So the colonists settled problems locally whenever they could, and when they had to appeal to English authorities they tended to bypass the London interests, appealing directly or through individual patrons.

The London interests, therefore, had very little information about the colonies which they could pass on to the government in exchange for favors. The English government found itself working in the dark: just when it was beginning its first tentative experiments in imperial control, it had to rely erratically on information from the colonists' individual patrons, a handful of self-seeking colonial servants, and commissioners occasionally sent out to investigate particular problems. By the same token the American interests had very little opportunity to make their needs known to the British government. Without the possibility of arguing their collective grievances at the appropriate level, they saw no alternative to local riot, rebellion, or simple evasion as a way to protest the effects of undesirable policies. The English lacked informed parties to consult on colonial conditions, and the colonists lacked intermediaries to take their case to the English government. Both colonists and policy makers could only react after the fact to decisions made on the other side of the ocean.

· · ·

English visitors to the American provincial capitals in 1690 would have found the mixture of new and institutional interests there quite familiar. Some of the traditional forms of interest group organization still existed: the colonial assemblies, the colonial towns, and Harvard College were institutional interests; so were the various companies such as the Atherton Associates of the New England Company; and so even were the legally established Puritan churches in the small towns of Massachusetts and Connecticut and the county courts in the south. The neighbors and relatives of the various proprietors constituted ascriptive interests, as did the isolated pockets of non-English settlers scattered throughout the countryside around the capitals.

Alongside the traditional groups in the larger towns, and undercutting the authority of the civic institutions to speak for a united populace (much as was the case in London), were the embryonic American groups in the future transatlantic interests, the newer associational ones. In New York City, for example, there was a flourishing Dutch Reformed Church, a Huguenot congregation, and a small group of Church of England members; the town also had a Quaker meeting, a Lutheran congregation, and scattered Jewish families. Merchants had been meeting together since 1670, at least, when Governor Lovelace had issued a proclamation about "keeping a punctual time for meeting at the Exchange."[1]

In Boston twenty to forty merchants met daily at eleven o'clock in a room under the Townhouse "for the more convenient and expeditious dispatch of Merchants' affayrs." More informally, the merchants met at two coffee houses where they could also purchase books, pick up the news, and learn of imminent sailings.[2] The Townhouse—in this case its library room—also served as a meeting place for the Anglicans until King's Chapel was built in 1686. The town also had a Baptist church, a Quaker meeting, and a Huguenot congregation.[3] Beyond these, Boston had also produced at least three labor organizations—the carters, the coopers, and the bakers—that were rudimentary but still more effective than those in other towns.[4] The carters, for example, were well enough organized to take on the town government on the question of responsibility for road repair, and win.[5]

Elsewhere in coastal towns, and particularly in the capitals, the diverse interest groups of Boston and New York repeated themselves. Newport, Rhode Island, had a Quaker meeting, a Baptist congregation, a Jewish congregation, and a tightly knit group of merchants.[6] Charles Town (Charleston), South Carolina, only eight years old in 1690, already had five different English church denominations and a Huguenot congregation;[7] Philadelphia, the same age as Charles Town, had only one church—the Quakers—but it also included three different ethnic communities and a group of fifty-six merchants.[8]

In 1690 interest groups were still confined almost exclusively to the larger towns: rural groups opposed pluralism in the communities they dominated. Small towns lacked the resources to support competing churches or economic specialization. New York had sixteen carters— enough for a distinct and effective organization—but Salem could afford only two, and the smaller towns called on any available farmer with a cart if they had goods to be transported.[9] Boston had five separate religious denominations by the 1680s, but only four other Massachusetts towns had the resources to support more than one.[10]

Thus small towns became centers of single economic, religious, and sometimes ethnic interests. Village groups sought not diversity but isolation and autonomy, the authority to turn out or keep out all who were not of the same mind.[11] They were usually left alone to pursue their single interests; seldom did two groups of a kind—two religious groups or two vocational or ethnic groups—coexist in small towns, for example, or other rural centers. In Maryland "the greatest part of the inhabitants [did] consist of Praesbiterians, Independents, Anabaptists, and Quakers, those of the Romish being different," but each of the five resided in separate localities.[12] In New Jersey there were five Baptist congregations, eight Quaker meetings, and five Dutch/French reformed churches, but only one town contained churches of two denominations.[13] Groups of French settlers were scattered throughout the colonies; except for those in Charles Town, they tried, even before their arrival in America, to get local authorities to promise to leave them alone, separated by at least five miles from the nearest settlement.[14]

Although as a general rule the interest groups were organized only at the local level, a few ecclesiastical organizations included more than one town. George Fox's visit to the colonies in 1672 had helped organize the Quakers, who by 1689 already had a yearly meeting in New England and monthly or quarterly meetings elsewhere.[15] Puritan ministers of New England revived their yearly meetings in the late 1670s, possibly in response to the Quakers' organization there.[16] Dutch Reformed ministers in New York met occasionally,[17] and Virginia's thirty-five Anglican ministers began meeting after the Bishop of London sent over Commissary James Blair to head them in 1689.[18] These meetings were generally held to discuss doctrine, discipline, and charity,[19] though Maryland Quakers also met for trade,[20] and Massachusetts ministers held their meetings when the General Court was in session so they could be informed of legislative proposals.[21]

All the interests, whether in towns or villages, were still in their infancy. They were inexperienced (the Charles Town and Philadelphia groups, for example, had begun only in the 1680s), poor, unstable, and divided. Many groups were still too poor to put up a regular headquarters, a meeting place where they might also possibly keep records, and this must have slowed down organization. The twenty families who constituted the New York Jewish community had no synagogue, for example, New York Anglicans had no church building; the Baptists there met in members' homes and the Quakers in a tavern. Huguenots in Boston met in the town's schoolhouse; Anglicans until 1686 met in the Townhouse library. The Boston Coffee House did, it is true, serve the same functions as the mercantile coffee houses in London, but nowhere outside Boston did merchants have a coffee house to meet in; only in Boston and possibly New York did they even have an Exchange. Only in Boston did interests (and only some interests, at that) have access to a printing press. Only in New England and Virginia did lay or ministerial representatives of the churches have the money to meet regularly; the ministers of the Dutch Reformed Church in New York, one of the strongest churches in that colony, wrote their superiors in Amsterdam that "personal conferences once a year would be very useful to us, although this is not yet quite possible. The expense involved . . . cannot yet be well met."[22]

Whatever organization could be achieved suffered from the instability of shifting and ill-defined memberships. The lack of a clear division of labor in many areas, a problem common to developing areas, meant that mercantile interests were often indistinguishable from the rest of the community. Mercantile and landed interests fused and separated, overlapped and pulled apart. Merchants "formed not a singular social entity, but a spectrum, not a clearly defined block of like-minded individuals with similar attitudes and styles of life but a combination of [different] people."[23] The governor of New York lumped together "merchants, planters, and inhabitants to the number of 2,000" when describing the colony to authorities in England.[24] Broadly inclusive petitions like those from "divers Merchants, Masters of Ships and others,"[25] or "divers of the Gentry, Merchants and others,"[26] or "the Gentlemen, Merchants, and Inhabitants of Boston and the Country adjacent"[27] suggest that the New York governor was thinking the same way the colonists were: there was as yet no clearly identified, distinct mercantile interest.

Religious interests also overlapped, as membership frequently shifted.

"Of all sort of opinions there are some, and the most part none at all," wrote one contemporary.[28] The cohesion of both religious and ethnic communities depended on the leadership of their ministers, and given the chronic shortage of ministers in the colonies (a facet of the chronic shortage of professionals in developing areas), the necessary leadership was often lacking. When a minister died, moved away, or became disabled or disenchanted with his congregation, the group could quickly disintegrate. In October 1681, the leading Dutch Reformed minister of New York wrote urgently to the Classis of Amsterdam, seeking a replacement for the recently deceased incumbent at Newcastle. A year later he wrote saying it was too late: there were now too few Dutch Reformed communicants at Newcastle to support a minister. Quaker preachers had appeared, and the Dutchman wrote that he "would not advise anyone to come over as ministers there amid the uncertainties of these present waves of enthusiasm."[29] Only the Quakers did not depend upon ordained ministers, a fact that may explain the ease with which they were able to proselytize among leaderless late seventeenth-century congregations and appeal to "the people of the world," by which they meant non-Quakers.[30] The very success of the Quaker "revival" in this period and its rather abrupt decline once other churches began supplying ministers reflect the general instability of contemporary religious interests.

Despite their instability, their poverty, and their local orientation, by 1690 a few—very few—of the interests were going beyond the level of provincial organization and developing connections in London, some quite formal, others considerably less so. Since most colonial churches were offshoots of English denominations, since most colonial export merchants had to have English correspondents, and since a number of non-English groups in the colonies had arrived via London where members had stayed long enough to develop English friendships this was not surprising. The New England Yearly Meeting of Quakers and the Philadelphia Yearly Meeting corresponded at least once a year with the London Meeting for Sufferings;[31] Commissary James Blair of Virginia reported directly to the Bishop of London on Anglican affairs in that colony.[32] Less formally, individual Jewish merchants in London and New York shared ownership of ships,[33] and merchants of the Free Society of Traders (a Quaker company) in London and Philadelphia kept up a regular correspondence.[34] Boston Anglicans, though lacking the formal channel of a commissary, corresponded with the Bishop of London,[35] and London tobacco merchants sent relatives to live in Virginia in order to develop connections with the planters.[36]

Some of the London groups went further than correspondence and actually offered the colonists help in provincial affairs, filling their pulpits, lending them money, arranging for them to purchase land. As one could expect, the most helpful such groups were the strongest of the Restoration interests: the Huguenots, Quakers, Anglicans, and Virginia merchants. The French Committee of London helped a group of Huguenot emigres settle in Virginia.[37] the Free Society of Traders extended generous credit when it helped supply Quakers in Pennsylvania.[38] London merchants bought land in various colonies for resale to Huguenots at reasonable rates.[39] London Congregational churches raised funds for the relief of victims of King Philip's War and a Boston fire that followed.[40] London merchants served as bankers for provincial correspondents. After George Fox returned from his colonial tour in 1673, English Quakers began sending an average of one "visitor" to the colonies every nine months.[41] Under the Bishop of London the Anglican Church managed to send at least twenty-four new ministers to Virginia between 1665 and 1680, despite the shortage of Anglican ministers at home and the reluctance of ministers to go to the colonies.[42]

Beyond these occasional instances of help, however—and they are about the only examples we have—there was very little cooperation between London and American provincial interests during the Restoration era. What is particularly striking is the fact that Londoners rarely offered the Americans political help, though they were already beginning to function as political lobbies, starting to offer help to provincial interests in England. But they rarely lobbied with the government on behalf of American provincial interests and there is little evidence that the Americans ever asked them to. London merchants trading to Virginia appealed to Parliament several times against raising the tobacco duties, an issue on which they shared the same views as their Virginia correspondents.[43] Other London merchants helped the mercantile community in New Hampshire bring down Governor Cranfield.[44] A group of Quakers was probably behind Charles II's short-lived instruction to Massachusetts in 1661 prohibiting the persecution of Quakers in that colony. London dissenters introduced Increase Mather to some of James II's advisers when he came over to protest the Dominion of New England. Beyond these instances, London interests seem to have given the colonists little help.

One reason English lobbies rarely appeared on the Americans' behalf was that as late as 1689 few issues affecting specific interests in specific colonies came openly before the English government. From 1660 to 1696 the Privy Council considered only a handful of issues which involved English interest groups with American connections. On the two most important, the drafting of the charter for Pennsylvania and the creation of the Dominion of New England, the Duke of York exerted his personal influence and did not consult the appropriate interests at all. Six other issues affected only three groups. In the 1660s the New England Company, established to convert the Indians, applied once for a renewal of its charter and once for permission to hold a national charity collection. In the following decade Newfoundland merchants sought protection for their fisheries and convoys for their ships, and in the 1680s Huguenot emigres assisted by the French Committee sought aid in moving to the colonies.[45] Later on the English government began reviewing colonial laws, deciding whether to let them stand or not. But in the 1680s only Virginia of the mainland colonies sent its laws to be reviewed in London. Later interests took advantage of English connections to press for the appointment of royal officials they liked or the removal of those they did not. But until 1685, when New York became a royal colony, only Virginia and New Hampshire among the mainland colonies were royal colonies whose appointees were subject to royal removal. New York became a royal colony that year, and the Dominion of New England was created shortly after, but the Dominion's permanence remained a subject of strong doubt.

Another reason English interests did not take up many colonial issues was that the colonists didn't ask them. Sometimes this hesitation was a reminder of friction between London and provincial groups earlier in the century. London merchants trading to New England had repeatedly appeared at the Lords of Trade seeking a stricter enforcement of the Navigation Acts against the New England merchants, and London dissenters had been openly dismayed by the intolerance of their New England counterparts. The merchants trading to Virginia did not openly oppose the interests of their tobacco-growing correspondents, but they alienated the tobacco planters when they claimed the planters would support an act prohibiting the export of bulk tobacco. "conceiving such a law made here would answer their Prtcular Interest & profit & thereupon using all endeavors to procure the same did boldly and presumptuously undertake to petition his Majestie without our privities knowledge & agreement in the least in our names as well as their own therein setting forth on our behalfes that it would be much for the advancement & good of this country."[46]

Often the hesitation resulted from the weakness of the colonial interests themselves. Immature, unstable, divided on political issues, most colonial interests lacked the resources to appeal to England on any but the most vital and least divisive concerns. The cost of appealing was too high. If they wanted English associates to make a case for them before the government, they had to collect and send evidence. If they wanted a petition or an address sent or a case followed through Parliament or one of the boards, there were fees to be paid, which the English passed on to the colonists. If they sent over special agents, that cost more, though ecclesiastical agents like Increase Mather were able to make up part of the cost by preaching in London churches, and merchants were sometimes able to develop useful trading connections in London.

The cost of appealing, moreover, was not only a financial one. There was bound to be some stigma attached to groups or individuals who appealed over the heads of the local majority to a distant imperial power, thereby advertising their acceptance of London as the center of imperial power. As a Massachusetts leader wrote, contentions were "very much unbecoming a people in our circumstances."[47] Quakers in Massachusetts found this out when they appealed to London and found their appeal published in the *Boston Newsletter*. At their further request the Board of Trade criticized the newspaper report for "containing reflections upon their proceedings here in England."[48]

What made the costs particularly prohibitive was that even the established colonial policies in Restoration England were likely to be altered or repealed without notice, often because of obscure backstairs politicking. In 1661, for example, the King warned against the persecution of Quakers in Massachusetts; the following year, under English pressure, he cancelled the warning.[49] In 1672 a charter was prepared in England establishing an Anglican diocese in Virginia, and the King was prepared to nominate a bishop; then, with no explanation, the matter was dropped. After a brief interlude when Charles II accepted agents of the New England colonies as emissaries from semi-autonomous governments, his brother James (the new King) abruptly ended the procedure by creating the Dominion of New England.[50]

Finally, even if colonial groups had been able to cover the cost of seeking help from the Londoners, they could not always decide what to ask for. Even when interest groups did develop some organization and a stable and distinct membership, they were often so badly divided over questions of practical policy that they could not present a united front on issues of political importance. Merchants in New York and Boston, for example, disagreed sharply over whether to welcome, tolerate, or oppose James's attempts to combine the New England colonies and New York in the Dominion of New England.[51] Quakers and Huguenots, knowing James to be a Catholic and suspecting that his aid to Protestant dissenters in England and America was a temporary political expedient, divided over whether to support the King or not. For groups that did not even have the money to build a meeting place and pay for provincial meetings, and for groups that had little consensus on political issues, it was a rare issue that was worth the effort of appealing to England.

As the Restoration went on, several issues appeared which certainly had to be settled at the imperial level, and were important enough and nondivisive enough to enlist the interests' efforts. After New York became an English colony in 1664, there was no shortage of issues to be settled by imperial authorities: resident Huguenots, for example, sought naturalization so they could trade in compliance with the Navigation Acts, and the governor needed instructions from London about how to proceed; New York merchants were concerned about duties on New York products charged by other provinces. Elsewhere companies wanted colonial boundaries settled in their favor, something that could be done only by imperial authorities. Interests argued for and against bringing New England colonies under royal control; the decision had to be made in London.

On all these issues it paid the colonists to make their desires clear to authorities in England. But in their dealings colonial interests tended to bypass London interest groups, either substituting influential individuals or appealing directly to imperial authorities themselves.[52] In the colonies they gravitated to roving commissioners, governors, customs collectors— any representative of the British government who appeared there was fair game for the entreaties of interests who didn't know where else to turn; he could rarely escape being drawn into local disputes. When the New York City Huguenots who were not yet naturalized citizens wanted permission to take up trade despite injunctions against this in the Navigation Acts, they sought permission not by going to the French Committee but by petitioning the governor and having him forward the petition to the Lords of Trade, applying "to your Lordship as to a channel through which the King's favors flow to them."[53] Quakers distrained for support of Congregational clergy in Massachusetts appealed to Governor Andros of the Dominion of New England; so did Huguenots in the Narragansett country, whose hay was stolen by English settlers. Both groups got what they wanted from Andros directly.[54] When Congregationalists sought relief from Andros himself they sent Increase Mather, who quickly approached the King in person.

In England the interests sought help through highly placed individuals—colonists who had returned to London, friends or relatives who had never left it, anyone who might be able to navigate the uncharted channels of Court politics. New York merchant Robert Livingston, despite his acquaintance with a number of London merchants trading to New York, was helped in his petitions for reimbursement by the Earl of Peterborough and by William Penn.[55] Pennsylvania farmers complained to Penn himself, not to London Quakers in general, about the duty imposed on their wheat when they shipped it from Maryland ports.[56] The cases of Livingston and the Pennsylvania farmers may have been special. After all, Livingston was arguing a private case, and Penn was the proprietor of Pennsylvania. But there was nothing special about the fact that Huguenots in various colonies looked for political assistance not to the French Committee of London but to Dr. Daniel Cox and one or two aristocratic patrons at the Savoy Church. When John Winthrop went to London on behalf of the Atherton Company and the colony of Connecticut (he was disputing Rhode Island's claim to the Narragansett Country as he sought a new charter for Connecticut in 1661), he was helped by personal friends and correspondents—Robert Boyle, Samuel Hartlib, Sir Kenelm Digby, Sir William Brereton, Lord Say and Seal— men who had no special interest in the Atherton Company.[57] Increase Mather described the help he got when he was in London negotiating for the return of the original Massachusetts charter, which Charles II had abrogated by *quo warranto* proceedings: "Providence ordered my acquaintance with such persons as did exceedingly advantage me for a most successful management of my negotiations. In King James' time my acquaintance with . . . Mr. Lob proved a mercy to New England . . . After the Revolution my intimate acquaintance with Sr. Henry Ashurst proved a singular mercy."[58] In all these approaches the colonists were still relying on friendship networks, the precursors of interest groups.

Significantly, the colonists most likely to have friends highly placed in Restoration England were colonists of considerable means of influence themselves—a few New England merchants, individual Chesapeake planters, friends and relatives of proprietors, and certain New England leaders. Before the development of connections between London and the provincial interest groups, political influence in the colonies belonged only to the well-born and the well-connected and only periodically, at that.

As the last decade of the seventeenth century began, the looseness of English interest group networks thus left room for the Americans to fit in and function in ways quite similar to provincial interests in England. Since London interests had begun to function as political lobbies, it is conceivable the Americans could have looked to them to lobby with the English government on matters of concern to colonial interests. On the whole, they did not. On marginal issues that might be settled at the town, provincial, or imperial levels the Americans generally opted for local solutions because they did not have the resources to appeal to the English government. On questions that had to be settled at the imperial level, Americans tended to bypass English interests, going directly to imperial authorities, because they lacked confidence in either the power or the trustworthiness of English groups.

Colonial interests had virtually no say in the drafting of the Navigation Acts, surely the most important legislation affecting them in this period, nor did they have any more real influence on the backstairs deliberations preceding the creation of the Dominion of New England: the kings worked with court politics rather than colonial interest groups in mind. The Lords of Trade collected volumes of information, almost none of it from interested parties who might have warned them in advance that certain policies were likely to produce trouble; their information-gathering was largely reactive to events in the colonies. They sent commissioners to New England after some New Englanders had complained that the colony was acting independent of English authority. They sent commissioners to study Virginia after the Virginians had rebelled. They heard lengthy testimony about the merits and weaknesses of the Dominion of New England—after it had failed. They suffered from the lack of American input into imperial decisions; Americans suffered from not being able to give it.

CHAPTER 4

The Development of English Interests, 1690–1714

The Glorious Revolution ended half a century of conflict at home and began a quarter of a century of conflict abroad. Both the domestic and the foreign changes helped the voluntary interests, most especially those with American leanings. Once monarch and Parliament reached accommodation over the actual control of government, a rapid expansion of administration was possible, and the new generation of government servants was far more conscious than their predecessors of the importance of system and information, both of which the interests could help provide. The two long wars with France (1689–1714) required the government to get both financial support and information from the interests, the more so from interests with colonial connections because North America was now a theater of war. The day-to-day "management" of colonial affairs in peace and war fell to the King and his servants rather than Parliament. This benefitted transatlantic interests, which found their small-scale lobbying far more effective when confined to particular royal appointees considering particular issues affecting particular colonial regions.

In the aftermath of the Glorious Revolution the interests found their own positions more clearly defined; they no longer had to function as states within the state but could now behave as recognized political units influencing national politics rather than evading them. The interest groups grew in organization (though less in numbers because their own rate of growth continued to slow as the overall rate of London's growth did), and colonial interests were the beneficiaries of the reciprocal redefinition of relations between London interests and the state. The old interests entered the competitive political arena with a variety of other new interests. Some of the new groups—English voluntary associations like hatters or iron mongers, or institutional ones like the Royal African Company or the Hudson's Bay Company—they were likely to encounter in Parliament. Others, like the American mainland interests, they were more likely to confront at the Board of Trade. "Imperial" interests like the Irish lobby or the West Indians they faced in several places.

.   .   .

In the thirty-five years before 1696 only two London interest groups, the London merchants trading to New York and the London merchants trading to Virginia, had sought parliamentary help on questions of interest to their American correspondents. In the nineteen years after that date, Parliament received twelve such petitions. Between 1697 and 1709 the newly created Board of Trade received fifty-one petitions from English groups on behalf of American interests; in the same period the Privy Council heard appeals from six different London interest groups on nine separate issues. In the years before the late 1690s there had been few occasions on which Londoners had interested themselves on matters of concern to the provincials; in the years after that there were more and more.[1]

For an explanation we must begin with London. Nowhere was the development of interests more noticeable. Between 1690 and 1715 the Palatine Relief Committee, a lobby of sorts, was established; the General Baptists, the ministers of the Three Denominations (Presbyterian, Congregational, and Baptist), the Sephardic Jewish community, and merchants trading to Pennsylvania, New England, the Carolinas, and probably New York became able for the first time to lobby effectively; and the Virginia merchants, Quakers, Huguenots, and Anglicans developed far more sophisticated methods of lobbying than they had used before.

Several factors explain the sprouting of London's interest groups. One was simply the continued growth of greater London in the late seventeenth and early eighteenth centuries, though at a somewhat slower rate than before. The suburbs were growing while the City proper was not. The population of greater London grew by an estimated 75,000 over the first half of the eighteenth century, from 575,000 to 650,000, but this was a far lower rate of increase than had taken place in the second half of the seventeenth century.[2] Still, with a population somewhere around 575,000, London in 1700 was bound to contain a greater variety of interests than towns of provincial England, the largest of which, Bristol, numbered only 20,000, or the towns of provincial America, the largest of which, Boston, numbered only about 7,000.

Such a concentration of population allowed London to support interest groups even out of proportion to its numbers. By 1700 there were at least a thousand merchants there trading to America. In the first quarter of the eighteenth century 398 merchants signed petitions on questions relating to individual American colonies, but this was clearly only a fraction of the total number of merchants involved in American commerce. A map of English dissenters would have shown an extraordinary concentration in London—20,000 or more, enough to support eighty-eight dissenting churches as against only forty-six Anglican churches and chapels—a lesser concentration in provincial towns, and a rapid thinning toward the countryside.[3] The population of non-English communities in London is impossible to estimate over a twenty-five-year period, because emigres arrived in waves, some remaining in London, others moving on to the English and American provinces, but the non-English population in London probably never fell below 10,000 in the late seventeenth and early eighteenth century. In 1686 and 1687, 15,000 Huguenots had entered London as a result of French persecution. They immediately set to building French churches—eight new ones between 1690 and 1700—while the congregation of the old Threadneedle Street Church swelled to 8,000. Early in the eighteenth century some Huguenots began assimilating into London society, losing their separate character and interest, but in 1710 the non-English population of London was expanded by the sudden arrival of 13,000 Palatine German emigres.[4]

The various interests tended to concentrate in particular neighborhoods, making organization easier; for example, of the twenty dissenting churches in the City proper, eleven were within 500 yards of Dr. Williams's Library on Red Cross Street. French churches (some dissenting, some Anglican) remained concentrated in Spitalfields and the Savoy; German churches, largely Lutheran, were in the Savoy and along the waterfront. Similarly, there was a slight tendency for merchants trading to the same colonies to be concentrated in the same part of the City. Their coffee houses were all within a five-minute walk of the Royal Exchange, but their counting houses were concentrated in other parts of the City—Chesapeake merchants around Tower Hill, Pennsylvania merchants on Grace Church Street, the newer Carolina merchants settling in the northern and western parts of the City.[5]

For some of the religious and ethnic groups organization was made not only feasible but imperative by the fact that London was the place to which foreign refugees generally came first, and their rapid but sporadic influx forced the communities to tighten their organization to distribute available resources. The arrival of thousands of French refugees into London after the revocation of the Edict of Nantes in 1685 had greatly complicated the work of the French Committee,[6] and the influx of hundreds of Ashkenazic Jews into an area of a few blocks in London in the same decade had presented an enormous challenge to the leadership of the existing Sephardic community.[7] Crises required organization; once they were over and the newcomers had either moved on or been assimilated and employed, then the communities had further resources to tap. Thus the London ethnic groups were more likely than those in the provinces to have numbers and wealth sufficient to produce surplus resources, which could be used either for lobbying or for direct financial assistance to colleagues elsewhere. The size and wealth of London, the geographical concentration of interests within the City, the need of interests to maximize resources to manage a transient population—all these helped London's growing interest groups.

In the new environment interest groups began to develop organizations, varying from the loose and informal to the sophisticated and complex, and to deploy the resources which were to give them political leverage in colonial as well as English politics. The two strongest groups were the two that were already structured, the Anglicans and the Quakers. The Anglican Church, closest of the religious groups to the center of power, created a number of new officers and subordinate societies, some of which related to the colonies. In 1689 the Bishop of London appointed his first representative to the colonies: James Blair was sent to Virginia as the Bishop's Commissary empowered to call meetings of priests in the colony. After 1702 the church also organized the Society for the Propagation of the Gospel (S.P.G.), a group whose missionaries reflected zealously the Anglican interests in America, and the Society for Promoting Christian Knowledge (S.P.C.K.), whose continental connections led it to focus its attention on helping non-English communities in America. Both groups were capable of very effective lobbying, though this was not their primary responsibility.[8]

The Yearly Meeting of Quakers, which had been established in 1675, created a committee in 1701 to "watch the laws which are before Parliament"; it included some American members and assumed responsibility for Quakers in all the colonies except Pennsylvania, which was left to William Penn while he was active. Meanwhile the London Meeting for Sufferings had appointed a committee to correspond with yearly and monthly meetings in the provinces, and the committee also kept abreast of laws affecting the colonies.[9]

Other ecclesiastical groups also organized, though much more informally. In 1702, after a false start some ten years earlier, ministers of the three main dissenting denominations in London (Baptists, Presbyterians, and Congregationalists) began meeting, at first only intermittently, but by 1715 they did seem to have associated with them a group of prominent laymen including Sir William Ashurst, Thomas Holles, and Lord Barrington, who served as political liaisons.[10] The Baptists, who had been meeting regularly since 1686, even had their own coffee house, the Hanover, by 1714.[11] The Lutheran Church in London was not formally organized by 1715, but the first Lutheran chaplain to the Royal Court had already been appointed by Queen Anne.[12] In 1690 the Great Synagogue was built at Bevis Marks, and by 1702 the Sephardic Jewish community had created a Committee of Deputies "to attend to the business of the nation which is before Parliament."[13] Meanwhile the French Committee continued to distribute the Royal Bounty and initiated a correspondence with American churches in 1699.[14] (The Dutch Church at Austin Friars also corresponded with Dutch Reformed churches in New York, though there is no direct evidence of their political activity.)

The loosest groups of all belonged to the merchants, most of whom did not get beyond coffee house gatherings early in the century. In 1702 appears the first formal record of three colonial mercantile coffee houses, the Pennsylvania, New England, and Carolina,[15] and it seems likely from appearances and testimony on key issues that the new centers had a member or two—Nathaniel Paice for the New England merchants and Joseph Boone for the Carolinians are likely candidates—assigned to watch the affairs of Parliament and the Board of Trade. There may even have been a fourth new gathering place sometime after 1689, the New York coffee house. The fact that New York merchants petitioned Parliament or the Privy Council three times between 1689 and 1702; that in 1703 they sent to Parliament a petition signed by men "living at and trading to New York"; and that they were able to guarantee to the Board of Trade the attendance of prominent New York visitors to London all suggest that there was a regular gathering place and a more formal organization than appears on any records.[16]

Best organized, of course, were the Chesapeake merchants, already establishing political committees. By 1712 the Virginia merchants were meeting regularly at the Exchange or at their coffee house, choosing a committee of leading members to collect dues, hire counsel, draft petitions, and organize their appearances before the Board of Trade.[17] A year before that a group of Maryland merchants, constituting an informal committee of sorts, asked the Board of Trade to instruct the government of Maryland not to pass any law relating to commerce unless eighteen months was allowed before it took effect, so the merchants could review it.[18]

Overlapping the committees within the interests, sometimes but not always synonymous with them, "core groups" of distinguished members began to emerge in the first two decades of the eighteenth century. Core group members were men of affluence and influence, men with connections at Court and in Parliament, men of enough standing within the interests to organize "subscriptions" to defray expenses. It became the custom for them to seek the "good liking of the administration" before the interest group as a whole approached the government.[19] In addition, a number of the interests had agents with varying responsibilities, everything from serving as filing clerks, getting the agenda for upcoming

Board of Trade or Privy Council meetings, searching records for vital information, to coordinating efforts with groups in the English and American provinces. Between them the core groups, the agents, and the committees handled the most delicate work involved in extracting concessions from ministers and lesser bureaucrats.

All three types maximized what parliamentary support they had by developing far more sophisticated techniques than Restoration interests used for influencing potential friends in Parliament as well as the Board and the Privy Council. Core group members went over the voting records of M.P.s and called on those who might be sympathetic. (The Quakers were particularly effective at this.) The Quakers were also adept at organizing letter-writing campaigns to M.P.s and on at least one occasion a group of Quakers waited just outside the doors of the House of Lords and actually negotiated with Lords standing near the door for a change in the wording of proposed legislation.[20] Merchants called on M.P.s from London and the outports; dissenters reminded particular M.P.s of dissenting votes among their constituents. On special occasions the merchants were able, as Jacob Price has shown, to influence M.P.s from London and the outports to support their measures, and to turn out surprisingly large numbers of M.P.s (313 showed up to vote on the French treaty in 1707),[21] and the Quaker lobby was able to block passage of the bills for resuming charter colonies to the crown in 1701, 1702, and 1706.[22] On other occasions the interests were able to join other interests for successful log rolling: the West India sugar interests and the Irish linen interests did this early in the century and so did the tobacco and wine interests, each seeking a favorable treaty with France.[23]

By itself the growth and organization of the new interests could not entirely explain their political influence. Equally important was the unprecedented expansion of a government that had to be responsive to them. Freed from fundamental controversies over control after 1689, supported by new sources of revenue, and required to organize in order to mobilize national resources for two French wars in quick succession, the British government expanded with phenomenal speed. To a far greater extent than their predecessors in the Restoration the new generation of administrators realized that they needed to collect information systematically if they were to develop and implement policy and measure its effectiveness, and for this they needed the cooperation of all interest groups.

The need to support expanding wartime armies and collect the necessary funds stimulated the growth of the bureaucracy almost fivefold in twenty-five years, from about 2,500 just before the Glorious Revolution to about 12,000 in 1714. Particularly related to the transatlantic interests was the increase in the staffs of committees associated with trade and colonial administration. William III at first continued the old Lords of Trade and Plantations, replacing James's appointees with his own, but by 1692 the committee was in decline with scarcely a clerk. In 1696 the King appointed a new committee, the Board of Trade, to be responsible for day-to-day imperial decisions, and together with the Treasury and Customs they and other staffs came to sixty-five.[24]

The Board's duties were loosely defined: to "inspect and examine into the general trade of our said kingdom and the several parts thereof . . . to consider some proper methods for setting on work and employing the poor of our said kingdom," and "to inform [themselves] of the present conditions of the respective plantations."[25] With functions as vague as these the Board could work on any number of issues, but several of its activities particularly affected colonial interests. During wartime it recommended the best times for the sailing of convoys and the kinds of naval stores the colonies might produce. Over the longer run, it prepared instructions for the governors of the royal colonies, nominated colonial councillors, resettled foreign communities in America, and reviewed legislation from all the colonies to see if laws contained any provision inconsistent with the laws of the mother country or manifestly unjust to groups in the colonies.

The Board consisted of eight salaried and eight *ex officio* members, and as few of them had much expertise on colonial matters, they looked for interests for much of their information. The salaried officials were largely country gentlemen with little direct knowledge of the colonies.

Unlike Restoration councils, religious and mercantile, on which interests were represented directly (Clarendon's Committee of Foreign Plantations established in 1660 had ten merchants on it out of a total of 46 members) and unlike some of the councils proposed in the 1690s including one for elected representatives of trading constituencies, the Board had almost no members representing interest groups themselves. On the first Board there was only one merchant, and while the Bishop of London was a member *ex officio,* he rarely attended. Instead, the ministers' need to find jobs for their parliamentary supporters meant that the Board was composed mainly of men with some importance in English politics but very few connections with America and very little direct knowledge of American politics.[26]

In seeking direct knowledge about American conditions, moreover, the Board frequently had no other sources as reliable as the interests. American interests often had fresher information and more of it than government bureaucrats could get from official sources. Part of the reason was that the interests' coffee houses were often close to the wharves, certainly closer than Whitehall, and ship captains went there first to deliver their mail and drop off any colonial visitors who might have sailed with them. When mail or visitors brought unexpected news, coffee house patrons could assemble quickly, within a day or so if necessary, and decide which information to pass on to the government and what action to press for before the government servants learned the news themselves.

Furthermore, the interests had more American correspondents to provide them news than the government had. We have noted the rapid expansion of government in this period; what we did not note was that the number of officials in America did not grow proportionately. Out of 750 customs officials at the end of the period only 42 (2 percent) were in America, whereas American and West Indian trade was 32 percent of the value of all English trade.[27] There were about two hundred and forty English officials in the American colonies (.02 percent of the English government). At most there would have been about 20 officials each in royal colonies, and 12 of these would have been royal appointees to the colonial councils, men who had no obligation to write to the home government at all. The eight remaining officials were, moreover, unlikely to get along with each other and therefore likely to send conflicting information because their objectives were so different. Governors trying to win the good will of colonies by winking at their customs infractions were not likely to see eye to eye with customs officials; lieutenant governors were not likely to support the interpretations of governors they hoped to unseat. So committees at Whitehall had few first hand sources of American information from their own staffs, and the interpretations of royal appointees in the colonies were likely to be contradictory anyway.

In addition to lacking many reliable government firsthand sources of American information, the members of the Board also lacked official guidelines for determining or implementing colonial policy. The government had no clear, overarching policy, or rather most "policies" were so vague that they gave the Board little guidance. Take trade, for example. If there was any guiding principle of British colonial administration, it was that the colonies were to serve the economic interests of the mother country. A few implications of this principle were clear: colonial enterprises could not be directly competitive with English ones, for example. But on many issues that came up it was not at all clear how the principle should be applied. For instance, how much paper money could colonial governments issue without threatening the debts of British merchants and hence the economic interests of the mother country?[28] Clearly the best people to ask were the merchants.

One other example was religion. An English interpretation of the Toleration Act was simply inapplicable when considering laws of colonies whose religious mixture was quite different from England. How could the Act, which declared that legally registered members of English Protestant dissenting congregations were exempt from the penalties of the Test and Corporation Acts, be applied in colonies like Massachusetts and Connecticut? Confusion regarding the laws of almost all the colonies was enormous, and if it was to be cleared up at all, the Board needed a great deal of information from churchmen and dissenters alike.

Lacking personal familiarity with colonial affairs, reliable information from government servants in the colonies, and clearly applicable government guidelines to direct their interpretations, the Board of Trade members sought information *ad hoc* from London interests as issues came up. When was the best time for tobacco and sugar convoys to sail? The Board undertook endless consultations with tobacco and sugar merchants and spent countless hours considering their petitions and counterpetitions before settling on departure dates. What naval stores could the colonies produce? The Board again asked the merchants before recommending hemp, pitch, and tar in 1704. What tools would Palatine immigrants need if they settled in the colonies? The Board asked the New York and Virginia merchants. Was there a shortage of linen in Virginia? In 1708 they asked the Virginia merchants.[29] The Bishop of London and the S.P.G. gave them information on the persecution of Anglicans in the northern colonies; the London Meeting for Sufferings collected detailed information about fines levied on American Quakers.

The Board sought more than information from the various interests; it sought the opinions of the rank-and-file members on various questions. There is some evidence that individual members of the Board consulted privately with interests on particular affairs. At times the Board sent someone out to poll the interests: leading merchants, colonial agents, or agents hired by the merchants themselves were asked to solicit the opinions of merchants as a group on such questions as the placing of lighthouses or the timing of convoys.[30] Twice a week its meetings were opened to the public, and agents were sent to provide advance notices of hearings the rank and file of the interest groups might usefully attend.[31] Just how many people could squeeze in at any one meeting is not clear, but in 1711 the active members of the Virginia "trade" decided to attend *en masse,* and though there were up to 175 of them, they anticipated no trouble getting in.[32]

When the Board of Trade or members of other government committees did not solicit their information, interest groups often found it useful to volunteer it. To this end they usually appointed one of their own members or relied on their core group to serve as agents. Agents might in turn hire a solicitor for legal advice. It was the job of the agents to learn of the anticipated dates of hearings and prepare their presentations after gathering information.

The groups sometimes circulated manuscript pamphlets copied out by clerks, or broadsides which might be duplicates of broadsides printed in the provinces, excerpts from provincial newspapers printed separately, pamphlets written by members of the group or commissioned journalists. A number of the interests used their own printing presses in this period: the Virginia merchants, for example, contracted with their own publisher;[33] Bevis Marks Synagogue had its own press,[34] and the German community had its own press and book seller.[35]

The groups also worked on petitioning, which, after the Glorious Revolution, became for the first time unquestionably legal. Article five of the Declaration of Rights declared "That it is the right of the subjects to petition the King, and all commitments and prosecutions for such petitioning are illegal."[36] Petitions provided information, they politicized interest group members who might otherwise have paid little attention to what the government did, and they demonstrated to the government the breadth of the petitioners' support. Once petitioning became safe, it took little time for London interests to develop its techniques to the fullest.

The quarter-century after England replaced King James II with William and Mary in the Glorious Revolution was a watershed in the growth of English government; it was also, and for the same reasons, a watershed in the development of London-American interest group cooperation. The Revolution settlement, while far from definitive, did at least create a domestic environment in which voluntary interests were guaranteed safe functioning; the growth of London, while slowing, still facilitated their concentration and organization; and the growth of the government enhanced their political influence. London voluntary interest groups were beginning to blossom.

· CHAPTER 5 ·

American Interests, 1690–1714

To most American colonists, living in the British empire meant something quite different after 1710 from what it had meant a quarter-century before. No longer were the colonies reacting to policies concocted rather capriciously in the private councils of the monarchs, and finding that the most effective reaction was often to pay no attention at all. By the second decade of the eighteenth century the colonies were becoming integrated into an empire that was both more openly responsive to their demands and more assertive of its own authority.

Seven of the mainland provinces had become or were in the process of becoming royal colonies, their governors appointed and instructed by the crown. All the colonies had to send their laws to England for review by the Privy Council, and many were the object of imperial efforts to stop piracy and smuggling, resettle non-English groups within their lands, and utilize their resources, particularly their naval stores and new manpower, in times of international conflict.

Why did the colonists come to accept arrangements after 1689 that they had either ignored or resisted before? Not because the arrangement was imposed on them by force: the British army in the colonies was there primarily to fight the French, not subjugate the colonists, and the government servants, while there in greater numbers than during the Restoration, still did not amount to more than a handful. The empire was run by compliance, not coercion.

What, then, explains the compliance? Many things, of course—economic benefits, military protection, a large measure of continued self-government, a strong sense of being English, for example.[1] But along with these was another reason why the colonists were willing to accept a more integral position in the empire—they were acquiring influence over the way that the empire was run.

In securing this leverage the transatlantic interests had become crucial.

Along with groups like the newly appointed British officials in the colonies and agents representing the colonial legislatures in London, they became one of the main conduits for the exchange of information in the empire. In the decades after 1689 voluntary interests in the American colonies increased in membership, organization, and political consciousness to the point where many of them were ready to seek some kind of cooperative relationship with their counterparts in London. They were especially directed this way because of the number of imperial functions that now directly affected them. The early years were a period of trial and error as the Americans were learning what issues were appropriate for appeal, what supporting material was needed, and what correspondents should be addressed, while the Londoners were learning which departments of the post-Revolution government would handle particular questions. Both sides also learned that one of the Londoners' strongest resources in English lobbying—their access to information the government needed—was, if anything, even more important in lobbying on colonial issues than on domestic. Little by little the English and American interests began to develop patterns of effective cooperation.

.   .   .

The interests developed from a variety of backgrounds. Some of them were new; some represented the consolidation and development of small, often impoverished, and weakly organized groups that had existed earlier. Some of the new ethnic interests continued to develop on the frontier on tracts of land large enough to allow whole communities of foreigners to live for a while in semi-isolation, preserving their culture against the English influences that surrounded them. But more of the interests continued to result from the growth of cities that provided the numbers and wealth required for interests to flourish. Boston grew from 7,000 in 1690 to 12,000 in 1720, Philadelphia from 4,000 to 10,000, New York from 3,900 to 7,000, and Charles Town from 1,100 to 3,500.[2]

Accuracy in estimating the size of various interests varies from group to group. Mercantile groups can be estimated fairly accurately since occupation was often listed on tax lists: we know, for example, that 53 men were counted in Philadelphia's merchant community in 1710, 110 in New York in 1702/3, and 150 in Boston in the 1690s.[3] With churches and ethnic groups we are generally much less certain because church records are unclear or incomplete, and it is difficult to track down ethnic origins from the family names on tax lists. In New York City, the only place with a Jewish community at this time, the number of Jewish families grew from twenty in 1690 to forty in 1715, in part accounted for by the immigration of a number of wealthy Jewish merchants such as Pacheco, Levy, and Franks.[4] In the same city, among the surnames on the 1703 tax list 374 were probably Dutch, 190 English, and 74 French.[5] But there the precision ends. When we get to Boston we have only a rough estimate of 500 to 700 Scots Irish arriving at the end of the period, and a slightly smaller number of Palatines.[6] In the colony as a whole there were estimated to be 2,000 French.[7] For the other cities we really cannot estimate the distribution of various ethnic groups at all.

For churches we are in even worse shape. We can assume that a church must have grown in numbers if it became rich enough to erect a building—or a second one—in the period. A rule of thumb was that it took forty families, an average of two hundred people, to finance a church, but it is unwise to go beyond this to estimate numbers. New York City's tiny Anglican congregation had worshipped in the town's fort in 1690; by 1697 they were able to build Trinity Church.[8] By 1717 there were enough Presbyterians to build a church on Wall Street at Broadway.[9] In Boston the Church of England grew so rapidly that by 1710 King's Chapel had become "too small for the congregation and strangers that dayly increase," and it had to be enlarged.[10] Quakers built their first meeting house in 1694 and fifteen years later had to expand into a second building. Baptists were wealthy enough and numerous enough to have a permanent minister in 1708. French Huguenots were finally wealthy enough to build a church in 1715. Philadelphia, exclusively Quaker before 1690, had a Presbyterian Church and an Episcopal one numbering 500 before the decade was out. Charles Town Congregationalists built a church in 1690, Quakers built a meeting house there in 1699, and a second Episcopal Church went up in 1702, and we have an estimate of 2,950 dissenters, 2,550 Anglicans, and 500 Huguenots living in that city in 1700.[11] But there are no reliable statistics for any of the churches.

With new members and new meeting places came the opportunity—indeed, the necessity—for stronger organization, and the quarter-century after 1689 saw the rapid organization of many colonial interest groups. Before 1689 the organization of Puritan ministers in New England had waxed and waned. In that year they were organized enough for twenty of them to draft and sign a petition to the King seeking a restoration of the colony's original charter, which Charles II had taken away; from then on we see the Boston ministers, themselves representing a spectrum of theological opinion, slowly assuming the leadership of their colleagues in Massachusetts and New Hampshire. By 1717 the Associated Ministers of Boston seem to have been meeting regularly, hearing appeals from disputes in other congregations, publishing pamphlets, and speaking for the rest of the Congregational-Presbyterian churches in negotiations with the governor.[12]

Far more clearly organized were the Anglicans, Presbyterians, and Quakers. The Presbyterians organized their first Presbytery in Philadelphia in 1706 and in 1717 their first synod.[13] In 1690 there was one commissary of the Church of England in the colonies, James Blair of Virginia; by 1715 the Bishop of London had also sent commissaries to Maryland, the Carolinas, New England, Pennsylvania, and New York, and Anglican clergy to every colony except Rhode Island. Connecticut and New Hampshire were usually meeting once a year.[14] Perhaps the best organized church in the colonies, better organized even than the Anglicans, were the Quakers, who created a hierarchical organization unmatched by any of the other colonial interests. By the first decade of the eighteenth century Quakers in all colonies were organized into monthly meetings, and representatives from the monthly meetings attended the yearly meetings. The Newport Yearly Meeting was coming to be recognized as the center of New England Quaker organization, while the Philadelphia Yearly Meeting more quickly became dominant in the middle colonies.

Similarly, toward the end of the seventeenth century growing numbers of non-English communities in the colonies began to organize. Foreign groups settled on the frontier found that the very needs of the community forced them to create some kind of organization, however unstable it might be. In cities the non-English groups began to organize around churches and clubs; there was a French club in New York City, for example. Huguenots did not organize beyond the club or congregational level, but each congregation was formed into a corporation whose members met twice a year.[15] Dutch ministers in New York met annually or in times of crisis.

Finally, it was the generation after 1690 that developed the major mercantile coffee houses. In 1690 only two towns, Boston and New York, had any coffee houses at all; by 1720 there were four coffee houses in Boston, three in New York, one in Philadelphia and a tavern in Newport where merchants met.[16] At these the merchants collected mail, bought insurance, held auctions, and arranged commercial transactions; here also they drew up and signed petitions and prepared broadsides for public distribution.

Once they had come together as groups, the interests sought out London connections in a variety of ways, most often through letters, agents, or requests passed through colonists who were visiting London on business. Sometimes they added requests for help to ongoing correspondence, as did Quakers when they described troubles in their yearly epistles or merchants when they added paragraphs to letters primarily about business arrangements. Sometimes colonial interests sent agents to win London support on particular missions; Increase Mather picked up friends among London dissenters when he went over trying to get back the Massachusetts charter in the years surrounding the Glorious Revolution, and Comissary James Blair went to England and worked with the Anglican Church there to unseat Governor Nicholson of Virginia. Sometimes the colonial interests wrote friends in London for advice and ended up hiring a Londoner to work on their behalf with the relevant English groups (Sir Henry Ashurst was liason for a number of dissenter associations). There was certainly a lot of trial and error in the early efforts at cooperation. Colonial visitors were not always sure where to seek the appropriate lobbyists. Colonial agents sometimes approached the wrong people in government, colonial correspondents sometimes asked for help on issues that were out of date or never came up.

Over the decades after the Glorious Revolution, however, most London and American interests managed to establish long-term connections and to figure out what issues to appeal and which branch to appeal to. Most particularly, they learned to work with the Board of Trade. (Only a few individual lobbyists such as William Penn and to a lesser extent Increase Mather developed good connections among the ministers of state at this time, and most of the interests preferred not to work with Parliament where, among other things, they were likely to run up against purely English interests. At the Board they found it easy to make connections, and they were likely to confront only other American interests there.) On each of its functions the Board showed its responsiveness to Londoners with American connections. Sometimes they needed help in the drafting of governors' instructions, for example. The Bishop of London helped draft the Maryland Act of 1700 establishing the Anglican Church in that colony. The act was drawn up in London and transmitted to Maryland through the governor's instructions.[17] Quaker pressure was responsible for New York Governor Hunter's instruction in 1709, "you take care that an Act be passed in the General Assembly of your said Province to the like effect as that past here in the 7th and 8th years of his late Majestie's reign Entitled an Act that the Solemn Affirmation and Declaration of the People called Quakers shall be accepted instead of an Oath in the usual form."[18] It is difficult, in fact, to find examples of ethnic and religious groups being turned down on their requests for particular instructions, and there are only a few such cases regarding the merchants.

At other times the interests sought influence in getting favorable nominations to colonial councillorships, though here it is difficult to be quite certain about how successful they were. Merchants usually passed their nominations on through individual members of the Board, and the names of the merchants are not usually mentioned directly in the surviving lists of councillors and the men who nominated them. One exception is the list of men nominated for councillorships in Maryland in 1691, on which 21 of the 36 candidates were nominated by "the merchants" or "Lord Baltimore and the merchants" or "Colonel Copley and the merchants."[19] Probably merchant nominations in general accounted indirectly for 10–20 percent of the colonial councillorships (the Bishop of London accounted for another 5 percent). This did not seem a small percentage to contemporaries. Governors, who thought such nominations essential to the power of the governorship, were outraged by it.[20]

One can further see the interests' influence by looking at the resettling of foreign communities in America. There had been two major efforts to help continental migrants get to the colonies in the 1680s, and both were privately managed. One had been the Quaker effort, financed by the Quakers' Free Society of Traders, to help European Quakers move to Germantown, Pennsylvania;[21] the other had been the Huguenot effort, directed by the French Committee, to aid victims of Louis XIV to settle in various parts of the colonies.[22] When Christoph von Graffenried first attempted to establish a Swiss/Palatine settlement in New Bern, he got both public and private help, some coming from the minister of a German church in London, some from London merchants who advanced transportation costs, and some coming from Queen Anne.[23] When the German refugees arrived from the Palatinate in 1710, however, so many came at once that the German community of London was overwhelmed and had to approach the Board of Trade for help. In the end it was the Board, not the German community, that managed the German settlement.[24] Frequently thereafter the Board negotiated with ship captains for reasonable transportation of non-English groups across the Atlantic, and with governors and assemblies for assistance to refugees once they arrived in the colonies.

On the review of laws passed by the colonial assemblies, the Board's records mention specifically only two cases where non-English representatives were consulted on particular provincial legislation,[25] but it is difficult to find any provincial acts that do not reflect the outcome non-English groups would have wanted. Governor Spotswood referred to the Board's deference to merchants in 1718, when he complained that the London merchants trading to Virginia might as well draw up their own version of a tobacco inspection act to be passed in the colony, "otherwise there is no pleasing them."[26] The governor's complaint was fair enough: the only occasions on which the merchants' views were disregarded were rare ones on which they were clearly ill informed or those that concerned local affairs on which the Board thought it was not proper to interfere.[27] Most striking of all was the churches' role in legislative review. In the first twenty years of the century, five of the colonies passed laws severely limiting the rights of religious minorities, and all five saw them disallowed by the Board.

Despite the increased government authority over them, however, despite the willingness of London connections to help, and despite the government's responsiveness to the London lobbies, not all the colonial interests took advantage of the chance to use informal London influence.

Some of the groups, like the carters and porters, had few concerns beyond the town level and no incentive to form London connections.[28] Other groups, especially the towns and assemblies, lacked natural allies among the London interests so they hired men, either colonists or Englishmen, to take their case straight to the English government. New York City did this in 1698, when it sought a repeal of the colony's law which ended its flour-bolting monopoly. The Common Council voted "that the sum of fifty pounds Sterling be Raised upon ye Credit of ye Citty to be imployed by an agent att home in England for ye Representing the State of this City unto his Majesty and the Lords Commissioners of Trade and Plantations."[29] Between 1690 and 1696 five colonial governments or parts of them did the same thing, and petitioned the King directly.[30]

Some groups that did have natural English connections still resented becoming dependent on London intermediaries. One senses this feeling even with the New England Yearly Meeting, for at one point they considered sending copies of a pamphlet to London for advice on its publication, and then decided to send it to the Philadelphia meeting instead.[31] Other groups appealed particular issues to England but did not ask their London counterparts for help in doing so. South Carolina dissenters appealed to the House of Lords against a provincial act establishing the Anglican Church, but they did so through London merchants, not any dissenting group.[32] The Anglican ministers of Virginia, surely one of the best connected groups, appealed one issue through the governor rather than the Bishop of London.[33] Early in the period even the Virginia tobacco planters by-passed the London merchants when they protested to Parliament against the high tobacco duties. The very fact that the Virginia tobacco planters, the Virginia Anglicans, and the New England Quakers, three of the colonial lobbies with the strongest London connections, declined to use them from time to time on issues where they reasonably might have done so, suggests that London-colonial lobbies were still a long way from functioning smoothly.

On marginal issues, moreover, which could be handled at either the provincial or the imperial level, colonists still often found that it was more convenient and less expensive to build up local support. They could attempt to play the role of "swing voters," for example: Huguenots played this to considerable success in Charles Town in the first decade of the eighteenth century, and they also had some success in New York City.[34] They could also attempt to expand their political support by forming coalitions. Huguenots were often in coalitions with Anglicans and with a section of the mercantile communities; dissenting groups sometimes formed coalitions with each other and with groups of merchants.

With any workable base of local power colonial interests would try to keep issues handled within their province, even issues that far more naturally should have been handled by imperial authorities. In one case, the governor of New York required a Presbyterian minister to pay the full costs of his trial on charges of preaching without a license, even though the minister was acquitted; New York dissenters subsequently got the provincial legislature to pass a law forbidding a man being compelled to pay the costs of prosecuting himself.[35] That question, certainly, could have been handled at either the local or the imperial level;[36] but other problems approached locally much more clearly concerned imperial questions. New York merchants petitioned the governor, not the Admiralty, against the Admiralty's order for victualing British ships at Boston. Boston merchants petitioned their governor in 1704/5 against their ships being carried off;[37] in 1709 they sent a representation to the same governor asking for the further encouragement of the production of naval stores.[38] New York Huguenots petitioned again against provisions in the Navigation Act restricting overseas trade to British nationals. In due course the petitions were appropriately forwarded to the Board of Trade, but it is significant that these local interests, all of which had considerable strength through connections in London, tried to handle their problems on the provincial level first.

Little by little, however, by trial and error, in a variety of ways, and for a variety of reasons, the newly organizing American interests began after 1690 to explore the kinds of help that corresponding groups in London might give. Through business partners, relatives, friendship networks, visits to England, conversations with merchants, ministers, or Quaker visitors who stopped briefly in the colonies and then returned to London, and sometimes, if they were well enough organized to support the expense, through agents sent to London specifically to work with the London interests, the colonists tentatively investigated the uses of London connections.

We can get a sense of the way in which transatlantic cooperation developed by looking at three randomly chosen groups. The New England Quakers appealed to the London Quakers for help in fighting persecution in Massachusetts. Anglicans in Pennsylvania did not face discrimination, but they did seek London assistance in their open competition against other churches. Feuding groups within the New York mercantile community each appealed to the London merchants. Every experience was quite different from the others but each group, after an early period of false starts, learned by trial and error the value of London allies.

The New England Quakers sought imperial protection against local discrimination. From 1690 on, the Quakers of the New England Yearly Meeting corresponded with the London Meeting of Sufferings at least once a year. Routinely they "returned ye Sufferings of several friends to be recorded and sent for London."[39] Usually these "sufferings" concerned penalties for refusal of military service or distraint of property to support the local Congregational minister; they were not requests for help, and while the London Meeting for Sufferings kept a record of them, there is no indication that they did anything else. In 1697 the New England meeting sent its first actual request for help, asking the London meeting for contributions to help meet "the necessityes off pore ffriends to ye Eastward."[40] But this first appeal apparently came to nothing: there is no evidence that the London meeting sent anything. Four years later the New Englanders tried again, this time drawing up a petition seeking help against "warrants writ to straine for the maintenance of ye priest" at Salem,[41] which they asked the London meeting to send on to the King. The London meeting did, but because they had little political experience, neither the Londoners nor the New Englanders knew that an act which had once received the King's assent could not later be repealed. In this case the distraint was authorized by an act which the King had approved many years ago, without the meeting's noticing it.[42]

Over the next three years the Quakers rapidly expanded their information and honed their lobbying skills, and in 1705 the New England Quakers had better luck than before: they petitioned the Queen for disallowance of a Connecticut law against "Hereticks" (primarily Quakers and Rogerenes, whom the London Quakers mistakenly lumped together). The law was an old one, but it had recently been reissued and was therefore being reviewed; when it came before the Board of Trade the London meeting not only petitioned against it but sent two agents to plead the Quaker cause and present the Board a book entitled *New England Judged*. Whether they read the book or not, the Board members found the Quaker case convincing and ruled in favor of disallowance.[43] With gratitude and recognition of the London meeting's new-found lobbying skills, the New England meeting acknowledged that "we are glad to heare that friends in England have obtained so good an interest in the Government."[44]

By 1715 the Quakers had moved a step farther. No longer content to wait until a law was passed and then protest against it, they sought to head off a Presbyterian appeal before it ever reached England. That year the New England meeting, "being Acquainted that the Presbyterian clergy in Boston's government are about to solicit the Government of Great Britain to have the Presbytery Church Government established in Boston as it is in North Britain," set up a committee "to acquaint our Correspondents at London" with the threat.[45] A year later the Londoners answered, informing the New Englanders that the proposal had been defeated in Boston and had never reached England, but assuring the New Englanders of their constant vigilance on such matters.[46] By 1716 the London-American Quaker lobby, which had scarcely existed in 1690 and was ineffective as late as 1702, had become one of the most sophisticated of the metropolitan-provincial lobbies.

Anglicans in London and Anglicans in Pennsylvania also developed a lobby in this period, but for somewhat different reasons and in a somewhat different way. The Anglicans in Pennsylvania were never persecuted, for Pennsylvania always enjoyed religious toleration, so they never had occasion to seek the help of London Anglicans in getting provincial laws disallowed. Instead they looked to the Londoners mainly, though not exclusively, for supplies and for government assistance in proselytizing among other churches.

In 1690 the Anglican Church did not exist in Pennsylvania; Philadelphia was entirely Quaker and there were no Anglican enclaves outside the city. By 1697 thirty-six men (probably representing slightly under two hundred people, if their families are included) sought an Anglican minister, but instead of asking the Bishop of London they worked through Governor Francis Nicholson of Virginia, who prided himself on being a leading patron of the Anglican Church in the colonies.[47] Once the minister arrived the church grew so quickly that by 1700 it had 500 members, too many to fit into the old church, as its ministers reported to the Archbishop of Canterbury.[48] Shortly after this the church expanded to Chester and began proselytizing among the Quakers there. By 1704 the Society for the Propagation of the Gospel had sent an Anglican minister to Chester and was underwriting his salary, something the vestry had sought because "We were loth to venture the loss of such as have but lately returned from Quakerism to our Communion by pressing upon them to joyn along with us to their charge and expense."[49] By the following year the Chester Anglicans, still with Quaker conversions on their minds, were pressing the Archbishop of Canterbury, this time for help building a school because "the great numbers of young Quakers in this country who are not provided for by People of their own Persuasion . . . necessity would oblige them to send where they might embibe such principles as afterwards they could not easily forget."[50]

From there the Anglicans moved into politics and, like the Quakers' early attempt, their first venture seems to have ended in failure. Through the S.P.G. they tried to get the Chester minister's salary paid from customs duties in 1704, but the Customs Commissioners apparently would not agree. In later years, however, the Pennsylvanians persuaded the Bishop of London to use his influence in London to keep a local Anglican minister from being tried in a Quaker court where the witnesses against him, all Quakers, would not have to swear on oath that their testimony was true. The Bishop succeeded and the case was moved.[51] Like the New England Quakers, the Pennsylvania Anglicans, whose church did not even exist in 1690, were using to the fullest their connections with S.P.G., the Archbishop of Canterbury, and the Bishop of London. By 1715 they had learned quickly the uses of imperial connections.

Different from both the New England Quakers and the Pennsylvania Anglicans—more different from them, even, than they were from each other—was the New York mercantile community. Unlike the other two interest groups, the New York merchants began the period badly divided. Each wing sought support from the London merchants trading to the colony, and in the process they temporarily caused a rift among the merchants of the London coffee house. When news of the Glorious Revolution reached New York in 1689, the New York merchant Jacob Leisler, in command of the local militia, had overthrown the governor appointed by the deposed King and ruled the colony on his own; the New York mercantile community was sharply divided over whether to support him. The divisions did not heal after Leisler's death, and for the next quarter century each New York governor in turn had to decide which of the two factions he would support. Once a governor had made his decision, the offended party would begin working for his removal.

When the period began neither mercantile faction had effective London connections. Both sent petitions to London, either directly to the King or indirectly through particular London merchants the New Yorkers knew. There is no evidence that Jacob Leisler, Jr., worked with Leislerian merchants when he came to London to seek the repeal of his father's attainder in 1694. But in 1698 Nicholas Bayard and several other anti-Leislerians went to London and sought the merchants' help in getting their testimony before the Board of Trade.[52] Thereafter both the Leislerian and the anti-Leislerian merchants usually had an agent in London, coordinating petitioning efforts and appearances before the Board of Trade. Bayard signed London mercantile petitions during the several years he was in the City;[53] a 1703 petition from Leislerian merchants signed by merchants "living at and Trading to the Province of New York"[54] attests to the transatlantic cooperation between the groups. Together the agents and merchants focused on particular issues such as the dates of convoys, provincial revenue acts, removal of New York from the military command of New England, but each of these also became a partisan issue, brought up with the recognition that a series of defeats in London would undermine the incumbent governor. Governors Fletcher and Cornbury, opposed by Leislerian merchants and governors Bellomont and Hunter, opposed by the anti-Leislerians, learned this to their regret.

Between 1690 and 1715, then, Anglicans in Pennsylvania, Quakers in New England, and merchants in New York City had all learned the value of connections with interest groups in London, but they had done so in different ways and had emphasized different reasons. The differences are important here. The reasons that led these three groups to seek London connections—need for imperial help against local discrimination, need for London resources to compete against other churches, and need for London support in internal conflicts—were the sort of reasons that most often impelled other colonial interests to seek London associations during the period.

The New England Quakers exemplified the minorities existing in virtually every colony that looked to the imperial government for protection against hostile local majorities. In every colony except Pennsylvania, Rhode Island, and the northern part of Carolina, Quakers constituted a minority; this was true for every church outside the Presbyterian/Congregational establishment in Connecticut and Massachusetts, and every church outside the newly created Anglican establishments in New York, Maryland, and South Carolina. Jews were a small minority in New York and Rhode Island; Palatine Germans who came in 1710 were a minority in New York and Pennsylvania, and small Huguenot communities were scattered throughout the colonies. For most of these groups the royal disallowance of laws that discriminated against them and, in royal colonies, the royal appointment of governors sympathetic to them, were their greatest protection in local politics. But obtaining the royal favor depended on the groups' having good lobbyists before the English government, and for this the colonial interests were learning how to use their London associates.

The New York merchants were an example of a divided colonial interest in which the feuding sides sought London's help in their local conflicts; they were not alone in trying this, for merchant communities were among the least cohesive interest groups in the colonies. At the very least they were rent by social differences.[55] They were also segregated along the lines of the goods they sold, and these divisions were naturally represented in the London groups with whom the merchants did business. When the merchants dealt primarily in distinct goods and worked in separate places over a long period of time, as did the merchants of Albany, New York, who handled furs, and the New York City merchants who handled grain, then clearly we should consider them separate interests, and not parts of a divided community. But where the merchants' interests shifted around and the whole community worked and even met together, as did the merchants of Portsmouth, New Hampshire, some of whom specialized in lumber and some of whom worked in naval stores, it is legitimate to assume that they did constitute a single interest group, however bitterly divided.[56] Merchants also split along religious lines; the Quaker merchants who had monopolized Philadelphia's trade, and the Dutch Reformed and dissenter merchants who had dominated New York and New England respectively, were increasingly challenged by newcomers from the Anglican and Huguenot churches in this period. Finally in Charles Town, Philadelphia, and Boston, as well as New York, the merchants were divided along political lines. Philadelphia merchants, for example, hired rival agents to represent them in London, one agent representing the merchants who supported William Penn, the other representing the agents who opposed his proprietorship.[57] Just how formally the Boston and Charles Town merchants were divided is unclear; it is not known whether the separate factions sent formal agents. Certainly Charles Town merchants supporting proprietary government in South Carolina and merchants opposing it went over as individuals to work with London merchants on particular issues, and Boston merchants, divided on a galaxy of issues, from the relationship of Massachusetts with the imperial government to the merits of a particular governor, almost continually had rival groups or individuals in the imperial capital.[58]

The merchant communities were not the only colonial interest communities whose protracted disputes led both sides to appeal to London. Dutch reformed leaders in New York quarreled over the governor's right to appoint their ministers; both groups tried to appeal to the Duke of Marlborough through the Amsterdam Classis.[59] Presbyterians in New York City disagreed over the merits of a minister sent them from England; both sides appealed to London Presbyterians.[60] Virginia's Anglican ministers divided over support of the royal governors. Commissary Blair, who had the ear of the Bishop of London, opposed most of the governors during the period, but the governors also had their supporters among the clergy, who did not hesitate to write to the Bishop on the governors' behalf.[61] In the struggles within the Palatine communities of New York and Pennsylvania the fact that some leaders had influence enough in London when the original arrangements proved unsatisfactory gave them the upper hand.[62]

If the New York merchants exemplified the divided interest group whose factions each appealed to the London interest for support in the local encounters, the Pennsylvania Anglicans exemplified those ecclesiastical and ethnic interests which appealed to their counterparts in London for help in the intensely unstable world of the colonial churches. Given the transient, unsettled nature of the churches' peripheral membership, help from London in the form of ministers or money for schools, church buildings, or burial grounds could be vital in keeping their membership intact. Jewish communities, for example, had a pattern of starting, dissolving, and starting again before a lasting group could be established; that consolidation often occurred once the Jews bought a common burial ground.[63] French churches, unable to train their own ministers in the colonies, plagued by periodic crises when ministers died or retired, and losing second-generation members to Anglican or Presbyterian churches anyway, were virtually dependent upon London's Threadneedle Street Church for money and a supply of French-speaking ministers.[64]

Even among the English churches, people were remarkably willing to switch from one denomination to another if their own minister left, the church building was inconveniently located, or a less "expensive" denomination moved into town—a variety of reasons large and small. If London churches could send over a minister (the Quakers sent visitors)— better yet, if they could subsidize his salary and supply him with Bibles and plate—the peripheral members would be less likely to think of switching to other churches.[65] In Philadelphia, for example, a recent study has suggested that the Quaker church in this period consisted of a core of devout Quaker immigrants from England surrounded by new converts holding a variety of radical opinions, who had joined when the church was the only one in town but were willing to switch when it was not.[66] In Salem and in Newbury, Massachusetts, Anglican churches were created for no other reason than that a number of parishioners did not like the location of the Congregational meeting house.[67] The Newbury missionary wrote of the Congregational Church the "No. of Dissenters I know not but tis very great; what religion they are of I cannot find. It is an admixture of several opinions." Anglican ministers even referred to "selling the Church" to other denominations,[68] and the Rev. Benjamin Colman wrote of his own Congregationalists, "yt there happen a discontended person or two in ye place . . . immediately they propose to Yourselves Let us send over for a minister of Ye Church of England."[69] In the intensely competitive world of colonial churches, Baptists, Anglicans, Presbyterians, and Quakers—indeed any church that was not supported by local taxation and even some that were—needed London subsidization if they were to compete for new members and keep their own from drifting off to more attractive churches.[70]

In the quarter-century after 1690, therefore, the development of London-American interest group cooperation was far from steady. Nevertheless, it was beginning. At first it proceeded by trial and error: sometimes the colonists neglected to seek London help on issues where it would clearly have been in their interest to do so; sometimes they sought help on impractical issues—the repeal of laws that had expired or were only rumored to exist. Sometimes the London groups were too ignorant or inefficient to be of help. Bit by bit, however, the provincials and the Londoners were learning to work together. In the two decades after the "merchants and planters trading to and interested in the plantations of Virginia and Maryland" petitioned Parliament in 1696, London-American interest group cooperation began to blossom.

· CHAPTER 6 ·

The Colonial Governors and the Interests at the Beginning of the Eighteenth Century

Beginning in the quarter-century after 1690, the world in which the colonial governors worked was shaped in vitally important ways by the influence of London interests. Colonial groups which supported particular governors could pass on their approval to their counterparts in London, which would in turn pass it on to the British government. Those that disapproved of a governor's policies could do the same thing, and the Londoners would bring pressure on the imperial government to make the governor change his ways. The interests worked on governors indirectly, suggesting councillors to the Board of Trade, advising the Board on the wording of instructions, or urging the acceptance or disallowance of colonial laws, and directly, calling on the governors before they left London, seeing that they were greeted once they arrived in their colonies, and working with the appropriate colonial interests to put local pressure on them.

The influence of the London interests and, equally important, the perception of their influence varied among the provinces depending in turn upon the strength of local interests. A study of the three most important governors in the period—Joseph Dudley (Massachusetts, 1702–1715), Robert Hunter (New York, 1710–1720) and Alexander Spotswood (Virginia, 1710–1720)—shows the variety of ways in which London-American interests functioned from colony to colony and the variety of ways in which the governors responded.

· · ·

The actual appointment of governors was rarely susceptible to the influence of these interests in this period: the governors still owed their appointment to individual patrons—generally the principal officers of state—who were more concerned in finding jobs for unemployed military officers in this generation of intermittent war than they were with gratifying particular London interests. Only occasionally were the London or provincial interests consulted in the selection of a colonial governor. The Massachusetts Congregational leader Increase Mather, for example, nominated Governor Phips for that colony,[1] and the appointment of Joseph Dudley had the endorsement of the Bishop of St. Asaph and of London merchants trading to New England.[2] But when the Board of Trade passed on to the Privy Council the nomination of one Tobias Bowles to be governor of Maryland, "Having been recommended to us by some of the Principal Merchants residing there and trading to Maryland,"[3] the Council paid no attention, and there is little indication that they would have responded to any other recommendations.

Once the governors were nominated, however, various interests in London and America went to work on them at once. The minister of New York City's Anglican Church wrote to express his hope that "the Bishop of London with other friends will recommend me and my church to the favor and protection of the new Govr, and that affectionately,"[4] and dissenting ministers, merchants, and leaders of the Quaker meeting all expected their English associates to do the same. As the period wore on it became the custom for representatives of London interests to call upon governors before their departure, urging support for their colonial correspondents. If the governors were unlucky enough to put into one of the West Indian Islands for repairs to their ship before getting to their assigned colony, they might meet, even there, some advocates for mainland interests. When Governor Bellomont of New York and New England was forced to stop at Barbados, he ran into a Presbyterian minister who "took the freedome, when alone to assure his L/ship if he would protect and countenance N.E. in their Religion and Liberty, he would be happy in that Government."[5]

When the governor arrived in his colony, he was bound to be greeted by spokesmen for various interests offering food and entertainment, lodgings while his house was put in order, gold boxes, or simply addresses.[6] The reluctance of interest groups in Massachusetts to greet Governor Phips was quite remarkable;[7] so was the failure of anyone in Philadelphia to show up and greet Governor Blackwell.[8] Far more typical was the experience of Virginia's Governor Spotswood, greeted by "abundance of Company" within hours of his arrival at Williamsburg,[9] or New York's Lord Cornbury who wrote, on the very day of his arrival, that "I find at my coming hither great complaints of hardships suffered by many people."[10] Clearly, Cornbury had been besieged by various interested parties from the moment he got off the ship.

In time provincial interests found various ways of exerting local influence on the governors, as well as on their councils and legislatures. Their technique centered mainly on offers of electoral support, political sermons, petitions, coffee house speeches, club meetings, and addresses of praise, whose main value was that the governor could send copies on to the Board of Trade or his English patrons as evidence of his local popularity; he could also send them to the relevant London interests to help gain their active support in keeping him in office.

The churches were particularly adept at applying pressure. When the governor was already a member of a church (most governors were Anglican), the church had considerable leverage over him from the beginning. The Bishop of London instructed vestries to appoint Anglican governors to memberships immediately upon their arrival. As a member of the congregation the governor had regularly to listen to sermons on church politics; if he paid insufficient heed to them he could be ostracized from the church's activities (Governors Hunter and Bellomont of New York were virtually driven out of the Anglican Church of New York City).[11] Churches of all dominations could send favorable addresses to London. So important could these addresses be that one of Governor Nicholson's detractors complained "that he used to send presents to the ministers and churches . . . whenever he wanted any of their flattering commendations."[12]

If the governor was not considered sufficiently supportive, the local groups could turn their meetings, resolutions, petitions and addresses, and their other local weapons against him. Ministers could preach against him (the minister of Trinity Church in New York City preached so effectively against Governor Bellomont's efforts to convict some political leaders of treason that the trial was speeded up to give the minister fewer days on which to preach),[13] and they could leave him out of their prayers. They might meet together to draw up pamphlets or broadsides against him.

In any event, well before they had exhausted their local resources, interest groups who were disappointed with a governor would have appealed back to London for help, seeking to destroy the confidence that his patrons, the Board, and the Privy Council had in him.

Just as governors forwarded favorable addresses and publicized favorable comments, their opponents sent copies of local petitions and addresses to concerned interests in London and gave local publicity to the Londoners' responses. The New York agent Samuel Baker received a copy of a grand jury address against Governor Hunter, instigated by New York City merchants. Hunter was sure "Mr. Baker has laid it before your Lordships (the Board of Trade) for I am informed that he has laid it on the tables of most coffee houses in the city." The London merchants' letters, he reported, "have been dropt in the streets and copys thereof sent to most of the counties."[14] When Anglicans in Braintree, Massachusetts, were taxed for the support of the Congregational

Church, they appealed to the S.P.G., whose secretary immediately wrote Governor Dudley: "The Society . . . apprehend it is very much in your Excellency's power to do and procure to be done that which is just and equal to such as are so oppressed."[15]

By the late 1690s some of the London-American interests were sophisticated enough in their techniques to go beyond complaining on particular issues and attempt the total discrediting of certain governors with an eye to bringing them down. Governor Bellomont of New York was probably the first governor so targeted. Soon after his arrival in New York, Bellomont alienated the principal merchants of New York City by cracking down on their collusion with pirates.[16] Soon after that he alienated both the Church of England and part of the Dutch Church by sponsoring legislation to take back lands granted to them with questionable wisdom, if not legality, by his predecessor, and by refusing to the Anglican minister the subsidy from the colony's treasury which Bellomont's predecessor had also granted.[17] When he failed in his efforts to win over the Huguenots of New Rochelle and New York City by hiring a supporter of his who was also a Massachusetts Huguenot minister to serve them, he also cancelled the government's subsidy to the Huguenot minister.[18] Within a year of Bellomont's arrival in the colony the Bishop of London was opposing him, some of the merchants had already sailed for England in order to work with their London correspondents for the governor's dismissal, the Dutch Church had sent one of its merchant members, Nicholas Bayard, to work against Bellomont with the Dutch Church at Austin Friars, and the Huguenot Church of St. Esprit had opened up correspondence with the French Church on Threadneedle Street.[19] Had Bellomont not died suddenly on March 5, 1701, it is likely that he would have been the first gubernatorial victim of out-and-out interest group hostility.

By the time of Bellomont's death, then, it was clear that colonial governors had to be both opportunistic and defensive in dealing with the increasingly sophisticated London and provincial interests. The dangers and the opportunities varied from colony to colony, governor to governor. The three governors who survived longest in this period—and did so in part because they came to appreciate the need for careful maneuvering in the minefield of London-American interests—were Joseph Dudley of Massachusetts, Robert Hunter of New York, and Alexander Spotswood of Virginia. Each developed an awareness of which provincial interests were important to cultivate, which were marginal, which could be divided and thus neutralized, and which were not worth bothering with. Each used what patronage he had to favor the leaders of important interests, each entertained extensively (when Dudley invited Boston's Congregational ministers to his home, Cotton Mather complained that "they were eating of his Daintees and durst not reprove him");[20] each went as far as he could to grant the interests' various political demands. In these ways their approaches were similar. But they survived for different reasons and with different experiences. Spotswood dealt with a dominant Virginia tobacco aristocracy, whose English connections were powerful. In the time Dudley governed Massachusetts the Congregational-Presbyterian majority he had to work with actually had weaker London connections than did the minority opposing it, and it was Dudley's objective to make just enough concessions to the opposing interests to be able to utilize their English connections without entirely alienating the Congregational-Presbyterian local majority. Hunter, by contrast, worked among complicated sets of rival New York interests, each articulate locally and well-connected in England. Each governor had constantly to reassess the relations of his political patrons with the leaders of London interests for and against him. And each, for all his dexterity, was either brought down or worn down by the interplay of transatlantic pressures. A brief survey of the three men's gubernatorial careers shows the different ways in which London-American interests functioned from colony to colony.

Of the three Spotswood had the least room to maneuver. Spotswood governed a colony dominated by a homogeneous Anglican tobacco planter aristocracy, and there were few, if any, other interests in the colony that he could use as a counterweight.

The planters, if not deeply committed to Anglicanism as a faith, were a least agreed in their support of the Anglican organization, so there was no chance of building an ecclesiastical power base to rival the Church of England. As for the other churches in the colony, we have Robert Beverley's comment that "They have no more than five conventicles amongst them, namely three small meetings of Quakers and two of Presbyterians. 'Tis observed that those counties where the Presbyterian meetings are produce very mean tobacco and for that reason can't get a minister to stay amongst them."[21] There was little point in developing support from these groups and Spotswood did not even try. He considered the Quakers "obstinate," complained of their "unaccountable behavior," and then left them alone because most of them lived in remote areas near the Carolina border.[22] Spotswood never had anything to do with the small Presbyterian congregation at Elizabeth River or the handful of Presbyterian families on the Rapahannock and York rivers.[23] They were too small and too distant to be included in the Presbyterian synod of Philadelphia, established in 1712.

Similarly, there were no non-English groups with whom Spotswood could usefully ally. A proposed Swiss settlement never materialized, though Spotswood did try to help it;[24] a German settlement that Spotswood himself encouraged finally drifted away,[25] and at Manakin town there were only three hundred Frenchmen, whom Spotswood treated with contempt.[26]

Nowhere, moreover, was there a community of merchants that Spotswood could work with to offset the economic power and mercantile connections of the wealthy planters. The colony included lesser planters in great numbers and with interests quite distinct from those of the great planters, but they were not organized as a group; moreover, the merchants they dealt with in England tended to be far less politicized that the merchant factors of the wealthier tobacco growers.

Lacking any alternative base of power, Spotswood had to try to develop what influence he could within the planter aristocracy. He tried, among other ways, to win over the Anglican clergy. He took up correspondence with the Bishop of London and became a member of the Society for Propagation of the Gospel. By passing an act establishing the value of tobacco in relation to the value of coinage, he helped stabilize clerical salaries that were paid in tobacco in the colony. Perhaps most important, by insisting that parishes must accept and support ministers appointed by himself Spotswood got the clergy's support by freeing them from dependence on the whims of their parishioners. Not all the clergy welcomed the governor's assistance, but enough of them did to keep Commissary James Blair from organizing a clerical offensive against Spotswood.[27] By attempting to weaken the vestries, however, Spotswood raised an issue which was bound to create tensions between the clergy and their parishioners, thereby weakening the local influence of his clerical supporters. Patronage could be used to neutralize the clerical interest, not to bring it to the solid support of the governor.

When Spotswood attempted to build up his own support within the planter aristocracy, first by pushing for a tobacco inspection act and promising inspectorships to key politicians, and then by granting a monopoly of the Indian trade to a company of planters in return for their support, his efforts came to grief. The men who had been promised inspectorships were turned out of office in the next election, and the opponents of the Indian company appealed to England and got the act creating the company disallowed. William Byrd, one of the leading local opponents of the governor's Indian Trade Act and his Tobacco Inspection Act, went to London to work with the London merchants trading to Virginia in getting both acts repealed. He was completely successful. When the hearings were held at the Board of Trade, none of the merchants appeared on Spotswood's behalf, while "several" sent a protest and memorial against him.[28] Byrd wrote smugly of "having a hand" in the merchants' activities.[29] Both acts were disallowed, and Spotswood bitterly complained that "it is very well known that the merchants never ceased teazing your Lordships till both these acts were destroyed whether they were pushed on by the remonstrances of their correspondents here . . . I shall not now determine."[30]

Thus Spotswood, who arrived in Virginia determined to wrest some reforms from the tobacco aristocracy that represented all the important interests of the colony, soon found that he had no local interests worth building up to counterbalance it, no way of using patronage or social influence to work on it from within, and insufficient resources to fight its connections in England. In his final years as governor he did the only thing practical at the time—capitulated and joined the group he could not dominate from outside. By 1719 he sent the Board of Trade "the Voluntary and Deliberate Testimonys of the principal Gentn and Inhabitants of 21 out of 25 countys of Virginia,"[31] and in his final year in office he spoke to the Burgesses with praise for the "concord and application to Business . . . good temper and generous disposition."[32] Clearly, Spotswood had come to terms with a dominant provincial aristocracy in which all major local interests with London connections overlapped.

In one or two ways Governor Joseph Dudley of Massachusetts was worse off than Spotswood: a colonist himself who had lived for a time in England, he was associated with several Massachusetts interest groups so weak locally that they had little political clout, even on those rare occasions when they worked together. Dudley's associations were with very moderate Puritans, Huguenots, and a small, largely Anglican group within the merchant communities; during his administration he also gave some help to Quakers. These small groups, generally clustered in a few seaboard towns, were no political match for the overwhelming Presbyterian-Congregational majority of the colony, lesser merchants and tradesmen or farmers living in small agricultural towns with one Puritan church. Dudley's conversion to Anglicanism made him anathema to the Congregationalists, his identification with a select group of wealthy merchants was not popular with the farmers and lesser tradesmen, and his earlier support of James II's Dominion of New England had brought him considerable unpopularity among the small townsmen of Massachusetts, who wished to have as little to do as possible with the mother country. So the governor was at a disadvantage locally before he even entered his administration.

Dudley, moreover, lacked Spotswood's patronage: since the Massachusetts Council was elected by the lower house, he lacked the power to nominate its members; he never had any patronage comparable to Spotswood's short-lived tobacco inspectorships; and he lacked the power of appointing and inducting ministers in the established church, a power Spotswood had been able to use to neutralize the clergy of Virginia.

In another sense, however, Dudley was luckier than Spotswood, for the Quakers and Huguenots with whom he cooperated and the Anglicans and wealthy merchants with whom he identified had connections with powerful London interests, while the small-town Congregationalists farmers and tradesmen who were likely to oppose him had far weaker London connections than the tobacco planters Spotswood had to deal with. As yet the dissenters in London were poorly organized for lobbying: their ministers met sporadically and occasionally addressed the Queen, but they lacked sustained political organization. They were, moreover, not in sympathy with the attempts of the Massachusetts government to compel members of other denominations to support the Congregational Church in each locality. When London Quakers complained about Massachusetts taxation of Quakers to support the established church, Cotton Mather complained that "an Account was addressed . . . unto us . . . by the Independent Ministers in London, as if we had persecuting Lawes among us,"[33] while the Quakers themselves acknowledged that the London ministers "seem to shew their great dislike to their Brethren in New England's proceedings agst. our friends there."[34] Faced with a London lobby that was neither particularly supportive or particularly well organized at this time, the New England Congregationalists relied heavily on individual agents like Henry Ashurst and Jeremiah Dummer to put their case before the government. Even by the end of Dudley's administration they still had not developed a lobby comparable to that of their ecclesiastical and mercantile rivals.

Although his circumstances were different, Dudley had little more room to maneuver than Spotswood had. His strategy was soon clear: make the minimum concessions necessary to retain the support of his Massachusetts associates and their London lobbies while trying not to antagonize the Congregational majority. By and large, the strategy worked.

His approach is evident with a number of groups. He managed to retain the support of the bulk of London merchants trading to New England, many of whom he had met earlier during his long periods of residence in England. (Many of them had petitioned for his appointment in the first place.[35]) He did this by giving patronage and contracts to their biggest correspondents in Boston and by supporting their demands that ships in the British navy cease carrying certain commercial goods, but the favors cost Dudley the support of the lesser Boston merchants and cost the larger merchants their newly acquired leadership of Boston politics.[36] Dudley may well have found that the cost of maintaining the friendship of a Boston mercantile clique was greater than the rewards of the London support it brought.

The governor's handling of the Huguenots, the Quakers, and the Anglicans makes his strategy clearer. Dudley had been the friend of the leader of the Huguenot settlement at Oxford, Massachusetts, at least since 1688 when he had arranged for the Huguenots' purchase of the land. Shortly after Dudley's arrival in the colony the settlement's very existence was threatened by Indians, and the settlers sought Dudley's help. Dudley sent thirteen soldiers—enough to protect the village for a short while, not enough to arouse criticism among the other colonists, and not enough to keep the town from being abandoned a year or two later.[37] When the settlement was abandoned, many of its inhabitants joined the existing Huguenot community in Boston. The greatly expanded Boston French Church needed a new building, so Dudley helped push through the General Court an act subsidizing its construction. But the act lasted only one year, and sensing opposition in both the General Court and the town of Boston, Dudley did not press for another though the Huguenots were clearly short of money.[38] He had given the Massachusetts Huguenots the least that he could, but it was enough to bring him a favorable association with London's Threadneedle Street Church, a favorable petition from "Gentlemen concerned in providing Masts" which included a number of Huguenots, praising his care in handling the mast trade,[39] and the testimony of the Huguenot leader that "J'ay sacrifie tous mes intérets pour m'attacher aux vôtres, avec toute la passion d'une véritable affection."[40]

For Anglicans, too, Dudley had kind thoughts and not much practical help. Dudley's administration coincided with a period of steady if not very spectacular growth of the Anglican Church in Massachusetts. In 1702, when Dudley took office, the only organized Anglican Church in the colony was in Boston, though there was a small group of Anglicans in Braintree without a minister. In the next thirteen years Anglican churches were organized in five other towns and the S.P.G. sent over three missionaries to help them out. By the end of Dudley's administration there was as yet no formal organization of ministers, but it was generally acknowledged that the Reverend Samuel Myles of Boston was their leading spokesman.

Dudley himself, though raised a Puritan, was a convert to Anglicanism, a member of the S.P.G., and a corresponding member of the Society for Promoting Christian Knowledge. The Bishop of St. Asaph had been one of the supporters of his appointment,[41] and Dudley kept up his connections in the S.P.G. well enough that Reverend Myles could write the secretary, "The Governor tells me you are his friend and that on my writing to you, you will oblige me,"[42] and Dudley himself could write that "I truly desire by all methods of their Directions as well as by a good example personally to put forward Religion and the Church of England as I ought."[43]

Of actual help to the Anglicans, however, Dudley gave very little. In

1703 the Braintree Anglicans, still lacking a regular minister, protested against paying taxes to the Congregational Church; there was very little Dudley could do to help them. Ten years later they were still protesting to Dudley; he referred them to the General Court where it was clear they could expect no help, and excused himself to the S.P.G. by explaining that they still had no permanent minister and therefore did not constitute a legal church.[44] In Newbury a wing of the Congregational Church, annoyed at the relocation of the church building in a place they found inconvenient, petitioned the S.P.G. to send them over an Anglican minister. When they continued to be taxed to support the Congregational Church they appealed to Dudley, who first offered his "opinion" to the local justices against such taxation and then freed the Anglican leaders when they were jailed anyway for failing to pay the taxes. The issue was finally decided when the precinct voted to excuse the Anglicans from paying taxes.[45]

The religious group that was organizing fastest during Dudley's administration was the Quakers; and they, also, got rather nominal help from the governor. Guided by visitors from the London Meeting for Sufferings, the New England Yearly Meeting began taking over the authority and functions—including appeals to England—that had previously been exercised fairly randomly by various monthly meetings and even by individuals. It was also during Dudley's administration that the New England Yearly Meeting began sending agents to London to work with the London Meeting for Sufferings on the repeal of New England laws offensive to Quakers. In response the London meeting established both a committee to handle parliamentary affairs and a committee (largely composed of Quaker merchants trading to the area) to correspond with New England Quakers.[46]

Here, as with the Anglicans and the Huguenots, Dudley had a delicate line to draw in working with a strong transatlantic lobby on the one hand, and an implacably hostile local majority on the other. His concern to keep on good terms with the English Quakers is shown by his making sure that they knew of his reprimand of a Boston newspaper editor who printed an article critical of Quaker lobbying in England. But the limits of his ability to give practical aid to Quakers also became clear early in his administration: an act passed by the Massachusetts General Court in November 1706 ordered Justices of the Peace to present the names of all towns destitute of a (Congregational) minister. If towns failed to appoint and support a minister, then the General Court was to appoint one, levy and collect taxes, and pay the minister. The act particularly hit the Massachusetts town of Dartmouth, a Quaker center whose magistrates refused to collect the rates and were, predictably, thrown in jail. When they first petitioned Dudley he greeted them warmly and agreed to write to the Board of Trade about their case (which he did, in fairly neutral terms). Accordingly, the Quakers then sent on to the London Meeting for Sufferings a petition to be forwarded to the Queen. Dudley then had the Quaker assessors discharged from jail. The strategy worked: the London Meeting for Sufferings did not forward the petition, but the Congregational majority in the General Court did not complain. Dudley had done just enough for the Quakers to win their "Salutation of re-spect" and "acknowledgements of his severall ffavors and kindnesses" and to preserve their good will for the rest of his administration.[47]

Rather than saying that Dudley did the least required to neutralize the increasingly effective transatlantic organization he faced, it might be fairer to say that, confronted with a hostile majority in the court and the council, he found it impossible to do more than use his executive office to advise, serve as a conduit for messages to the Board of Trade, and release prisoners from jail. Like Spotswood, he had confronted a homogeneous majority in his colony; unlike Virginia, the Massachusetts majority was not particularly well connected in London, while its op-ponents were. Spotswood had virtually no room to maneuver because the dominant group in the colony was the only group with English connections able to help them; Dudley had only slightly more room because the local Congregational majority could bring far more pressure on him than could the English allies of their opponents.

In contrast to both Dudley and Spotswood, Governor Robert Hunter of New York had a good deal of room in which to maneuver. In 1710, when Hunter took up his administration, he found himself operating in a network of London-American interest groups that were certainly the most complex of the period: with its heterogeneous ethnic, religious, and even mercantile background New York contained the richest variety of interest groups in this period, enjoying the most complicated relations with interest groups overseas.[48] Instead of a homogeneous majority (in which several interests overlapped) opposed by hopelessly small alter-native groups, New York had a number of large interest groups; in New York City, for example, about 50 percent of the population was still Dutch, 35 percent English, 15 percent Huguenot, and there were about 40 Jewish families.[49] Most of the groups, moreover, were further cross-cut into sub-interests by geographical distinctions, class lines, and party divisions dating back to Jacob Leisler's administration. Not only did the merchants of New York City and Albany have different interests, but within New York City the merchants met in rival Leislerian and anti-Leislerian coffee houses.[50] Not only were the Huguenots split between those in New Rochelle who had accepted Anglicanism and those in New York City who had not, but the New York City French themselves met in different clubs.[51] Not only were the Dutch Reformed churches divided between those (generally Leislerians) who accepted the right of governors to collate ministers to their churches and those (anti-Leislerians) who did not (and it followed, between those who did and did not want to appeal over the governor's head to the Classis in Amsterdam and the Dutch Church of Austin Friars in London), but when Hunter took office the Dutch Church in New York City was still divided along Leislerian/anti-Leislerian lines.[52]

The Leislerian and anti-Leislerian banners spread out to cover two groups of roughly comparable local strength. The Church of England members, some wealthy Dutch leaders, wealthy Huguenots, thirty of the forty leading merchants in New York City, and later some of the Palatine settlers were anti-Leislerian in sympathy;[53] Presbyterians, Quakers, less wealthy French and Dutch, and the small but strong group of New York City Jews tended to be Leislerian.

Unlike Governor Dudley, Hunter was not committed to any one set of interests by previous experience in the colony, and well after his arrival he was still trying to play a neutral role. But neutrality could not work forever, and after several months Hunter committed himself to the Leislerian grouping. On the face of it, he appeared to have made a disastrous mistake, for though the two groups were fairly equally balanced in provincial politics, the anti-Leislerian groups had potentially far stronger support in London. The Church of England had the Bishop of London and the S.P.G.; the wealthy Huguenots corresponded with the Threadneedle Street Church in London;[54] the wealthier members of the Dutch Church corresponded with the Classis of Amsterdam and with the London Church at Austin Friars far more than did the less wealthy fragment of the church, the anti-Leislerian merchants had the support of a majority of the politically active London merchants trading to New York, and the Palatines had the support of merchants, court chaplains, the S.P.C.K., and the remnants of the London committee set up to help them in 1710. Against them Hunter's allies had only a mixed bag of London supporters. Strongest were the Quakers; Hunter had pushed hard for an act allowing them to take a solemn affirmation instead of an oath in New Jersey, even though "Our men of noise have excited their talent against the Act."[55] Behind them were the Presbyterians: they were not very well organized in London but what strength they had went to Hunter, "their particular friend."[56] Jewish support—and this possibly included support from the London synagogue at Bevis Marks—came when Hunter pushed through the assembly special acts giving the Jews naturalization.[57]

Except for the Quakers, this combination did not give Hunter a particularly strong nucleus of support, so he had to maneuver with his potential enemies. If they had all worked together they would have been almost unbeatable—as they had been against Bellomont. But they never did work effectively. Partly by strategy and partly by good luck Hunter was able to make the most of hitches in the transatlantic cooperation and lack of cohesion within the groups.

Two of the groups he neutralized locally, the French by befriending and entertaining their leaders (he had lunch several times in one week, for example, with John Fontaine, a visitor with distinguished connections in the French L'Eglise du St. Esprit),[58] by pushing through the New York Assembly a bill declaring that the children of aliens who had settled in the colony by 1683 were deemed naturalized respecting their right to hold inherited lands, an act which benefitted Huguenots and Dutch,[59] and by restoring the Huguenot minister's salary which Bellomont had cut off. The Dutch he neutralized by declining to press the governor's right to appoint their ministers, thereby eliminating the main issue of contention with earlier governors. Hunter was helped by the disappointment of the Amsterdam Classis, which had expected to work through the Dutch ambassador's influence on the Duke of Marlborough, the leading British minister. Marlborough was dismissed from office in 1710, however, and the Classis had no way to influence his successor. New York Dutch had mixed reactions: they complained to the Classis that the "public Declaration and Confession of your impotence does great harm and is very injurious to the General condition of the church," but they had also to admit that "by a change of administration [in New York] a change for the better came to us."[60]

Rather easily Hunter had disarmed the Dutch and French leadership. But his striking successes came with the Anglican Church, the London merchants, and the Palatines. With the Anglican Church he was quite fortunate in the long run. The local leaders were anti-Leislerlian and so opposed to him, but Hunter was able to divide the church and neutralize their power. In both New York and New Jersey the Anglican Church served a small minority of the inhabitants (1,200 out of 45,000 in New York),[61] but this minority included leading politicians with strong English allies. They had strong connections with the S.P.G.; many were friends of Hunter's predecessor, Lord Cornbury, who had returned to England and was chairman of a number of S.P.G. committees that took up issues relating to the Anglican Church in New York.[62] The minister of Trinity Church in New York City and the minister of the Anglican Church in Burlington, New Jersey, had close connections with the Bishop of London and the Archbishops of York and Canterbury. Under the leadership of the same rector of Trinity Church, the Reverend William Vesey, the Anglican clergy of New York and New Jersey met regularly to discuss church affairs, reporting all complaints against the governor back to the S.P.G., the bishops, and the Queen. Under Vesey's leadership the Anglican community of New York City led the smaller congregations of the two colonies in making the most of their Anglican, anti-Leislerian connections in London.[63]

But Hunter himself was an Anglican, a member of the S.P.G., a friend of leading Anglican bishops such as Swift, and he was just as aggressive in courting Anglican support as were the anti-Leislerians in Trinity Church. By personal appeals he won over to his side the two other leading S.P.G. members in the colony, Lewis Morris and Caleb Heathcote; through them and through his own correspondence with the Society he won over part of the S.P.G.;[64] he rebuilt the old Anglican Chapel in the Fort and set up a rival Anglican Church there, attracting members away from Trinity Church.[65] When Vesey called meetings of the clergy, Hunter summoned rival meetings at the same time.[66] He was careful to present his side of every question in regular correspondence to the S.P.G., and he pressed for an Anglican bishop in the colonies, someone whose authority would supersede that of self-appointed local leaders.[67]

Thus Hunter was able to divide the English bishops, the S.P.G., the New York ministers, and even Trinity Church itself. The long-run result was a stalemate; for the last part of Hunter's administration the Anglican interest in New York was neutralized. Three main issues came up. One concerned Jamaica, New York, where a predominantly dissenting community forcibly took over the Anglican Church and parsonage and refused to pay the salary of an Anglican minister who had been forced upon them in accordance with a rather ambiguous provincial law establishing the Anglican Church; the outcome of this issue was clearly a success for the New York Anglicans: they got the S.P.G. to prevail with the Queen to send Hunter a strongly worded additional instruction allowing the clergy to appeal their salary problems, however small in amount, to the provincial court (where it would be expected that the governor would appoint sympathetic judges).[68] A second issue concerned Hunter's approval of a New Jersey act granting Quakers the right of affirmation in lieu of an oath. The New Jersey Anglicans petitioned the S.P.G. against the act; the Society in turn petitioned the Queen. But Hunter strongly supported the act in letters to the Board of Trade, and the law was allowed to stand.[69] The final issue concerned Trinity Church's opposition to one Elias Neau, a catechist to New York City blacks, whose work Hunter continued to support even after there had been a widespread slave rebellion in the city. Once again the Anglican rector complained to the S.P.G., but this time the Society did nothing.[70] In 1716 Vesey went to England to present his case against Hunter to the S.P.G. and the Bishop of London. The Society, after some consideration, decided they could do nothing to unseat Hunter, since Vesey was not one of their missionaries.[71] Soon after this, however, Vesey was appointed commissary to the Bishop of London, an appointment which gave him nominal leadership over the other clergy in New York with power to convene meetings of the clergy and check on clerical discipline.

Thus Vesey had got some help in England, but not as much as he had hoped for; Hunter was safe, but spoke bitterly of knowing "the cause of the Bishop's spleen."[72] Both men and their supporters realized that an impasse had been reached in local ecclesiastical affairs. For the remaining five years of Hunter's government there was a superficial peace, as each man consciously passed up opportunities to attack the other.

It is possible that once Hunter had reached a rapprochement with the Anglican minister, the governor's political opponents switched their ground from ecclesiastical to mercantile affairs. In any event, there were no mercantile issues on which the governor disagreed with the merchants during his first five years in office, and it was only after he had come to terms with the church that he ran into serious trouble with the merchants concerning an "act for discharging the public debts and creating bills of credit." What the merchants objected to was the act's partiality in paying back more colonial debt to Leislerian supporters than to their opponents. Hunter soon learned of their appeal to the London merchants: "one Mr. Baker a Merchant there has had a Sum of mony remitted him from hence to Enable him to oppose some or all our Mony bills at Home,"[73] and warned the Secretary of the Board of Trade, "I'll deal plainly with you if there is too easy an Ear given to such Representations as some self-interested little Merchants there or some Spiteful ones here may happen to give of our affairs and Acts, it is to no purpose for me to remain on this side."[74] Hunter, at least, thought the merchants of London had pulled out all the stops, circulating petitions from New York among the coffee houses, petitioning the Board of Trade, sending them a memorial on the subject and writing up their "objections" after that, calling as a group on the Board's legal adviser, and finally, when the adviser and consequently the Board had recommended decisively in favor of the act, petitioning to be heard at the Privy Council against it.[75] Indeed, the merchants' crusade against the New York debt act was one of the clearest cases in the period of a London group acting on behalf of provincial correspondents on an issue in which the Londoners were not at all concerned.

But the merchants' effort backfired, ironically because of their very disinterestedness, and this in itself revealed another limit to the uses of London influence on provincial issues. "The merchants of London trading to New York are not proper to object to what debts ought to be allowed or disallowed"[76] was the opinion of the Board's legal adviser, and the Board itself agreed that regarding a law affecting individuals in the province, "the said merchants, not being inhabitants within the colony, cannot pretend to be affected."[77] The Board thus decided that this was a purely provincial matter, an in-group fight unrelated to imperial principles, and it therefore refused to be influenced by London interests. Just how the Board reached this decision is not clear, since the Debt/Revenue Bill also involved an excise on liquor, and the profits of liquor merchants surely did affect their trade to Great Britain. On the other hand, as Hunter himself said, almost any issue could be interpreted as affecting the trade of Great Britain, and a line between local and imperial issues had to be drawn somewhere.[78]

The Huguenots, the Anglicans, and the merchants were the core of the governor's opposition. By taking them on at different times, by capitalizing on differences between London and provincial interest groups, and by confining his differences with the New York merchants to narrowly provincial grounds, Robert Hunter was the most successful of the governors in neutralizing the efforts of his local opponents to capitalize on London connections. His successes showed that there were limits to the help provincials could expect from Londoners—but those limits were likely to be realized with an exceptionally able and lucky governor, working with a variety of interest groups so his opposition could be fragmented.

Thus in the quarter-century after 1689, the very effort to placate London-American interests taught the colonial governments some of the limits of their power. But for the interest groups, too, the period was one of learning, of trial and error. In attempting to influence governors the interests experimented with methods that revealed their own limits.

Several factors were responsible for these limits. For one thing, governors were appointed and removed by the leading ministers of state; as most London-American interests of the period lacked influence at the ministerial level, they had no direct leverage over the appointments. In a period of intensely partisan Whig-Tory strife in English politics the ability of patrons to get colonial governorships for their clients depended on their party's power and on their own influence within the party, rather than on their connections with interests.

In this period, moreover, interest groups were still experimenting with techniques for influencing newly appointed governors before they left London; by 1715, for example, they had not yet developed forms of public entertainment which they later used to extract expressions of open support from the new appointees. The fact that many governors appeared to have been caught by surprise by the complaints of various interests when they arrived in their colonies suggests that Londoners had been less than urgent about acquainting the new governors with the needs of their provincial colleagues.

Once the governors arrived in the colonies, they found interest group pressures less strong than they might have been because the London interests were themselves often divided along Whig-Tory lines, coinciding to some extent with High Church-Low Church divisions. Hunter in particular was able to escape the full weight of their influence for this reason. With the exception of the Chesapeake merchants, London merchants trading to America were divided roughly along the lines of the colonists they traded with—pro- and anti-Leislerian in New York, pro- and anti-Proprietary in Philadelphia, Anglican versus dissenter in Boston and Charles Town—as Anglican and Huguenot merchants were moving up the social ranks in the seaport towns and were joining or supplanting Dutch merchants, English Puritans, or English Quakers at the top of the social scale. Divisions of other kinds among the non-English ethnic groups also kept them from concentrating their efforts in the period. In London there was a three-way social division between the French of the Threadneedle Street Church, those of the Savoy, and those of Spitalfields; an ecclesiastical division between those who became Anglican and those who became Presbyterian; and a political division between colonial Huguenots who tended to be Tory and Londoners who were Whig.[79] Jews divided their allegiance between the Sephardic leaders at Bevis Marks and the Ashkenazic ones of small synagogues; Germans were either aristocrats with their own society or poorer people with no connections there.[80] All of them were in various stages of assimilation and as such had different ideas about supporting the demands of their provincial counterparts for isolation and autonomy within their colonies. Indeed, in this period only the Quakers and the Virginia merchants seem to have enjoyed unity, and even the Quakers were temporarily split by the Keithian schism.[81]

A far more important factor in the equation was that governors in colonies still dominated by a homogeneous majority lacked the power to do much for minority interests, however much pressure their colleagues applied from London. Dudley could do little for Massachusetts minorities except release them when they were imprisoned for breaking provincial law; Spotswood rarely tried to do anything. Significantly, more was done for minorities in New York, where the blocs in the assembly were closely matched. In assemblies where particular minorities could produce swing votes on crucial issues (as was true of the Huguenots in South Carolina) they were in a strong position, but this was rare. Thus before 1715 the influence of London interests was strongest on the middle colonies and on South Carolina, societies too varied to be dominated by any single group in which a variety of interests overlapped.

In 1715 an American colonist visiting London would easily have noticed the recent proliferation of London interest groups with American connections. Half a century before, there had been no such groups;

thirty years before only three or four. Now there were well over a dozen. With the exception of the Moravians, the Dissenting Deputies, and interests clustered around the founding of Georgia, all of the London-American interests that remained important down to the Revolution were established by 1715. Interests in the provinces looked to Londoners for help on questions they could not handle at the provincial level. They were learning, with some resentment, that Londoners were better equipped to handle such problems because of their proximity to the capital, their position at the center of an information-gathering network, their enhanced ability to function in London's pluralistic society, their greater concentration of wealth and numbers. Londoners, meanwhile, were learning that they could still influence decision-making on American as well as English issues, and some political value attached to serving as spokesmen for interests throughout the provinces.

As one would expect from their development, most of the connections between interests were in the experimental stage, a stage that involved trial and error with the means of communication, forms of organization, and types of pressure, as the groups tested the various institutions of government to find which were most responsive and probed the limits of their influence. As one would also expect, their successes were uneven. They had proved more successful in dealing with the British government at home than with the governors in the provinces, more successful in working with the Board of Trade than with Parliament, the King, or the ministers, and more successful in the pluralistic middle colonies than in the homogenous colonies of the Chesapeake and New England. But rough though they were, the groups were ready to press further with their transatlantic lobbying in the years after 1715. Thanks to the responsiveness of English institutions, interests in England and America were beginning to establish that stable relationship with the government so essential to the placid administration of Walpole, Henry Pelham and the Duke of Newcastle in the heyday of London-American interests that was soon to come.

CHAPTER 7

The Heyday of London Interests

For London interests with American concerns the height of political influence came in the period 1721 to 1754, a relatively tranquil era between the appointment of Sir Robert Walpole as leading minister and the death of his successor Henry Pelham. In these years the Londoners were able to lobby effectively with the Board of Trade and establish long-standing connections with the leading ministers. In this generation, more than any other in the colonial era, American interests had influential spokesmen in the British capital and through them a chance to participate in making the decisions that affected their world.

One reason for this was that the increasingly structured organization of the interests themselves allowed for the emergence of recognized leaders who could double as informal ministerial advisers and interest group spokesmen. Moreover, because the triumvirate of leaders—Sir Robert Walpole, Henry Pelham, and the Duke of Newcastle—dominated the chief offices of state so continuously through the period, the interest-group leaders could develop long associations with them bordering on real friendships.

Ministers were particularly receptive to advice from the lobbyists because they realized the essential role played by interests in maintaining the rather fragile government stability. That stability depended upon popular acceptance of the Hanoverian monarchy, which had succeeded the Stuarts upon Queen Anne's death in 1714, upon the monarch's acceptance of the ministers, and upon the ministers' abilities to command parliamentary majorities for policies they and the monarchs agreed upon. The ministers got their majorities by carefully distributing patronage to M.P.s, their relatives and colleagues, and by adroitly ducking major issues which might unite the splintered parliamentary opposition, cost them the financial backing of London's "money'd men," and provoke hostility out of doors. The delicacy of their position, the uncertainty of popular support, and at times even the precariousness of government was shown by three uprisings or major plots against the monarchy in this period (1715, 1722, and 1745), two major defeats for the ministers in Parliament (over the Excise crises and the Spanish War), and the repeal of two major laws (on gin consumption and the naturalization of Jews), which produced so much popular defiance they could not be enforced.[1]

In these circumstances the cabinet members and their associates on the Board of Trade had great incentive to develop smooth working relations with the representatives of transatlantic interests. The interests could, among other things, suggest what decisions would or would not go down with provincial colleagues and anticipate sources of discontent—laws or appointments that would be particularly unpopular in the provinces, creating disturbances that might spill over into national politics, embarrass ministers, and jeopardize the delicate political stability.

In return the interests expected favors: anything from favorable legislation and beneficial trade treaties at one extreme, to administrative concessions and financial assistance on pet projects at the other. The interests pressed their demands; the government decided how many they could afford to grant. Usually the interests we are dealing with were not strong enough to win major legislation, but they were able to negotiate lesser concessions. The dissenters did not get the repeal of the Test and Corporation Acts they sought, but succeeded in getting members let off fines when they were chosen for local offices they could not accept. Foreign communities could not obtain the naturalization arrangements they sought, but they did get government support when they organized charity drives to benefit continental refugees. Quakers did not get the act they wanted allowing them to affirm rather than swear in legal proceedings, but they were allowed to subscribe to government loans. Merchant groups had somewhat better luck; some joined in the successful opposition to Walpole's Excise Scheme of 1733 and others—a different section—pressed for the war with Spain in 1739. But merchants also did better with administrative requests in general, submitting to parliamentary commercial regulation they did not like but obtaining government assistance in building lighthouses or dismissing unpopular officers.

There was bound to be some tension in the lobbyists' relations with the ministers, the London rank and file, and the provincials for whom they claimed to speak; there was some grumbling, some gratitude, but the work of the transatlantic interests was never better. To understand how the Londoners came to serve so effectively as liaisons between the provincials and the government it is necessary first to examine their growth and then to look at their relations with provincials in England.

·   ·   ·

The growing strength of the interests themselves seems to have derived from tighter structuring rather than from any overall growth in numbers, something one might expect given the leveling off of London's population growth in the first half of the eighteenth century. Indeed, taken together, the available estimates suggest a decline in total membership of London interests, though the increase or decrease varied markedly from group to group.

The three main dissenting churches all declined, for example, from an estimated 41,000 people served by 158 ministers in 1727 to an estimated 33,000 served by 127 ministers in 1749, to 25,000 hearers and 96 ministers in 1765.[2] But the rate of decline was not the same from church to church: the Baptists lost two-thirds of their members while Presbyterians and Congregationalists lost a third each.[3] The number of politically oriented merchants (men interested enough in American affairs to sign at least one petition on the subject) fell from 389 in the twenty-five year period 1689 to 1714, to 293 in the longer period 1715 to 1750.[4] But while most of the various merchant groups lost members, and the Virginia merchants dramatically so, (falling off from 261 signatories to 9) the South Carolina merchants, who had scarcely worked together at all before 1715, grew to include 144 active merchants.[5] The percentage of foreign-born in London's population fell from an estimated 2–4 percent early in the century to 1.6 percent by the time of the American Revolution, but again, the decline was not evenly spread.[6] Huguenot immigration tapered off, so the number of Huguenot churches fell from 30 to 21 over the first half of the eighteenth century.[7] But Salzburger Germans began immigrating in considerable numbers, so the number of German churches grew from three to eight.[8] The London Jewish community increased nearly twelvefold, from well under 1,000 to about 8,000,[9] and the Irish (if one counts them, like the Jews, as "foreign") swarmed into London in uncounted numbers.[10]

Despite the ups and downs in the membership of the interests, their organizations did not suffer. There was often, in fact, an inverse correlation between their size and the strength of their organization. The faster a group was shrinking, the more urgently it needed organization to preserve its safeguards; the faster a group was growing, the less easily could it assimilate new members and also develop structurally.[11]

Regardless of their size and their expansion or contraction, many of the interests developed similar structures, with levels rising from counting houses and congregations to coffee houses, to clubs to umbrella organizations. At the base were the congregations, the counting houses, and the Royal Exchange where rank-and-file members met, probably with few thoughts about politics at all.[12] Many of these members might also visit a coffee house, the next layer up. They might well go simply for a theological discussion, for business reasons, or just for sociability, but at the coffee houses they were likely to meet men who also shared political concerns.

Merchants tended to gather at coffee houses named after the area to which they traded—the Virginia Coffee House, the Carolina Coffee House, and so on. Dissenting ministers along with some dissenting merchants who used the coffee houses as offices gathered at Hamlin's, the Amsterdam, and the Independent, and the Quakers had several coffee houses where they put up out-of-town visitors when the Yearly Meeting was in session. Coffee houses for the non-English communities were usually located either near the community centers (for example, Spital-fields for the French) or near the offices of merchants trading to the mother country. Most of the other houses associated with American interests were within a small area one block north and south of Cornhill, from Seething Lane to Threadneedle Street to Fish Lane and down to Birchin Lane, a location determined far more by its proximity to the Royal Exchange and the Post Office than by the convenience of individual patrons, many of whom had churches or counting houses some distance away. (The Virginia Coffee House, for example, was a center for tobacco merchants whose firms increasingly clustered on Tower Hill).

What initially attracted customers to the coffee houses was a combination of conversation and business. Merchants visited the houses once or twice a day to pick up mail, get up-to-date market information, buy and sell cargoes and insurance, exchange bills, serve notices, and talk over colonial affairs with other merchants and newly arrived ship captains and colonial visitors. Congregational ministers met formally twice a year at the Amsterdam, though they must have come together informally much more often since the house was known for its theologically oriented conversation.[13] Presbyterian ministers assembled on Tuesdays at Hamlin's; here, too, they must have gathered more often in informal discussion, for the ministers who met at the Independent considered Hamlin's too Arminian for their taste.[14] The Independent Coffee House attracted Baptists and a smattering of Presbyterians who went to Hamlin's for meetings and the Independent for conversation; we do not know how often the Baptist ministers held regular meetings.[15] We do know that all the dissenters' coffee houses had the reputation of incessantly discussing "free will, election, and reprobation."[16]

In their particular coffee houses Londoners found themselves drawn into political discussions. For one thing, in addition to providing convenient centers for business, conversation, and reading newspapers, the coffee houses also served some governmental functions. The Privy Council posted notices of hearings, the Board of Trade asked agents to poll the merchants there, and ministers and merchants circulated petitions. When the Reverend Samuel Davies, leader of the Virginia Presbyterians, came to London to get the government's support for itinerant preaching in that colony, he circulated a petition among the dissenting coffee houses and in little more than a month had the signatures of more than half of London's dissenting ministers.[17] At mercantile houses "they treat of matters of state, make leagues with Foreign Princes, break them again and transact affairs of the last consequence to the whole world," wrote one critic, but then added somewhat more sympathetically: "In a word, tis here the English discourse fully of everything, and where they may in a very little time be known."[18] Friends could argue, enemies could plant rumors, people who might not otherwise have bothered with politics could become politicized.

Over the years some of the more active patrons of mercantile coffee houses created a third layer of organization—the club—often moving to the upper floors of the houses where they could make decisions that were binding and make them in private. By 1734 at least four different groups of London merchants—the Chesapeake, Carolina, New York, and New England merchants—had formed clubs.[19] The Pennsylvania merchants may also have done this, though the Quaker merchants trading to Pennsylvania tended to work through the London Meeting for Sufferings rather than mercantile organizations. Sometime after 1735 the Congregational ministers meeting at the Amsterdam began calling themselves a Board, keeping minutes in which they recorded procedural resolutions and arrogating to themselves a good deal of authority: "Resolved, that no petition be recommended by any minister of this Denomination until it be presented to this Board on a Tuesday evening and signed by five of the members."[20] The merchants' clubs do not seem to have been this formal, but they did meet once or twice a week to collect dues, publish pamphlets, hire agents, and divide up lobbying among members—things they could do far more easily in that setting than while meeting at a coffee house.

Far better known than either the coffee houses or the clubs was the top layer of the interest structures—the umbrella organizations that served to bring together larger collections of merchants, churchmen, dissenters, and ethnic minorities. Here the American merchants lagged behind the other groups: only briefly did they develop any kind of umbrella group, and that was during the mid-1740s when England was again at war with France. A committee of sixteen, four representatives each from among merchants trading to North America, South America, the East Country, and the Italian "straights," met to "consider the numerous captures of ships and the prevention of the same for the future."[21] The group apparently did not last very long: some years later, when the government was distributing money to "Suffering merchants" who had lost ships or cargoes in the current war with France, it nominated a commission of four men, something it presumably would not have had to do if the older committee was still in existence.[22] Beyond this committee and the Commission of 1746, the American merchants do not appear to have developed any overarching organization, largely because they did not need one: there were few issues coming before Parliament that involved merchants trading to all the mainland colonies, and the Board of Trade considered issues on a colony-by-colony basis.

In contrast to the merchants, some of the ethnic and religious leaders either modified and refined their London-wide organizations or developed entirely new ones. Only two groups stayed the same, the Society for the Propagation of the Gospel and the Committee of Representatives of French Churches in London, but these had been well organized from the beginning of the period. The S.P.G. continued to hold its annual February meeting for the election of officers, and its monthly meetings presided over by the Archbishop of Canterbury or the Bishop of London and attended by about twenty members. In practice much of the work fell to the secretary and to a handful of London members who frequently met during the period between the monthly meetings.[23]

Two other groups, the Jews and the Quakers, made only minor changes in organization over the first half of the century. The Quaker Yearly Meeting and the London Meeting for Sufferings were well established by 1715. There were no major structural changes after that, but the practice of assigning particular jobs to different committees of two or three individuals and sharing the work around as widely as possible gradually disappeared, and a group of 30 to 35 men came to handle all of the major questions of the London meeting. The same names appear again and again on committees to obtain copies of parliamentary laws, committees to correspond with overseas yearly meetings, committees to arrange attendance before the Board of Trade, and committees to consider complaints of provincial suffering.[24] In 1749 they also appointed a parliamentary agent.[25] The Sephardic Jews had also been organized before 1715, but by 1740 they had established a Committee of *Deputados* to watch political developments that might affect them and a committee to watch over the activities of the Aldermen of London.[26] They also had a Committee on America.

The newest organizations belonged to the dissenters: the Three Denominations represented the clergy, and the Dissenting Deputies represented the laity. The Three Denominations was organized first. In 1727, after several false starts in earlier decades, the Baptist, Congregational, and Presbyterian ministers organized a general body representing all dissenting ministers within ten miles of London. The whole group met once a year; to handle affairs in the interim they elected a committee of nineteen, fairly equally balanced among the three denominations. The committee usually met about once a month, but it could be summoned on other occasions if a coffee house meeting of ministers of one denomination asked for it; the committee in turn could call special meetings of the general body. One of the committee's most important functions was lobbying: in 1732 the General Body agreed "yt wt ever related to ye General Interest of ye Dissenters and about wch it may be necessary to advise with any minister or ministers of state be laid before ye Committee" and henceforth the committee cultivated ministerial connections, especially with the Duke of Newcastle.[27] As time went on the main body was supplemented by *ad hoc* groups, as for example the committee to enquire whether there were clauses in a particular parliamentary bill "that may affect . . . the rights and Priviledges of the Protestant dissenters,"[28] but the members of the *ad hoc* committees were scarcely distinguishable from those of the standing committee.[29]

In 1732 the laymen among the dissenters organized the Dissenting Deputies, composed of two representatives from each dissenting congregation within ten miles of the City. At first the deputies were simply a special organization to run a campaign for repeal of the Test and Corporation Acts, but over the years they continued to meet regularly, usually once a month. They chose a committee of twenty-one men (later twenty-five) who met every two weeks, initially to plan a strategy for the repeal campaign but later to handle a variety of other matters. In a short period of time the Deputies, far more politically active and more interested in American affairs than their ministerial counterparts in the Three Denominations, had a secretary, a treasurer, and an agent-solicitor.[30]

Just as there were layers in the organizational structures of the interest groups, so too there were layers among the membership, as measured by the intensity and effectiveness of their political activity. At the broadest level were merchants and members of English or foreign groups who really didn't care very much for politics at all, but might occasionally be talked into signing a petition.

At the next level were men who were interested in politics and achieved a measure of influence through hard work. They were not particularly wealthy or well connected nor did they hold positions of great prestige. They knew a lot about the American colonies from first-hand experience, however—most of them were either ex-colonists or Englishmen who had resided in the colonies for some time—and a number of them had served at some time or another in the capacity of agent for a colonial government. Networks of correspondents kept them up to date on American affairs; their friends in Parliament provided them with such accurate information that they were able to have petitions, memorials, and testimony prepared at the right time; the Board of Trade used them to poll particular interests or round up attendance; and they were willing to follow the Board's deliberations doggedly day after day, when issues of particular importance came up. The group included Richard Partridge, a transplanted New Englander who became a Quaker merchant and was also the London meeting's parliamentary liaison as well as being agent for Rhode Island and Pennsylvania,[31] the lawyer James Abercromby, formerly Attorney General of North Carolina who returned to London and became confidant of the Chesapeake merchants and agent for Virginia and South Carolina,[32] and Henry Newman, another transplanted New Englander who was named Secretary to the Society for the Propagation of Christian Knowledge, was one of the chief organizers of the Salzburgers' settlement in Georgia, and became an indefatigable correspondent with colonists in all parts of America.[33] Partridge, Abercromby, Newman, and perhaps half a dozen others like them became important because they were the workhorses of the interest organizations.

At the top level of membership were two other sets of interest group figures, one the ethnic or religious leaders who tended to develop comfortable working relationships with the King or his ministers, the other the wealthy mercantile leaders whose relations with the King and Cabinet were less consistent.

The top ethnic or religious figures had parlayed their positions as group spokesmen into positions of influence with the leading politicians. In a variety of ways they had become acquainted with the King and his ministers and had translated the formal introductions into long-standing friendships, which they could use both for themselves and for their group. The Quakers John Hanbury, David Barclay, and Dr. John Fothergill were in this category; so were the Stennetts, father and son, Baptist ministers at the Little Wild Street Church; Samuel Holden, Dr. Benjamin Avery, heads of the Dissenting Deputies; Reverend Fredrich Michael Ziegenhagen, the Lutheran court chaplain; the DaCostas, Moses Hart, and Aaron Franks from the Jewish community; Edmund Gibson, Bishop of London; and the occasional Huguenot leader who was appointed one of the chaplains to the King.[34] They lobbied almost exclusively with the King or his ministers (it is very rare to find them testifying before Parliament or supplying papers to the Board of Trade), and except for Gibson, who broke with Walpole in 1736, they generally worked behind the scenes.

Other than a few religious leaders who also happened to be merchants, these individuals did not derive any of their influence from wealth; they were men of middling salaries and without independent means. They met leading politicians in various ways. Some became acquainted with the King and his ministers through their jobs: the court chaplains and the Bishop of London would have had that opportunity. Others served in delegations that met with leading ministers on issues to come before Parliament. Others may initially have met one of the ministers when they had to arrange ceremonial appearances at court. When groups presented formal addresses to the King on special occasions like the birth of a royal heir, the conclusion of peace, or the defeat of a rebellion, they had to arrange the timing and the details of presentation ahead of time with the Secretary of State, and for many of the religious leaders this may have been their first ministerial encounter.[35] Others got to meet the leading ministers through charity drives: one of the best ways to promote a charity drive was to get a contribution and an endorsement from the King, and getting these usually required assistance from two or three of the most important ministers.

In contrast to the religious and ethnic leaders, the mercantile giants found their relationship with ministers far from clear; it varied from individual to individual depending on whether or not the merchant was active among City of London politicians who were the backbone of opposition to the national government. Unlike the religious leaders, the outstanding merchant lobbyists were men of wealth, often acquired with breathtaking speed, and were frequently described as the richest men in their trade. Some of them were important holders of government stock; all of them were influential enough for ministers to want their support. But despite their wealth the leading American merchants were identified—and identified themselves—with a community of middle-rank merchants in the City of London, a group which generally formed the core of opposition to the Walpole-Pelham governments in the City.[36] Quite probably these American merchants were less inclined to oppose the ministry than other mercantile groups were; there is not hard evidence. Still, it was risky for any merchant hoping for election to City office— and many of the leading American merchants did hope for it—to identify himself too publicly with the ministry.

So the mercantile leaders spent their time—a very great deal of it in fact—working directly with all branches of government, but while their activities with Parliament were quite open, in negotiating with ministers they were likely to cover their tracks. They spent endless hours "attending constantly at the offices," preparing reports, gathering information, giving testimony, and circulating petitions.[37] Since many of the merchant leaders were awarded government contracts during the mid-century wars with France, patronage for their more important correspondents, and parliamentary action on issues which required ministerial backing, they must have spent time attending the ministers, but they have left us very little information about it. One can easily surmise, however, that relations among merchant lobbyists, the City, and the national government were always tricky.

Relations of all the leading lobbyists—mercantile, ethnic, and ecclesiastical—with the groups they represented could also be tricky. One area of ambivalence concerned the primary source of their influence: where exactly did it come from? Lobbyists who developed connections with ministers, M.P.s, and members of the Board of Trade achieved their influence both as individuals and as spokesmen for their groups, and the relationship between the two roles was never entirely clear. The other area of ambivalence concerned the benefits of lobbying: who got them? Lobbyists who devoted extraordinary energy to cultivating ministerial influence might expect some of the benefits of that influence to go to themselves as well as to the group. Both issues—the sources and the objects of influence—were potential subjects of friction.

The lobbyists' influence derived from both personal and group resources. A few leaders were able to develop a comfortable working relationship with ministers in part because they had wealth enough to contribute to politics (William Baker comes to mind here), free time enough to consult with ministers "at a moments' notice" (Baker's words),[38] provide quarters adequate for entertaining (George II watched London parades from the window of a wealthy Quaker merchant),[39] and congenial personalities (Newcastle insisted that dissenting and Anglican leaders get along with each other as well as "persons of note").[40] But they could never have achieved the influence they had if they had not been able to reflect accurately the views of the interest groups with whom they were identified. They polled the rank and file, they summarized votes, they condensed the most current information down to manageable proportions. Ministers found it easier to summon two or three individuals to talk over an issue than to consult with a much larger group or seek their collective attendance before a hearing, but only if those individuals were capable of presenting the ideas of the whole group. Ministers got more information from questioning individuals than from reading between the lines of a petition, but only if the individuals were well informed. Obtaining accurate information was dreadfully time consuming, however. Micajah Perry, one time "dean" of American lobbyists, went bankrupt, in part because he spent so much time lobbying.[41] Reverend Frederick Michael Ziegenhagen was "pestered nearly every day" by Germans in London pressing him to get government help,[42] and Samuel Holden, chairman for a time of the Dissenting Deputies, had to decline the offer of the Massachusetts Assembly to serve as its agent "on acct of his being already so much engaged" and the following year resigned the chairmanship of the Deputies themselves, having "neither . . . strength or leisure" to continue.[43]

Similarly, it was hard to draw the line between the benefits of lobbying to the groups and to the lobbyists themselves. Leading merchants might work disproportionately hard to get bounties for particular colonial exports but then they stood to gain disproportionately by transporting the goods involved; wealthy dissenters might work extraordinarily hard to get groups of dissenters excused from paying taxes to the Anglican Church, but they stood to gain more than their poorer associates by such exemptions. To be "finger next the thumb" to someone like Sir Robert Walpole brought prestige;[44] it brought the freedom to send unsolicited suggestions on a variety of issues, and often patronage. The most influential merchants got contracts to transport immigrants to the colonies in peacetime or military supplies in wartime; the most influential churchmen went up the ladder of preferment and leading churchmen and dissenters were put in charge of important charities. In 1746 four of the most influential merchants were named a Commission for Distributing Moneys to Suffering Merchants, those who had lost ships or cargoes in the current war with France.[45] From at least 1736 a small group of ministers of the Three Denominations were entrusted with "the receiving of money from persons in power . . . and distributing it in charities."[46] And, of course, the French Committee continued to administer the royal bounty.

Contracts, patronage, administration of charities: all these brought prestige and power to the leading lobbyists. But they could also create resentment, suspicions, and inflated expectations about the individuals' influence in ministerial circles. If ministers repeatedly concluded that "the time was not yet ripe" to repeal the Test and Corporation Acts, the authority of the dissenting leaders was bound to be compromised within the larger group. If ministers made clear their view that a scheme of sending bishops to the colonies (put forth by the Bishop of London) would immediately become "the topic of all conversation with a spirit of bitterness and acrimony," the Bishop was bound to suffer some embarrassment with his colleagues.[47] If lobbyists misrepresented or oversimplified the views of the larger groups—as the wealthier merchants appear to have done in condemning colonial paper money far more rigorously than the lesser merchants would have had them do—there was bound to be resentment among rank and file; if ministers or merchants administered funds for charity, there was bound to be controversy over the way they did it. Consider these minutes of a General Meeting of the Three Denominations, April 6, 1736:

> A motion being made that the receiving of money from persons in power by Dissenting ministers and distributing it privately in charities with account is disapproved by the Assembly.
> The previous question whether it shall be considered at this time? was putt it was caried in the negative.

A motion being made that the names of those ministers might be mentioned who receive the money from the Gentlemen in power.

Another motion was made for adjourning, and carry'd in the affirmative.

In this case the committee escaped uncensored, but the very effort to
expose it, revealed in this brief minute, gives us some idea of both the
perils and opportunities that lobbyists faced.[48]

.   .   .

Just as there were tensions between leaders and rank and file, there was
also tension between the Londoners and the English provincial interests.
London groups did not represent formal national organizations, but they
did have informal connections with corresponding groups in the provinces or the outposts. They knew about, and generally shared, provincial
concerns. Since Londoners were close to the seat of government and
therefore well informed and able to act quickly, and on the whole
wealthier than their provincial colleagues, it was customary for them to
lobby on behalf of the provincials. Cooperation between the two groups
was not always smooth, but on the whole the Londoners did an efficient
job and the provincials appreciated it. None of the London groups except
the Quakers and the S.P.G. had anything like a national organization
(both the Quakers and the S.P.G. had national meetings and a national
treasury), but most had means of corresponding with similar groups in
the provinces or the outports. The Dissenting Deputies had a committee
to correspond with provincial dissenters, and provincials visiting London
after 1740 had a standing invitation to attend meetings.[49] The Huguenot
Committee administered charity to Huguenots in clusters outside London, and German churches had a network of agents to report on German
immigrant groups in the channel ports. London merchants' clubs seem
to have had committees of correspondence; they sent members to poll
the outport merchants on issues of common concern; outport merchants
hired agents to consult with London merchant clubs and coordinate with
London agents; and sometimes London and outport merchants hired the
same agents. Between 1700 and 1750 twelve of the thirty-five Bristol
petitions to Parliament and seven of the twenty-three Liverpool petitions
were almost identical to petitions sent by the Londoners, suggesting a
high degree of cooperation.[50]

Occasionally, as one might expect, there was friction between the
Londoners and the provincials. Sometimes there would be differences of
substance: London and outport merchants were, after all, competitors,
and it would have been surprising if they had always agreed on issues
or policy. More often the differences concerned procedure. The Londoners were far more sophisticated lobbyists than the provincials, and they
insisted, not always tactfully, on directing provincial efforts as well

as their own. The ministers of the Three Denominations circulated among provincial dissenters a list of three "arguments to be insisted upon in . . . Petitions."[51] The same group along with the Dissenting Deputies, the London Meeting for Sufferings, and the Bishop of London insisted on having the final say about whether provincial writings were worthy of publication and provincial petitions worthy of presentation to the appropriate people. They did not hesitate to criticize provincial efforts, nor indeed did they hold back from reprimanding wayward provincials on any issue where the local groups attempted to act independently.[52] When Yorkshire Quakers wrote M.P.s asking for an additional provision to a bill before Parliament, the London Meeting for Sufferings voted unanimously that this was a mistake, sent four of their own members to tell this to the particular M.P.s, and reprimanded the Yorkshire meeting for acting independently in the first place.[53]

The reprimands were not all in one direction. Provincials for their part, often felt that the Londoners were too slow, too cautious, and too capable of sympathizing with ministers. From the provincial perspective the Londoners accepted all too well the slow turning of government wheels and did nothing to speed it up. Liverpool dissenters, who evidently had very little idea of the difficulties of seeking parliamentary legislation, complained to the Dissenting Deputies against their "applying to the Gv-t M-n privately" and waiting on their directions before applying to Parliament for repeal of the Test and Corporation Acts in 1736, and they went on to add, "Nor can we have that Confidence in your watching favourable seasons, as to think ourselves excused from watching along with you."[54]

These recriminations aside, the Londoners seem to have done an efficient job on behalf of provincial interests, and the provincials recognized it. The Dissenting Deputies organized a strong, though ultimately unsuccessful, campaign for repeal of the Test and Corporation Acts in 1736 and an even stronger one (though also unsuccessful) three years later.[55] They also lobbied to get dissenters excused from sheriff's duty, to get protection for dissenters against local riots, and to have sympathetic appointees engaged in the Attorney General's office.[56] In 1757 the Three Denominations campaigned successfully to defeat a provision in the Milita Act authorizing Sunday drilling.[57]

In 1736 the London Meeting for Sufferings and the London Yearly Meeting campaigned for an act requiring all cases involving amounts under £10 to be handled by local Justices so Quakers could avoid expensive hearings before the Exchequer Court. They helped counsel to prepare a brief, coordinated provincial appeals to M.P.s, worked with parliamentary supporters on their responses to amendments proposed in the legislature, gathered information, lobbied with M.P.s, and even called on some of the bishops seeking their support. Though their measure was ultimately thrown out in the Lords, the London Quakers had mounted an extraordinary campaign.[58] For two years the London merchants trading to the American mainland colonies held off the passage of the Molasses Act. They did so by calling on M.P.s, hiring counsel to testify and testifying themselves, and repeatedly petitioning (their opponents in the West India interest did the same).[59] The West Indian merchants finally won, but the contest showed to both sets of merchants the value of having London allies.

Provincials put up with London supervision in order to get favors they needed, and the periods of tension seem not to have lasted very long: English provincials grumbled, but they were grateful. The years 1715 to 1755 were the time when the loose London-provincial networks in England were at their most effective. The same was true, as we will see in the next chapter, for London and provincial groups in the colonies.

CHAPTER 8

The High Point of London and American Interest-Group Cooperation, 1721–1754

The years between 1721 and 1754 were years when relations between London and provincial interests were at their best. The London interests' connections with leading ministers, the Board of Trade, and the Privy Council made them a vital influence on royal administration of the colonies at a time when the resources of the colonies continued to outgrow the resources of the British government to run them. American population expanded sixfold in those years, from a quarter-million in 1700 to a million and a half in 1760, and it expanded inland, away from the centers of imperial authority and the ports where the British navy could call. By mid-century, indeed, colonial population was more than a quarter that of England and Wales and one more mainland colony, Georgia, had been established. In the first sixty years of the century colonial exports grew by almost four times and imports from Britain by six.

Yet British colonial administration did not keep pace. The army in America remained minuscule except in times of war. The number of customs officers increased by 30 percent, hardly enough to keep up with the growth in colonial trade. Georgia's establishment added some new royal officials, but Maryland's return to the proprietor in 1715 took some away. Governors in the royal colonies increasingly saw their powers whittled away in compromises with aggressive local assemblies and disputes with other colonial officials, yet despite the growing discrepancy between the number and power of administrators and the number and power of those to be administered, the American empire remained fairly tranquil, in part because American interests had continued influence on the making of decisions that affected them.

Even in this period, however, the high point of London-American cooperation, there were ominous suggestions that the tranquility would not last. As long as colonial government remained primarily in the management of the kings and their councils and advisers, the London interests could make the most of their own personal contacts, their information, their patient willingness to be on call through endless deliberations. But gradually, episodically, not even very clearly, the very growth of the American colonies came to mean that a number of issues slid from the royal councils to Parliament, and Parliament took up a number of other new issues directly. The steady erosion of the Board's ability to handle colonial problems by instructions, legislative review, and gubernatorial threats, the growing colonial competition with English economic interests, the growing colonial currency problems which left provincials strapped to pay off British creditors, all produced parliamentary legislation that at least some interests did not want. The Hat Act and the Iron Act, for example, passed despite opposition from the transatlantic lobbies; it showed that resources that served the interests so well with the royal administration were inadequate on major parliamentary issues.

These straws in the wind were in various ways obscured at the time. First, for every alarming law Parliament passed in the face of their opposition, the interests could point to a favorable one passed with their support or to a potentially unfavorable one that they blocked before it reached the legislature. Second, the effect of unfavorable legislation was blunted by weak enforcement, and here the interests could still be effective: without an extension of imperial administration many of the new laws depended on provincial acts for their implementation, and provincial acts could be shaped by the Board of Trade through instructions, legislative review, and gubernatorial pressure. Parliamentary intervention in colonial affairs did not decrease the amount of business handled by the Board, and the Board of Trade's power seemed deceptively to increase with Lord Halifax's efforts to strengthen it at the very end of the period.

The American interests grew in two ways. One way, which applied to mercantile and smaller church and non-English groups, was through the creation of more pluralistic societies in the established towns; the other, which affected the larger ecclesiastical and ethnic denominations, was through the repeated creation of new settlements composed of colonists with similar interests. With few exceptions the colonists did not develop new types of organization, but they did consolidate the old ones.

As they consolidated their organization over ever-expanding numbers, the American interests developed demands on the provincial governments. If the groups could obtain these demands locally, they were happy to do so. But if local governments could not or would not meet their desires, interests with good English connections and money for expenses appealed the issues to the British government.

Since occasional issues ended up in Parliament, London interests that were used to confining their lobbying to the Board now found themselves lobbying with Parliament as well. They had to develop new techniques to do this: learning Parliament's agenda ahead of time, cultivating the ministers' support, fitting their proposals into the parliamentary calendar, and soliciting the support of as many M.P.s as possible.

As the interests undertook their work with Parliament and continued their work with the Board of Trade, they and the politicians they lobbied with developed some common assumptions about the nature of legitimate interest group activity. Lobbies were to be based on existing institutions whose functions were not primarily political. Interests were narrowly based and generally worked on their own, not developing larger organizations with interests of different types. Their relationship with the government was a cooperative one; they appealed neither to the opposition politicians nor the general public. They lobbied only on questions of their own interests, rather than on general causes. As ministers and interest group leaders came to accept these assumptions, most of them became comfortable working with each other. American interests truly had a part in the process by which imperial decisions were made.[1]

·   ·   ·

The growth of American interests in this period took place in two different ways. As the established towns grew in population and wealth and were able to support an increasing variety of interests, society grew more pluralistic. Mercantile communities were one kind of group that flourished in the seaport towns. Boston merchants had by 1750 organized a club meeting in the British Coffee House. Somewhat later, when they formally organized a society, it had 146 members.[2] New York merchants met on the second floor of the newly built Exchange after 1753.[3] Charles Town had about 200 merchants[4] and Philadelphia perhaps 260; they probably met in a tavern.[5] Whether there were any merchant organizations that extended beyond the city lines is impossible to say. It would not be surprising if they did since many of the urban merchants had connections with merchants in the smaller towns, but the evidence of any formal organization is simply lacking.

Another type of transatlantic interest in established towns consisted of the smaller churches, some new and some old, that expanded in this period. The tiny Jewish community in New York City had grown to 100 families by mid-century and had sent offshoots to Newport, Rhode Island, in one direction and Philadelphia in the other. By mid-century there were synagogues in Newport, New York City, and Charles Town.[6] Baptist groups, also tiny, were springing up predominantly in rural areas in the wake of the Great Awakening. Philadelphia and Boston had Catholic chapels ministering to the Irish immigration, and Philadelphia, to serve its German immigration, had Lutheran, German Reformed, and Moravian churches.

The other way in which colonial interests grew was through the repeated creation of new settlements, which in their early stages tended to be composed of people with fairly similar interests. This was the main way for the ethnic groups and the major religious denominations to expand. When New Englanders went off to found new towns centered around a church, they were, in a sense, forming a new branch of an established interest. Far more dramatic and numerically more important was the settlement of non-English immigrants in isolated areas where they were not likely to be assimilated for a while, part of the process by which the negligible numbers of non-English in the colonies in 1715 came to be one-third of the population by the Revolution. When Scots moved into unsettled areas in rural Massachusetts, when Salzburgers settled communities in Georgia, when Germans, Scots Irish, and others moved down the Great Wagon Road establishing settlements in the back country, they too were establishing new interest group centers.

The pattern of church growth varied from denomination to denomination. In the port cities most of the larger denominations had at least one church or meeting, but when the denominations expanded into the smaller towns, they traveled different routes. The Anglican Church, for example, followed two different paths. In colonies where Anglicanism was legally established, the church organizations expanded with the expanding population, new communities founding churches when the distance to their former church became too great to travel. Elsewhere, and especially in New England, Anglicanism tended to expand in circles out from seaport centers as urban missionaries of the S.P.G. began preaching in surrounding smaller towns. The Anglicans were not very strong numerically in the cities—usually the dissenters outnumbered them—but they increasingly attracted families of wealth and social leadership, which gave them an urban influence out of proportion to their numbers. Once their city bases were established, S.P.G. missionaries began establishing missions in towns up to fifty miles away (occasionally even farther if the towns were along a road), where they attracted hearers who were disenchanted with the town's existing church.[7] Once the Anglicans in the town became numerous enough to build a church and buy a plot of land for a minister of their own, the S.P.G. sent one out, and the new minister, in turn, began proselytizing in the towns to which he could travel.

If Anglicanism spread out in circles from coastal towns, the most visible growth of Presbyterianism and Lutheranism was through a north-to-south movement in the back country. In each of the major seaport towns Presbyterianism grew steadily, expanding to fill another church or two in this period, and the Lutherans, sometimes in cooperation with other German sects, formed a church of their own. But the two denominations grew fastest through the movement of Scots Irish and Germans down the Great Wagon Road from the Pennsylvania frontier to Georgia.

As Presbyterians and Lutherans moved south, Quakerism moved north. It actually declined in Philadelphia (it fell to a quarter of the population there) and elsewhere in the middle colonies, but made up for this by expanding up the Hudson River and further in Rhode Island, Massachusetts, and Maine. We have no statistics on its membership, but a Quaker visitor to New England in 1754 attracted crowds of 1,000 to 4,000. A number of these were surely non-Quakers who came out of curiosity, but the fact that the Newport Yearly Meeting for a while came to surpass the Philadelphia meeting suggests that great numbers who came actually were Quakers caught up in the brief but rapid movement of Quakerism to the north.[8]

The interest groups varied in organization from the loose to the fairly structured. At the "loose" end of the spectrum were planters and farmers. The leading ones must have met as members of the legislature and, more locally, they must have gathered at church and court. On crucial issues they seem to have developed a gentleman's agreement to share the expenses of lobbying, but it is doubtful whether they ever went farther and set up clubs, as one South Carolina planter suggested planters do in his own colony.[9]

Slightly better organized were the merchant groups. Only one, the Bostonians, created a club during the period. The rest still seemed to meet at the coffee houses. They appear not to have established committees, but they did come together often enough to determine stands on political issues and they seem to have been able to collect substantial sums of money.

By far the best organized of the colonial interests were the churches. The non-English immigrants generally socialized through their congregations, and their church organizations pulled together at varying speeds over the period. The churches that were already established experienced few changes in organizational structure. At the very beginning of the period, in 1716, the Presbyterians established the Synod of Philadelphia (which later split in two over the Great Awakening[10]); toward the end the Quakers' quarterly meeting took on more authority as it evolved into a yearly meeting;[11] and several Baptist associations were meeting annually.[12] Beyond these there were almost no changes in the structure or the procedure of the various churches.

So for the established church organizations this was a period of consolidation rather than innovation. It was also a period when more of the groups developed a stable, highly visible, respected leadership. The same men (such as Thomas Richardson, who retired after forty years as clerk of the Newport Meeting) were elected again and again to clerkships and treasurerships of the Quaker meetings.[13] Year in, year out, Benjamin Colman was moderator of the meetings of Congregational ministers in Boston, and it was Colman to whom congregations in the smaller towns turned when they needed the Boston ministers to handle a local dispute.[14] About ten men, the most important of whom was Rev. Francis Alison, dominated the Presbyteries of Philadelphia and New York, each serving at least one term as moderator and one as clerk.[15] Henry Melchior Muhlenberg was undisputed leader of the Lutheran Church; Isaac Backus was beginning to be recognized as preeminent among New England Baptists, and James Blair, Alexander Garden, and their fellow commissaries of the Anglican Church reached the highest point of their authority in this period.

Although it is known that colonial interests grew in numbers and consolidated organizations, it is hard to say what percentage of the population was included in them. In one sense virtually every adult was in some kind of interest group simply by virtue of his ethnic background, his vocation, or the way he did or did not worship. If we specify organized interests and thereby disqualify, say, housewives, village doctors and blacksmiths, small-town merchants, the farmers who had no chance to organize, and the people who didn't attend church, we are still at a loss to guess the numbers of interest groups with any accuracy. The incompleteness of the records of English and non-English churches and the absence of any mercantile group's records for this period make it impossible to know how many people were active members and how many showed up only when they wanted to get married, baptize a child, arrange a burial, or in the case of mercantile clubs, when they wanted to get information about particular conditions of trade that would affect their own shipping. Even among active church goers, congregations were still not stable: their members were frequently on the move, they fragmented over the Great Awakening, and even in good times most of them were still so short of ministers that when an incumbent died or left there might be a long delay in replacing him; during this gap the congregation would switch churches rather than go without pastoral services altogether. One must give up the attempt to pin down exact numbers of members relative to the whole population.

The kinds of political issues in which the groups were interested varied according to their situations, but from colony to colony the church demands, at least, were fairly consistent. All groups sought the appointment of sympathetic governors and the removal of hostile ones. Minority churches wanted to be let off paying taxes to the established church. In the established churches ministers on fixed salaries wanted protection against having their salaries reduced by the assemblies either by direct legislation or by inflationary issues of paper money. Churches short of ministers wanted itinerant preaching made legal so remote congregations could have the services of a minister at least occasionally. A few Anglicans wanted a bishop appointed for America; dissenters wanted protection against such an appointment. The larger churches and the universities wanted to be incorporated so they could handle money; and at some time or other nearly every church needed a lottery to raise money for new buildings.

Merchants and ethnic groups were slightly less uniform in their political demands than were the church goers. Merchants everywhere opposed import duties and local excises. Most merchants wanted some encouragement of foreign immigration because more immigrants meant more consumers, and the enthusiasm for such encouragement increased as one moved south. Most merchants argued that some paper money was useful to their colony's economy, but they did not agree on how much. Charles Town merchants were particularly concerned with the regulation of auctions, where interlopers might undersell them;[16] Philadelphia merchants were more interested in regulating the dimensions of wooden staves and the quality of flour.[17] Finally, merchants in all the colonies wanted bounties on local products so they could profit from increased export trade.

Most of the immigrant groups wanted help for friends and relatives still waiting to come to the colonies. For European emigrants this meant getting permission to leave the home country, exemption from tolls along the way to the nearest port, and making interim living arrangements in Holland, London, or one of the southern English ports if they were stopping there.[18] For all emigrants this meant also the guarantee of a safe passage, with the government subsidizing the trip and extracting guarantees from captains that passengers would not be badly treated. When the immigrants arrived in the colonies they wanted to settle on land already surveyed and to be exempted from taxes until they got their settlement under way, usually seven years. Often, they asked also to be left alone—but not completely, for they also wanted help with defense if their settlement was on the frontier.[19]

Similar types of interests shared roughly similar concerns throughout the colonies. But it was not always initially clear which of these concerns were safely left to local authorities and which were best appealed to England. Some issues—bounties, foreign negotiations, or the appointment of a bishop, for example—could obviously be handled only at the imperial level; others, like the regulation of auctions and the size of staves, were considered local issues on which the British government rarely interfered. But the bulk of the issues were in between, neither exclusively local or exclusively imperial; they could be handled at several levels. When Philadelphia merchants wanted to oppose Lord Baltimore's claim to three counties in Pennsylvania, they first petitioned the city of Philadelphia asking it, in turn, to petition the Pennsylvania assembly. Ultimately, the matter was handled by the Privy Council.[20] When immigrant groups wanted land surveyed, they could go to the Board of Trade for instructions to the governor to arrange the surveys or ask that the surveys be handled by the British government. A religious minority seeking exemption from paying taxes to the established church would probably appeal first to the local assessor, next to the collector, next to the legislature for legal recognition of their exemption, and finally to the Privy Council for disallowance of the original law and instructions to the governor to get a less discriminatory law in its place.

Whether groups found it necessary or useful to appeal questions to the home government depended on a number of things. The first consideration was the strength of the group's English connection and its willingness to help out on particular issues, and here the American interests varied greatly from group to group. Associations of mechanics or groups of porters and carters, for example, had no English connections. Ethnic charities or social groups such as the Hibernian Societies, Sons of St. Patrick, Sons of St. Andrew, and so on, had no natural connections in England, but occasionally a social group like the Fellowship Society of Charles Town managed to get, through personal contacts with London merchants, support for a local policy it wanted.[21] The poorer tobacco planters, and the poorer farmers in general, did business with English merchants who were not interested in politics.

Other groups had a hard time with English connections but still managed to make them. London merchant clubs, as far as we know, had no corresponding committees, so colonial merchants and planters had to rely on letter-writing campaigns to influence them. Presumably the American merchants gathered at the local coffee houses to organize a large-scale campaign: when the South Carolina assembly passed an act levying heavy import duties in 1744, Robert Pringle was confident that "every person here in trade will write to their friends at home about said tax bill."[22] On important issues the merchants, like the religious groups, could go farther than this and collect money to hire an agent. The Boston, Gloucester, and Marblehead merchants sent Christopher Kilby to London to oppose a liquor tax.[23] Governor Hunter of New York complained that "one Mr. Baker, a merchant there, had had a sume of money remitted him from hence to enable him to oppose some or all the money bills at home . . . we may guess at his employers by his correspondence."[24]

Wealthy planters, like the poorer farmers, had no continuing organizations, but when they had to they could like the merchants, develop highly effective letter-writing campaigns with the relevant London merchants. "I believe most of ye Gentm in Virginia are urgent with their correspondents to come into this good design," wrote Robert Carter about the intended repeal of the parliamentary prohibition on stemming tobacco in 1728,[25] and he was right: the planters not only wrote urgently but sent over an agent to work with the London merchants.

The most systematic connections between Londoners and Americans were in the church groups. American yearly meetings of Quakers corresponded with assigned members of the London Meeting for Sufferings, American dissenters exchanged letters with the Dissenting Deputies' Committee of Correspondence, and American visitors were allowed to attend both the Deputies' meeting and the Quaker Yearly Meeting.[26] Anglican missionaries corresponded regularly with the secretary of the S.P.G., as did the Anglican commissaries with the Bishop of London, and when they particularly wanted information the commissaries came back to London to talk over colonial issues with the Bishop and the Archbishop of Canterbury.[27]

If the desirability of appealing issues to England depended first on the Americans' London connections, it depended next upon the cost. When English groups helped out Americans, they expected them to pay at least part of the costs of preparing petitions and paying fees as they went through various offices. Expenses could run up to £100 plus carriage fare and stationery; more, if the group sent over its own agent to work with the Londoners. This was a substantial amount—well over a year's salary for a minister, for example—and for less organized groups it could involve considerable sacrifice.[28]

Additionally, much depended on how well the group was able to get what it wanted in local politics without appealing to imperial authority, and this varied greatly from group to group, colony to colony, and time to time. The success of interests with colony governments depended not only upon their numbers, but upon their ability to form coalitions with other interests. The opportunities for coalition were greatest in the middle colonies, where the greatest number of interest groups existed: by mid-century political factions in New York, New Jersey, and Pennsylvania were emerging as interest group coalitions, loose enough so that particular interests got leverage by threatening to abandon ship.[29] Even in the New England and the southern colonies, however, coalition politics were possible, and upon their success depended a few interest appeals to England. Anglican ministers in Virginia cooperated with well-to-do tobacco planters to get a tobacco inspection act, which kept up both the price of tobacco and the monetary integrity of clerical salaries, and they had little trouble getting the act approved in England. But when the planters opposed the ministers, as they did when the planter-dominated House of Burgesses passed an act reducing clerical salaries in 1758, the ministers appealed straight to England without contesting the bill locally at all.[30] In Massachusetts Quakers, Anglicans, and Baptists, all adversely affected by the same law taxing them for the support of the established Congregational Church, were unable to form any kind of coalition against it, so each one separately had to appeal to correspondents in Britain for help with bringing pressure on the governor to push for more favorable legislation.[31]

Finally, the success of interests in dealing with colonial governments depended upon the efficiency of the governments themselves, and this also varied from colony to colony. Despite the American legislators' aggressive assertion of the assemblies' institutional powers vis-à-vis the governors, their constituents were accustomed to getting things done at the town and county rather than the provincial level until well into the century, about the time of the mid-century wars. Early eighteenth-century assemblies in general were loosely structured organizations dealing informally with a variety of matters, major and minuscule, judicial and administrative, as well as legislative. Petitions on all manner of subjects, from individual pensions to banking and currency, from the repair of church pews to religious toleration, were given more or less equal attention by the *ad hoc* committees to which they were referred.[32] Since legislative sessions were short—sometimes no more than a few weeks—the enormous amount of time spent on trivia could delay the enactment of major legislation sometimes by several years. In addition, some laws were hardly enforced at all where opponents constituted a local majority.[33] Groups exasperated by the inability of colonial legislatures to get the things they wanted done, groups penalized when assemblies did get something done—these, along with colonists concerned about issues that could be handled only at the imperial level, were the people who looked to London interests for help with the British government.

Like their counterparts in the English provinces, the Americans complained that Londoners were "slow and dilatory,"[34] resented on occasion being deprived of "that help we relied on with the greatest assurance,"[35] disliked being told that their pamphleteering efforts were not good enough for English publication, and were annoyed to be informed that their indiscretions "will not fail of being represented here [in London] to our as well as your disadvantage."[36] Americans, like English provincials, had constantly to bear in mind that the final decision about how and whether the London groups would handle lobbying belonged to the Londoners alone.

Nevertheless, on issues that had to be handled at the imperial center,

Americans were likely to allow English interests to intercede for them. Twenty-two petitions to the King concerning American interests can be identified between 1715 and 1720, and none came directly from the colonies. In the next two decades there were some colonial petitions, but they were outnumbered three or four to one by those from English groups.[37]

The bulk of the issues remained questions of management. They were handled by the Board or the Privy Council, where interests were most comfortable because they dealt with a government that was responsive to them on particular issues, having no overriding colonial policies. Here their opposition came largely from other interests that had no advantage over them—from other colonial voluntary interests,[38] from colonial assemblies or proprietors acting as interests,[39] and occasionally from English associations no better equipped than they were to provide American information, hire counsel versed in American affairs, or organize patient attendance in the boards and chambers. So much did the interests prefer working with the Board that at times they considered it a measure of success just to get the Board or the Privy Council to decide issues at all, without passing them on to Parliament. When the head of the Dissenting Deputies learned that "nothing would be done [on the question of appointing American bishops] without the maturest deliberation" and that "the Affair was farr from being concluded on," he exulted that the issue was not likely to come before Parliament that session.[40]

Some issues did come up before Parliament in the 1730s and 1740s, however, their numbers increasing gradually, though not at the expense of the total volume handled by the Board. They represented rather an expansion of the colonial business handled by all sections of the government: growing colonial trade brought the North American colonies into greater importance in the imperial economy and greater competition with other parts of the empire, increasing the colonial production engendered conflict with competitive English producers, and expanded areas of settlement made colonies a more important arena of conflict in the mid-century wars with France.

Some parliamentary measures on the American colonies came from appeals of the colonial interests for special legislation. Moravians wanted naturalization,[41] producers of indigo and naval stores wanted bounties, South Carolina rice growers wanted permission to ship directly to Europe,[42] wealthy Virginia tobacco growers wanted an end to prohibition on shipping stemmed tobacco.[43] On such issues the London interests needed patience (the rice exporters waited ten years before Parliament took rice off the list of enumerated commodities), money (the Quakers spent £1,000 on their own campaign against the Tithe Bill in 1736),[44] and hard work lobbying several hundred men rather than a handful, but eventually they were likely to get the measures through.

If a group was working for favorable legislation, it had first to win assurance that ministers would support their measure or at least not object to its being brought up. Campaigns for measures must be undertaken "with the good likeing of the administration" rather than in opposition to them; "appealing to Parliament [unsupported] is no compliment to an administration."[45] On the issue of the Moravian bills this meant going directly to ministers themselves; the bill allowing rice growers to export rice directly to southern Europe, on the other hand, was probably supported by the ministers mainly because it was backed by the Board of Trade.

Once ministers gave their assent, the lobby's next step was to work with them in pushing the measure through Parliament. The lobbyists themselves often helped prepare legislation. In 1755 William Baker, by then a member of Parliament himself, drafted legislation for the "regulation for the rights of Hudson's Bay" and sent it to Newcastle "in conformity by your commands."[46] In 1736 a committee of the London Meeting for Sufferings drafted a bill making it obligatory for tithes and church rates under 40 shillings to be handled by Justices of the Peace rather than by Exchequer or Ecclesiastical courts.[47]

Lobbyists also had to work with ministers and the Speaker of the House on the parliamentary calendar, preferably a week or so before the session began. Timing was tricky: if a bill was presented too early, it might get lost amidst discussion of budget or other subjects of greater importance to the government. If a bill was presented too late, it ran the risk of being postponed until after Parliament adjourned, as there was little time for M.P.s to read petitions and addresses and hear expert testimony.

Once the preliminaries were set, the rest of the lobbyists' work consisted in bringing influence to bear on the M.P.s. Before M.P.s left their country homes for London, committee members called on them, and lobbyists approached them again once they reached the capital, urging leaders to give active support and imploring less active ones at least to show up and vote. London merchants called on M.P.s from London and the outports; dissenters reminded particular M.P.s of dissenting votes among their constituents. Lobbyists also delivered information to Parliament as a whole, in the form of petitions and expert testimony; they hired counsel to testify before Parliament, often to respond to planted questions. Lobbyists also distributed a great variety of information to M.P.s at home or at the door of the House: manuscript pamphlets copied out by clerks, broadsides which might be duplicates of broadsides printed in the provinces, excerpts from provincial newspapers printed separately, pamphlets written by members of the group or commissioned journalists. Occasionally the interests resorted to log rolling: it is significant that the London merchants trading to South Carolina got nowhere with their demands for the direct export of rice to southern Europe until they got the support of the Spanish and Portuguese merchants.

Time-consuming issues could drag out over years, sometimes more than a decade, but the wait was often worth it, especially if the lobbyists did not face opposition from any other lobbies, English or American, which thought their own interests were jeopardized by the proposal.

Where the Londoners had considerably less success was helping their American counterparts on legislation that developed from interests in conflict. Some parliamentary proposals came from English interests—the hat makers and the iron mongers come to mind here—opposing American competition; others emerged when competing colonial interests, generally economic, appealed against each other on issues that had implications for the running of the empire. On the Bubble Act, which shut down the Massachusetts Land Bank in 1741, and the Currency Act, which restricted the issue of paper currency in the New England colonies a decade later, the New England merchants had not acted as a group but had sent opposing petitions. New Hampshire merchants had divided over the White Pines Act restricting the cutting of masting pines to the Royal Navy. New York and New England users of molasses, particularly the rum manufacturers, bitterly opposed the Molasses Act, but the Act was proposed in the first place by the West India lobby.

If a London group feared that Parliament might take up legislation discriminating against its friends in the colonies, its first job was to appoint a committee or an individual agent to get advance notice of bills to be proposed. The committee or agent might pay a regular fee to clerks of the House of Commons or they might check with Arthur Onslow, the mid-century speaker of the House of Commons who was "always . . . kind" to special interests with American connections.[48] Ministers or members of the Board of Trade could tip off groups about bills that were in the works. Some groups had their own members in Parliament. Anglican gentry dominated the Commons, but over the period 1715 to 1754 twenty-eight dissenters sat in Parliament and about five American merchants. (A total of 198 merchants were M.P.s; it is not always clear how many among them classified themselves primarily as American merchants, but usually at least one or two in any given session).[49] Sometimes the interests were able to anticipate Parliament's agenda fairly clearly: when it was "strongly suggested" to the Quaker merchant Richard Partridge in 1748 that a paper currency bill would come up in the next session of Parliament, Partridge planned his opposition accordingly.[50] At other times the lobbyists' information was far more vague, as when they got wind of "threatenings . . . against charter governments" in 1754.[51] But one way or another the interests almost always managed to get warnings about intended parliamentary legislation that would affect their correspondents in the colonies.

Once the issues were raised and the parliamentary agenda set, however, London interests were hard-pressed to defend their American colleagues on an issue where the government was responding to the pressure of even stronger interests. They could hire counsel, circulate counterpetitions, distribute information, and call on the leading ministers, hoping they might signal indifference if not disapproval in debate. Sometimes, as when some of the New York merchants acceded to limitations on hat making in the colonies in return for not having furs put on the enumerated list, they could get a compromise. Sometimes, as with the Iron and the White Pines acts, the legislation was unenforceable without local cooperation. Sometimes, as with the Molasses Act and the Currency Act, the interests could delay the passage of laws. But compromise, delay, and encouragement of noncompliance were the best the lobbyists could do against powerful English lobbies, the government, or both.

For a time the lobbyists' ability to maneuver, the unenforceability of some of the laws, and the fact that the Board of Trade not only continued to handle its usual volume of work, but even obtained additional powers briefly at the end of the period, blurred the potential threat to the effectiveness of transatlantic interest groups inherent in Parliament's intrusion into colonial administration. It remained less important to colonists that they won or lost on particular issues, than that they were represented in the competition.

As the committees and individual agents of the various interests worked with members of Parliament and the Board of Trade, both lobbyists and politicians developed some common assumptions about the extent and limits of legitimate interest group activity and the proper relationship between government and interests. One such assumption was that lobbies were based on existing institutions—coffee house clubs, churches, and charities—whose functions were only incidentally political. Merchants came to coffee houses to buy insurance, pick up mail, and exchange information; religious groups met for worship; ethnic groups met to provide housing, food, credit, and other help for recent immigrants and worship for the whole community. They were not immediately concerned with politics, but once assembled, the merchants, worshipers, and ethnic groups could be made aware of issues affecting them that were currently before Parliament, and they could be asked to sign petitions, make financial contributions, or appear before Parliament as witnesses.

Another assumption was that the interests remained specific, fairly narrowly rooted throughout the period. With three exceptions—the cooperative efforts of Presbyterians, Congregationalists, and Baptists in the Three Denominations and the Dissenting Deputies, and the committee representing merchants trading to four continents who met to consider ways to prevent the capture of ships during the French war of the

1740s—the various denominations, ethnic communities, and mercantile clubs kept their organizations separate from one another. They might cooperate briefly with other groups, but the cooperation never involved any change in organization.

Lobbyists did not need to develop cooperative organizations since most issues coming before Parliament or the Board affected one merchant group or denomination (or rather, one each on opposing sides) or one ethnic group. The Board of Trade handled colonial appointments, legislative review, and instructions to governors on a colony-by-colony basis; in helping to settle non-English immigrants they negotiated with governors and through them the colonial legislatures. In Parliament the various ethnic and religious groups were seldom interested in the same issues at the same time. Quakers were interested in the settlement of tithe disputes and in getting colonial Quakers exempted from taking oaths (the issue came up in a number of subjects including the naturalization of Quaker immigrants to the colonies). Moravians were also interested in obtaining naturalization without taking oaths, but their parliamentary campaign came ten years later. Jews and Quakers were both interested in amending an act for naturalizing immigrants to the colonies passed in 1739, but the amendments they wanted were entirely different. Most parliamentary issues affecting the merchants concerned only one colony or one colonial region. Even issues that at first sight appeared to be of general mercantile interest turned out on closer examination to have concerned only the members of one or two particular coffee houses. Robert Walpole's excise scheme of 1733, for example, was apparently not opposed across the board by merchants trading to all colonies but only by those trading to Maryland and Virginia.[52] American signers of two petitions critical of Walpole's unpreparedness against the Spanish in 1739 and 1742 were largely Carolina merchants; many of the neighboring Chesapeake merchants refused to support them.[53]

Another assumption shared by lobbyists and the government was that the relationship between the two on American issues was basically a cooperative one. Lobbyists rarely lobbied in opposition to the known opinion of ministers on American issues: except for extraordinary cases like the tobacco merchants' defeat of Walpole's excise tax in 1733, interests would have no chance of winning without ministerial support.

If there was little point in opposing ministers on particular issues, there was even less point in joining the parliamentary opposition on a long-run basis. For most of the period 1715 to 1755 the parliamentary opposition was too weak to be of any use to the interests. Against the ministerial combination of personal followers, landed aristocrats, and moneyed men the opposition could not develop an effective coalition. Moreover, they did not seek interest group support, for the backbone of the opposition was the country gentleman, a man convinced that England was a homogeneous Anglican agrarian society in which everyone shared, or ought to share, the same ideas about the common good. There was no room in his thinking for diverse interests, and no opposition leader could convince him to enter any long-run combinations with groups as different as the dissenters or the urban merchants.[54]

The transatlantic interests did not usually appeal to the parliamentary opposition; neither did they go over the heads of the ministers and appeal to the public. Except for the merchants active in City politics, interest group leaders pointedly disassociated themselves from any kind of popular opposition to the government—any "spirit of political madness," as a Presbyterian leader described popular opposition to the Duke of Newcastle in 1756.[55] Appealing to the public was "endangering the quiet of the kingdom," as Governor Holden of the Dissenting Deputies warned provincials in 1733.[56] As the American-connected groups saw it, to bring pressure on Parliament by raising a public clamor (a very bad word in eighteenth-century politics) was to "play the politician," to usurp Parliament's deliberative role.[57] When the agent of the assembly of Virginia brought over a petition supporting Walpole's proposed tobacco excise in 1733 and had copies of it printed and circulated for publicity, the merchant Micajah Perry demanded to know "how he came not to present his representation to this House as it is addressed, but chose to print it and make it an appeal to the people."[58] Writing for newspapers and magazines was sometimes done but its legitimacy was questionable, since newspaper readership was not selective. Archbishop Secker advised an American missionary not to publish a piece in the *London Magazine,* because flaunting the issue in a public magazine would "draw down the contempt of" the politicians the missionary was attempting to influence in private.[59] By the same token, to circulate copies of pamphlets at newsstands, while it was also done on occasion, was to "publish them to the world," and hence in poor taste. General tracts on political theory and even journals directed toward a general criticism of the government were quite legitimate publications, but pamphlets designed to arouse an informed public to put pressure on Parliament were not.

The best strategy of interests, therefore, was to assume that on American issues the government would try as much as possible to placate them, and that on these matters they should assume the role of advisers, never the role of potential adversaries. Few of the interest group leaders went as far as John Hanbury when he bought the seat at Bristol for a government supporter.[60] But most would have agreed with the Quaker committee that in 1734 advised Quakers in the country to appeal only to M.P.s "who are esteemed to be well affected to the Present Government."[61] Whenever possible, they cleared petitions with ministers before presenting them. (Custom required that the Speaker of the Commons see a petition before it was read in the House.)

Since they could not properly appeal to opposition at any level, lobbyists found that their greatest strength continued to come not from political pressure but from their access to certain kinds of information the government needed. When the Board of Trade wanted information about French Protestants who had landed at Jersey on their way to America, they consulted with French ministers in London;[62] when they wanted information about the working of South Carolina's township law over the 1730s, they consulted merchants trading to the colony.[63] When Moravians wanted Parliament to exempt their coreligionists in the colonies from oaths and military service, they petitioned Parliament, mentioning that many of the Moravian settlers had already met with approval in America and going on to give information about Moravian beliefs, history, and settlement;[64] when South Carolina merchants wanted to export rice directly to southern Europe, they explained that when rice was reshipped to the Continent from Britain, "it is frequently spoiled (being a grain of tender nature) by the length of time necessarily taken up by two voyages."[65]

Finally, it was assumed that lobbies tried to influence the government only on questions that directly affected their own interests. There was a crucial difference between interests, which it was legitimate to take up, and "causes," political principles, "general issues of humanity," which it was not.

As interest groups came to accept these assumptions, ministers came to accept the legitimacy of interest group lobbying as part of the political process. Mid-eighteenth-century London interests with American connections were notable for the ease with which they approached ministers and the contentment with which they viewed government. Dissenters were "generally well affected and indeed necessary supports to ye present establishment in State;"[66] they spoke of the Duke of Newcastle as "the Bulwark of our Religion and Liberties."[67] A merchant signed a personal note to Newcastle, "I cannot more faithfully be . . . your Grace's most obedient and most humble servant;"[68] a Jewish leader wrote to a friend that London Jews "as they think themselves happy under ye present government circumstances . . . will not start a thing they think not necessary for their preservation."[69] Dissenters "suitably prize[d] the blessings we have of Protestant Religion and legal government and resolve to stand fast in defense of them as they are."[70]

Thus, in general, London interests with American connections were comfortable working with the British government in the mid-eighteenth century. Occasionally American issues, such as Sir Robert Walpole's proposal for an excise on tobacco in 1733, the quarrel with Spain over the Georgia boundary which provoked calls for war in 1739, and the mismanagement of the early part of the Seven Years' War, created a parliamentary crisis, intensified the connection of some mercantile leaders with the City's opposition to the government, and unsettled the government's relations with important interests. By and large, however, the government was able to keep them happy by supplementing English concessions with less costly American ones. Particular American groups did not always win in the give-and-take of London's interest group politics, but they were part of the process by which decisions were made. They, too, had reason to feel represented at the highest levels of imperial decision making. London-American interest groups were an important factor in stabilizing politics in England and America.

CHAPTER 9

The Colonial Governors and the Interests, 1720–1750

During the heyday of London-American cooperation, colonial interests continued to use their English connections to get leverage with governors they could not adequately influence in the provincial capitals. As more and more groups in the colonies developed London connections, governors were increasingly forced to cultivate interest group support for survival. With interests able to influence their instructions, their councils, and the review of their legislation through the Board and Parliament, and with interests also having some influence on prolonging or terminating their appointments, governors had to be even more careful of interest group relations after 1715 than they had been before.

At the beginning of the century governors in the southern colonies and in New England had had little room for maneuver. Of the three governors we looked at for the first quarter of the century—Hunter of New York, Spotswood of Virginia, and Dudley of Massachusetts—only Hunter governed a province so pluralistic that he was able and in fact required to work with a variety of transatlantic interests; the governors of Massachusetts and Virginia could not. By the 1730s, however, Virginia and Massachusetts were developing pluralistic societies, at least in and around the capital cities, and their governors had considerably more opportunity and more need to play off interests than had their predecessors. We can see this most clearly in two of the longest administrations of the period, William Gooch's in Virginia, 1727–1749, and Jonathan Belcher's in Massachusetts, 1730–1741.

Both Gooch and Belcher initially owed their appointments largely to the personal choices of leading ministers, but once in office they had to work with interest groups for political survival. Gooch was an Anglican country gentleman running a colony of would-be Anglican country gentlemen; Belcher was a Congregational/Presbyterian merchant administering a colony dominated by merchants of a similar religious background. Each man, however, discovered that politics involved more than a superficial identity with one interest or another.

Of the two governors Gooch was by far the more successful: at the very least he lasted twice as long in tenure. Admittedly, he had some resources that Belcher did not have, the most obvious being enormous tact. Belcher was surely one of the least charming governors of the entire colonial period: his talent for cursing out his enemies was every bit as great as Gooch's talent for complimenting them.[1] The Board of Trade had to recommend to him "more temper and coolness."[2] Gooch also had stronger political patrons in England. Belcher's acquaintance with the King may have helped his initial appointment, but his main patron among political leaders left office about a year after the governor began his administration.[3] Gooch had a regular salary; the lack of a regular salary proved a volatile issue throughout Belcher's tenure. Gooch had only one legislature to contend with; Belcher had two—New Hampshire as well as Massachusetts.

But when all these advantages are acknowledged, it still remains the case that Gooch was extraordinarily skillful—or extraordinarily lucky—in handling interest groups. He had to deal mainly with the planter aristocracy, the London merchants they did business with, and with the Anglican Church, which was legally established in the colony. But he also had to work with other interests, ethnic, religious and economic. New groups were appearing in Virginia mainly in the Piedmont and the Valley. They differed from the dominant Anglican gentry not only in religion (some were Quakers but most were German Lutherans or Pietists and Scots Irish Presbyterians) but also in the work they did (they raised livestock and produced hemp and saltpeter rather than tobacco).[4] The new groups were never strong enough or active enough politically to give the governor a viable alternative to alliance with the tobacco planters, but they had to be reckoned with, and it is a measure of Gooch's political acumen that he was able to persuade the colony's Anglican planter gentry of the need to make concessions to the newcomers. So successful was Gooch that he was still in office when he died, over two decades after his arrival, at peace with the interest groups that surrounded him.

Gooch recognized early in the game—earlier than his predecessor Spotswood had—that the Anglican planter interest must be satisfied if his administration was to be a peaceful one. Locally Gooch's greatest resource was his own extraordinary tact: there was hardly anyone, except perhaps the London merchant Micajah Perry, who did not succumb to the governor's personal charm, a charm that made him "mighty well beloved and respected by the country."[5] Gooch was able to persuade most of the influential planters most of the time that his policies—the regulation of the quality of their tobacco being exported, for example—were for their advantage, and he reinforced his support among the planters with gracious entertainment and generous land grants to many of them.

In England Gooch also took pains to keep up his connections with the mercantile and ecclesiastical friends of the Anglican planters. Gooch came to Virginia with the support of the Virginia-trading merchants of London and kept it throughout his administration except for a brief period around 1732–1733; indeed, so much confidence did the lobby ultimately have in him that by the 1740s they were content to trust Virginia affairs to the governor, and their lobby had become temporarily inactive.[6] Gooch's religious background was both Anglican and Scottish Presbyterian, and through his brother, later Bishop of Norwich and Ely, and his friend the Bishop of Bangor, Gooch had good connections with the Anglican Church. He corresponded with his brother and the Bishop of London; and even more important, perhaps, he cultivated his connections with James Blair, commissary of the Bishop of London in Virginia. He did not much like Blair but still, as he wrote to his brother, "We are good Friends and I intend to keep so if I can, which will be difficult."[7] Blair himself wrote of Gooch, "There is a perfect understanding betwixt him and me that makes all things easy both with clergy and laity."[8] Moreover, it certainly did not hurt that Gooch was a former neighbor of Sir Robert Walpole, Prime Minister for over half the period of Gooch's administration.

On behalf of the new groups, the Lutherans and Presbyterians who produced meat and hemp on the frontier, Gooch pressed the Burgesses for both economic and religious concessions. He won tax-free land grants for the newcomers, and laws regulating the quality of exported meat, limiting the travel of cattle to the northern colonies, and creating bounties for the production of hemp and saltpeter, all of which they wanted. On these economic issues the Burgesses did not take much persuading.

With regard to the toleration of religious groups, however, Gooch's achievements are less clear, particularly with the Quakers. The Virginia Quakers, of English and German Pietists stock, increased in numbers enough to have three monthly meetings by the year of Gooch's death. Early in Gooch's administration the Burgesses passed a law providing that when Quakers refused to pay taxes for the support of the local Anglican minister, their possessions would be taken and sold at auction. The auction sales were particularly prejudicial to the Quakers since they brought low prices and thereby necessitated enormous confiscations to compensate for the taxes. Exactly what Gooch's role was in helping the Quakers is unclear, but he seems to have sympathized with them; by

1759 they had been granted partial exemption from "priests' taxes" because "men of great note" (presumably Gooch had been among them) are "moderate and willing to assist us."[9]

With the Presbyterians Gooch's role is a little clearer, although not much. Down to the 1740s there was little open trouble. In the 1720s the occasional Presbyterian minister served in Virginia to a small congregation, complained of discrimination, and was not able to do anything about it. In the early 1730s Scots Irish Presbyterians began settling in Virginia in great numbers, and one group asked the Philadelphia Synod to intervene with Gooch on their behalf. Gooch assured the Synod that "no interruption shall be given to any minister of your profession who shall come among them."[10] He required only that ministers qualify themselves for protection under the Toleration Act by swearing to certain of the Thirty-Nine Articles, and since all of the ministers coming in the 1730s complied, there was no difficulty accommodating Presbyterians in that decade.

In the 1740s, however, the situation became more complicated and Gooch had to use all of his considerable talents to keep the "Presbyterian question" from becoming a deeply divisive issue in Virginia politics. The Scots Irish migration swelled dramatically. At the same time the Presbyterian Church began dividing into two wings, the "old-light" conservatives and the "new-light" evangelicals, and the new lights became increasingly troublesome. Some refused to qualify themselves for the protection of the Toleration Act, some qualified in the court of one county but neglected to do so in other counties where they served as itinerants, and some began proselytizing Anglicans in their itinerant travels. The Presbyterian Synod of Philadelphia made clear its disassociation from them in 1745, and leading Anglicans in Virginia began openly questioning whether the Toleration Act applied to them.[11]

A lesser politician might have been cowed by the situation, but Gooch made the most of it. When the new-light ministers first arrived he "received them with Candour and Respect, and granted them Liberty to preach in Hanover."[12] Later when the old lights and some of the Anglicans voiced their objections to the evangelicals, Gooch wrote cordially to the Philadelphia Synod expressing approval of the old-light position and issued a proclamation requiring local magistrates to suppress the activities of itinerant preachers. At the same time he talked the Council into giving Samuel Davies, a leading new-light preacher, a license to preach in several churches, and he later tried his best to get the same permission for Davies's assistant.[13] As a result of his compromise and conciliation Gooch managed to stave off an Anglican, an old-light, and a new-light Presbyterian appeal to England before he died. His death in 1749 was admittedly well timed, but he had managed to maintain the reputation of faithful supporter of the Anglican Church while developing cordial relations with the old lights and showing, by Davies's own account, "the greatest Aversion to persecuting Measures."[14] At Gooch's death all the major interests in the colony, along with their English allies, thought the governor had probably done the best he could for them.

Jonathan Belcher did not do as well in Massachusetts as Gooch did in Virginia, but he did manage to last eleven years as governor and to get another governorship later, despite his tactlessness, his lack of a primary patron, and his tricky administrative position. A partial explanation of his success lies in his manipulation of transatlantic interests. For nearly ten years he managed them fairly well, until a pair of bank crises united the Boston and London merchants against him and neutralized the English dissenters who had friends in the Boston mercantile community. In 1741 Belcher fell, partly because a rival got the ear of the Secretary of State, but just as much because powerful interests wanted him removed, and sympathetic interests could not organize enough support for him.

Belcher was acutely aware of, and quite blatant about, the importance of cultivating connections with the London-American interests. Not that Belcher handled all his contacts gracefully; he did not. He once invited two Anglican ministers to dinner and quarreled so violently with one of them that the minister refused to meet Belcher socially any more.[15] But successful or not, his acutely self-conscious nonstop efforts to placate lobbies made Belcher the epitome of the interest-group politician.

Belcher's self-consciousness was unusual, but his techniques were not. He entertained merchants and ministers and dined with Boston Quakers soon after his arrival. He solicited gifts for various institutions—books for Harvard, plate for an Anglican Church.[16] He attended the Anglican Church on occasion as well as the Congregational. He sought favorable legislation for religious minorities. He tried to get jobs for relatives of influential English lobbyists.[17] He made sure they got copies of local election sermons favorable to Belcher,[18] encouraged local groups to address British authorities in his favor,[19] sent his son to "pay his respects" to the leaders of various interests,[20] sent fish, plants, and other gifts to them,[21] and encouraged his brother-in-law (Richard Partridge) to seek supportive petitions from English interests.

Belcher's success was, at the very least, uneven; he did better with the ecclesiastical lobbies than with the merchants. His prime identification was with the Congregational and Presbyterian churches. (His personal religion was somewhere in between and his "pticular friend," Reverend Benjamin Colman, admitted to a friend that Colman looked at religion with "Presbyterian eyes.")[22] In England Belcher counted among his fairly good friends the leaders of the Presbyterian and Congregational wings of the Three Denominations, who dined with him before he left London and wrote affectionately of him to friends in Massachusetts.[23] At the time Belcher was appointed governor the Dissenting Deputies did not exist, but right from the beginning of his administration Belcher culti-vated connections with the leading dissenting layman, Samuel Holden, who became the first chairman of the Deputies in 1732.[24] Belcher's son, brother-in-law, and his friends Colman and Henry Newman assured Holden that Belcher was a "great Honr and Blessing to his country" and counted on his interest "among ye Ministers of State that are about ye Throne."[25] Holden's influence seems to have saved Belcher's job at least once when the governor was under attack.[26]

Belcher's strong connections with London dissenters helped compen-sate for his uneven popularity among the clergy of Massachusetts. Mas-sachusetts clergy seldom presented a united front on anything, and during Belcher's administration the clergy was often divided between the Colman wing, which supported Belcher, and its opponents, who did not. Belcher entered office at a disadvantage because he was closely associated with a former governor whom most of the ministers disliked. In addition Belcher antagonized some ministers by his "zealous adherence to ye King's Instructions" (probably both the instruction to obtain a fixed salary for himself and the one to obtain liberty of conscience for Prot-estants outside the Congregational Church). As a result the clergy's praise of Belcher was "lean" in the one address we know of.[27] In 1737 some ministers among the anti-Colman group published in London papers a letter expressing joy at Belcher's rumored removal, a letter that Colman and his friends took pains to refute.[28] Certainly the clergy divided sharply over Belcher, but Colman's wing had the better connec-tions and Colman kept their allegiance.

Of the two other important English religious lobbies, the Quakers and the Anglicans, Belcher had far more success with the Quakers, though he probably overestimated their importance to his administration and their determination to help him.[29] His brother-in-law and London agent, Richard Partridge, was a Quaker, active, as we have seen, in the London Meeting for Sufferings. Before he left London Belcher was waited on by a delegation of Quakers who were "very well received,"[30] and within a few months of his arrival in the colony he had got through the Massa-chusetts assembly an act exempting all Quakers from paying taxes to the Congregational Church. (Earlier they had been exempt only if they lived within five miles of a Quaker meeting and made a statement of allegiance to the government.)[31] It was not all the Quakers wanted, but it was enough to get Belcher a message of thanks from the London Yearly Meeting.[32] When the governor's position began to slip in 1740 he counted, perhaps too much, on "the great interest of the Quakers, together with the Dissenting clergy [to] be too hard for my stubborn enemies at last."[33] The London Meeting for Sufferings did not address the King, as he had hoped, but Quakers in at least two English counties, prompted by Partridge, did petition on Belcher's behalf.[34]

With the Church of England Belcher had his weakest connections: his hope was mainly to neutralize the Church by cultivating a few influential leaders in Boston and England. His two chief English acquaintances were the bishops of Lincoln and London. He worked on Lincoln through personal visits of Jonathan Belcher, Jr.; Belcher also tried to get a job for the bishop's son.[35] The Bishop of London he waited on in person, calling on him several times before he left London. Once in Massachusetts Belcher seems to have exchanged fairly cordial correspondence with the bishop while urging Jonathan Jr. to pay his respects and bring gifts. Apparently the approach worked well enough to neutralize the bishop. Belcher had gall enough to ask the Bishop of London to attend the Board of Trade in favor of the governor's accepting a temporary salary rather than the permanent one the Board demanded.[36] The bishop would not do it, but when Belcher got into a fight with the bishop's commissary over the governor's appointing a fast on an Anglican feast day, the bishop sided with Belcher, not the commissary.[37] To offset the local influence of the commissary Belcher got the support of the commissary's irascible rival Reverend Timothy Cutler, rector of Christ Church (he attended the church from time to time and helped get them plate from England),[38] and his more genial subordinate Reverend Thomas Harwood (he offered Harwood land for a new church).[39] He also obtained a law returning to Anglican churches taxes paid by Anglicans to the local religious establishment.[40] When the final crisis of Governor Belcher's Massachusetts administration developed, he did not look to English Anglicans for help, as he did to Quakers and the three dissenting denominations, but the Anglicans were not active in bringing him down.

Although Massachusetts Anglicans and Congregationalists were divided, within each group Belcher managed to ally himself with a faction well connected with England, and the Quakers on both sides of the Atlantic were quite firm in his support. At worst the ecclesiastical lobbies were neutral; at best they were quite helpful.

The same cannot be said of the mercantile lobby: with them his relations showed the limits and complexity of interest group relations. Belcher himself had been the leading merchant in Boston, and he had a coterie of Boston merchant supporters with good English connections.[41] He got the support of London's Quaker merchants through his brother-in-law, a Quaker merchant himself, and of dissenting merchants through the Dissenting Deputies. When Belcher left London for his government he was given an impressive, not to say riotous sendoff by eighty merchants who honored him at dinner with an awesome number of toasts,[42] and once in Massachusetts he hoped to keep their support by not putting his heart into the enforcement of the Navigation Acts and by backing reforms in the Boston markets.[43]

Early in his administration, however, Belcher lost the support of an influential part of the New England merchants in London, the merchants trading to New Hampshire. When he disputed the land claims of the New Hampshire masting interests, John Tomlinson, their chief correspondent in London and a merchant who had been unenthusiastic about Belcher's appointment in the first place, began building up opposition to the governor in the New England Coffee House.

Since the New Hampshire merchant group was a small part of the New England lobby, Tomlinson might not have got far had it not been for the problem of Massachusetts currency. In 1739 a group of Massachusetts entrepreneurs created a land bank, threatening to issue an enormous number of exchange certificates with the only security being the value of the entrepreneur's land. The land merchants objected vigorously, and fifty-eight of them—nearly three-quarters of the number who had caroused with Belcher before he left for the colony—petitioned against it.[44] Belcher himself dealt ruthlessly with the land bankers, an action which ought to have brought him the London merchants' support. He also opposed a silver bank, however, even though it was sponsored by his own well-connected mercantile supporters in Boston. Their antagonism, along with the antagonism of the New Hampshire masting merchants, was enough to keep the London merchants trading to New England from supporting Belcher despite his stand on the land bank.

In the spring of 1741, with a sizable part of London's merchant community backing a rival candidate, with dissenters, never unanimous in their support of Belcher anyway, now taking no role, and with Quakers petitioning only at the county level, Belcher did not have the London support he needed to face a competitor. He was replaced.

Belcher's experience with the London merchants showed just how complex interest group relations could become. It was possible for a governor to do just what a London interest wanted on a major issue and still not get their support if he opposed them on another issue or antagonized their American correspondents. Together, Belcher and Gooch illustrate the importance of interest group politics to Anglo-colonial government after the second decade of the eighteenth century, even among those colonies that had not had pluralistic societies a few years before. A governor's experience with interests depended on his own tact, the groups' strengths, unity, and transatlantic connections, the stability of the British government, and, admittedly, on just plain luck.[45]

CHAPTER 10

The Coming of the Revolution:
The English Side

In 1749, when the Dissenting Deputies inquired of ministers about the possibility of an American bishopric, they were assured that the ministers "would be glad to hear objections to the idea of a bishopric from Persons of any Consequence."[1] In 1773, by contrast, when a committee of merchants called upon Lord North to discuss American politics, they were told to "return and set quietly in their counting houses."[2] Separated by only two decades, the encounters were nevertheless an imperial mindset apart. The empire had been based on voluntary compliance by the Americans, but this compliance in turn had been based on the expectation of responsive restraint on the part of the British. It was a system of give-and-take in which transatlantic interest groups had played an identifiable role. After 1754 they and their recognized functions progressively collapsed, the victim of interlacing developments that originated on both sides of the Atlantic.

Some of the reasons for the collapse can be traced back to the 1750s. In England Henry Pelham's government ended with his death in 1754. It was followed by a series of ministries so short-lived that interest groups had no time to establish comfortable connections with them. The Board of Trade, with which the interests had enjoyed their greatest influence, lost much of its power in the Seven Years' War, 1756–1763, and never got it back. Some of the interests, including the Quakers, the Dissenting Deputies, and the Virginia merchants were hampered in the same decade by quarrels with their American correspondents.[3]

Far harder to pinpoint are more general changes, beginning in the 1760s, in British attitudes to the management of colonial problems— changes that reduced both the government's flexibility in law-making and law enforcement and its responsiveness to solicitations from the interests. Just how the attitudes came to change is not very clear, and, indeed, contemporaries were far from clear themselves. English political leaders shared both appreciation and apprehension about mainland America's growth, and they had confused and even contradictory ideas on how to handle it. They recognized that American population was growing with great speed—from 1,200,000 in 1750 to 2,100,000 in 1770—that American trade was growing even faster—faster, in fact, than trade with any other part of the empire—and that American settlement area was expanding so rapidly that after the peace of Paris gave Britain lands to the Mississippi, there was very little to keep Americans from occupying the whole area within a few years. They worried that such growth demanded some sort of regulation—regulation, for example, to prevent conflict between the expanding settlements and Indian tribes in the territory awarded to Britain, financial regulation forcing the increasingly wealthy Americans to relieve hard-pressed British taxpayers in reducing the national debt, regulation even to head off a possible shift of the center of imperial power from England to America. To the extent they had given the matter much thought, the political leaders probably guessed such reforms should come sooner rather than later. The habitual American compliance was now reinforced by the presence of the British army in America after the Seven Years' War; the national government in Britain was fortified by four decades of comparative stability at home; and by 1765 the reformed customs service had succeeded in increasing collections by fifteen times. All these suggested that the metropolitan government was in a strong position to force regulation on the colonies.[4]

Finally, most politicians agreed that such regulation should be undertaken by Parliament, not the King, to protect, as they said, the rights of Englishmen from the unchecked expansion of monarchical authority.[5] And so it came to pass that Parliament at the end of the Seven Years' War undertook major legislation to define and regulate the colonies' position within the empire. No longer were laws easily delayed or modified and exceptions made in response to pressure from American interests. No longer were laws put on the books as a concession to one interest, and then ignored as a concession to another. The laws were fragments of an American policy meant to be enforced.

The transatlantic interests, whose electoral support in Britain was not expanding,[6] continued to find it difficult to influence legislation applying to several or all the mainland colonies at once. They found it less and less possible to convince the various ministries that laws would prove unworkable or that exceptions should be made to laws once passed; nor could they compensate for their weakness with Parliament by winning administrative concessions from the Board of Trade, for the Board itself continued in eclipse. Distanced from the Board of Trade, the ministries, and even their own colonial correspondents, the interests lost the leverage they had once gained from providing information. Distanced from this important source of information, ministers found themselves miscalculating American opinion and legislating in the dark.

Just as it was becoming clear that their old relations with ministers were no longer tenable and their old resources no longer effective, the interests were confronted with a further problem. John Wilkes and his supporters began creating a new type of association in the late 1760s— the public opinion lobby. Predicated on new ministerial relations and the use of new resources, Wilkes's lobby called into question all the assumptions that lobbies had developed over the first half of the eighteenth century. Rather than representing an existing organization whose functions were not primarily political, Wilkes's lobby was a new, loosely defined group whose purpose was exclusively political. Rather than defending the concerns of particular interests, the Wilkeites espoused a general cause. Rather than seeking the cooperation of ministers, the lobby was from the start openly hostile to them. If existing lobbies had to seek widespread support, would they have to adopt Wilkes's methods and assumptions? The interest groups were temporarily immobilized by the divisive nature of this question.

The changes just described were not visible all at once but developed gradually stage by stage. The first stage lasted roughly from Henry Pelham's death in 1754 to the very early 1760s and the beginning of the political instability that characterized George III's first decade. It contained the beginnings of later problems but was marked most visibly by a decline in the interests' relations with the Board of Trade. The second stage lasted (again, roughly) until the late 1760s. In this period the Board of Trade declined further, the last of the consistently sympathetic ministers left office, and Parliament took up new intercolonial questions. The third stage lasted from then until the American Revolution, and in the course of it the interests fragmented over the radical new methods and assumptions about lobbying introduced by Wilkes's Bill of Rights Society.

·   ·   ·

Pelham's death, ending a generation in which interests had established stable ministerial contacts, was the initial destabilizing event. Its full importance was obscured, however, by the continuation in office of ministers sympathetic to colonial interests and by the Seven Years' War, which pushed to the background some long-simmering colonial issues. For the thirty-three years before Henry Pelham's death English politics had been dominated by the triumvirate of Pelham, Walpole, and Newcastle; for all but two of those years Walpole or Pelham had been Prime Minister. Walpole's retirement and then Pelham's death left only Newcastle, and he did not command the confidence of Parliament and the

King that the other two had enjoyed; over the eight years from 1754 to 1762 there were four different ministries.

The importance of the ministerial turnovers, however, was not as immediately evident to the London lobbyists as it might have been, in part because the ministers most responsible for colonial administration continued to have interest group connections. For all but seven months of the period the Duke of Newcastle served as first commissioner of the Treasury, the office that had come to be identified with the prime ministership. Though he did not exert the influence that his predecessor did, Newcastle did keep up the interest group connections that he had developed over many years. Extracts of letters from the colonies, particularly Virginia, were regularly "Left at Newcastle House by J. Hanbury," the Quaker merchant.[7] When working on the budget Newcastle consulted the merchant John Barnard; on American military affairs he consulted Sir William Baker, and he gave Baker a lucrative contract for supplying the army in New England.[8] Baker, Barnard, and Hanbury in turn gave Newcastle electoral support. The Baptist leader Joseph Stennett, who addressed the Duke as "My very dear Lord," gave Newcastle political advice from the English provinces, looked to him for patronage, and, more abstractly, prayed "for the continuation of all those blessings on your Grace, that may render you still the great support of his Majesty's government, the bulwark of our religion and liberties."[9] Benjamin Avery, head of the Dissenting Deputies, continued to look to Newcastle for patronage and for the exemption of dissenters from fines incurred when they could not accept local offices; in return he recommended Newcastle's candidates in constituencies where dissent was strong.[10]

Two other ministers particularly responsible for American affairs also had strong connections with American interests. In the "Glorious Ministry" from 1757 to 1761, Newcastle's Secretary of State for the South was William Pitt, the overwhelming favorite of London's middling merchants among whom were most of the merchants trading to America. To the merchants Pitt offered hope (as his predecessor had not) that the war with France, which began in 1755, would be prosecuted effectively in America as well as in Europe. As their insurance rates on American properties went down, their investments in the war effort went up, a fact that Pitt was not slow to acknowledge. Like Newcastle, Pitt had friends among the merchants, William Beckford, for one, but he was at his best—and better than Newcastle—in dealing with groups such as the delegation of representatives from several branches of the American trade who called upon him to congratulate him on his American victories in 1758.[11]

Pitt's cordiality to the merchants is well known. What is less well known is his cordiality to dissenters: his negotiations with representa-

tives from the Three Denominations on the Militia Bill of 1757 were a
classic example of mid-eighteenth-century cooperation between ministers
and interests. In January 1757 a delegation from the Three Denominations waited on Pitt to protest against a proposed clause in the Bill
appointing Sunday for militia drills. Pitt greeted them graciously, sympathized with them, and "thought it might not be amiss that the sense
of the Dissenters should be made known, in the most public manner,
and that as early as possible."[12] The committee drew up a petition to
the House of Commons, but they were careful to show it to "a Person
of Great Character,"[13] presumably Pitt himself, before asking a member
of the Commons to present it. At Pitt's suggestion they reworded part
of the petition, and shortly after the petition was presented they were
able to report that "on Thursday, Febry 24 the Blank in the Militia Bill,
was filled with Monday by a very large majority."[14]

Besides Pitt and Newcastle at least one other highly placed politician
had important interest group connections in the 1750s. This was Earl
Granville, President of the Privy Council continuously from 1751 to
1763. Granville's most important connections were with the Quakers,
and his most important contribution to them came in 1756, when he
delayed a parliamentary measure disqualifying Quakers from colonial
assemblies; there seems to be little argument that Granville was the
Quakers' chief ministerial supporter in the 1750s.[15]

Except for a very brief period, 1754–1756, when Secretary of State
Henry Fox managed to antagonize the London merchants trading to
America by his indifference to American defense, the relations of London
interests with the ministers most actively involved in American affairs
appeared to change very little in the decade of the fifties.[16] Their relations
with Parliament hardly changed either. If anything, interests had less to
do with Parliament in the period 1754 to 1760 than they had had before,
because Parliament passed an average of only one American measure
every two years as opposed to three every two years in the decades
before; the decline resulted from wartime exigencies rather than preven-
tive lobbying by the interests.

The one area where interest group relations with government clearly
began to suffer soon after Henry Pelham's death was, rather strangely,
in their dealing with the Board of Trade, the very institution with which
they had previously had the greatest success. The Board had been no-
toriously responsive to interests before 1754 and invaluable in supporting their needs before Parliament, the Privy Council, and the ministers.
The Board's power was at its greatest just at the time of Pelham's death,
when the Earl of Halifax, President of the Board, had added to its powers
the nomination to colonial governorships and the exclusive correspondence with the colonial governors.

Having increased the Board's authority as much as he could, however, Halifax saw it erode after 1754, in good measure because of the Seven Years' War. With the government dependent upon colonial contributions of money and manpower, the Board could not afford to be sticky in its review of colonial legislation, especially when it related to taxation. Because it was essential for colonial governors to understand military affairs, Halifax had reluctantly to give in and appoint some military commanders to the governorships, and in practice these commanders had to correspond with British military leaders as well as with the Board. The colonial issues that Parliament did take up during the war emanated from the Treasury and the Customs Commissioners far more than they did from the Board; between 1754 and 1763 the Board actually presented only one set of papers to Parliament. The number of reports it prepared for the Privy Council declined from twenty-six in 1755 to eight in 1760. As the Board's work declined so did the number of meetings it held each year, from 114 to 70. The Board never did regain the power it had had in 1754; from that date on it became less and less capable of responding to interest group pressure.[17]

There is also some evidence that the Board's members themselves became less willing to respond during the same period. Between 1754 and 1756 there was a turnover of seven members—almost the whole Board—and the new members appear to have been somewhat less well connected to the American interests. A particular loss for the dissenters was Lord Dupplin, a close friend of a number of dissenters including the Baptist leader Joseph Stennett, and also a close personal friend of Halifax. Dupplin had advised dissenters how to approach the Board, and interceded with Halifax on their behalf.[18]

Halifax himself remained at the Board until 1761, but since very little of his correspondence has survived, it is hard to be sure just what his own connections were. Benjamin Avery, head of the Dissenting Deputies, had easy access to him, as did the Archbishop of Canterbury and the Quaker leader Dr. John Fothergill. Halifax certainly shared John Hanbury's eagerness for war in America, and he sent James Abercromby to sound out the opinions of Virginia merchants on various questions.[19] But at the same time Avery was turned down rather gracelessly when he recommended a candidate for a colonial appointment.[20] Hanbury was the subject of some critical remarks when he sent Halifax some American information, though providing information was one of the customary functions of interests. The Quakers in general were so convinced of Halifax's hostility that they tried to avoid negotiating with him whenever possible.[21] Halifax in turn was alarmed by the aggressive partiality for Pitt against Fox shown by the London merchant community. In general Halifax's determination to bring system to colonial administration inclined him to resist on general principle the pressures brought by particular interests on particular issues.

The decrease of the Board's powers and the disinclination of some of its members to favor special interest groups were straws in the wind in the late 1750s, suggesting the political decline of London-American interests. But the situation was somewhat obscured by the presence of sympathetic ministers at the cabinet level and by the fact that interests did not have to lobby very much at the parliamentary level. Over the mid-1760s, however, the problems of the interests became much more visible, as the sympathetic ministers left office, the Board of Trade's authority was further reduced, and Parliament rather rapidly took up a number of American questions on a scale too large for traditional lobbies to handle.

The first loss of a sympathetic cabinet member was the departure of William Pitt in October 1761, but when Newcastle was squeezed out of office seven months later, the interests faced a more serious dilemma. For years Newcastle's party had been synonymous with government; lobbyists had grown used to working with them and no one else. To many lobbyists it was almost unthinkable to abandon Newcastle even when he was in opposition. For the first few months they rationalized that Newcastle's exit was just temporary; he would soon prove indispensable to government as he had done on several occasions before. By December 1762, however, it was clear that Newcastle would not be back in office anytime soon, nor would his political followers. Interest group leaders had to decide whether to go into opposition with Newcastle or transfer their attention to the new ministers. The Archbishop of Canterbury and the Bishop of London had direct access to successive prime ministers and so they, along with most bishops, stayed with the government. The dissenting leaders to whom Newcastle had turned over the administration of the Regium Donum (royal charity) were dismissed by the new government, so they remained loyal to Newcastle.[22] Others managed to make connections with later secretaries of state. It is hard to say how many of the merchants followed Newcastle: well known merchants like Sir William Baker, Barlow Trecothick and John Tomlinson certainly did, and enough others to make it easy for Newcastle and the Rockingham ministry which he joined in 1765 to work closely with the London merchant community. Of all the leading merchants whose political views we know, the largest group by far associated with Newcastle and the Marquis of Rockingham.

Newcastle's departure was followed by nearly a decade of confusion and upheaval, as six ministries were appointed in seven years. In self-defense most interest group leaders had to attempt some kind of working relationship with the various ministries, and they seem to have had better luck with some than with others. With all cabinets they confronted younger men who were less experienced in interest group politics than the lobbyists were used to, and since the ministers averaged only a little more than a year in office the lobbyists were hard pressed to open up channels of communication. Not surprisingly they had their best luck with the Rockingham ministry of 1765–1766. Newcastle returned to office and renewed his friendships with church and mercantile leaders. Lord Dartmouth, President of the Board of Trade, was a close friend of the dissenting leader Dennys De Berdt and the Quaker leader Dr. John Fothergill. Edmund Burke, Rockingham's secretary, served as liaison with merchants,[23] and Rockingham himself became friends with a number of merchants, to one of whom, Sir William Baker, he offered the post of Chancellor of the Exchequer.[24] But the Rockingham ministry was the only one after 1763 to represent even a partial throwback to the Walpole-Pelham era, and Rockingham survived in office only thirteen months.

Pitt, now Earl of Chatham, followed Rockingham in office, and some members of his Cabinet were also well connected with the American interests. During his brief term of office he sought meetings with mercantile leaders, and his Secretary of State, the Earl of Shelburne, was a leading patron of dissenting writers. But soon after his appointment Chatham took ill and withdrew from politics. Shelburne lost much of his power in a cabinet shuffle and was finally dismissed, and the leaderless cabinet drifted on without direction. Interests cultivated connections with other ministries as best they could (Lord North, for example, met at some time with all the groups), but the rapid cabinet turnovers before 1770 made this difficult; there was not enough time to develop the comfortable individual relationships like those that had evolved in the Walpole-Pelham generation. When lobbyists did develop connections with one ministry they were suspect in the next.

Nor could the lobbyists shore up their sagging influence by reviving their earlier relationship with the Board of Trade, for the Board itself became the pawn of the unstable political factions of the 1760s. Indeed, one of the last great closet battles of the mid-century was fought in 1762–63, just at the time it was becoming clear that Newcastle's departure from government would be long-lasting, and the Board's position was beginning to deteriorate rapidly. The behind-the-scenes lobbying for and against the Massachusetts Act of 1762 creating a Congregational missionary society to rival the S.P.G. was conducted in classic eighteenth-century fashion, with the S.P.G. making the rounds of the Privy Council and the Board of Trade against the bill, and the Dissenting Deputies working similarly in its favor.[25] The Bishop of London and the Archbishop of Canterbury also lobbied against the act, as much as they could do discreetly, since they were not members of the S.P.G. For his part Thomas Hollis, a leading dissenter but not a member of the Dissenting Deputies, secretly financed dissenting publications on the subject.[26] In the end the act was disallowed, but from then on Anglicans and dissenters failed to lobby on American issues before the Board of Trade.

At the Board nine new presidents were named in ten years, which meant that they, too, had no time to establish ties with interests. In the delicate negotiations that preceded the formations of each new ministry the powers of the Board were redefined, and since the prospective heads of the Board were rarely strong enough to outface prospective cabinet members who wanted to share the Board's authority, the Board lost progressively in most negotiations. In 1761 it lost the appointment of colonial governors and probably most of its remaining patronage to the Secretary of State.[27] In 1766 it lost direct correspondence with colonial governors, which meant it was cut off from direct access to important information. It lost the right to make original representations to the crown, which meant that it lost the authority to recommend what issues were to be sent to Parliament.[28] Two years after that the Board became simply an adjunct to the Secretary of State's office.[29] Already then, on issues that the Board had recommended to Parliament, the House of Commons had begun consideration without waiting for the Board's full report. By 1768 the Board was reduced simply to reviewing laws, and even on this it did not have complete independence: in 1773 Parliament actually applauded it for disallowing a Massachusetts act. In reviewing laws members could well have continued to reflect pressure from interests but they did not: advised by the Attorney General, they confined themselves to judging colonial acts only according to their compatibility with English law.[30]

Accordingly, the influence of interest groups with traditional American connections declined in the 1760s. The number of appearances of interest group representatives before the Board of Trade fell by only four—from 14 in the 1750s to 10 in the 1760s—but five of the later appearances were on the one issue of timber bounties and occurred within a three-week period. Three others were on another issue, paper money.[31] Not a merchant appeared to testify on American affairs before the Board after 1764, and not one merchant petition was submitted to them. The last successful single petition on a religious issue came from the Baptist leader Joseph Stennett in 1771; Stennett petitioned against a Massachusetts law taxing the Baptists of Ashfield to pay for a Congregational meeting-house there.[32]

Time and again the Board reviewed laws affecting colonial or British interests without the appropriate Londoners in attendance, something that would have been inconceivable only a few years before. There were at least thirteen such occasions between 1764 and 1772. A Pennsylvania law on commerce and navigation, for example, was recommended for disallowance in 1766 not because the merchants objected to it (they were not consulted), but because it exceeded "the Bounds of the Authority vested in them by their Constitutions."[33] The following year the Board recommended disallowance of a Massachusetts act which set aside "the security of the foreign creditor," but no merchant attended while the act was under consideration.[34] The same year a Pennsylvania act providing for construction of a lighthouse was recommended for disallowance without consulting the merchants. A decade earlier a Virginia law on the same subject had been circulated among the Virginia merchants for their opinion before the Board made its determination.[35] When Quakers did show up to protest a Virginia act on slavery, the President of the Board told them their opinion was not wanted.[36] As the Board's flexibility shrank, its contacts with interest groups shrank disproportionately.

Not only were the London interests unable to work with the Board, the one institution they were used to influencing so effectively; they also found the Board's functions increasingly handled by Parliament, more and more displaying an inflexible attitude toward colonial law enforcement that did not give the interests much room to maneuver. Parliament's attempted reform of the customs service in the Revenue Act of 1762, its expansion of the jurisdiction of vice-admiralty courts which did not use local juries, and of the power of customs officials in the Sugar Act of 1764, along with the ministry's moving British regiments from Canada to the seaboard towns, all signaled a shift in emphasis toward enforcing colonial obedience to laws, however unpopular, and away from working with interests either to prepare laws the colonists would comply with voluntarily or to wink at selective evasion.

In addition, some of the parliamentary activity, both domestic and imperial, required new methods of lobbying. After the end of the Seven Years' War Parliament took up several major questions of policy affecting all or several colonies at once, and directly or indirectly affecting the interests of London merchants trading to America. Altogether in the years 1763 to 1767 there were nine issues on which London merchants trading to several colonial areas petitioned Parliament or negotiated with ministers. Somewhat later, in 1772 and 1773, Parliament three times took up a domestic issue, consideration of the Thirty-Nine Articles, that affected the religious lobbies, Anglicans and dissenters.

To lobby effectively both the churches and the merchants had to develop new methods of bringing pressure, but the new methods themselves proved divisive and the increasing divisions brought about the third stage in the lobbies' decline. The further the new methods took

the groups from the customary characteristics of eighteenth-century lobbies, the closer they brought them to an entirely new concept of lobbying
as represented in the Wilkeite "public opinion" lobby, and the deeper
the divisions within the groups became.

Of the three main groups of London lobbies with American connections the least visibly disrupted were the non-English communities. They
witnessed in silence the legalistic reversal of colonial laws favoring their
friends in America, as when a Maryland law allowing naturalized citizens
the same rights as native born was shot down as being "repugnant to
the laws of this realm." They even had to put up with instructions sent
to colonial governors in 1774 forbidding them to approve acts of naturalization passed by their local assemblies. They did not, however, have
to deal with any parliamentary legislation nearly as extensive as the
Stamp Act, and even if they had it was almost unthinkable for them to
attempt any umbrella organization involving many different non-English
communities in London.[37]

Of the other types of interests it was the merchant groups who suffered
the first divisions, since the mercantile issues were the first to come
before Parliament. As early as 1765, a group of fifteen or twenty leading
men emerged in the forefront of the new efforts to represent all the
coffee-house interests. They were notable both for their breadth of interest and for the continuity of their efforts. As a general rule, two or
three represented the merchants trading to each mainland colonial area,
and the same men continued to represent their fellow merchants throughout the prerevolutionary years.[38] In the major crises of the decade, from
the Stamp Act to the preparation of petitions against the stagnation of
trade in March 1774, merchants' committees were chosen to coordinate
efforts at mass meetings of the rank and file, and the same men were
consistently on the committees. From time to time their position was
confirmed by new elections, but they never appear to have had any
competition, and turnover of members was rare. In addition to heading
the mass meetings, the committee members also met frequently among
themselves: between 1765 and 1775 there is clear evidence of at least
sixteen such meetings, though this number is undoubtedly too small.

The merchants' committee was composed of wealthy, highly respectable merchants who had several well-established precedents for organizing themselves as they did. This suggested that they would pursue a
largely traditional approach to lobbying, and so, for the first several
years, they did. While the committee itself was an informal association
sustained only by reelection at mass meetings, its constituents were
members of the individual coffee houses. With the appointment of Rockingham as Prime Minister in the summer of 1765, the merchants began
a four-year period of cordial relations with successive ministries: Rock-

ingham, Chatham, and the Duke of Grafton all consulted the merchants' committee on questions pertaining to American trade. When the Rockingham ministry revised the Navigation Acts, for example, it worked so closely with the committee that Capel Hanbury had to "request our Friends to excuse our not now entering into the answering . . . letters . . . [because] we are now very closely engag'd in endeavouring to procure beneficial extension regulations of the American Commerce."[39]

In addition, when the merchants did petition Parliament, their early petitions concentrated on providing information about conditions of trade. The Stamp Act petition, for example, stressed the inability of American customers to pay their debts; the message of the petition against the Townshend Duties was "that this commerce so necessary to afford employment and subsistence to the manufacturers of these Kingdoms, to augment the public Revenue, to serve as a nursery for Seamen, and to support and increase our navigation and Maritime Strength, is at present in an alarming State of Suspension."[40] The information was directed toward explaining the merchants' interest, rather than justifying the Americans' cause.

Even though the merchants' committee tried to follow mainly traditional methods of lobbying, its very attempt to consolidate the coffeehouse lobbies in a larger group was alarming to some of the merchants. Particularly disturbing were the lobby's size, its intercolonial base, and its impersonality. There had been fringe benefits to coffee-house participation that mass meetings at the King's Arms could not offer. Coffee houses had newspapers, the inevitable presence of ship captains, the latest mail, insurance dealers, and the like; they were places where some merchants carried on their entire business and others came to discuss the trade. In the normal course of business the merchant would naturally attend the coffee house, where fellow merchants could exert a friendly pressure that King's Arms orators could not.[41]

Despite the attempt of the merchants' committee to preserve traditional methods of lobbying, the essential departures from tradition they did accept were enough to discourage some merchants in the committee's early years. The lesser merchants found that lobbying activities brought them no extra business in America and did not even produce the fringe benefits they were used to from coffee-house lobbying in London. After 1769 it became increasingly difficult for merchants to pursue any of the traditional methods at all, as the Wilkeite movement posed fundamentally divisive questions about what a lobby should be and how it should function in contemporary politics.

The divisions arose during two crisis periods, 1769–1770 and 1774–75. In each case the merchants responded slowly to parliamentary legislation affecting the American colonies—the Townshend Duties in the first period, the Coercive Acts in the second—because as was customary they hesitated to criticize the acts directly and were waiting for an American economic response upon which they could base their petitions for repeal. In the period when they were waiting, London radicals in the Wilkeite movement did take up the American issues, attacking the government directly upon political grounds, and when the merchants finally met, they faced the choice of sticking as nearly as possible to traditional methods or of using Wilkeite activity as a model for their own. In the first period, the bulk of the merchants considered Wilkeite methods and, on the whole, seem to have rejected them; in the second, the merchants were far more sharply divided. In the early months of 1775 they continued to reject the Wilkes model, but by late in the year the Wilkeite pressure had become so strong that the mercantile lobby split apart.

The first crisis began in spring of 1769, nearly two years after the Townshend Duties were passed. That year Wilkes's repeated exclusions from Parliament, despite his repeated elections as M.P. for Middlesex, gave London radicals a new personal leader, and the establishment of the Bill of Rights Society to support Wilkes and pay his debts introduced a new kind of institution in British politics—the public opinion lobby. One of the most significant (but least studied) effects of the Wilkeite movement was that it forced existing lobbies to consider whether they would be better off abandoning traditional methods and developing new ones, using the movement as a model.

The question was particularly pointed in the case of the mercantile lobby, because within three months of its establishment the Bill of Rights Society had added American grievances to those of the electors of Middlesex. In May 1769 the Middlesex freeholders' petition, prepared under Wilkeite direction, linked the ministry's mismanagement of American affairs with its violations of subjects' rights in England.[42] But the Wilkeites went even further than merely superimposing American grievances on their own list: at one level they blended American complaints inseparably with their own. They applied the American demand for "no taxation without representation" to the plight of the unenfranchised in England, using it as the rationale for demanding an expansion of the English electorate.[43]

Despite the Wilkeite interest in American affairs, the London-American merchants were, as a whole, hesitant to take up the program or methods of lobbying, both of which diverged sharply from the merchants' traditional approach. The mercantile lobby, for example, had derived support only from members of the London coffee-house communities, men directly or indirectly involved in the American trade; the Wilkeite movement, by contrast, appealed to "the public" by means of mass meetings indiscriminately attended, "fortuitous concours[es] of people," as the *Annual Register* described them to distinguish them from "lawful assemblies" like the merchants' meetings.[44] The merchants had cultivated a cooperative, advisory relationship with the government; the Wilkeites assumed a position of open hostility to the ministry, successfully urging the Middlesex freeholders to include in their May 1769 petition a plea to discontinue the existing ministry.[45] The merchants had defended their own practical interests, providing government with information it might not otherwise have about them; the Wilkeites, by contrast, espoused a cause—"the cause of Constitutional liberty," "Mr. Wilkes' cause," "the public cause"—and they provided constitutional theory, not practical information.[46] Their support, moreover, for the political principle of "no taxation without representation" was clearly offensive to merchants who prided themselves on "never meddling with politics."

Inevitably the Wilkeite innovations raised disturbing questions. Should the merchants expand their base to include, for example, lesser tradesmen unconnected with the American trade? Could they continue lobbying in the face of ministerial hostility? Did they take up American issues as a cause?

Merchants first debated these questions in 1769–70 and disagreed about them, but down to 1775 they were able to keep the differences papered over. In that year, however, the receipt of the Continental Congress's resolutions anticipating a third nonimportation agreement among American merchants again raised questions about whether the merchants should adopt Wilkeite methods of lobbying against government measures. This time the questions were no longer muted but were debated publicly in mercantile meetings and in Parliament. This debate seems to have polarized the lobby much more decisively than the debates of 1769–70, some merchants joining the Wilkeite lobby, some digging in their heels against it, and some dropping out of political activity altogether.

Between January and March 1775 the merchants petitioned Parliament or the King four times, three times on the Coercive Acts and once on the act restraining New England's trade; each petition followed a debate that produced new clarification and new bitterness. Three issues—whether membership in the lobby should be open to men not directly involved in the North American trade, whether the lobby should espouse a cause rather than explain an interest, and whether the lobby should continue its efforts in the face of ministerial hostility—sharply divided the London-American merchants in this period.

The crisis of 1775 ended the mercantile lobby's usefulness to the Americans, though it did not, as it turned out, put an end to the lobby itself. In the last years of the American Revolution the lobby reemerged in a role in which it was comfortable, pressing in traditional ways for government assistance in collecting American debts. The question of debt was clearly one of practical interest that could not be elevated to a "cause," and it was one on which ministers needed specific information that only the merchants could give. During the Revolution the Wilkeite mercantile leaders had fled to the Continent; the mercantile leaders who remained in England dissociated themselves and the lobby from the new radical reform movements of the early 1780s. For fifteen years at least— the records are unclear after that—the lobby continued to press the government on debt and related questions with considerable success.[47]

The problems of the various church lobbies began slightly later than those of the merchants, but they were just as divisive, and along many of the same lines. Open rifts among the Anglicans and dissenters did not develop until 1772, when members of both groups petitioned Parliament for relief from the Thirty Nine Articles. The petitions brought into the open long-simmering theological differences in both groups. But they also provoked the same kinds of arguments that the merchants had had over such issues as expanding the lobbies to include people who were not members of the immediate interest group, advocating causes rather than espousing an interest, and lobbying in the face of ministerial hostility. American issues themselves were not among the initial causes of conflict, but the churches did divide over them, with the less traditional ministers favoring the Americans. By 1775 the pro-American sympathizers represented only a fragment of the earlier church lobbies: the ecclesiastical interests, like the mercantile ones, were in disarray.

Throughout most of the 1760s church groups did not have to face the organizational questions the merchants faced because they already had long established organizations. The Quakers and dissenters already had London-wide meetings, and the Anglicans had the S.P.G. There were few divisive issues, and American questions, like the Stamp Act and the Townshend Duties, did not bear on religion directly, though some dissenters linked them to the attempts to appoint a bishop for the colonies as common efforts to subvert American liberties.[48] But even the effort to obtain an American bishop, for all the literature it produced, was not as divisive as it might have been since it was really a lost cause: successive secretaries of state made it clear to dissenters and Anglicans alike that they intended to "avoid anything of a religious nature" which might set the dissenters in a political opposition.[49]

It was not until the early 1770s, then, that church organizations took up campaigns which altered their traditional relations with the government and hence divided members over their propriety. A very brief narrative of ecclesiastical lobbying on the eve of the American Revolution suggests some striking innovations—innovations indicating that the ecclesiastical lobbies responded to the Wilkeite model, and then disagreed over their response. Did they limit their appeal to members of established institutions, or did they seek to arouse "the public"? Did they act only with the cooperation of the ministry, or did they dare work in opposition? Should they espouse only their own interest or could they take up a general cause? The issues divided the ecclesiastical lobbies as they had divided the merchants; dissenters and Anglicans showed similar patterns in their responses.

Consider the Anglicans first. The issue which initially divided the church was not colonial but domestic—the required subscription to the Thirty Nine Articles. Divisions over the acceptability of the articles had produced a pamphlet war in the late 1760s between rationalists in the church, who opposed them, and Calvinists, who did not mind. But no active effort for relief was made until 1771, when the Reverend Francis Blackburne published his *Proposals for an Application to Parliament in the Matter of Subscription.* On July 17, 1771, a group of "conscientious and learned clergy" formed the Feathers Tavern Association[50] and drew up a petition asking to be "restored to their undoubted right as Protestants of interpreting Scripture for themselves."[51] The petition was then circulated widely throughout the country to get signatures of clerics, doctors, lawyers, and university students, all of whom had to subscribe to the articles. (About forty or fifty of the 250 signers were not ministers.)[52]

Shortly before the petition was to be presented to Parliament (January 31, 1772), leaders of the Feathers Tavern Association called upon Lord North to sound out his opinions. North was unalterably opposed to the petition,[53] but at a meeting February 2–4 the association decided to go ahead with the petition anyway. Despite their tireless lobbying with members of Parliament, however, the petitioners found the full weight of government against them, and the petition was rejected by 217 votes to 71.[54]

Even such a cursory recounting of the fate of the Feathers Tavern petition reveals a new pattern. The association itself was an *ad hoc* group sanctioned neither by tradition nor the authority of the Anglican Church, and the signers of their petition were not even limited to the members of the association. They petitioned not as a group with a specific interest but as a group behind a general cause, the defense of the "rights" of Protestants. They did not consult with the Prime Minister before circulating the petition, and when he expressed disapproval they proceeded despite his hostility. Open membership, espousal of a "cause," and a hostile relationship to government: these were precisely the sources of mercantile consternation, and the Anglicans fragmented similarly.[55]

Shortly afterward the dissenters split in similar fashion. In the debates on the Feathers Tavern petition several members of Parliament had suggested that while they could not support giving Anglican ministers relief from the Thirty Nine Articles, they would support a request of dissenting ministers and teachers for relief.[56] (In order to qualify their churches under the Toleration Act, dissenting ministers had to subscribe to all but three of the articles.) And so, shortly after the Anglican failure, several leading members of the Three Denominations of Dissenters called a meeting to discuss petitioning Parliament that they might be allowed to substitute subscription to the Bible for subscription to the articles. They were in a stronger position than the Anglicans when they began, not only because their request had been encouraged by members of Parliament but also because a number of government supporters represented constituencies where dissent was strong, and the government dared not risk losing these constituencies by insisting that their representatives support the articles.[57] In the early stages of preparing petitions they could argue "that administration appears disposed to take off the subscription."[58] Buoyed by evidence of support, a majority of the Three Denominations favored petitioning Parliament for relief.

They were opposed, however, by a strong and quite determined minority made up of two groups. One group was more Calvinist in thought and like the Calvinistic Anglicans did not regard subscribing to the articles as a hardship.[59] The other group were ministers whose government connections had won for them control of the Regium Donum, or royal charity; the courtiers with whom they worked had convinced them that the government was not in fact willing to abandon the subscription, and they feared that petitioning would cost them their government patronage. They were the "Acham's Wedge" in the dissenters' camp, as one contemporary described them.[60] "A Regium Donum man . . . goes and expresses his concern . . . lest adm-n should deprive them of their money on that acct."[61] While supporters of the appeal called on acquaintances in the Commons, waited once or twice on every member of the House of Lords, and organized a massive letter-writing campaign among dissenting ministers throughout the country[62] (but particularly London and its environs), opponents distributed anti-petition tracts at the door of the House of Commons and wrote the Bishop of London that a "great and respectable part of the Dissenting ministers oppose the application."[63] In vain did Israel Mauduit write that "no one measure has been adopted by the body of London ministers for the fifty years past which has been undertaken and prosecuted with more general concurrence":[64] it was abundantly clear the dissenters were seriously divided.

Thus far, however, the divisions had been rather conventional. It was not new for the government to seek influence within an interest group by giving favors to some of its leading members, only to end up estranging those members from the rest of the group. Neither was it new for Londoners to disagree with provincials, though in this case the customary roles were reversed: the Londoners were moving faster than the provincials rather than being pressed by them to speed up their efforts.

Over the next year a novel division among dissenters did appear, one paralleling in a number of ways the divisions among merchants and Anglicans. Although the petition of 1772 had failed, the General Body resolved to try again, and their second campaign included dissenters who thought that both the original demands and the rationale for supporting them had not gone far enough. The 1772 petition had asked to substitute subscription to the Bible for subscription to the Thirty-Nine Articles; the new group argued that since not all dissenters could accept all of the Bible, they should simply petition for removal of the subscription requirement without offering a substitute.[65] Moreover, while supporters of the 1772 petition had simply argued that dissenters could be good Christians without accepting the required articles, some supporters of the 1773 petition now defended it "upon the common principle of liberty,"[66] because "No human authority has a right to impose articles of faith upon any individual in the community."[67] Supporters of the 1772 petition had thought they had the support of administration because North did not actually say he would oppose them; the 1773 petitioners knew from the vote in the House of Lords, where the earlier petition had been thrown out by government supporters, that the ministry opposed them. The 1772 campaign was run by a committee of the General Body on behalf of dissenting ministers; some of the 1773 campaigners claimed to speak for "any individual of the community."[68]

Once again, the familiar issues appear: should the lobby speak for and include people not immediately in the interest, should a lobby take up a general cause, and should it persevere in the face of ministerial hostility? And once again the lobby was divided. In the meetings at which they decided upon a second appeal to Parliament the ministers of the Three Denominations voted on several motions; the majority varied from 43 to 55 but there was always a minority of 13 to 19, and it is clear from the crossings-out and the motions expunged from the minutes that the discussions were extremely heated.[69] When the decision to petition was made, the minority broke off and formed the Society of Protestant Dissenting Ministers. (The ministers of the Three Denominations referred to themselves as The General Body.)[70] And once again the petitioners were defeated in Parliament; the issue of subscription did not come up again until 1779, when North's administration abolished compulsory subscription to the articles to compensate dissenters for the relief of British Catholics from several clauses in the penal code that had been voted the year before.[71]

Like the Anglicans and the merchants, dissenters found their differ-

ences spilling over to American issues. American issues did not feature
in the early campaigns except in Anglicans' arguments that "the persons
applying for this extraordinary indulgence for themselves" were keeping
the American Church of England under actual persecution by opposing
the establishment of a bishop in America.[72] But by 1774, after the
passage of the Intolerable Acts in the spring and before the general
election in the fall, members of the group who had favored a less
traditional approach to a public opinion lobby began equating American
problems with those of the English dissenters. Joseph Priestly wrote,
"Do you imagine, my fellow citizens, that we can sit still, and be the
idle spectators of the chains which are forging for our brethren in
America with safety to ourselves?"[73] Thomas B. Hollis addressed the
Americans, "We have no hopes but in your zeal, the same measures
pursued against you will return upon us with greater force if they succeed
in America."[74] What percentage of dissenters actually supported the
Americans is difficult to estimate. Contemporaries certainly identified
dissenters with American support: a government agent in Nottingham
reported that it was difficult to raise troops there during the Revolution
"owing in great measure to the whole corporation . . . being dissenters,"
and another agent at Portsmouth complained that he could not get an
address in favor of government because "We are beset with Presbyterians
and dissenters of every kind."[75] Long after the event a contemporary
concluded that "a dissenter and a Wilkeite were synonymous,"[76] but
this was far from the case. In 1763 there were 83 dissenting churches in
London, each with at least one minister, yet only 17 dissenting ministers
signed a pro-American petition of October 1774. Probably the core of
these were Baptists: the Reverend John Rippon, who was in a position
to know, later reported that all but two of the Baptist ministers in
London supported the American cause.[77]

The Quakers, who did not participate in the Dissenting Deputies or
the Three Denominations, nevertheless found themselves also in disagreement over American issues. After the passage of the Intolerable
Acts the London Yearly Meeting petitioned Parliament for reconciliation
with America, and the Quaker leaders John Fothergill and David Barclay
wrote several times to Lord Dartmouth seeking conciliatory measures
that would end the American crisis.[78] The same leaders also wrote
American Quakers, who were urging nonresistance to British measures,
to tone down their extreme opposition to American resistance.[79] But
two things make us wary of calling the English Quakers solidly pro-
American, though at first glance they would appear to be. First, the
English Quakers in 1775 and 1776 were not solidly anything. Friends
were sharply divided between reformers and nonreformers, the reformers
being strictly pacifist and the nonreformers opposing pacifism if it was

not in their own best interest.[80] Many of the so-called American supporters were in the reform wing, and they pressed for American negotiations because they wanted to avoid war rather than because they espoused any American "cause," though for men like Fothergill and Barclay these motives were certainly muted. The divisions among the Quakers, then, were new but ran along conventional lines within the Society.

Thus by 1776 merchants, Anglicans, dissenters, and Quakers all found themselves splintered along a spectrum, fragmented by issues which partly involved the Americans and partly reflected indigenous divisions over the nature of interest group lobbying. American issues divided them, but local issues about the nature of lobbying divided them more and prevented any of them from effectively representing any American "cause."

The crucially timed eclipse of London lobbies with American connections, which substantially reduced the government's access to American information, was both cause and effect of the imperial realignment. The influence of transatlantic interest groups was a casualty of the shift of imperial decision-making to Parliament, a change which left other parts of government, voluntary associations used to working with them, and even members of Parliament themselves off balance in a critical period.

· CHAPTER II ·

The Coming of the Revolution:
The American Side

Long used to looking to London lobbies for the prevention of unpalatable laws, connivance in their evasion, or help in getting exemptions, American interest groups now watched the progressive paralysis of their London correspondents with bewilderment. They sensed a shift in the locus of imperial decision-making that brought their earlier expectations into question, but the various interests did not know what role if any their own correspondents played in the shift, nor could they see how the change would affect the system of limited, responsive government in which the Londoners had represented them so effectively. They read their newspapers, flocked to newly arrived ship captains and other transatlantic visitors for news, shared their information in drawing rooms, shops, and counting houses, and filled their letters to London with comments about political miscellany—cabinet changes, local elections, Wilkes's escapades—any detail of English politics that could serve the double purpose of conveying their own concerns and eliciting an explanation of their correspondents' positions.

American interests were disturbed by the Londoners' inability to head off broad restrictions, primarily the work of Parliament, and similarly by their silence on more narrowly local questions, primarily topics handled by the Board of Trade. The Londoners seemed helpless to avert general new policies that were immensely harmful to the Americans. The Proclamation Line of 1763, for example, an administrative policy which cut off westward expansion, thwarted the plans of non-English communities hoping to move west, of religious groups wanting to expand their geographical base, of merchants seeking business on the frontier, and of land companies (which were just setting out to seek English connections at this late date). The prohibition on colonies' printing money (the Currency Act of 1764) affected ministers' salaries and merchants' business. Efforts to enforce the collection of customs meant, among many other things, more British officials in the colonies who could provide to the capital the kind of information that interests had previously dispensed to cultivate influence.[1]

Americans worried that their erstwhile lobbyists were not only victims of political changes but contributors to them. Were the Londoners becoming indifferent to the problems of their American correspondents? When American Presbyterians and Congregationalists warned the Dissenting Deputies of a new plan to establish bishops in the colonies, the Deputies did not even bring the subject up at their meetings. In 1766 the Deputies refused, or didn't bother, to consider an application from colonial Presbyterians for help getting the Presbyterian Church in New York City incorporated. New York City Huguenots petitioned the Threadneedle Street Church for a new minister in 1772, and were told that none would serve. The Virginia tobacco growers' efforts to pass a series of currency acts they considered essential produced seven years (1757 to 1764) of acrimony with their London factors.

The American interests tried both threats and cajolery; neither worked. The Americans then tried developing their own connections with the British government, bypassing the London interests; that didn't work, either. Direct appeals brought no benefits from the imperial government, and since they were made over the head of provincial legislators, they brought increasing criticism in the colonies. In the absence of the informal representation the colonists were used to, the idea that more formal representation was necessary took on appeal.

Disappointed by the turn of London politics, American interests now turned to provincial governments to get things done and found that by mid-century assemblies were becoming more efficient, more aware of the need to let interests know what they were doing, and more responsive to interest demands. So the interests shifted their focus from London to the provincial capitals, repairing the splits caused by earlier problems (the religious revivals, currency issues, demands of defense), tightening their local organization, appointing lobbyists, and looking for coalitions with other interests.

Before they could fully develop their local effectiveness, however, they ran up against the challenge of a new, more inflammatory type of colonial lobby working to mobilize public opinion against parliamentary legislation. These public opinion lobbies were very much in the line of Wilkes's Bill of Rights Society, and the established interests divided over them in much the same way that London lobbies split over Wilkes.

Like the London groups, the established American interests broke up, in stages, over the methods espoused by the new lobbies. In the first period following the Stamp Act radical new lobbies appeared—the Sons of Liberty and the nonimportation associations—but the established lobbies, which also opposed the Stamp Act and were willing to cooperate briefly with nonimportation, suffered little loss of cohesion. The second stage followed passage of the Townshend Duties. The radicals then wanted to revive nonimportation, which had been abandoned once the Stamp Act was repealed. Radicals appealed outside as well as inside the merchant community, on the principle of public good rather than mercantile interest. The merchant leadership divided sharply over whether they should cooperate with the radicals or not.

The more serious rifts, affecting now the churches as well as the mercantile groups, came after Parliament's passage of the Boston Port Act in 1774 and the colonial election of the Continental Congress in response. Most of the American denominations tried futilely to support both Parliament and the Continental Congress before caving in to differences of opinion among ministers and parishioners alike. Merchant groups divided similarly over support of the Continental Congress, and they splintered further over the question of working with radical groups of nonmerchants they could not control. In the end, organizational pressure or not, each colonist's decision whether or not to support the Revolution was largely a personal one.

·   ·   ·

In the decades after the accession of George III in 1760 Americans, and particularly American merchants, began to feel that the London mercantile community was becoming "cool" toward helping them and that it was hopeless to try to do anything about it. The initial response of American merchants was to put greater pressure on the English, but most merchants were uncertain how best to do this. Some of them thought about shifting business to political sympathizers, and at least one London merchant pleaded with his American correspondents to do just this: "Does it not occur to you as a measure absolutely requisite to be adopted in America, to agree in supporting those Merchants effectually and only, who have openly and avowedly espoused your cause with infinite danger to themselves while so many have been busy in traducing you and forwarding the late iniquitous measures with all their force?"[2]

This advice proved only partially workable. If a London merchant failed to obtain the proper favors for a correspondent or changed something like his credit arrangements, he would expect to be dropped, but not if he failed to take an active role on general American measures. For one thing colonists could not always be sure they had the right information about the political activities of the merchants they dealt with, since some merchants took the opportunity to spread rumors about their competitors. One of James Russell's correspondents chastised him for being politically inactive in the summer of 1774, but allowed that the account he had received of Russell's inactivity might be a very partial one calculated to serve some private purposes.[3]

But even if colonists were fairly certain of having the correct information, it was still not rational to punish or reward political activity. The largest London firms had at most three partners, and Americans frequently worried about their being so overburdened with work that they could not give individual customers adequate attention.[4] If some Americans shifted their business selectively, the merchants to whom they moved might be so overloaded that they could not give the new customers enough time. Americans who continued to trade with unsympathetic merchants would stand to profit because of the extra time their English associates had for taking care of their business; the Americans who shifted initially would be forced to return to their original correspondents.

So right down to the Revolution, when Congress voted "not to give any orders in future to those merchants who have publicly or privately favored those measures that are inimical to the trade and liberties of the American continent,"[5] American planters and merchants either adopted nonimportation agreements which discriminated equally against all English merchants or traded with sympathetic and unsympathetic merchants alike.

Unable to put the economic pinch on merchants who were indifferent, inactive, or hostile on American issues, colonists had to fall back on wheedling, threatening, or cajoling. "What then, in the name of common sense can be the reason that you have not long before this . . . presented a petition to the King and Parliament?" wrote one.[6] "I cannot help thinking that you are tired of the Virginia trade," complained another.[7] The same planter urged another correspondent to "bestir yourself . . . to procure a redress of our grievances. It is [your] Duty to do it; it is [your] interest to do it."[8] How effective such pressure really was is hard to say. James Russell, the merchant accused of criticizing the Continental Congress, took pains to send a letter to the Maryland Provincial Assembly denying the charges, perhaps because he received a number of similar letters at the same time, and within six months was assured that "you at present stand fairer with the people here, than any merchant in the trade."[9] But Thomas and Rowland Hunt, whose correspondents angrily suggested that they must be getting tired of the Virginia trade, did nothing to disabuse the colonists of the impression that they were anti-American (indeed, they went on to sign an anti-American petition in 1775), and yet they stood as fair with the Virginians as Russell stood in Maryland.[10] The American importunings seem to have been effective only with those merchants who inclined to support the Americans anyway.

Given the growing difficulty of trying to influence English interests, it was natural for Americans to consider bypassing them altogether both on local and on continental issues and going straight to the British government, and that is exactly what they did. Between 1715 and 1764 the American interests had rarely petitioned the King or Parliament directly nor had American assemblies done so: voluntary interest groups appealed only three times in the 1750s, for example, and assemblies did not petition at all.[11]

Between 1764 and 1774, by contrast, colonial groups petitioned the King or Parliament on at least eight different occasions on both local and imperial matters.[12] Some of the petitions, though they were properly handled at the imperial level, were on questions of purely local importance. In 1766 the New York Presbyterians, for example, seeking incorporation for their church, petitioned the King in Council directly;[13] a few years earlier Albany merchants had petitioned against a land grant to British soldiers in northern New York.[14] In 1773 the New York hatters, the most important hat-making group in the colonies (admittedly unconnected with any London association), petitioned against an act limiting English importation of American hats, and another New York group appealed for permission to manufacture steel.[15] Most of the other petitions were against statutes or proposed statutes affecting all or several of the North American colonies—the Sugar Act, the Restraining Act, the Commercial Reform Act of 1766, the proposal to create American bishoprics, and, of course, the Coercive Acts.[16]

In each case the appeals were drawn up not by Londoners acting on behalf of Americans but by the Americans themselves. In 1768 the agent for Massachusetts wrote an unknown correspondent in the colony suggesting that he pay £10 a year directly to the House of Commons for advance notice of bills affecting American interests;[17] earlier this would have been handled by the London groups themselves. On at least one occasion an American group—in this case the Presbyterian Synod of New York and Philadelphia, worried that the Dissenting Deputies were not working actively enough to prevent the appointment of bishops—considered appointing their own agent as an alternative to relying on the English.[18] When the Americans in London petitioned against the Coercive Acts, they actually declined to accept English signatures on the petition.[19]

With Americans feeling more and more the need to bypass London interests and work directly with the British government, and with colonial decision-making shifting from the Board of Trade to Parliament, it was natural for all groups, but particularly the colonial assemblies, to think about developing their own parliamentary connections, especially through the colonial agents, whom the assemblies chose. One can see this development in the changes among the colonial agents. At mid-century most of the agents were merchants, because assemblies, as well as mercantile and agricultural interests, looked to London mercantile lobbies for help. James Crokatt, agent for South Carolina, Robert Charles, agent for New York, Richard Partridge, agent for Rhode Island and Pennsylvania, Jasper Mauduit, agent for Massachusetts, all were merchants. By the eve of the Revolution Crokatt had been replaced by Charles Garth (who also became agent for Maryland), Charles was succeeded by Edmund Burke, and Connecticut had hired as their agent Richard Jackson; Garth, Burke and Jackson were all Members of Parliament and none was a merchant. Ben Franklin, not himself a Member of Parliament but influential there, had succeeded Partridge for Pennsylvania and Mauduit for Massachusetts. An agent well connected with Parliament could get petitions presented; an agent in Parliament could present them himself. Members of Parliament could be present in closed sessions and Committees of the Whole; they could sit on committees and draft legislation.

But the American efforts to develop influence within Parliament were clearly not a success. Only four Americans actually sat in Parliament, and they along with the three agents formed a group too small even to serve as effective swing voters when there was a strong opposition coalition.[20] Most of the American petitions were thrown out or sent to oblivion by tabling. And the effect of the American efforts on the already strained relations of the transatlantic interests was certainly negative. English groups resented the American attempts to act independently of them and relations between English and American lobbyists began to sour. English merchants disowned the New York merchants' protest against the Commercial Reform Act of 1766, for example.[21] Merchants who volunteered to sign the Americans' petition against the Coercive Acts were affronted when the Americans refused their offer. The Dissenting Deputies put down the New York and Philadelphia Synod's proposal to send an agent to work independently of the Deputies by advising that the administration would object: "they would look upon him as under the influence of the colonies as their agent."

If London lobbyists resented the colonists' by-passing them in appealing to the British government, colonial opponents attacked them for appealing to the government at all. The Massachusetts Baptists who successfully appealed against paying taxes to support the Congregational Church in Ashfield were told by local Sons of Liberty that the very act of appealing to England was unpatriotic. When the Reverend Samuel Peters decided to visit England, one of his critics remarked that he was "Under the influence of a strong and unnatural ill will which it is said you have shown to the land of your nativity."[22]

Even a moderate like Ezra Stiles, who had himself proposed establishing a regular correspondence between English and American dissenters some years before, was berating the Baptists and Quakers in 1775 for wanting to keep open their avenues to England.[23] The debate between "Antillon" and "First Citizen," which filled the pages of the *Maryland Gazette,* addressed itself to this question of the propriety of English appeals. And it was easy enough for mechanics or radical merchants to suggest that more conservative merchants who opposed the nonimportation agreements did so because they wanted to preserve close connections with their English correspondents. Appealing to England brought raised eyebrows (at the least), but more likely lost friendships, vilification in the press and in town meetings, and mob action. Increasingly, it wasn't worth it.

As the cost of appealing went up and the possibilities of success went down, some of the American interests that had frequently looked to London in the past began shifting their attention to lobbying in the colonies. Just how, and how successfully, they influenced local politics varied from colony to colony and group to group as it had earlier in the century, depending on the capacity of the colonial assemblies to respond to interest group demands, the interest groups' awareness of what the assemblies were doing, the number and strength of the groups themselves, and their opportunities for enhancing their own influence by coalition with other interests.

One thing was clear, however: from mid-century on, faced with problems of defense, transportation, and finance associated particularly with the Seven Years' War and led by aggressive speakers and increasingly experienced members, most of the assemblies took up more legislation and dealt with it better than before. Compared to their performance earlier in the century, most of the assemblies had become more efficient at handling legislation, more aware of the demands of their constituents, and hence more capable of responding to the needs of interests. They did this by concentrating increasingly on what we arbitrarily call "legislative activities,": drawing a line between legislation and judicial decisions, developing the capacity to initiate and consider legislation, and making the colonial public aware of what they were doing. The developments were occurring unevenly from colony to colony and region to region, with larger colonies tending to move more rapidly than smaller ones and southern and middle colonies on the whole moving more quickly than New England. Nevertheless, for most interest groups the changes meant more opportunities to get what they wanted in the local arena.

Legislative efficiency is, of course, difficult to measure with any precision. But three arbitrarily chosen criteria—the degree to which assemblies concentrated on legislative as opposed to judicial functions, the development of the committee system, and the emergence of experienced leaders, including strong speakers, suggest that between mid-century and 1775 a number of assemblies were already fairly sophisticated and capable of responding to the demands of various interests. As the assemblies began divesting themselves of their judicial functions, they developed far greater efficiency in drafting legislation than they had had before. Nearly all the colonies made some improvements in their committee organization (crucially important since legislation was now invariably drafted in committee), and several, particularly in the South, improved their committee systems substantially. Everywhere but in New England colonies developed standing committees, leaving the members of select committees (which normally drafted bills, in all but the Chesapeake colonies) more free to concentrate on legislation.[24] Committees new and old, standing and select, were thus functioning more efficiently in the 1760s,[25] as they were increasingly dominated by small groups of experienced legislators reelected time and again by their constituents.[26]

In the twenty-five years before the American Revolution, moreover, assemblies also made greater efforts to let constituents know what they were doing. Nine of the colonial assemblies published compilations of their laws; all the colonies (except North Carolina) that had not previously published their journals and their laws after each session now started to do so. The published journals made clear to readers just who was drafting legislation, and enabled interest groups to guess who was likely to have supported or opposed legislation affecting them. (The assembly journals of Massachusetts, Maryland, and New York occasionally carried division lists.) The journals did not include debates, but on key issues these were "leaked" in newspapers or pamphlets.

Not only were interests better informed about the assemblies; they also came increasingly to be consulted as part of the legislative process. For example, the Massachusetts General Court adjourned to solicit constituents on the excise bill in 1753; Pennsylvania assemblymen urged colonists to petition on the issue of financial support for war in 1759 and again on the assembly's request for royal government in 1764; the New York assembly consulted constituents on the governor's budget several times after 1753; the Massachusetts General Court again adjourned to consult constituents about a bill offering indemnity to the Boston Stamp Act rioters in 1766. The Maryland assembly consulted constituents on a tobacco inspection law, and Massachusetts legislators consulted them on a bill incorporating the Society for Relieving Widows and Children of Congregational Ministers.[27]

Constituent opinion was fed into the consideration of bills in various ways. Assemblies printed up copies of controversial bills under consideration. When members went home during adjournment, they often simply brought back personal impressions, no doubt somewhat randomly obtained. But constituents were sometimes urged to go further and petition for or against proposed measures. By the 1760s adjourning to solicit petitions was not unlike holding a referendum, with numbers of signatures being analyzed as an indication of public feeling. The adjournment of the Pennsylvania assembly to seek public response to the assembly's petition for royal government, for example, was followed by an exchange of pamphlets by John Dickinson and Joseph Galloway, each analyzing the number of signatures contained in the various local petitions.

For interest groups the legislatures' new efficiency and their new responsiveness to constituents' demands meant that the interests had more chance than they had earlier of getting things done locally; by the same token, so did their opponents. Given the new opportunities and possible new challenges and given the decline in their influence in British politics, most groups no longer had the luxury they had enjoyed until the 1750s of deciding whether they were better off handling issues at the local or imperial level. For self-improvement or self-defense they had to begin cultivating influence in the assemblies.[28]

To do so required tighter or broader organization for provincial interests. Some of the traditional transatlantic interests organized on a larger scale than before, some tightened existing organizations to create specialized institutions for lobbying, some approached other organizations about the possibility of coalitions, some appealed to the public, and some did all of these.

In the capital cities, merchants who previously had had only coffee house organizations now began to establish clubs, societies, or chambers of commerce. Occasionally they spoke for a "mercantile interest" throughout their colonies, but there was no formal colonywide or statewide organization of merchants until well after the Revolution. In most of the larger capitals, however, the merchants were organized far more formally than they had been before. Philadelphia merchants who continued to have only sporadic meetings down to the Revolution, nevertheless established a committee to lobby the legislature.[29] Boston merchants established the Society for Encouraging Trade and Commerce, which also chose a committee to handle lobbying.[30] New York (1768) and Charles Town (1774) merchants established chambers of commerce.[31] Mercantile organization was limited to the separate larger towns. So probably were the ethnic organizations like the Sons of St. Patrick, Sons of St. Andrew, and the German Friendly Societies founded largely though not entirely for charitable purposes (and still lacking London connections).[32]

Ecclesiastical organizations, by contrast, developed at the provincial and even the interprovincial level, though the network was sometimes seriously hampered by internecine quarrels stemming from the Great Awakening.[33] Two groups, the Quakers and the Methodists (the Methodists being the only new denomination before the Revolution), moved toward creating organizations which linked all the mainland provinces. All the Methodist ministers in the colonies—admittedly a small number before the Revolution—met annually.[34] Quakers continued to hold regional yearly meetings, but the Philadelphia Yearly Meeting became the predominant one and served as a clearing house for the ideas of the rest. The Methodists apparently had no specialized committee for lobbying; the Philadelphia Yearly Meeting established a Meeting for Sufferings in 1756, "to apply to the Government or Persons in power on their behalf."[35]

The Presbyterians and Baptists, the fastest growing denominations in the colonies as they spread to the frontier, organized in smaller geographical areas.[36] Like the Quakers, however, they each had some kind of committee for political activity. The Hanover Presbytery, founded in 1755, sent two delegates to Williamsburg when the House of Burgesses was in session.[37] Three years later the Presbyterian Synod of New York and Philadelphia was established; by 1766 they had eight ministers in attendance and the following year they united in General Convention with the Consociated Congregational Churches of Connecticut.[38] Most of their political work was done by *ad hoc* committees, but the convention did have a standing committee of correspondence. Baptists met in regional associations, the most important of which was the Warren Association, begun in 1767. The Warren Association in turn elected a Grievance Committee, quite similar to the Quaker Meeting for Sufferings.[39]

Church of England ministers also organized locally. They had met irregularly at the summons of their commissaries earlier in the century and now started holding annual, provincewide conventions, beginning with New Jersey in 1758.[40] They chose presidents, clerks, and "standing secretaries"; the president was the chief lobbyist. Whether they had standing committees on politics is unclear, but certainly they had *ad hoc* committees. A very effective one lobbied "day and night" with the New York councillors against a proposal to incorporate the Presbyterian Church in 1767.[41] The incorporation was voted down.

Besides lobbying with members of the legislature, the politicized merchants and members of various denominations undertook another fairly new kind of political activity. They began to seek coalitions with other interests that agreed with them on important issues. Interests in the middle colonies had already begun to do this. A number of other colonies followed after 1770 and especially after 1774. The New York elections of 1768 and 1769 were choices between coalitions of long-standing interests; elections in many colonies after 1774 were fought between rival slates combining traditional and newer interests: planters and mechanics in South Carolina, for example, merchants and mechanics in Massachusetts.[42]

As a corollary of their new political organization the interests also intensified their appeals to the public, particularly in Boston and the middle colonies. In New York especially mercantile and ecclesiastical interests alike appealed for support of sympathetic candidates at election time, with pamphlets entitled "Reasons for a Union of New York Dissenters Against the Episcopal Church,"[43] "Defense of the Church of England,"[44] "Friends of Trade Against Lawyers for the Assembly."[45] Merchants published their appeals to Parliament and to London merchants, as well as their nonimportation agreements. Religious denominations published eight times as many pamphlets between 1765 and 1773 as they had between 1754 and 1765, and the great bulk of the increase came in the publication of pastoral letters and association minutes. The Philadelphia Meeting for Sufferings published its first epistle in 1775,[46] and the Presbyterian Synod of New York and Philadelphia published its first pastoral letter in the same year.[47] The year before, the Anglican clergy of Connecticut decided for the first time "to lay before the public the sentiments of this Convention," and as the revolutionary crisis intensified,[48] other conventions felt it necessary to do the same thing. From the time they were first established the Baptist Associations usually published their minutes. A larger or tighter organization, specialized institutions for lobbying, attempts at coalition, electoral activity, public circulation of minutes, resolves, and letters all helped to increase the local political influence of the once London-oriented interest groups.

The growing local effectiveness of established interests was counterbalanced by two new kinds of colonial groups developing in the same period: interests with a purely local orientation and lobbies espousing a radical "cause." One of the sets was not a serious threat: it simply included a large number of local interests—ethnic societies, societies providing insurance, library supporters, social and intellectual clubs, labor organizations, military and professional associations, land companies, and the like—that had developed since 1750 with few if any English connections.

This is not to say that no such interests existed at all before 1750: Sons of St. Andrew had existed in several cities, for example; at least two cities had medical societies; two had charitable Irish societies; and carpenters,' porters,' and carters' organizations existed in some places though the longevity of such groups is not clear.[49] Nor is it to deny that any of the groups had English connections. The St. Andrew's Society of

Philadelphia, for example, thanked two London merchants for the gift of a seal,[50] and Charles Town's Fellowship Society won the right to incorporate because two merchants took the trouble to guide the provincial act of incorporation through the proper English offices.[51] Most of the charitable, intellectual, and social groups included wealthy merchants with English connections.[52] Nevertheless there was, after 1750, a period of explosive growth of local interests largely unconnected to England. Groups that had once been London-oriented became a smaller part of the existing colonial interests, and they faced stiff competition for local political influence.[53]

The other set of new interests was considerably more dangerous. In opposition to parliamentary legislation of the 1760s and 1770s, particularly the Stamp Act, the Townshend Duties, and the Boston Port Act, colonists from a variety of interests and some acting on their own organized radical public opinion lobbies much like John Wilkes's Bill of Rights Society in England. The new lobbies included the Sons of Liberty and the nonimportation associations, increasingly radical in their orientation. Debate over their new methods split and eventually paralyzed many of the traditional interests as the imperial crisis worsened from 1765 to 1776.

American interests, like their London counterparts, suffered collapse by stages. In the beginning of the crisis, from 1765 to 1768, both the mercantile and the church groups looked at the new lobbies apprehensively but cooperated in petitioning against the Stamp Act and agreeing to stop the importation of British goods temporarily. In the second stage, 1768 to 1774, the church groups remained cohesive, papering over incipient differences by issuing noncommittal statements, but the mercantile lobbies began to crack. They differed over how best to oppose the Townshend Duties (passed in 1767). Some favored only petitioning, some were willing to revive nonimportation, and some, much to the disgust of other merchants, favored bringing men outside the mercantile community into the opposition by citing American rights rather than the mercantile interests. The worst fragmentation occurred in the third stage, 1774 and after, when church and mercantile groups alike added to their earlier differences the new question whether their primary allegiance was to the crown or to the newly elected Continental Congress, and the resistance to British authority that it encouraged.

For the period 1765 to 1768 most of the interests were as united as they had been for much of the century; there was not much to disagree about. Nearly every group agreed on the need to explain to their London correspondents just why the Americans felt aggrieved by the Stamp Act and why it was in the Londoners' interest to work for repeal. Colonial merchant groups agreed to cancel orders of British manufactures until the Stamp Act was repealed and wrote to groups of London merchants asking them to use their influence with Parliament against the Stamp Act.[54] The Presbyterian Synod's pastoral letter of 1766 lamented the "unusual taxes" threatening America with "inevitable ruin,"[55] and even the Anglican ministers at their annual convention in Connecticut wrote the Bishop of London bemoaning "these difficult times."[56]

When the Stamp Act was repealed, merchants and planters were careful to retain the Londoners' confidence and heed their advice not to "triumph as if it (repeal of the Stamp Act) was a victory gained over the British Legislature."[57] They subsequently "acknowledged the noble efforts of the merchants in London and elsewhere which were so seasonably and so successfully exerted on this occasion."[58] Philadelphia merchants thanked the London Quaker merchants who had helped them, and the Presbyterian Synod of Philadelphia thanked George III for the confirmation of "our liberties."[59]

Throughout the campaign the interests' emphasis had been on decorum, propriety, and convention: in 1766, when Ezra Stiles proposed a union and an annual convention of Baptists, Quakers, Presbyterians, and Congregationalists, he was opposed by ministers in all denominations because they feared the convention would be so similar to the Stamp Act Congress that it would arouse distrust in Britain.[60] The particular motives for opposing the Stamp Tax varied from individual to individual within each of the various interests, but the combination of widespread dislike of the tax and the exercise of restraint in the protests and thanks sent to England made most interests capable of presenting a united front during the crisis.

This was not true of the crisis over the Townshend Duties. The churches on the whole did not have to take a stand but merchant groups did, and they were no longer capable of appearing to be united. The question was not whether the duties themselves were acceptable—almost everyone agreed that they were not—but what means could properly be used to oppose them. Should nonimportation be tried again? Many merchants said no; wet-goods merchants and established merchants with large inventories generally accepted the duties with mere annoyance, expecting to petition against them and ask the London merchants for help. Meanwhile they simply planned to pass the duties on to their customers through higher prices. Others—the new merchants and those who dealt in dry goods—wanted a revival and expansion of the nonimportation agreements and a broader appeal for support.

In towns where the merchants disagreed over the fairness of nonimportation agreements, or where the mercantile community was small, the merchants who favored nonimportation had to go beyond the purely mercantile community and seek support from "gentlemen," "traders," "mechanics," or simply "other inhabitants."[61] At first the outsiders accepted the merchants' lead, but by 1770 the other groups were beginning to act independently, and the original merchant leaders were badly divided over whether they should give in or not. At any rate it was seriously questionable, in America as in England, whether they actually still spoke for a merchant "interest." Moreover, for nonimportation to work it had to be observed by all merchants, not just those who had voted for it; recalcitrant merchants had to be pressured with increasing harshness in late 1769 and 1770, by a group that had no legal standing.[62] Finally, to justify coercion, merchants in the colonies as well as England had to argue that they were acting not on self-interest but on the principles of public interest. In appealing to nonmercantile groups, coercing dissidents, and claiming to act on public principle, American merchants were breaking with tradition; American mercantile groups were fragmenting along roughly the same lines as their British counterparts.[63] The divisions were evident in Boston almost as soon as notice of the Townshend Duties was received in late summer of 1767; beginning in the winter of 1767, first New York and then Philadelphia, Charles Town, Annapolis, and Baltimore merchants split over nonimportation.

The situation was exacerbated following the Parliamentary Act shutting Boston Harbor, news of which arrived in May of 1774; it sparked the next crisis and opened a new stage of colonial opposition to British measures which ultimately worked into Revolution. For American interest groups the Boston Port Act inaugurated two years of chaos, during which it became virtually impossible for members to remain neutral. Since other colonies sympathized with Boston but were unwilling to give help unilaterally, a Continental Congress was chosen to concert measures of resistance, and it became an alternative and rival to the authority of King and Parliament. The established interests, both ecclesiastical and mercantile, wrecked on the question of where their allegiance lay. To the colonists the Boston Port Act was evidence of British intention to repress them with unprecedented severity. It was particularly harsh because the Bostonians were given no chance to avoid the punishment by paying for the tea first. The Port Act was also shattering because it received the support of the King and Lord Dartmouth, the two people from whom the colonists had hopes of sympathy if not open support. Disillusionment with the King and Dartmouth was followed closely by disillusionment with the London mercantile interest. Throughout the summer and fall the colonial merchants continued to write their London correspondents that "it's in the power of the merchants and Manufacturers to get the act repealed."[64] When the London merchants failed to obtain repeal of the Port Act—indeed, they did not even try in 1774— the American merchants gave up hope that the Londoners would ever lobby for them again. The last letter the London merchant James Russell received from a colonial correspondent urging the Londoners to lobby on the colonists' behalf was written in December 1774;[65] after that the colonists invoked the help not of merchants in particular but of "right-thinking Englishmen" in general.

The churches, as before, had an easier time preserving unity when the crisis began, but even they succumbed before long to serious rifts. The first specific problem for the churches appeared when the Continental Congress invited an Anglican minister, the Reverend Jacob Duché, to preach before them. Anglicans had a brief moment of soul searching.[66] Had Duché declined, he would have been branded an enemy of the country; his acceptance implied his public support of the Congress. Elsewhere, particularly in Massachusetts, local committees demanded that Anglican ministers in particular declare their support of Congress or face banishment, and several left their parishes as early as the spring of 1775.

It was the Quakers who were thrown into greatest confusion by the Congress. By distinguishing as early as 1774 between the legitimate activities of the assemblies and illegitimate activities of the Congress, the Quakers became the first denomination to take a public stand on radical activity and, not surprisingly, the first to disagree over it, and with considerable bitterness. The Philadelphia Yearly Meeting declared its intention to "keep as much as possible from mixing with the people in their human policy and Contrivance and to forbear meeting in their Public Consultations."[67] The key words here were "human" and "public consultation." They applied to committees of correspondence, nonimportation associations, conventions, and the Continental Congress itself; they did not apply to legally established and traditionally recognized institutions like the provincial assemblies. The Friends denounced the Congress and the nonimportation associations as being "manifestly repugnant to the peaceable Principles of our Christian Profession,"[68] but this did not mean that they withdrew from politics altogether. Edward Biddle noted acidly that they "moved heaven and earth to support the election of moderates to the Pennsylvania Assembly."[69]

Locally, Quaker leaders such as Thomas Mifflin defied the Yearly Meeting and took part in the nonimportation association; others, John Reynell for one, refused to participate. Despite the Meeting for Sufferings' declaration against "illegal assemblies,"[70] even the conservative Quaker James Pemberton was willing to work with members of the Continental Congress if they discussed the question of religious freedom.[71] Of the active radical leaders in Pennsylvania in 1774 and 1775, 29 percent were Quakers, a drop off of only 11 percent from the Stamp Act agitation during which the Meeting for Sufferings had taken no stand.[72] By the end of 1775, 163 members of the Society in Pennsylvania had been investigated by the meeting for accepting political office, engaging in some military activity, or both, and Pemberton lamented that "we are become here a people disunited in Sentiment and Conduct."[73]

While the Quakers were disunited over the Philadelphia Yearly Meeting's demand for noninvolvement in extra-legal politics, other churches tried to avoid open divisions in 1774 by straddling the fence between imperial and local legislatures, by defending "legal authority" without ever saying what legal authority actually was, and by "addict[ing them-selves] to no party," as John Wesley advised the Methodist preachers.[74]

The Presbyterians came closest to openly supporting radical measures when the Synod of New York and Philadelphia advised their members to "adhere firmly to their resolutions [those of the Continental Congress]; and let it be seen that they are able to bring out the whole strength of this vast country to carry them into execution."[75] In several towns the radicals were known as "the Presbyterian party," and it was the Presbyterians to whom John Adams was referring when he wrote in 1775 that "The Clergy, this way, are . . . now beginning to engage in politics." (Adams was referring to a letter that the Synod of New York and Philadelphia had written to Presbyterians in North Carolina defending the Continental Congress.[76]) But the same pastoral letter which urged adherence to the congressional resolutions also professed loyalty to the King. This was perfectly natural—the colonists were still acknowledged subjects of George III in 1775—but it also indicated a strong undercurrent of support for moderate measures among Presbyterians of the middle colonies.[77]

The Baptists, like the Presbyterians, tried to paper over divisions by coming out for both George III and the Continental Congress. In general Baptists in the south supported radical resistance, and Baptists in the middle colonies were inclined against it, though neither group was close to unanimous. The New England Baptists appear to have been the most seriously divided since they had recently been beneficiaries of English help against the Congregational establishment in Massachusetts.[78] In 1774 Massachusetts Baptists sounded out members of the Continental Congress about the possibility of legislation restricting religious persecution in New England, but at the same time a leading Baptist predicted: "If no redress is granted from government [here] they {the Grievance Committee} will, I suppose, apply to the King and Council through their agents in London."[79] Two years later, when the Massachusetts Baptists appealed a case to the provincial convention, they were berated by the Philadelphia Baptists for an act that might antagonize George III. Like the Presbyterians and the Congregationalists, the Baptists found it difficult to adopt a united front over measures of imperial resistance.

Finally, among the major denominations, even the Anglicans were torn by internal conflicts as well as conflicting pressures from England and local Patriot committees. Anglican ministers in the south tended to support the Patriot cause, but a substantial minority, probably around a quarter, did not. A majority of the S.P.G. missionaries in the north were inclined in the opposite direction though it is hard to estimate their position accurately: by the spring of 1775 many of them were under strong local pressure to commit themselves to the Patriot side or quit their posts, and by May several had already been forced to leave. The political attitudes of the remainder during this period are not always clear. A missionary who wrote that he "dares not write his sentiments on the subject fully, lest letters shd fall into their hands whose tender mercies are cruelty,"[80] was clearly heading for the Loyalist camp, but one who wrote that "my mission stands as fair as any in the province"[81] might either have Patriot sympathies or be writing with the expectation of having his mail intercepted. Most northern missionaries hung in as long as possible, trying to avoid politics but preaching to increasingly radical congregations because, as Reverend Richard Peters explained, "Should we refuse, our principles would be misrepresented and even our religious usefulness destroyed among our people."[82] Anglican ministers were finding it more and more difficult to assemble, but when they did the double problem of public relations and genuine personal uncertainty inclined them, like the Presbyterians and the Baptists, to hide behind a defense of "superior authority" without saying what that authority really was.

Once Independence was declared the job of keeping the churches together became harder, in some cases impossible, both at the ministerial level and at the level of rank-and-file membership. The crisis of 1774–75 had revived old divisions and created new ones in the churches, and in so doing had weakened the ability of colonywide or intercolonial organizations to speak for their members. From the summer of 1776 many organizations could not even meet at all because of disruptions caused by the Revolution; others met sporadically and suffered from bad attendance and unreliable information. The Philadelphia Yearly Meeting of Quakers continued to meet annually, but without many of its leaders who were in exile in Virginia. Baptist associations met as best they could. Dutch Reformed ministers met twice during the war, lamenting "the lack of reports from all the particular meetings."[83] Presumably Congregational groups like the Boston Consociation continued to meet, but there is no evidence; there *is* clear evidence, though, that conventions of Anglican clergy ceased to meet altogether.

Whether the conventions of ministers attempted to meet or not, the Revolution confronted churches with problems affecting lay churchgoers which in themselves sufficed to undermine provincial ecclesiastical interests. It dislocated congregations or split them up when members had to flee from British armies or local mobs, it weakened the authority of ministers who found themselves at odds with a majority of their congregations, and it created such differences of opinion that even when associations or conventions did meet they were ineffective in regulating their members' activities. "Good God," wrote one minister, "what should we do or whither shall we turn?"[84]

Divisions among the mercantile groups appeared almost as soon as news of the Boston Port Act arrived. They occurred over both policy and procedures: policy disputes revolved initially around the advisability of nonimportation agreements as a weapon against the British and soon after over the question of recognizing the Continental Congress and provincial conventions as possible alternatives to British authority in London and the legally established provincial assemblies. The procedural disputes, if this is what they should be called, were along two lines. One split was between moderates who wanted to stay active in politics in order to retain as much influence as possible, and conservatives who lost heart and dropped out, sometimes leaving the towns altogether, sometimes staying but declining political activity. The other split was between the moderate merchants who tended to think there was such a thing as "merchant interest," and the radical merchants who attempted to stay on top of the even more radical mechanics' politics. The policy disputes developed at more or less the same time in different towns; the procedural disputes developed first in Boston and then moved south from 1774 to 1776.

When news of the Boston Port Act arrived in Boston the town resolved, naturally enough, on unilateral nonimportation; they also resolved to request help from other American ports. The local nonimportation proposals divided merchants along the same lines that they had previously done: dry-goods merchants (opposed) versus wet-goods merchants (for); smugglers (opposed) versus nonsmugglers (for); and opponents of coercion versus merchants who thought that coercion was the only way to get their recalcitrant colleagues to cooperate in resistance. Nonimportation did not stand alone as an issue for long, however.

In the summer of 1774 New York merchants raised a host of new issues by proposing that nonimportation be implemented by a continental congress of representatives from all the colonies. Mechanics and merchants immediately disagreed with each other and among themselves. Who should vote? Should the congress be recognized as a possible alternative to the British government? Should the provincial conventions being chosen at the same time, and often for the purpose of electing delegates to congress, be considered themselves as legitimate alternatives to the legal assemblies? How much coercion could the nonimportation association authorized by the congress properly use?

The alignments are not always clear: a meeting of Boston tradesmen in mid-June was "much divided in sentiment and some smart altercations ensued," but we do not know the sides.[85] In New York William Smith warned against "clapping or hissing" and hoped that "if a division should be necessary . . . such division may be made . . . with all possible order and decorum."[86] The divisions were primarily between merchants and artisans but the merchant groups also lacked consensus. At least two members of the Philadelphia merchants' committee of the town did not serve on the committee to pick the delegates; James and Drinker dropped out of mercantile politics, sarcastically calling the Continental Congress this "August Assembly, the saviors of America."[87] When a New York public meeting chose a committee of correspondence in July, some merchants did not want to serve on it. Two weeks before a member of the merchants committee had published an advertisement in the papers for a public meeting, and the committee split sharply when a majority disavowed the ad.[88]

One by one the conservative merchants dropped out of the resistance movement, unable to accept decisions made at mass meetings, unable to condone the meeting of a general congress, unable to serve on a coercive nonimportation committee if it were authorized by the congress. Some remained in the cities; others began moving to the country as early as the summer of 1774. As conservative merchants pulled out and the mechanics became more active there came a point at which the leadership of resistance switched from moderate to radical men. From this point on moderate merchants had to decide whether to stay in the movement and retain what influence they could, or give up.[89] Increasingly, they gave up.

Throughout the colonies the withdrawal of moderate merchants from politics was both cause and effect of the decline of mercantile influence. The decision whether to stay active or not and in the end whether to join the Patriots or not was influenced by several factors. The merchants who withdrew early or ended up Loyalist tended to be older and wealthier than those who stayed and took up the Patriot cause; in Philadelphia they were often Quaker (though we have seen the limits of Quaker influence) and in Boston, disproportionately Anglican. Merchants were more likely to be Loyalist in some cities than in others. In the smaller ports like Newburyport they were more likely to be Patriots, but that might simply have resulted from greater community pressure driving conservatives out. In Newburyport, for example, there were virtually no Tories among the merchant community, but there was also a large turnover of the top mercantile families between 1765 and 1790, suggesting that merchants who opposed resistance to England may have quickly left.[90] In New York City, by contrast, 48 percent of the merchants were Loyalist and in Annapolis about 23 percent.[91] Whatever unity existed in the smaller ports, the larger mercantile communities were deeply divided.

But although we can isolate a few factors that seem to have influenced merchants' loyalties, in the end their decision to go for or against the Revolution was a very personal one. What can explain why the wealthy Boston merchant John Rowe, who wrote categorically in June of 1774 "The Committee [of Correspondence] are wrong. The Merchants have taken up against them,"[92] would become a Patriot, while his good friend John Amory, who had cooperated far more with the nonimportation associations, would become a Loyalist?[93] Why did the Quaker merchant Thomas Wharton, who wrote emphatically warning his London correspondents that American anger was widespread against the Intolerable Acts, end up a Loyalist while another Quaker, Thomas Mifflin, became a Patriot leader?[94] The Revolution separated the members of American interest groups along political lines for profoundly personal reasons, but the important thing is that it did separate them. When the Reverend Mather Byles lamented in 1775 that "I write in confusion—everything round me is confused,"[95] he reflected the uncertainty, even the agony, that many interest group leaders shared throughout the war.[96]

CHAPTER 12

After the Revolution:
The Lobbies Go Their Separate Ways

In 1783, as the Revolution ended, many of the prewar interest group members actually expected to reestablish their earlier transatlantic associations. They recognized that American independence would bring fundamental changes in their political positions; that the Americans would, for example, no longer need London associates to lobby for them when the English government was reviewing colonial laws or appointing colonial officials. Still, they hoped somehow to recreate the former Atlantic ties almost as if the Revolution had never taken place.

Particular expectations drew the merchants and religious leaders to seek the old connections. Some of the merchants wanted the convenience of doing business with firms whose methods they knew and trusted; some thought they had to renew dealings with old firms in order to get extended credit while paying off prewar debts; others simply wanted to work with old friends again. The Church of England parishioners faced immediate practical questions about the Americans' separation from the English state; dissenters wanted to talk about doctrine and finance. As soon as it was safe to cross the Atlantic, therefore, English and American firms rushed back to do business with their leading prewar correspondents on the other side of the ocean. Ecclesiastical groups exchanged correspondence and representatives, and the dissenters sent fundraisers to the British Isles. Only the non-English seem to have lost their London connections.

It did not take long, however, before merchants, churchmen, and dissenters came to realize that although American churches were starting to grow rapidly and American trade with England would soon approach prewar levels,[1] the difficulties of reestablishing prewar correspondence were far greater than they had anticipated. In the first place, immediately after the war ended the interests realized how badly the conflict had scattered their members, ruined their groups, and destroyed their cohesion. The second stage of their disappointment began a year or so after the first, once the new postwar problems further disturbed efforts to reopen old lines of communication. New merchants with new methods made prewar relationships obsolete. New institutions for established American church denominations made transatlantic organizations, especially for supplying ministers, also obsolete. American groups slowly reached out to start national networks. London interests sought firmer connections in the English provinces. Reluctantly, even painfully, members of many interests had to abandon the idea that American independence did not have to make a difference.

.   .   .

As soon as it was safe to cross the Atlantic, English and American merchants optimistically sought out ship captains to deliver letters to correspondents they had not been able to address for seven years. The London merchants Christopher Court and Thomas Eden, for example, reestablished their business with prewar tobacco growers in Maryland;[2] John Blackburn wrote his old correspondents in the United States that "I shall flatter myself with the favor of your preference to my house."[3] Mary Hayley, widow of the prewar merchant George Hayley, solicited orders from her husband's "old friends,"[4] and representatives of no fewer than six London firms visited Nicholas Brown of Providence seeking the favor of his preference for their particular firms.[5] New England firms rushed back to do business with the leading prewar houses in London—established firms like Lane, Son, and Fraser, or Champion and Dickason. New York merchants wrote hopefully to trusted merchants like John Blackburn or Fludyer, Hudson, and Streatfield; the Annapolis tobacco exporter Wallace revived his prewar partnership with Joshua Johnson in London.[6] Tobacco planters sought out their former consignment merchants: even Jefferson planned to resume business with Carey, Moorey, and Welsh, though he didn't much like them,[7] and Robert Beverley switched only because his prewar factor had declined to shepherd Beverley's oldest son through English schools in the usual mid-eighteenth-century fashion.[8]

Ecclesiastical spokesmen rushed as quickly as merchants and planters to resume transatlantic correspondence after the war. Diverse and sometimes competitive Anglican representatives went to London trying to win for themselves or their friends an appointment as bishop and with it the prestige of starting an independent American church. Quaker "visitors" as well as yearly letters from England and American crossed the Atlantic;[9] the London Meeting for Sufferings continued to send yearly letters to American Quakers meeting in Philadelphia, Virginia, the Carolinas, Maryland, New England, and New York.[10] The General Assembly of the English Baptist Church reestablished its Corresponding Committee[11] for America and the leading Baptist Association in America, the Warren Association, sent copies of its minutes, with back copies to 1779, to ministers associated with the General Assembly.[12] John Wesley, after appointing a superintendent for Methodists in America, addressed a letter of "advice and instruction" to American Methodist preachers and thereafter exchanged frequent letters with "Our Brethren in America."[13] Even the Vicar Apostolic of the Catholic Church in England resumed his correspondence with American Catholic missionaries.[14]

American church fundraisers toured Britain on behalf of universities. American Baptists solicited the "further patronage of English Baptists for Rhode Island College,"[15] Benjamin Rush revived old correspondence with English dissenters to raise funds for Dickinson College in Pennsylvania,[16] and John Witherspoon visited English Presbyterians on a fundraising drive for the College of New Jersey (later Princeton).[17] American church groups as well as mercantile ones sought their old connections and their old habits.

This rush to revive the prewar correspondence can be explained in various ways. Religious denominations simply found it hard to give up the idea of united, Anglo-American communities. American churches, especially those with affiliated universities, needed books and financial assistance. Quakers and some Presbyterians on both sides of the Atlantic were brought together by common efforts to abolish the slave trade.[18] American Methodists, Moravians, Mennonites, and Anglicans all needed English help in getting their own bishops and even looked to the English for their nomination. By habit some American churches even looked to English advisers to solve their internal disputes.

Of all the religious societies, it was, predictably, the American Anglicans who needed the most help. Like other groups they urgently needed a bishop of their own to ordain other clergy, a bishop who did not have to acknowledge the King as the head of his church. They also needed help protecting American lands given to the church by colonial governments before the war and now claimed by dissenters to belong to the public,[19] and English legacies which might be nullified by Independence. Missionaries pleaded with the S.P.G. for "the continuance, and in some instances the extension, of the Society's bounty,"[20] once America was no longer part of the British Empire. The S.P.G. itself decided the last question, and fairly soon, when they voted in 1785 to cut off the salaries of missionaries who remained in the United States.[21] But the other problems, along with the question of bishops, were handled at the highest levels of state in England and America, and the Americans needed a great deal of help from traditional London sources. Together with these, items such as the missionaries' requests for relocation and parishioners' requests for the replacement of Bibles and plate that were lost during the war filled the letters of Anglicans on both sides of the ocean.

The merchants' initial motives were three: credit, confidence, and convenience. James Barr summed them all up, when he described the non-English ships which crowded Philadelphia's harbor seeking to attract postwar business as being owned by "intire strangers both to the trade of this country and the customs . . . as there is such a number of strangers in amongst us . . . there is no such thing as any credit to be obtained."[22] Convenience and credit were overlapping reasons, but merchants weighed them differently. Those merchants and planters who gave greatest weight to the convenience of returning to familiar ways and well-known territory expressed considerably more enthusiasm than those who thought they had to return to prewar houses because they were dependent upon them for current credit and reasonable arrangements for paying off past debts. Robert Beverley explained that he stuck with the same merchants from habit because "my disposition leads me, when I once begin a correspondence, never to change without the most forceable reasons."[23] The Bromfields confidently sought to renew "our concerns . . . with Houses that are undoubtedly solid."[24] Jonathan Jackson, on the other hand, was considerably less enthusiastic about returning to Lane, Son, and Fraser to buy goods on credit: "I hold on to Mr. L[ane's] Ho. for they do to me in a kind of way, but they have all the tremor of an old woman and not much more understanding."[25] With even less enthusiasm than Jackson, Thomas Jefferson explained that Virginia tobacco planters returned to business with prewar factors only because they had to: "they find it necessary to give their English merchant the benefit of the consignment of their tobacco to him (which is enormously gainful) in order to induce him to continue his indulgence for the balance due."[26] One wouldn't expect Jefferson to exult over returning to business with a group of English merchants that he claimed had rendered him a species of human property, but there is no doubt that many of his fellow tobacco merchants returned to their old correspondents because it was the only way they could think of to arrange for paying off their debts.

In addition to credit and confidence for the merchants, and organization and fundraising for the religious leaders, there was another reason that impelled the interest group leaders to renew their prewar connections. They simply wanted to be in touch with old acquaintances again, to work once more with "friends of tried honor and character." Henry Bromfield, a Massachusetts merchant, exulted over a chance to pick up his old connections: "I hope the dawn now opening will increase to a brighter day."[27] At almost the same time the Massachusetts merchant Stephen Higginson was writing that when Britain reopened its trade to

Americans, it would "revive old habits, [and] call forth former feelings and attachments."[28] President Manning of the Baptist College of Rhode Island resumed his prewar correspondence with John Ryland, one of the most important Baptist philanthropists in England, with the remark that "I suppose Mr. Ryland has no less affection for his American brethren than heretofore,"[29] while Rev. Bela Hubbard, an Anglican missionary in Connecticut, wrote a London friend: "One good arises from the general evil that is brought on by the separation of the countries—a door is opened for a freer intercourse with one's friend."[30]

In 1783, therefore, it was far from clear whether "old habits, former feelings and attachments built up over decades" would prove durable enough to function in the vastly changed postwar world, or whether new types of ecclesiastical organizations, new approaches to business, and a new relationship of interests to government would evolve in the wake of the Revolution. Men like Bromfield had reason to hope that the old habits would last a long, long time.

It did not take long, however, before interests on both sides of the ocean came to fear that old ties were harder to renew than they had expected. As early as the summer of 1783 interests came to realize that revolutionary upheavals had altered the very makeup of the prewar groups. The organizations as such survived, but many of the members accustomed to arranging transatlantic cooperation were no longer there. In the second period, about a year later, the interests faced new problems growing out of American independence from the empire.

Almost as soon as the fighting stopped it became evident that men who had been active in interest groups before the war were no longer there. The war had dislocated individuals and disrupted groups. Merchants began to realize this when they sought out earlier correspondents only to find that some had died, some had retired, some had failed, some had switched into other trades, and some had quit business altogether. The "reconditioned character" of mercantile society was evident on both sides of the Atlantic.[31]

The American mercantile communities were particularly transient in Charles Town, New York, and Philadelphia, all occupied by the British during the war. In these towns merchants who had supported the Revolution had to flee to the countryside during the war; if they returned at all after the war they were likely to find that the British had occupied their quarters and used up their inventories, and the merchants could get no compensation. Loyalist merchants, on the other hand, often had to flee when the British armies evacuated the seaport towns; if they returned after the war they were likely to be shunned by their former customers. So the war produced a turnover of merchants: in New York City, for example, the Chamber of Commerce of 1779 had only 41 percent of its prewar members, and at the end of the war only 40 percent of the 1779 group were doing business.[32] Boston's wealthiest merchant by the end of the war had not even lived there in 1776.[33] Philadelphia had 60 percent more merchants in 1785 than in 1774.[34] Even in towns that were not occupied there was considerable merchant turnover. Only nine of Annapolis' seventeen leading firms in 1774 were still there in 1783.[35] Only five of the twenty-five wealthiest residents (merchants) of Newburyport in 1790 bore any relation at all to the top twenty-five of 1767.[36] A Newport resident summed up the situation when she wrote, "This succession of military armaments has drove numbers of the wealthy from their homes to which they never mean to return." Then she added that, for her own part, "Newport will not answer."[37]

In England there was also a turnover of merchants trading to America, many of them being reluctant to return to a business they had abandoned for six years. Gerardus Beekman, a New York merchant who had dropped out of business and retired to the country during the war, returned to town when the Revolution was over and wrote to three of the firms he had dealt with before 1775, announcing his intentions of going back into trade. He found that one merchant, John Blackburn, was ready to resume trade, though Blackburn had taken on a new partner. One other firm, Cooke and Ralph, had gone bankrupt, and the third, Fludyer, Hudson, and Streatfield, replied that had they continued in trade they would have been happy to handle Beekman's orders, but their late house had broken up.[38]

Beekman succeeded with one out of three; a random sampling of prewar London firms suggests that this was about par. Christopher Court, Thomas Eden, John Blackburn, Thomas Land, Alex Champion, and Davis Strahan and Company survived the war and returned to American trade. The old tobacco merchant Daniel Mildred, like many of the Quaker merchants, became a banker.[39] William Telfair and Basil Cooper went bankrupt,[40] Phyn and Ellis took up Canadian trade,[41] DeBerdt, Dearman, and Co. became "Brokers, for the Purchase and Sale of American Stock and Lands,"[42] Carey and Moore died,[43] and John Norton's heirs did not continue their trade after Norton's death during the war.[44]

As early as 1783 there were two different committees of merchants trading to America. One consisted of the "old merchants" trading before 1776, the other included merchants in business after 1783, and the overlap was small. Of twenty-three London firms signing a petition favoring the appointment of a consul to New England in 1786, only ten had been involved in prewar American trade.[45] Edward Payne, chairman of the new merchants' committee, had been a middling tobacco merchant before the war. Duncan Campbell, John Nutt, and William Molleson were chairmen of the old merchants' committee. Campbell was a prewar tobacco merchant who tried to shift his postwar trade to New England before becoming a government contractor; Molleson served on several government commissions; and though Nutt's postwar vocation is unclear, he does not seem to have returned to the American trade.[46]

The revolution in commercial relations was paralleled, if not as dramatically, by changes in ecclesiastical relations. Ministers as well as merchants learned from their first postwar efforts to reestablish transocean contacts that the difficulties were far greater than they had anticipated. One reason was apparent immediately—the great dislocation of ministers and congregations as a result of the war. English ministers who went to renew correspondence with Americans after the war did not find them there. Some people died, some fought in the war and never came back to their homes, some moved out permanently from war-torn areas, some switched churches.[47]

It was the Anglicans and Quakers who were on the whole most opposed to the war and hence most disrupted by it. Statistics for the percentage of Loyalists among the Anglicans do not exist for all the states, but those that do suggest a high correlation. One out of four Anglican ministers in Virginia, for example, was a Loyalist. Anglicans comprised 14 percent of the total population of New Jersey, but they made up 50 percent of the Loyalists there. Loyalist ministers were sometimes turned out by patriotic congregations; Patriot ministers found that Loyalists in their congregations had to flee Patriot committees, and a serious postwar problem was matching up ministers and congregations. After receiving letters like one from Rev. Ebenezer Diblee complaining of "the diminution of my parish by the flight of numbers,"[48] or one from Reverend Oliver Wiswall lamenting that "his congregation at Horton having deserted him . . . he discontinued his going there and has never since received any invitation from them,"[49] the S.P.G. set up a committee specifically to consider what should be done with displaced American ministers.[50]

With Quakers as with Anglicans it is hard to measure the extent of wartime disruption. Pacifism certainly did not predispose Quakers to support the Revolution; many openly opposed it. In 1777 Congress recommended to the various states that they apprehend all Quakers; most did not bother but Pennsylvania arrested forty-one men, including the leading Quaker politicians, and confined them in jail without a hearing. In Pennsylvania the Quaker organization also cracked from within. There 908 Quakers were disowned by the Society for cooperating in the war effort, and this number must represent only a small fraction of the revolutionary sympathizers, since in Philadelphia alone over 1,700 of the town's estimated 3,500 Quakers supported the Patriot side.[51]

Those Quakers who supported the Revolution were expelled from meetings; after the war, the expelled Quakers formed the Free Quaker Society and petitioned the state legislature for joint ownership of buildings and gravesites. As a result of the split and the jailings, as well as because of the general unpopularity of their opposition to the war, Quakers lost forever their prewar political dominance in Pennsylvania.

Other churches were less hard hit than the Quakers and the Anglicans, but they too were disrupted by the war. Ministers left and were not replaced, churches were destroyed in the fighting and not rebuilt. Congregations broke up and did not reassemble.

On the face of it the Presbyterians and Congregationalists should have had the greatest unity, and probably they did, though here again we have very few statistics. Patriots were called the "Presbyterian party" in Philadelphia; James Manning called the Revolution a Presbyterian war. The Anglican minister Charles Inglis wrote of Presbyterian ministers in October 1776, "I do not know one of them who did not, by preaching and every effort in their power, promote all the measures of the congress, however extravagant." On the other hand there were pockets of Presbyterians in the colonies, especially in the southwest, who had not supported the Revolution; it was to these that John Witherspoon referred when he said that his countrymen did not make good revolutionaries. Even the various provincial organizations experienced divisions, especially in the larger towns. In Philadelphia, for example, about a third of the Presbyterians seem to have been Loyalist. In Boston almost 40 percent of the Congregational merchants became Tory, and Congregationalists also joined General Burgoyne's army in considerable numbers, though we do not know exactly how many did so.

Bela Hubbard, an Anglican minister in Connecticut, wrote with relish that "many of ye dissenting parishes are vacant and likely to continue so."[52] One out of four Connecticut Congregational churches had no minister in 1784, and Ezra Stiles estimated that all told there were a hundred and twenty vacancies in Congregational churches throughout New England.[53] Similarly the Presbyterian Church Convention in 1785 lamented "the scarcity of ministers to fill our numerous congregations."[54] Far from unusual was the musical-chair game reported by the Coetus of the German Reformed Congregation in Pennsylvania: "Mr. Helfenstein left Lancaster and took charge of his old congregation in Germantown . . . Mr. Faber has accepted Lancaster; he left Gosrenhoppen because they did not give him the necessary support. Mr. Dubbendorf left Germantown and accepted a congregation, Lykens Valley, which is far distant."[55] Both congregations and ministers took what they could get.

If the first difficulties about restoring prewar mercantile and religious connections appeared as early as the conclusion of peace, the second set was not long in coming. Those men who did manage to salvage their prewar connections temporarily, now found new difficulties that made the transatlantic associations all but impossible. In the mid-1780s new business methods undercut old mercantile relations, new American church institutions undercut the ecclesiastical ties.

At this point both English and American merchants who tried to perpetuate the prewar system of consigning cargoes to individual factors found themselves undercut by new competitors—now including foreigners as well as English and Americans—using methods more efficient than the old consignment system. After the war Americans were no longer bound by imperial restrictions requiring them to trade in their own or English ships. A Philadelphian noted as early as the summer of 1783 that "oure harbor is filled with vessells allmost from every part of the Globe,"[56] and a Virginia planter was "just told of a considerable number of arrivals from Europe."[57] Both American and English merchants experimented with new business methods, some selling manufactured goods directly to American planters and farmers and buying their produce on the spot, some selling American products at auction in London considerably under the prices of the consignment merchants. New Virginia merchants moved to Norfolk, where they set up stores buying from the tobacco planters directly and selling them imported goods.[58] In Maryland, the firm of Wallace, Johnson, and Muir took away the customers of the prewar London merchant William Molleson by doing the same thing. Wallace, Johnson, and Muir were representative of new American practices in another way: as partners of the Philadelphia merchant Robert Morris they were among the growing number of American merchants, especially in the corridor between Richmond and Philadelphia, with business connections in several states.[59]

As soon as travel was safe, English and American merchants crossed the Atlantic in considerable numbers, each to settle in the other's territory and compete with local firms. English merchants flocked to growing ports—to Norfolk, to Charles Town, to Philadelphia—and set up their own businesses there. One English merchant took note of "the desire that prevails . . . for visiting America" and "the many applications to me for introductory letters to my friends."[60] So many came to Boston that the Boston merchants protested to the state legislature against "certain British merchants, factors, and agents from Britain, now residing in this town . . . who have received large quantities of English goods."[61] New York merchants complained of the "number of British Merchants residing here, who have it in their power to undersell us."[62] A Philadelphian lamented the decline of property values and the numerous bankruptcies in the town.[63] Rufus King predicted that the American resentment of the British mercantile invasion was so generally shared in all port cities that "the flame will communicate from state to state."[64]

Prewar London firms themselves faced an invasion though just where the new forces came from was open to question. Jefferson's acquaintances reported that in the City the American trade had been taken from the old established houses and thrown into the hands of London merchants who conducted public sales of large batches of low-priced American tobacco.[65] The letters Jefferson received implied that the new merchants were English, but Thomas Blount, an American then in London, attacked "the villainous conduct of some Americans (I may say most of them) who came over immediately after the conclusion of the war and got largely into business here."[66] The difference might be explained by the fact that Jefferson was talking about tobacco merchants (his acquaintance Edmund Pendleton in Virginia mentioned "some very low sales of tobacco from Britain at this time"[67]) while Blount was talking about others. Whichever trade they were talking about, Jefferson and Blount agreed in urging their American associates to have nothing to do with the new merchants. But it was already too late. The consignment system was headed for obsolescence.

Prewar London firms that could not survive the new competition went down in two waves: a number crashed suddenly in the crisis of 1784 and 1785, while the ones that survived this period failed over the next seven years. As early as August 1784 "no less than five great American houses tumbled in the city yesterday, one to the tune of £140,000."[68] A year later one of John Hatley Norton's correspondents noted that "several failures have lately taken place in London particularly among the American merchants and many more are expected."[69] Blount spoke of "the amazing number of bankruptcies that happen almost daily in that line." "It appears to me", he added, "that at least half the Merchants in the world must fail. We hear of little else from any quarter."[70]

Nowhere are the postwar changes revealed more clearly than in the letter book of Robert Beverley, a prewar Virginia tobacco planter who switched both his crops and his method of doing business after the war. Before the war Beverley's London factor had been Samuel Athawes. Toward the end of the Revolution, Beverley sent his oldest son to England to be educated and to cultivate useful mercantile friendships, but Athawes refused to give him help. In a fury, Beverley took his business first to Samuel Gist (who also noted the "succession of new merchants" in London in 1784) and then by 1786 to William Anderson. Over the next five years, Beverley continued to send some tobacco to Anderson, but he made two significant changes in his business. First, like many of his Chesapeake contemporaries, he began switching rapidly from tobacco into wheat (just how he handled the sales is not clear, but it appears, from the way he requests that Anderson send him information about wheat prices on various markets, that he was not consigning the wheat to Anderson). Second, by 1791 Beverley was working as Robert Beverley & Co., ordering goods for cash to sell at a local store run by Beverley's younger sons (who had never been to London). The following year Anderson sent one of his own relatives to open a store in Virginia, while Beverley's sons moved their store west to Culpepper County where tobacco planting was still strong and Beverley could attract business for his sons by taking up tobacco stemming. In 1792 he wrote of the "unexpected Revolution in the commercial and agricultural system"—a revolution Beverley himself certainly personified.[71]

Wartime disruption of American churches was evident as early as 1783; as with the mercantile communities the other difficulties in the way of reestablishing prewar ecclesiastical relations developed over the decade that followed. The most important change was that, one by one, the American churches decided it was more convenient to create their own institutions with their own constitutions and train their own ministers than it was to remain dependent on overseas sources for organization and personnel.

Baptists and Lutherans had begun organizing during the war. Within a three-month period, October to December 1984, at least four American denominations, the Dutch Reformed, Episcopal, Methodist, and Catholic, made clear their desire for separation from Europe rather than reunion. On October 8 the Synod of the Dutch Reformed Church in New York and New Jersey sent to the Classis of Amsterdam their own "measures and appointments," asking that body's approval and recognition of the Synod's independence.[72] In the same month a convention of Episcopal ministers resolved to be independent of all foreign authority, to regulate their own affairs, and to draw up a constitution.[73] They soon sent two priests to England to seek ordination as American bishops, hoping to convince English authorities that American hostility to bishops had ended with independence. In December a national convention of Methodist ministers met at Baltimore to draw up a constitution, their leaders having already written "dear old Daddy" John Wesley of their determination.[74] At the same time John Carroll set in train his own appointment as the first American Bishop of the Catholic Church by protesting vigorously, in response to a decree of the Congregation of Propaganda making Carroll simply the Superior of Missions, that American Catholic priests were not missionaries but national clergy.[75]

After the new federal Constitution had been drawn up, a number of the American churches used the creation of a strong national government as an incentive to create strong national organizations of their own and sever the last of their European ties. Upon his inauguration President

Washington received addresses from the General Assembly of the United States Presbyterian Church, the Methodist Church, the German Lutheran Ministers of the United States, the General Episcopal Convention, the Dutch Reformed Church in North America, the Yearly Meeting of Quakers from Virginia, Maryland, Pennsylvania, and Delaware, and the "Catholics of America."[76] Some of these groups, the Quaker Yearly Meeting and the Methodists, for instance, predated the inauguration; other were in the process of organizing. John Carroll had been chosen Bishop of the American Catholic Church but had not yet been consecrated. The Catholic address to Washington was signed by Carroll and four lay Catholic leaders, suggesting the beginning of a Catholic organization of clerics and laymen.[77] Shortly after the inauguration the first general assembly of the Presbyterian Church met at Philadelphia, intending "to comprehend all the future Pastors & Chhs. which may overspread the Territory from the Hudson's River westward to the Mississippi & southward to Georgia."[78] At about the same time a general convention of the Episcopal Church met, the first one in which all sections of the country were represented. Bishops from a southern and a middle state had by then been ordained in England and they were joined by a New England priest ordained, albeit somewhat questionably, in Scotland. The convention framed the constitution and canons of the Episcopal Church and by 1792 had ceased formal communication with the Church of England.[79] Also in 1792 the German Lutheran Church, which had flirted briefly with Anglicanism, established a separate organization,[80] and the same year the Warren Association approved the establishment of a general committee of Baptists in New England—hardly national but broader in scope than earlier Baptists organizations.[81] At the same time two other churches, the Dutch Reformed Synod and the German Reformed Coetus, broke from their moorings in Holland and established national organizations in the United States.[82] No one summed up better the changes in the various American churches than Edward Livingston, the head of the Dutch Reformed Church. "From being appendages of national churches in Europe," Livingston wrote, "they now become national churches themselves in this new Empire."[83]

To develop further their independence from foreign churches, American churches established or expanded universities (a number of the prewar universities had also to be repaired because of damage they received during the Revolution). These served not only to educate future ministers but also to give them a sense of unity arising from a shared educational experience. But when the universities sought to raise money through the traditional fundraising tour in England, they learned quickly that English donors were no longer responsive. Shortly after the war's end Eleazer Wheelock of Dartmouth and Benjamin Rush on behalf of Dickinson College were told by English friends that it was not worth coming over because they wouldn't get enough contributions even to cover the cost of their trip.[84] John Witherspoon actually did go to the British Isles to raise money for the College of New Jersey, and failed. He was even told in Scotland that it was inappropriate for wealthy American institutions to solicit money from impoverished Scots. When Witherspoon returned he reported to the Board of Trustees that he finally got several men in Britain to make what collections they should be able on behalf of the College and to remit it to the order of the Board, but they never did.[85] Four years later, when President Manning of the College of Rhode Island was planning to send over someone to raise money among the English Baptists, an English acquaintance warned him that he would not get any money.[86] American universities, therefore, were forced to become financially independent of England.

Meanwhile the Society for the Propagation of the Gospel had decided in 1785 to cut off the salaries of missionaries remaining in America, since the S.P.G.'s authority extended only to the British Empire.[87] Quakers too learned little by little of the changing balance between English and American wealth: in the forty years before the American Revolution far more English Quakers had visited America than American Quakers had visited England, but in a comparable period after the Revolution the figure was reversed.[88]

By the early 1790s the break between most English and American churches was complete. American Catholic, Episcopal, Methodist, Lutheran, and Presbyterian churches had established national organizations. Quakers, Baptists, and Jews had established regional organizations. Only the Congregationalists had no formal organization beyond the local level, but their ministers held informal statewide conventions. As the American organizations grew, their correspondence with English groups waned. There was less and less reason for any groups besides the Quakers to share information and exchange moral support. Even "dear old Daddy" John Wesley had stopped writing "dear Franky" (Francis Asbury, the first American Methodist Bishop) before his death. Only the Moravians could be called "appendages of national churches in Europe." Old friendships certainly remained, but as the channels of formal communication closed, the fundraising drives came to a halt, and the revival of prewar relations so eagerly sought in 1783 was no longer a possibility.

.   .   .

From now on the interwoven story of London and American interests breaks into many separate stories. In the United States the old interests stayed local in their political outlook for many years. Despite the creation of national organizations among the American churches, their lobbying efforts, like those of the merchants and the non-English, remained focused primarily on state and local politics. Their organizations, for the next decade at least, remained simple, a committee and a leader or two; their attention was directed to statewide issues and their objectives as well as their successes varied from state to state. The English interests' fortunes also varied, not from place to place but rather from group to group. Some of the interests turned their attention to broad crusades such as abolition of the slave trade (this became the cause of the Quakers and the Anglicans), became merely coffee house discussion groups (this happened to most of the mercantile lobbies), or disappeared altogether as members died or switched activities. Those that stayed active in prewar fashion, the Chesapeake merchants and the Dissenting Deputies, for example, had to regroup and reorganize as their provincial correspondents pressed the Londoners to allow them a more active role and establish truly national participation. By the end of the century politicians on both sides of the Atlantic were exploring the possibility of bringing together some of the interests in partisan coalitions, but that story belongs elsewhere—in another century and another book.

Abbreviations

Add. Mss.	*Additional Manuscripts, British Library, London*
A.P.C.	W. L. Grant and James Monroe, eds., *Acts of the Privy Council,* vols. I–VI (Liechtenstein, 1966, reprint of 1908–1912 eds.)
C.O. (P.R.O.)	Colonial Office, Public Record Office, London
C.S.P.Col, A.&W.I.	W. Noel Sainsbury, ed., *Calendar of State Papers, Colonial America and the West Indies, 1574–1732* (Vaduz, 1964, reprint of 1860–1939 ed.)
CSP	Publications of the Colonial Society of Massachusetts (Boston)
Eccl. Records, N.Y.	Hugh Hastings, ed., *Ecclesiastical Records of the State of New York,* (Albany, 1901–1916)
H.M.P.E.C.	*Historical Magazine of the Protestant Episcopal Church*
HSL*Publ*	Publications of the Huguenot Society of London
J.B.T.	*Journals of the Board of Trade* (London, 1969, reprint of 1920— ed.)
Lambeth-Fulham Mss	Records of the Bishops of London, Lambeth Palace Library, London
MHS*Coll*	Massachusetts Historical Society Collections, Boston
Minutes of Diss. Deputies	Minutes of the Dissenting Deputies, Guildhall Ms 3083/1, Guildhall Library, London
Minutes of Three Denominations	Minute Books of the Body of Protestant Dissenting Ministers of the Three Denominations in and about the Cities of London and Westminster. Dr. Williams' Library, London
NJ Col. Docs.	*Documents Relative to the Colonial History of the State of New Jersey.*
NY Col. Docs.	E. B. O'Callaghan, ed., *Documents Relative to the Colonial History of the State of New York* (Albany, 1850–)
NYHS	New York Historical Society

P.M.H.B.	*Pennsylvania Magazine of History and Biography*
PHS	Pennsylvania Historical Society
Presb. *Records*	*Records of the Presbyterian Church in the United States of America Embracing the Minutes of the General Presbytery and General Synod, 1706–1788* (New York, 1969, reprint of 1904 ed.)
Stock, *Proceedings*	Leo Francis Stock, ed., *Proceedings and Debates of the British Parliaments Respecting North America* (Washington, D.C., 1924–1941).
VHS	Virginia Historical Society
VHS*Coll*	Collections of the Virginia Historical Society
Virg. Mag.	*Virginia Magazine of History and Biography*
W.M.Q.	*William and Mary Quarterly*

Notes

Preface

1. Charles McLean Andrews, *The Colonial Period of American History: The Settlements* I (New Haven, 1964, reprint of 1934 ed.) I:xvi.
2. For a discussion of Andrews's critics see A. S. Eisenstadt, *Charles McLean Andrews: A Study in American Historical Writing* (New York, 1956), ch. 8.
3. *Essays in Colonial History Presented to Charles McLean Andrews by His Students* (New Haven, 1931).
4. Richard Johnson, "The Imperial Webb: The Thesis of Garrison Government and Militant Imperialism in Early America Re-examined." Paper read to Columbia Seminar on Early American History, New York, May 1984.
5. Review of Richard Johnson's *Adjustment to Empire,* in *Rhode Island History* 42 (1983):70.

Introduction

1. Seventeenth-century contemporaries did not use the term "interest group" at all; it is only in retrospect that historians have given it a categorical label. When in the early seventeenth century Englishmen spoke of interest, they meant only the profit gained by lending money. Later they spoke of interest as personal influence—one's "interest" with a highly placed Privy Councillor, for example. By the 1680s they had added a new concept, that of human motivation or concern—men were "bound by their own interest"—and this was indirectly transferred to groups. The "Protestant interest," a term used in 1675, seems to be the first application of this concept to a group. By the eighteenth century the term was used more often, but still applied only to people with broadly similar occupations or religious beliefs, and it referred mainly to the most visible groups in the House of Commons—the Church of England interest, the dissenting interest, the military interest, the landed and mercantile interests. As late as 1769, when Edmund Burke identified "a great official, a great professional, a great military, and a great naval

interest" as well as a landed and commercial interest in the Commons, he was still referring to very broad parliamentary groups, not the numerous special interests that were developing in England and America.

For some disagreements over the definition and role of interest groups see David Truman, *The Governmental Process: Political Interests and Public Opinion* (New York, 1962), p. 33. Truman's position is summarized in W. J. M. MacKenzie, "Pressure Groups: The Conceptual Framework," *Political Studies* 3 (1955):253, and is criticized in Roy C. Macredis, "Interest Groups in Comparative Analysis," *Journal of Politics* 23 (February, 1961):24–45. See also Charles Wilson, "Government Policy and Private Interest in Modern English History," in Wilson, ed., *Economic History and the Historian: Collected Essays* (London, 1969), pp. 149–155; Joseph La Palombara, *Interest Groups in Italian Politics* (Princeton, 1964), p. 18; Gabriel Almond and G. Bingham Powell, *Comparative Politics, A Developmental Approach* (Boston, 1966), p. 75. Samuel E. Finer describes an interest group as existing primarily for the convenience of members, not for lobbying, and distinguishes it from a lobby, which he describes as "The sum of organizations insofar as they are occupied at any point in time in trying to influence the policy of public bodies in their own direction; though (unlike political parties) never themselves prepared to undertake the direct government of the country" (*Anonymous Empire: A Study of the Lobby in Great Britain* [London, 1958], p. 3.) See also J. R. Western, *Monarchy and Revolution: The English State in the 1680's* (Totowa, N.J., 1972), pp. 166–167. Sir William Temple referred to "the public interest" in Graham Wootton, *Pressure Groups in Britain, 1720–1970* (London, 1975), p. 3. See also Edmund Burke, "Thoughts on the Cause of Present Discontents," *Works* (London, 1834), I:148. Recent political scientists would differ about whether Burke was really off the mark. Earl Latham (*The Group Basis of Politics* [Ithaca, N.Y., 1952], p. 35) considers the legislature a referee of group demands; James Burns (*Congress on Trial* [New York, 1949], p. 18) views legislators as elected lobbyists. See Harmon Ziegler, *Interest Groups in American Society* (Englewood Cliffs, N.J., 1963), p. 251. As for English politics in particular, Gabriel Almond and G. Bingham Powell argue that parliamentary committees constitute an unusually explicit form of interest group access (*Comparative Politics: A Developmental Approach* [Boston, 1966], pp. 83–84). For American politics note also Madison's identification (*Tenth Federalist*, p. 43) as "A landed interest, a manufacturing interest, a mercantile interest, a moneyed interest, with many, lesser interests."

2. "It hath ever been a policy of this State to reduce the trades of merchants of this kingdom into corporations and societies for the advancement of trade by the benefit of order and government" (*Free Trade* [1622], quoted in Ephraim Lipson, *The Economic History of England*, 6th ed. [London, 1956], II:193).

3. Robert Jackson, *Plural Societies and New States: A Conceptual Analysis* (Berkeley, 1966), p. 21. I have taken the distinction between institutional and associational interests from Gabriel Almond and James S. Coleman, *The Politics of the Developing Areas* (Princeton, 1960), pp. 33–35.

4. Compare this with similar local identification of premodern African interest groups, as described by Kenneth Little in "The Role of Voluntary Associations in West African Urbanization," (in Betty Zisk, ed., *American Political Interest Groups: Readings in Theory and Research* [Bellmont, Calif., 1969], p. 137).

5. Norman Brett James, *The Growth of Stuart London* (London, 1935). p. 475. J. R. Spurgeon notes that the goldsmiths and pewterers were entitled to exercise a "general control" over their trades throughout the kingdom as well as more stringent control over trade in the immediate area ("London during the Commonwealth," Ph.D. diss., University of Wisconsin, 1963, p. 7).

6. See Spurgeon, "London," p. 16.

7. By the mid-eighteenth century there were 198 churches in Greater London of which 69, fewer than half, were Anglican, 28 were Presbyterian, 26 Independent, 33 Baptist, 2 Quaker, 6 German or Dutch, 21 Huguenot (largely Anglican) and 3 Jewish. See E. S. de Beer, "Places of Worship in London about 1738," in A. E. J. Hollaender and William Kellaway, eds. *Studies in London History,* (London, 1969), p. 399.

8. G. D. Ramsay estimates that there were about 7,000 foreigners in London in the mid-sixteenth century, out of a total population of 80,000; *The City of London in International Politics at the Accession of Elizabeth Tudor* (Manchester, 1975), ch. 2.

9. Bryant Lillywhite, *London Coffee Houses: A Reference Book of Coffee Houses of the Seventeenth, Eighteenth, and Nineteenth Centuries* (London, 1963), passim.

10. For a brilliant general analysis of the importance of London's growth, see E. A. Wrigley, "A Simple Model of London's Importance in Changing English Society and Economy, 1650 to 1770," *Past and Present* 37 (July 1967):44–70. For disproportionate numbers of dissenters in London, see Harry Grant Plum, *Restoration Puritanism: A Study of the Growth of English Liberty* (Chapel Hill, 1943).

11. Robert P. Brenner, "Commercial Change and Political Conflict: The Merchant Community in Civil War London" (Ph.D. diss., Princeton, 1970) pp. 84, 200.

12. Ibid., pp. 340–341. One exception to the general point here concerns the Catholics, who found it far easier to flourish in London than in other towns. John Miller, *Popery and Politics in England, 1660–1688* (Cambridge, 1973). p. 25.

13. Brett James, *Growth of Stuart London,* p. 475.

14. J. P. Cooper, "Social and Economic Policies under the Commonwealth," in G. E. Aylmer, ed., *The Interregnum: The Quest for Settlement, 1646 to 1660* (London, 1972). pp. 130–131. See also Caroline Robbins, "Naturalization Under the Later Stuarts," *Journal of Modern History* 34 (June 1962):172. Peter Clark argues that migrants were unpopular in provincial towns, too ("The Migrant in Kentish Towns, 1580–1640," pp. 117–163 in Peter Clark and Paul Slack, eds., *Crisis and Order in English Towns, 1500–1700* [Toronto, 1972]).

15. See Peter Clark "Introduction," in Clark, ed., *Country Towns in Pre-Industrial England* (New York, 1981), p. 19.

16. W. T. Whitley, *A History of British Baptists* (London, 1923), p. 88.

17. Frances L. Bremer, "Increase Mather's Friends: Personal Relations and Politics in the Trans-Atlantic Congregational Network of the Seventeenth Century." Paper presented at the Organization of American Historians Meeting, April 1975.

18. After the Restoration the extension of the Thames River to the west made a connection between London and the western outposts by a system of river navigation that had not existed before.

19. For the importance of London's population, see E. A. Wrigley, "Simple Model," *Past and Present* 37 (July 1967):44–70. For the growth of inland transportation see William T. Jackman, *The Development of Transportation in Modern England,* Introduction by W. I. Chaloner (London, 1962, reprint of 1916 ed.), pp. 119–134; Edwin A. Pratt, *A History of Inland Transport and Communication in England* (London, 1912), pp. 64, 96, 97; J. A. Chartres, *Internal Trade in England, 1500–1700* (London, 1917), pp. 40–41, 46; T. S. Willan, *River Navigation in England, 1600–1750* (London, 1964, reprint of 1936 ed.), p. 133 and Maps I and II, p. 321.

20. Michael Kammen, *Empire and Interest; The American Colonies and the Politics of Mercantilism* (New York, 1970), p. 95.

1. The Civil Wars and Interregnum

1. On this subject see Jeremy Boulton, "Neighborhood Migration in Early Modern London," and Peter Clark, "Migrants in the City: The Process of Social Adaptation in English Towns, 1500–1800," in Peter Clark and David Souden, eds., *Migration and Society in Early Modern England* (Totowa, N.J., 1988) pp. 107–149, 267–291, esp. pp. 274–276. See also Roger Finlay and Beatrice Shearer, "Population Growth and Suburban Expansion," in A. L. Beier and Roger Finlay, eds., *London, 1500–1700: The Making of the Metropolis* (London, 1986) p. 50.

2. Valerie Pearl, *London and the Outbreak of the Puritan Revolution: City Government and National Politics, 1625–43 (Oxford, 1961), pp. 162–169.*

3. Ibid., p. 233.

4. Edmund Calamy, *An Historical Account of My Own Life, with Some Reflections on the Time I Have Lived In* (London, 1829), I:254. Valerie Pearl has found evidence of Scottish agents in contact with London Presbyterians in the early 1640s. "London Puritans and Scotch Fifth Columnists: A Mid-Seventeenth Century Phenomenon," in A. E. J. Hollaender and William Kellaway, eds., *Studies in London History Presented to Philip Edmund Jones* (London, 1969), pp. 232, 320, 323, 327–328.

5. J. E. Farnell, "The Navigation Act of 1651, the First Dutch War, and the London Merchant Community," *Economic History Review* 16 (1964):443–444; Robin D. Gwynn, *Huguenot Heritage: The History and Contribution of the Huguenots in Britain* (Boston, 1985), ch. 2. For the Dutch Church

see Ole Peter Grill, *Dutch Calvinists in Early Stuart London; The Dutch Church in Austin friars, 1603–1642* (Leiden, 1989) passim.

6. Irene Scouloudi, "The Stranger Community in the Metropolis," in Scouloudi, *Huguenots in Britain and their French Background, 1550–1800* (Totowa, N.J., 1987), p. 47; Patrick Collinson, "England and International Calvinism, 1558–1640" in Menna Prestwich, ed., *International Calvinism, 1541–1715* (Oxford, 1985) p. 219. Stephen Foster writes that "English Puritanism, in British historiography, has lost its capital 'P' and with the uppercase letter much of its distinctive agenda, except for brief periods of militance before 1603 and after 1633." *The Long Argument: English Puritanism and the Shaping of New England Culture, 1570–1700* (Chapel Hill, 1991), p. xiv.

7. Robert P. Brenner, "Commercial Change and Political Conflict: The Merchant Community in Civil War London" (Ph.D. diss., Princeton, 1970) p. 216.

8. Rowe is mentioned in Farnell, "Navigation Act of 1651," p. 442, and Pearl, *London,* p. 169.

9. Robert Brenner, "Civil War, Politics, and London's Merchant Community," *Past and Present* 58 (June 1973):54–55, 63.

10. Pearl, *London,* pp. 229–230, 270, 279.

11. K. N. Chaudhuri, *The English East India Company: The Study of an Early Joint-Stock Company, 1600–1640* (New York, 1965), p. 29; James A. Williamson, *The Caribbee Islands Under the Proprietary Patents* (London, 1926), p. 40. Conrad Russell suggests that in the 1630s Charles I raised his annual income to about £1,000,000 mainly through increases in customs. Russell argues that such an income should have been adequate to sustain the King, even in war, and it is therefore quite puzzling that the King had to call Parliament when war with Scotland broke out ("Parliament and the King's Finances," in Conrad Russell, ed., *The Origins of the English Civil War* [London, 1973], p. 108). The King's support of interlopers in the international trade was paralleled by his creation in 1636 of a new corporation in the City which included artisans and tradesmen. The new corporation was a potential rival to the City government. Reginald R. Sharpe, *London and the Kingdom: A History* (London, 1894), II:117. For more on the City's loans, see Robert Ashton, *The Crown and the Money Market, 1603–1640* (Oxford, 1960), pp. 127, 239, 132, 185.

12. Leslie A. Clarkson, *The Pre-Industrial Economy in England; 1500–1750* (New York, 1972), p. 140.

13. Theodore K. Rabb, *Enterprise and Empire: Merchant and Gentry Investment in the Expansion of England, 1575–1630* (Cambridge, Mass., 1967), pp. 35–70; 92–96.

14. Brenner, "Civil War Politics," p. 76.

15. Pearl, *London,* pp. 122–147; 154–157.

16. Brenner, "Civil War Politics," pp. 99–101. J. R. Spurgeon, "London during the Commonwealth" (Ph.D. diss., University of Wisconsin, 1963), passim.

17. William Kennedy, *English Taxation, 1640 to 1799: An Essay on Policy and Opinion* (London, 1964, reprint of 1913 ed.), pp. 24–28.

18. These titles are taken from Brenner, "Commercial Change and Political Conflict," pp. 228, 231.

19. Jan. 6, 1640–41 (House of Commons). Stock *Proceedings*, I:103.

20. Feb. 18, Mar. 18, 1640–41 (House of Lords). Ibid., pp. 105, 107, 109.

21. Letter of Mar. 17, 1645, read in House of Commons on Oct. 16, 1646. Ibid., pp. 182–183.

22. William Haller, *Liberty and Reformation in the Puritan Revolution* (New York, 1955), pp. 17, 23.

23. Claire Cross, "The Church in England, 1646–1660," in G. E. Aylmer, ed., *The Interregnum: The Quest for Settlement, 1646 to 1660* (London, 1972), pp. 100–103.

24. Haller, *Liberty and Reformation*, pp. 134–140.

25. Pearl, *London*, pp. 233–234.

26. See Farnell, "Navigation Act of 1651," pp. 441–442; Blair Worden, *The Rump Parliament, 1648–1653* (Cambridge, 1974), pp. 256, 230.

27. Mary Cathcart Borer, *The City of London: A History* (London, 1977), pp. 210–213.

28. November 29, 1653, and November 15, 1656. Stock; *Proceedings*, I:233, 238.

29. Albert M. Hyamson, *A History of the Jews in England* (London, 1928), pp. 163–166.

30. Cross, "Church in England," in Aylmer, *Interregnum*, p. 104.

31. Ibid., p. 117.

32. W. T. Whitley, *History of British Baptists*, (London, 1923) p. 88.

33. Cross, "Church in England," in Aylmer, *Interregnum*, p. 108; George R. Abernathy, Jr., "The English Presbyterians and the Stuart Restoration, 1648–1663," *Transactions of the American Philosophical Society*, n.s. 55, pt. 2 (Philadelphia, 1965):7.

34. B. R. White, "The Organization of the Particular Baptists, 1644–1660," *Journal of Ecclesiastical History* 17 (October 1966): 209–211, 226.

35. Whitley, *History of British Baptists*, pp. 88–90, 92–93.

36. William C. Braithwaite, *The Beginnings of Quakerism* (Cambridge, 1961), pp. 333–334, 337.

37. Abernathy, "English Presbyterians," p. 13.

38. Ibid., p. 17.

39. Hugh Barbour, *Quakers in Puritan England* (New Haven, 1964), p. 50.

40. White, "Particular Baptists," p. 226.

41. W. T. Whitley, ed., *Minutes of the General Assembly of the General Baptist Churches in England, 1654–1728* (London, 1908), I:1–2.

42. Abernathy, "English Presbyterians," p. 16.

43. Barbour, *Quakers in Puritan England*, pp. 199–200.

44. Christopher Hill, *The Century of Revolution, 1603–1714* (New York, 1966) p. 105.

45. Pearl, *London*, pp. 233–234.

46. Worden, *The Rump Parliament*, pp. 256–258.

47. Note Maurice Ashley's point that merchants in the Cromwellian period were tending to concentrate more on one line of business, though nothing

like the way merchants in the Netherlands specialized. Ashley concludes that "the question of specialization is very difficult." *Financial and Commercial Policy under the Cromwellian Protectorate* (London, 1962), p. 14.

48. Cross, "Church in England," in Aylmer, *Interregnum*, pp. 118–119.

49. Abernathy, "English Presbyterians," p. 13. Throughout the Restoration Congregationalists and Presbyterians were attempting to agree formally on terms of cooperation. (Roger Thomas, "The Break-Up of Non-Conformity," in Geoffrey F. Nuttall et al., *The Beginnings of Non-Conformity* (London, 1964), p. 34.

2. Restoration England

1. See Brian Dietz, "Overseas Trade and Metropolitan Growth" in A. L. Beier and Roger Finlay, eds., *London 1500–1700: The Making of the Metropolis* (London, 1986), esp. pp. 121–33; Ralph Davis, "English Foreign Trade, 1660–1700," in E. M. Carus Wilson, ed., *Essays in Economic History* (London, 1962), II:257–272, and J. M. Sosin, *English America and the Restoration Monarchy of Charles II: Transatlantic Politics, Commerce, and Kinship* (Lincoln, Neb., 1980) pp. 110–23.

2. [May 14], June 13, [Sept. 6], 1662; Jan. 8, 1668. *C.S.P. Col., A & W I* #301, 311, 365, 406.

3. March 7, 1670-71 (House of Commons). Stock, *Proceedings,* I:373–374.

4. One exception to this might be the merchants trading to Maryland. In the 1650s they appear to have met in the same coffee house with the merchants of Virginia. They may have continued to do so after 1660 though the name of the coffee house did not include Maryland. It is not clear whether the Virginia Coffee House is the old Maryland and Virginia Coffee House or a different building.

5. *C.S.P.Col., A & WI,* #28.

6. Jan. 21, 1675. Journals of the Lords of Trade, 1675–1677, I:63, PHS.

7. Ibid., pp. 70, 111. See also the petition of "several merchants," presumably those trading to New England, against the irregularity of New England trade (April 6, 1676). Ibid., p. 53.

8. June [ ] 1684. Ibid., IX:311.

9. Lillian M. Penson, *The Colonial Agents of the British West Indies: A Study in Colonial Administration, Mainly in the Eighteenth Century* (London, 1971, reprint of 1924 ed.), pp. 177, 178, 182–184.

10. Norman Sykes, *From Sheldon to Secker: Aspects of English Church History, 1660–1768* (Cambridge, 1959), p. 41.

11. Christopher Hill, *The Century of Revolution* (New York, 1966), p. 243.

12. Frank Bate, *The Declaration of Indulgence, 1672: A Study in the Rise of Organized Dissent* (Liverpool, 1968, reprint of 1908 ed.), p. 60.

13. Douglas R. Lacey, *Dissent and Parliamentary Politics in England, 1661–1689* (New Brunswick, N.J., 1969), p. 103. A. T. Gary, "The Political and Economic Relations of English and American Quakers, 1750–1783" (D. Phil., St. Hugh's, Oxford, 1935), pp. 20–21; Charles Edwin Whiting, *Stud-*

ies in English Puritanism from the Restoration to the Revolution, 1660–1688 (London, 1968), p. 220.

    On July 19, 1661, when the House of Commons was considering a bill "for preventing the mischiefs and dangers that may arise by certain persons called Quakers and others, refusing to take lawful oaths," several Quakers appeared at the door of the House with a petition against it. There is no evidence what meeting they represented. The act became law on May 2, 1662 (Stock, *Proceedings*, I:290, 305).

14. Lacey, *Dissent and Parliamentary Politics*, p. 107; Ethyn Williams Kirby, "The Quakers' Efforts to Secure Civil and Religious Liberty, 1660–1696," *Journal of Modern History* 7 (December 1935): 401–421.
15. Whiting, *Studies in English Puritanism*, pp. 95, 115.
16. Ibid., p. 63.
17. Lacey, *Dissent and Parliamentary Politics*, p. 104.
18. Dec. 5, 1686. E. S. DeBeer, ed., *Diary of John Evelyn*, (London, 1959), pp. 856, 363, 368, 446, 543.
19. See Malcolm Thorpe, "The English Government and Huguenot Settlement, 1680–1702" (Ph.D. diss., University of Wisconsin, 1972), pp. 130, 164 for collections. The money was to be distributed by the committee working with the Archbishop of Canterbury and the Bishop of London, among others. A. P. Hands and Irene Scouloudi, "French Protestant Refugees Relieved through the Threadneedle Street Church, London, 1681—1687," HSL *Publ* 49 (1971):1. For the refusal to help one particular Huguenot because he was not Anglican, see Ann Maury, *Memoirs of a Huguenot Family* (Baltimore, 1967, reprint of 1853 ed.), pp. 135–139.
20. Thomas Firman, *Some Proposals for the Employment of the Poor* (London, 1681), p. 29. See also David Owen, *English Philanthropy, 1660–1860* (Cambridge, Mass., 1964), pp. 17–19.
21. This is arguable. See J. R. Jones, *Country and Court; England 1658–1714* (Cambridge, Mass., 1978), p. 45. Improvements in tax collecting are discussed by Howard Tomlinson, "Financial and Administrative Development in England, 1660–88," in Jones, ed., *The Restored Monarchy, 1660–1688* (Totowa, N.J., 1979), pp. 100–101.
22. This explanation is drawn from C. D. Chandaman, *The English Public Revenue, 1660–1688* (Oxford, 1975), pp. 11, 87n, 91 and n, 264, 268, 270, 127, 348–349, 352–353, 356–357, and 360–361; C. A. F. Mekings, "The City Loans on the Hearth Tax, 1664–1668," in A. E. J. Hollaender and William Kellaway, eds., *Studies in London History Presented to Philip Edmund Jones* (London, 1969), p. 336; E. Lipson, *The Economic History of England*, 6th ed. (London, 1956) 11:247. City loans are listed in Reginald R. Sharpe, *London and the Kingdom: A History* (London, 1894), pp. 378, 389, 399, 403, 414, 455.
23. Frank Tomkins Melton, "London and Parliament: An Analysis of a Constituency, 1661 to 1702" (Ph.D. diss., University of Wisconsin, 1969), pp. 159–166; E. A. Wrigley, "Model of London's Importance," *Past and Present* 37 (July 1967):45–54. The marked decline in the European wool market hurt the Merchant Adventurers, men who had dominated and given

some unity of purpose to London's major livery companies, so badly that the organization became extinct by the end of the century. At the time of the Restoration in 1660 the King's royalist supporters were restored to power in the City, and the Court of Aldermen, dominated as it was by the companies, revived the traditionalist committee to examine parliamentary matters concerning the City. After 1671, however, the City Members of Parliament no longer worked with this committee but spoke on behalf of particular economic interests within the City.

24. Essential to understanding the voluntary interests' acquisition of power in the City government is Gary Stuart de Krey, *A Fractured Society: The Politics of London in the First Age of Party, 1688–1715* (Oxford, 1985) esp. pp. 76, 87, 99–106, 111–112, 125, 128, 136–141.

25. Basil Duke Henning estimates that 17 percent of the M.P.s were Presbyterian or "probably" Presbyterian, and another 9 percent were Independent. *The House of Commons, 1660–1690* (London, 1983) I:13.

26. June 1, 1685. Stock, *Proceedings*, I:425.

27. Lacey, *Dissent and Parliamentary Politics*, pp. 101, 104.

28. Ibid., p. 119.

29. Ibid., p. 113.

30. Ibid., p. 109.

31. Bate, *Declaration of Indulgence*, p. 60.

32. Ronald Hutton suggests this particularly for the Quakers: *The Restoration: A Political and Religious History of England and Wales, 1658–1667* (Oxford, 1985), p. 287. Richard L. Greaves, "The Radical Tradition in Britain, 1660–1688; A Retrospect" (paper given at the Millersville Conference, April 1991), discusses the limited participation of dissenters in "radical" riots.

33. Lacey, *Dissent and Parliamentary Politics*, pp. 160–162, 170–173. Tim Harris, *London Crowds in the Reign of Charles II: Propaganda and Politics from the Restoration until the Exclusion Crisis* (Cambridge, 1987), esp. p. 94.

34. John Brewer, *The Sinews of Power: War, Money, and the English State, 1688–1783* (Cambridge, Mass., 1990), p. 221.

35. J. H. Plumb, *The Growth of Political Stability in England, 1675–1725* (London, 1967), p. 13.

36. J. E. Neale, *Elizabethan House of Commons* (New Haven, 1950), p. 390. Ian Archer, "The London Lobbies in the Later Sixteenth Century," *The Historical Journal* 31 (1988):17–44; Edwin Green, "The Vintner's Lobby, 1552–1568, *Guildhall Studies in London History* 1 (April 1974):47–58.

37. Some of the most blatant forms of bribery were now being discouraged by the House of Commons. See Anchitell Grey, ed., *Debates of the House of Commons from the Year 1667 to the Year 1672* (London, 1763), I:16–17, 46.

38. [May 14], May 26, June 13, 1662. *C.S.P. Col., A. & W.I.*, #301, 307, 309.

39. Lacey, *Dissent and Parliamentary Politics*, pp. 99–100. Parliament passed an act forbidding "tumultuous petitioning."

40. March 4, 1671. Stock, *Proceedings*, I:371–372.

41. Lacey, *Dissent and Parliamentary Politics*, p. 103.
42. *The Diary of John Milward, Esq., Member of Parliament for Derbyshire, September 1666 to May 1668,* Caroline Robbins, ed. (Cambridge, 1938), pp. 165, 197, 203, 238–239. Carolyn Edie, "The Irish Cattle Bills: A Study in Restoration Politics," *Transactions of the American Philosophical Society* n.s. 60, pt. 2 (Philadelphia, 1970), pp. 50–57. H. Horwitz, ed., *The Parliamentary Diary of Narcissus Luttrell, 1691–93* (Oxford, 1972), pp. 169–352.
43. For merchants, see "Parliament and the Proposal for a Council of Trade," *English Historical Review* 54 (1939):41; "Letter to the Lord Mayor and Aldermen of London," August 17, 1660. *A.P.C.,* I, #448.
44. D. N. Griffiths, "Huguenot Links with St. George's Chapel, Windsor," HSL *Proc.* 22 (1976):498.
45. Bate, *Declaration of Indulgence*, p. 8. R. A. Beddard argues that "The Court worked hard and long to implement the Breda Declaration"; see "The Restoration Church" in Jones, ed., *The Restored Monarchy,* p. 160.
46. Ibid., p. 77.
47. Hugh Barbour, *Quakers in Puritan England* (New Haven, 1964) p. 227; Albert M. Hyamson, *A History of the Jews in England* (London, 1928) p. 174.
48. For a general background to this problem, see Betty Kemp, *King, Lords and Commons, 1660–1832* (London, 1957), and Kemp, "King and Commons, 1660–1832," in Joan Thirsk, ed., *The Restoration* (London, 1976), ch. 12.
49. Lacey, *Dissent and Parliamentary Politics*, pp. 184, 170–172.
50. Ibid., pp. 198–199.
51. Seen in the light of London interest group experience in the 1680s, the behavior of Massachusetts was little different from that of the others: after pushing the King to allow them to retain their charter, they sought alternately to ignore the King's authority, defend themselves in court against his *quo warranto* proceedings, and join with his enemies. Like all interest groups they were hampered by the King's vacillation as well as his objection to receiving petitions from any groups except legally established institutions, and his responsiveness to bribes so large that only the well established interests could afford them.

3. The Beginnings of Interest Groups

1. Carl Bridenbaugh, *Cities in the Wilderness: The First Century of Urban Life in America, 1625–1742* (New York, 1964, reprint of 1938 ed.), pp. 102, 39; Jerry Patterson, *The City of New York* (New York, 1978), p. 40; Thomas F. Archdeacon, *New York City, 1664–1710: Conquest and Change* (Ithaca, N.Y.), pp. 72–86.
2. Samuel Sewall reported discussing sailings with ship captains at the coffee house (Oct. 24, 1688; Halsey Thomas, ed., *The Diary of Samuel Sewall, 1674–1729,* 2 vols. [New York, 1973], I:181). Pamphlets such as *The Declaration of the Gentlemen, Merchants and Inhabitants of Boston, and*

the Country Adjacent (Boston, 1689) were advertised as being sold by Benjamin Harris at the London Coffee House.

3. Bridenbaugh, *Cities,* pp. 38, 103, 109, 95; Justin Windsor, ed., *The Memorial History of Boston: Early and Colonial Periods* (Boston, 1880), I:195–213.

4. New York carters organized to resist an order to remove dirt from the streets for 3 pence a load. They were threatened with discharge, submitted, and paid a fine. Mariana Van Rensselaer, *History of the City of New York in the Seventeenth Century* (New York, 1909).

   As late as 1704 Philadelphia's sixteen carters were summoned by the Common Council of that city and admonished to be careful in driving carts through the city, and four years later an ordinance against "excessive driving" was also passed by the Council (Dec. 1, 1704; Nov. 22, 1708; and Feb. 4, 1708/9). *Minutes of the Common Council of the City of Philadelphia, 1704 to 1776* (Philadelphia, 1847), pp. 6–7, 37, 59. For Boston bakers, see May 11 and Oct. 12, 1681, and August 12, 1685, in Nathaniel B. Shurtleff, ed., *Records of the Governor and Company of the Massachusetts Bay in New England* (1674–1686) (Boston, 1968, reprint of 1864 ed.), V:317, 322, 498–499.

5. For Boston's negotiations with the carters see the town records for Jan. 13, 1670/1; March 11, 1671/2; March 16, 1673; March 12, 1676/7; and Sept. 16, 1689. *A Report of the Records Commissioners of the City of Boston, Containing the Boston Records from 1660 to 1701* (Boston, 1881), VII:59, 66, 85, 99, 197.

6. Bridenbaugh, *Cities,* p. 104.

7. Ibid., pp. 95, 103; Arthur Henry Hirsch, *The Huguenots of Colonial South Carolina* (London, 1962, reprint of 1928 ed.), p. 51; Edward G. Lilly, *Historic Churches of Charleston, South Carolina* (Charleston, 1966), sect. 1 (no page given). Harriot Horry Ravenel, *Charleston: The Place and the People* (New York, 1931), pp. 18–20.

8. Bridenbaugh, *Cities,* pp. 95, 103–104.

9. Meeting of Selectmen, Dec. 23, 1690–91. *Town Records of Salem, Massachusetts, 1680–1691* (Salem, 1934), III:240.

10. Taunton, Salem, Marblehead, Newbury.

11. Patricia U. Bonomi, *A Factious People* (New York, 1971), pp. 26–28.

12. Rev. Yoe, May 25, 1676. Ernest Trice Thompson, *Presbyterians in the South, 1607–1861* (Richmond, 1963), I:18.

13. Peter O. Wacher, *Land and People, A Cultural Geography of Preindustrial New Jersey: Origins and Settlement Patterns* (New Brunswick, N.J., 1975), pp. 187, 188, 167. Wacher's maps for these groups generally cover the period up to 1700.

14. For the desire of Huguenot communities to be isolated see R. A. Brock, ed., *Documents, Chiefly Unpublished, Relating to the Huguenot Emigration to Virginia and to the Settlement at Manakin-town.* (Baltimore, 1962, reprint of 1886 ed.), pp. 54–60.

15. June 20–July 13, 1672. John L. Nicholls, ed., *The Journal of George Fox* (Cambridge, 1952); Arthur J. Worrall, *Quakers in the Colonial Northeast* (Nanover, N.H., 1980), pp. 63–67.

16. Robert Frances Scholz, "The Reverend Elders: Faction, Fellowship and Politics in the Ministerial Community of Massachusetts Bay, 1630 to 1710" (Ph.D. diss., University of Minnesota, 1966), pp. 223–224.

17. See, for example, Ministers of New York and Long Island to the Classis of Amsterdam (1680) lamenting that they cannot meet as often as once a year. *Eccl. Records, N.Y.*, II:754.

18. Blair later explained this in "Answer to Queries put by the Bishop of London to Persons who were Commissaries to my Predecessor" (1724), William Stevens Perry, ed., *Historical Collections Relating to the American Colonial Church* (Virginia) (Hartford, Conn., 1890) I:252.

19. See Worrall, *Quakers in the Colonial Northeast.*

20. Rufus M. Jones, *The Quakers in the American Colonies* (London, 1923), p. 294.

21. Scholz, "Reverend Elders," pp. 223–224.

22. Ministers of New York and Long Island to the Classis of Amsterdam (1680). *Eccl. Records, N.Y.*, II:754.

23. Bernard Bailyn, *The New England Merchants in the Seventeenth Century* (Cambridge, Mass., 1955), p. 190.

24. Governor Nichols's answer to queries, April 16, 1678. E. B. O'Callaghan, ed., *The Documentary History of the State of New York* (Albany, 1850), III:61.

25. June 2, 1692. "Proceedings and Acts of the General Assembly of Maryland, April 1684 to June 1692," in William Hand Browne, ed., *Archives of Maryland* (Baltimore, 1894), XIII:552.

26. "The Andros Tracts," 2, *Prince Society Publications* (New York, 1971, reprint of 1869 ed.), VI:236–237.

27. Nathaniel Byfield, *An Account of a Late Revolution in England* (Boston, 1689).

28. Governor Dongan to Lords of Trade, 1787, quoted in Jerry Patterson, *The City of New York* (New York, 1978) p. 40.

29. H. Selyns to Classis of Amsterdam, Oct. 28, 1682, and Oct. 21/31, 1683. *Eccl. Records, N.Y.*, II:829–830, 868.

30. Fox, *Journals,* pp. 620, 635, 641.

31. The establishment of the Corresponding Committees is recorded in Minutes of the New England Yearly Meeting, 14/4 mo. 1686. For a general discussion of the correspondence of English dissenters and New England Puritans see David Cressy, *Coming Over: Migration and Communication between England and New England in the Seventeenth Century* (Cambridge, 1987), pp. 228, 256–262.

32. Blair's correspondence is in Perry, *Collections, Virginia,* I, passim. See also Daniel Esten Motley, "The Life of Commissary James Blair," *The Johns Hopkins University Studies in History and Political Science* 19 no. 10 (Baltimore, 1901), and George MacLaren Brydon, *Virginia's Mother Church and the Political Conditions under Which it Grew* (Richmond, 1947) ch. 20.

33. Thomas F. Archdeacon, *New York City, 1664–1710: Conquest and Change* (Ithaca, N.Y., 1976), p. 72.

34. Marion Balderston, ed., *James Claypoole's Letter Book, London and Philadelphia, 1681–1684* (San Marino, Calif., 1967), p. 18.
35. The correspondence is in vol. VI, Lambeth-Fulham Mss.
36. Richard Beale Davis, *William Fitzhugh and His Chesapeake World, 1676–1701.*
37. Malcolm R. Thorpe, "The English Government and Huguenot Settlement, 1680–1702" (Ph.D. diss., University of Wisconsin, 1972), p. 90.
38. Balderston, ed., *James Claypoole's Letter Book*, p. 18.
39. William Fitzhugh to Nicholas Hayward, May 20, 1686; Davis, *Fitzhugh,* p. 189; *A Huguenot Exile in Virginia, or Voyages of a Frenchman Exiled for His Religion, With a Description of Virginia and Maryland* (New York, 1734, copy of 1687 ed.), p. 159.
40. Francis J. Bremer, "Increase Mather's Friends: Personal Relations and Politics in the Trans-Atlantic Congregational Network of the Seventeenth Century." Paper given at the Organization of American Historians Meeting, April 1978, p. 28.
41. Edwin Bronner, "Quaker Discipline and Order, 1680–1720," in Richard S. Dunn and Mary Maples Dunn, eds., *The World of William Penn* (Philadelphia, 1986), pp. 332–333.
42. Brydon, *Virginia's Mother Church*, pp. 225, 173–174.
43. March 7, 1670/1; March 29 and 31 and June 11, 1685. Stock, *Proceedings,* pp. 373–374, 381, 428.
44. David E. Vandeventer, *The Emergence of Provincial New Hampshire, 1623–1741* (Baltimore, 1976), pp. 135–136.
45. Until well into the Restoration, English authorities did not like to encourage local interests at the expense of colonial governments. See, for example, instructions to commissioners sent out to determine New England boundaries (To Governors of New England Apr. 23, 1664. (*NY Col. Docs.,* II:237).
46. Petition to James II, May 9, 1688. H. L. McIlwaine, ed., *Journals of the House of Burgesses of Virginia, 1659/60 to 1693* (Richmond, 1914), pp. 317–318.
47. Urian Oakes, *New England Pleaded With* (Cambridge, 1673), p. 36.
48. Governor Dudley to the Board of Trade, Feb. 28, 1706. C.O.5/912 ff175–176.
49. See J. M. Sosin, *English America and the Restoration Monarchy of Charles II: Transatlantic Politics, Commerce, and Kinship* (Lincoln, Neb., 1980) pp. 90–91.
50. Brydon, *Virginia's Mother Church,* p. 183.
51. Richard R. Johnson, *Adjustment to Empire; The New England Colonies 1675–1715* (New Brunswick, 1981), pp. 64, 137–143. Johnson refers to Increase Mather's "backstairs diplomacy" (p. 143).
52. A New York City petition to the Lords directed against Jacob Leisler in 1690 was signed by town councillors "as well as . . . the ministers and Rulers of the Reformed Churches and others the chiefest freeholders merchants of this province," but neither London dissenters nor London mer-

chants trading to New York supported it. (There is no mention of the petition in the correspondence of New York ministers in *Eccl. Records, N.Y.*, II:943–1007.) In their last ten years, 1686–1696, the Lords of Trade considered twenty-five issues affecting colonial interest groups. Twenty-one were appealed directly from the colonies.

53. Petition of French Protestants of New York to Governor Dongan, [ ] 1686/ 9. *NY Col. Docs.* III:419.

54. Council Minutes, June 1 and 23, 1687. Robert Nixon Toppan, "Andros Records," *Proceedings of the American Antiquarian Society*, n.s. 13 (April 1899 to April 1900) (Worcester, Mass., 1901): pp. 468–479; Huguenot Complaint, July 14, 1687, and Andros to Narragansett J.P.s, August 5, 1687. John Russell Bartlett, ed., *Records of the Colony of Rhode Island and Providence Plantations in New England* (Providence, 1858), III:227– 228.

55. Laurence H. Leder, *Robert Livingston, 1654–1728, and the Politics of Colonial New York* (Chapel Hill, 1961), pp. 185–190.

56. Nov. 24, 1697, *C.S.P. Col., A & WI* #56. For Penn's influence in gaining the Pennsylvania charter see "The Peaceable Kingdom: Quaker Pennsylvania in the Stuart Empire," in Dunn and Dunn, eds., *The World of William Penn*, pp. 173–194.

57. Richard Dunn, "John Winthrop, Jr.," *W.M.Q.* 3d ser. 12 (Jan. 1956):80.

58. Mather's friendship with Ashurst and others is detailed in Bremer's paper, "Increase Mather's Friends," p. 36. See Johnson, *Adjustment to Empire*, pp. 136–182, and Michael G. Hall, *Increase Mather, the Last American Puritan* (Middletown, Conn., 1988).

4. The Development of English Interests

1. These figures are derived from the *C.S.P. Col., A & WI* pp. 11–15, checked against the relevant volumes in the C.O.5 series. Parliamentary figures are derived from Stock, *Proceedings*, I and II. I have also used Dora Mae Clark, *The Rise of the British Treasury* (New Haven, 1960), p. 85, and a letter to me from Jacob Price, April 2, 1980.

2. E. A. Wrigley, "A Simple Model of London's Importance in Changing English Society and Economy, 1650–1750," *Past and Present* 37(1967):44– 70. For the ever-changing position of the mercantile interests in City politics see Gary Stuart de Krey, *A Fractured Society: The Politics of London in the First Age of Party, 1688–1715* (Oxford, 1985), pp. 125–137; Nicholas Rogers, *Whigs and Cities: Popular Politics in the Age of Walpole and Pitt* (Oxford, 1989), p. 142; and Henry Horwitz, "Party in a Civic Contest: London from the Exclusion Crisis to the Fall of Walpole," in Clyve Jones, ed., *Britain in the First Age of Party, 1680–1750: Essays Presented to Geoffrey Holmes* (London, 1987), pp. 191–192.

3. For the concentration of nonconformists in London see Harry Grant Plum, *Restoration Puritanism: A Study of the Growth of English Liberty* (Chapel Hill, 1943), p. 71. For London's help to the provinces see Duncan Coomer,

English Dissent under the Early Hanoverians (London, 1946), p. 56, and Carl Bridenbaugh, *Mitre and Sceptre: Transatlantic Faiths, Ideas, Personalities, and Politics, 1689–1775* (New York, 1962), p. 36.

4. The location of foreign and English dissenting churches is given in Walter Besant, *London in the Eighteenth Century* (London, 1925), p. 627, and for a slightly later period in E. S. DeBeer, "Places of Worship in London about 1738," in A. E. J. Hollander and William Kellaway, eds., *Studies in London History* (London, 1969), pp. 393–402. The locations are shown on Nicholas Rocque's map of London (London, 1746).

    For the Huguenot population in London see especially Malcolm Thorpe, "The English Government and Huguenot Settlements, 1680 to 1702" (Ph.D. diss., University of Wisconsin, 1972), p. 18; Robin D. Gwynn, "The Distribution of Refugees in England: London and Its Environs," HSL *Proc* 62:323; Raymond Smith, "The Archives of the French Protestant Church of London, a Handlist," HSL *Publ* 50 (1972):61.

5. The locations of the coffee houses are given in Bryant Lillywhite, *London Coffee Houses* (London, 1963), passim. In the years before directories the best source for addresses was the merchants' correspondence. This description was obtained by locating the available addresses on a contemporary map of London.

6. Thorpe, "The English Government and Huguenot Settlement," p. 71; Smith, "The Archives of the French Protestant Church of London," pp. 89–92; Roy A. Sundstrom, "Aid and Assimilation: A Study of the Economic Support given French Protestants in England, 1680–1727" (Ph.D. diss., Kent State University, 1972), passim.

7. Albert M. Hyamson, *A History of the Jews in England* (London, 1928), p. 88.

8. Bridenbaugh, *Mitre and Sceptre*, pp. 25–26. General histories are David Humphreys, *An Historical Account of the Incorporated Societies for the Propagation of the Gospel in Foreign Parts* (London, 1730), and Charles I. Pascoe, *Two Hundred Years of the S.P.G.* (London, 1901). W. K. Lowther Clarke, *The History of the S.P.C.K.* (London, 1959), ch. 1.

9. Douglas R. Lacey, *Dissent and Parliamentary Politics in England, 1661–1681* (New Brunswick, N.J., 1969), pp. 106–107; A. T. Gary, "The Political and Economic Relations of English and American Quakers, 1750–1785" (D.Phil. diss., St. Hugh's, Oxford, 1935), pp. 32–33; I. K. Steele, "The Board of Trade, the Quakers, and Resumption of Colonial Charters, 1699–1702," *WMQ* 3d ser. 23 (1966): 610n; Alison G. Olson, "The London Quakers' Lobbying for Pennsylvania Friends" (forthcoming, *P.M.H.B.*) London Meeting for Sufferings, Epistles Sent, II, 1704–1738, Index; Minutes of November 29, 1716 and August 4, 1717. In Friends Meeting House, London.

10. Bridenbaugh, *Mitre and Sceptre*, pp. 35–39; Address to New England ministers, Feb. or March, 1714–15, Cotton Mather to Dr. Daniel Williams et al. (1715); Thomas Reynolds to Cotton Mather, June 9, 1715; "Diary of Cotton Mather, 1709–1724," *MHS Coll* 7th ser., 7 (1912):300–303, 317–319.

11. See W. T. Whitley, *History of the English Baptists* (London, 1923), passim.

12. Garold N. Davis, *German Thought and Culture in England, 1700–1770* (Chapel Hill, 1969), p. 45.

13. *Bevis Marks Records: Being Contributions to the History of the Spanish and Portuguese Congregation of London; The Early History of the Congregation from the Beginning until 1800* (Oxford, 1940), p. 35.

14. Threadneedle Church Letterbook, Huguenot Society, London. Letters of August 27, 1699, August 25, 1700, May 19, 1700.

15. Lillywhite, *London Coffee Houses* pp. 387, 408, 147–148. Coffee house growth can also be attributed to the growing need for maritime insurance especially after the loss of the Smyrna fleet in 1693: insurance was sold at the houses. Harold E. Raynes, *A History of British Insurance* (New York, 1983, reprint of 1950 London ed.), p. 98.

16. London merchants to William Popple, 18 February 1698. C.O.5/1042 f10. Petition of the London merchants trading to New York to the House of Commons, 14 February 1699/1700. C.O.5/1042 f11, f107.

17. Micajah Perry wrote William Popple on October 11, 1711, that "The Trade have agreed yesterday at Exchange to be at Whitehall on Friday morning." C.O.5/1363 f333.

18. Memorial from merchants to Maryland, September 22, 1710. C.O.5/727 n.f.

19. N. C. Hunt, *Two Early Political Associations* (Oxford, 1961), p. 147. Core group lobbying was expensive. See John Brewer, *The Sinews of Power: War, Money, and the English State, 1688–1783* (Cambridge, Mass, 1990), pp. 236–237.

20. Ethyn Williams Kirby, "The Quakers' Efforts to Secure Civil and Religious Liberty, 1660–1696," *Journal of Modern History* 17 (Dec. 1935):413–420. The negotiation with the Lords occurred in 1696 on the bill to allow Quakers to make an affirmation in cases where they would otherwise have been required to swear an oath.

21. Jacob Price, *France and the Chesapeake: A History of the French Tobacco Monopoly, 1674–1791, and of Its Relationship to the British and American Tobacco Trades* (Ann Arbor, Mich., 1973), pp. 520–523.

22. I. K. Steele, "The Board of Trade, the Quakers and the Resumption of Colonial Charters, 1699–1702," *W.M.Q.*, 3d ser., 23 (1966):596–619. Steele attributes this to indifference rather than to the Quakers' active support.

23. One question I have not taken up in this analysis is, how important was it that Members of Parliament were not required to reside in the constituencies they represented? This may have increased the relative weight of London in national politics and with it the importance of interest groups there.

24. For the tremendous expansion in government and a breakdown of employees in administrative departments, 1692–1755, see Brewer, *Sinews of Power*, p. 66, and J. H. Plumb, *The Growth of Political Stability in England, 1675–1725* (London, 1967), ch 4. Ian Steele, *The English Atlantic, 1675–1740: An Exploration of Communication and Community* Oxford, 1986), gives

an excellent explanation of improved communications; see esp. pp. 113–188, 229–250.

25. The Board's Commission is published in *NY Col. Docs.* IV:145–148. See also Alison G. Olson, "The Board of Trade and London—American Interest Groups in the Eighteenth Century," in Peter Marshall and Glyn Williams, eds., *The British Atlantic Empire before the American Revolution* (London, 1980), pp. 33–50; I. K. Steele, *The Politics of Colonial Policy: The Board of Trade in Colonial Administration, 1696–1720* (Oxford, 1968).

26. Some of the English merchants who had originally pressed for creation of the Board in the 1690s had hoped that merchants might be represented on the Board, and some proposals went so far as to suggest an elected council of merchants (R. M. Lees, "Parliament and the Proposal for a Council of Trade, 1695–96," *English Historical Review,* 54 (1939):46–47. But had some groups been represented and others not, the Board would have been regarded as partial; had all the important interests been represented, politicians might have distrusted the Board as a rival to Parliament. For an earlier proposal along these lines, see the Letter to the Lord Mayor and Aldermen of London, 17 Aug., 1660, *A.P.C.,* p. 488.

27. The lists of customs officials for 1710 and 1760 are in Thomas C. Barrow, *Trade and Empire: The British Customs Service in Colonial America* (Cambridge, Mass., 1967), pp. 261–264. John J. McCusker and Russell R. Menard, *The Economy of British America, 1607–1789* (Chapel Hill, 1985), have very useful charts on English trade; see esp. p. 40. Note also R. P. Thomas and D. N. McCloskey, "Overseas Trade and Empire, 1700–1860," in Roderick Floud and Donald McCloskey, eds., *The Economic History of Britain since 1700* (Cambridge, 1981) I:87–102.

28. See Joseph A. Ernst, *Money and Politics in America, 1755–1775* (Chapel Hill, 1973), pp. 24–30.

29. Jan. 12, 1708. C.O.5/1632 ff336–40. May 21, 1708. C.O.5/121 f135.

30. For example, on Feb. 25, 1705/6, Mr. Blakiston was sent to poll the London merchants about the timing of convoys to Virginia. *J.B.T.,* 1704–1709, pp. 226–227.

31. The Board's weekly schedule was arranged and ordered to be posted "for the benefit of people who have business" on Nov. 20, 1717. *J.B.T.* 1714/15–1718, p. 296.

32. Micajah Perry to William Popple, Oct. 11, 1711, C.O.54/1363 f 333. In 1742 twenty Quakers attended the Board in a hearing on charges against the Pennsylvania assembly (John Kinsey to Israel Pemberton, 4 mo. 28, 1742, Pemberton Papers, PHS). In 1734 "a large number of Friends" attended on the Pennsylvania-Maryland boundary dispute. (London Meeting for Sufferings to Quarterly Meeting of Friends in Chester, Newcastle, and Kent counties, 28/12 mo. 1734, Epistles Sent, II, 495–496).

33. Before 1731 the merchants published fourteen pamphlets relating to the Virginia trade, but Arthur Bayley's "A Short State of the Virginia Trade in a Letter Occasioned by a Bill proposed to ye House of Commons for Commuting Tobacco for French Wines," written in 1708 (Egerton Ms. 921, ff9–10, British Library, London) was circulated in manuscript.

34. Cecil Roth, *The Great Synagogue, London, 1690–1940* (London, 1950), p. 44.

35. Davis, *German Thought and Culture in England*, p. 50.

36. Lois G. Schwoerer. *The Declaration of Rights, 1689* (Baltimore, 1981), p. 69.

5. American Interests

1. Philip Haffenden, *New England in the English Nation, 1689–1713* (Oxford, 1974), pp. 59–60; Richard Johnson, *Adjustment to Empire* (New Brunswick, N.J., 1981), pp. 306–363.

2. Carl Bridenbaugh, *Cities in the Wilderness: The First Century of Urban Life in America, 1625–1742* (New York, 1964), p. 143.

3. For Philadelphia see Gary Nash, "The Early Merchants of Philadelphia: The Formation and Disintegration of a Founding Elite," in Richard S. Dunn and Mary Maples Dunn, eds., *The World of William Penn* (Philadelphia, 1986) pp. 337–363. For New York see Thomas J. Archdeacon, *New York City, 1664–1710: Conquest and Change* (Ithaca, N.Y., 1976), p. 141.

4. Jacob R. Marcus, *The Colonial American Jew, 1492–1776* (Detroit, 1970), I:308.

5. Archdeacon, *New York City*, p. 45. The Anglican population of New York in 1695 was estimated at 90 families. J. Miller, *New York Considered and Improved, 1695*, V. H. Palsets, ed. (New York, 1903). Robert Hastings Nichols, *Presbyterianism in New York State: A History of the Synod and Its Predecessors* (Philadelphia, 1963), p. 19.

6. On this see Bridenbaugh's *Cities in the Wilderness*, p. 201.

7. John Albert Maynard, *The Huguenot Church of New York: A History of the French Church of Saint Esprit* (New York, 1938), p. 73.

8. Morgan Dix, ed., *A History of the Parish of Trinity Church in the City of New York* (New York, 1898), pp. 81–96.

9. Theodore Fiske Savage, *The Presbyterian Church in New York City* (New York, 1949), pp. 5–7.

10. Bridenbaugh, *Cities in the Wilderness*, p. 259.

11. Arthur Henry Hirsch, *The Huguenots of Colonial South Carolina* (Durham, N.C., 1928), p. 112.

12. In 1707 an "Address of the min*rs*" was presented to the Queen through Henry Newman, but there is no information about how many ministers signed. (Newman to Samuel Storke, June 7, 1707. Payne/Storke Corr., MHS *Coll*). For their organization see Carl Bridenbaugh, *Mitre and Sceptre: Transatlantic Faiths, Ideas, Personalities, and Politics* (New York, 1962), p. 66.

13. See Leonard J. Trinterud, *Presbyterianism: The Forming of an American Tradition* (Philadelphia, 1949), pp. 32–34; Rev. Richard Webster, *A History of the Presbyterian Church in America from Its Origin to the Year 1760* (Philadelphia, 1857), p. 95.

14. Alison G. Olson, "The Commissaries of the Bishop of London in Colonial Politics," in Alison G. Olson and Richard M. Brown, eds., *Anglo-American*

Political Relations, 1675–1775 (New Brunswick, New Jersey, 1970), pp. 109–124.

15. Hirsch, *Huguenots,* p. 48.

16. Bridenbaugh, *Cities in the Wilderness,* pp. 266–269.

17. Feb. 13, 1701 *A.P.C.,* II, #814.

18. C.O.5/995 f72, Instruction #60.

19. September 17, 1691. C.O. 5/713 f166. The same day Micajah Perry wrote John Povey commenting on a list of nominees Povey had sent him. Later in the day Perry wrote a second letter saying he had just talked with "John Hammon lately from Maryland" and as a result of the conversation added some more names to the list (ff161–162).

20. See Spotswood's complaint that "it is doing little honour to the Government to have its Council appointed in the Virginia Coffee House" (to Col. Blakiston, Dec. 1, 1714). R. A. Brock, ed., *The Official Letters of Alexander Spotswood, Lieutenant Governor of the Colony of Virginia, 1710–1722* (Richmond, 1888), II:79.

21. William I. Hull, *William Penn and the Dutch Quaker Migration to Pennsylvania* (Philadelphia, 1935), esp. pp. 324–387; Julius Friedrich Sachse, *The Fatherland: Part I of a Narrative and Critical History* (Philadelphia, 1897), p. 142.

22. "The Vestry Book of King William Parish, Virginia, 1707–1750," *Virg. Mag.* 6 (1903):289; R. A. Brock, ed., *Documents, Chiefly Unpublished, Relating to the Huguenot Emigration to Virginia and to the Settlement at Manakin-town* (Baltimore, 1962, reprint of 1886 ed.), p. viii, 17, 21, 38–42. Merchants "who lived in London and were very honest men, had been commissioned to offer lands at a reasonable price to any Frenchman wishing to come [to Virginia]." *A Huguenot Exile in Virginia, or Voyages of a Frenchman Exiled for his Religion, with a Description of Virginia and Maryland* (New York, 1734 copy of 1687 ed.), p. 159. "Archives of the French Protestant Church of London," HSL *Publ* 50:61. In 1686 scouts had arrived in New England anticipating Huguenot migration there. Clifford M. Shipton, "Immigration to New England, 1680–1740," *Journal of Political Economy* 44 (1936):227. See also A. P. Hands and Irene Scouloudi, eds., "French Protestant Refugees Relieved through the Threadneedle Street Church, London, 1681–1687," HSL *Publ* 49 (1971).

23. *Christoph Von Graffenreid's Account of the Founding of New Bern,* ed. Vincent H. Todd, (Raleigh, N.C., 1920), esp. pp. 221–231, 258.

24. The fullest account remains that of Walter A. Knittle, *Early Eighteenth Century Palatine Emigration* (Baltimore, 1965, reprint of 1937 ed.), chs. 1–3.

25. These occur after the period 1689–1715. On June 13, 1735, Perry's petition on behalf of a South Carolina appropriation act was considered favorably (*J.B.T.* 1734–1741, p. 25). On May 15, 1745, the Board consulted Moravian leaders about a New York act discriminating against them (*J.B.T.* 1741–1749, pp. 164–165). On Nov. 18, 1745, they read a letter from the Moravians sent in favor of a Pennsylvania naturalization act (Ibid., pp. 213–214).

26. Spotswood to Board, Sept. 27, 1718. C.O.5/1365 ff1767.
27. Merchants trading to Jamaica were scolded in 1736: "The Board then informed them that they are surprized the merchants should lay memorials before H.M. without having proof." April 15, 1736, *J.B.T., 1734–1741*, p. 102. On another occasion the legal adviser to the Board advised "I am of opinion that the Merchants of London Trading to New York, are not proper to object to what debts ought to be allowed or disallowed, this being a thing which is absolutely in the power of The General Assembly." West to Board, April 22, 1719. C.O.5/1124 ff64–71.
28. For examples of early porters and carters' petitions see April 22, 1691, and Dec. 10, 1695 *Minutes of the Common Council of the City of New York, 1675–1776* (New York, 1905), I:220, 393; Sept. 16, 1689, *A Report of the Record Commissioners of the City of Boston: Records from 1660–1701*, VII:197.
29. June 29, 1698. *Minutes of the Common Council of the City of New York*, II:33.
30. The petitioners included the House of Burgesses and Council of Virginia (May 22, 1691; *C.S.P. Co., A. & W.I., 1689–1692*, #1516, 1517), the Revolutionary Government of Maryland (July 11, 1692, ibid., #986), The Governor and Council of Pennsylvania (April 23, 1696, ibid., *1693–1696*, #343), the General Assembly of New Hampshire (April 6, 1693, ibid., #250) and the "Inhabitants" of Connecticut (Jan. 29, 1694, ibid., #846).
31. 11/4 mo., 1697. Minutes of the New England Yearly Meeting. Microfilm, Haverford College.
32. Address of the House of Lords to the Queen, 1705, with appended copy of Joseph Boones's petition "on behalf of himself and many other inhabitants of the Province of Carolina" signed by sixteen merchants. C.O.5/1291 f358.
33. "Humble Petition of the Clergy of Virginia to Governor Andros," June 25, 1696. C.O.5/1307 ff70–77.
34. Hirsch, *The Huguenots of Colonial South Carolina*, ch. 5.
35. Trinterud, *The Forming of an American Tradition*, pp. 32–33.
36. A group of landowners in Ulster, New York, agreed with an agent "either that he should prevail to get an act passed to deprive New York of the sole liberty of bolting flour or carry the cause to England." Deposition of Jacob Rutson enclosed in Lord Bellomont's letter to the Board of Trade, June 22, 1698. *C.S.P. Col., A & WI*, XVI:284.
37. The petition was enclosed in Dudley's letter to Secretary Popple, Oct. 17, 1704. C.O.5/911 f442.
38. "Representation from the Principal Merchants of the Massachusetts Bay to Col. Dudley." Jan. 31, 1709. C.O.5/913 f184.
39. The first such reference occurs as early as "the 14 day of 4 month, 1686." Minutes of the New England Yearly Meeting.
40. Ibid., 11/4 mo., 1697.
41. Ibid., 13/4 mo., 1701.
42. Arthur J. Worrall, *Quakers in the Colonial Northeast* (London, 1980), p. 114.
43. London Meeting to Board of Trade, Oct. 2, 1705. C.O.5/1291 ff204–209.

44. Minutes of the New England Yearly Meeting, 14/4 mo., 1706.

45. Ibid., 3/9 mo., 1715.

46. Dec. 18, 1716. London Meeting for Sufferings, Epistles Sent, II:238.

47. Col. Quarry and others to Nicholson, Jan. 18, 1697. William Stevens Perry, *Papers Relating to the History of the Church in Pennsylvania, 1680–1778* (n.p., 1871), p. 507. See also Bruce T. McCully, "Governor Francis Nicholson, Patron par Excellence of Religion and Learning in Colonial America." *W.M.Q.* 3d ser. 39 (April 1982):310–333.

48. Mr. Portlock to Archbishop of Canterbury, July 12, 1700. Perry, *Papers re Anglican Church, Pa.,* pp. 22–24.

49. N.d. but 1704; see ibid.

50. St. Paul's Church, Chester, to Archbishop (n.d., 1705). Ibid., pp. 27–29.

51. Note that the request came from a meeting of the Pennsylvania clergy, March 17, 1714. A letter from the governor and 103 Anglicans followed. Ibid., pp. 86, 87–89.

52. Merchants of London to William Popple, 18 Feb. 1698. C.O.5/1042 f10.

53. Merchants of London trading with New York to the King, Feb. 14, 1699/1700, and to the House of Commons the same day. C.O.5/1042 ff107–112.

54. Dec. 14, 1703. C.O.5/1120 f27.

55. Bernard Bailyn, *The New England Merchants in the Seventeenth Century* (Cambridge, Mass., 1955), p. 94. Given the reluctance of "men of substance" to argue their opinions before the lower orders and the avowed preference of British councils to consult "the better sort" rather than the "rabble," it is possible, indeed, probable, that the interests' major decisions were made by small groups of leaders. But given also the still primitive nature of colonial society, most colonial interests themselves represented a cut-through of several social ranks. The less fortunate as well as their betters appreciated the need to organize and the usefulness of transatlantic contacts.

56. See, for example, Bridges to Board of Trade, Feb. 1709/10. C.O.5/913 ff208–219.

57. George Willcocks to Board of Trade, Nov. 27, 1705. C.O.5/1291 f426.

58. For evidence of the activities of Boston merchants in London shortly after the Glorious Revolution see Elisha Cooke to Simon Bradstreet, Oct. 6, 1690, MHS *Proc* 45 (Boston, 1912):645, and Charles Lidget's extract of a letter from Boston, April 11, 1690, which he forwarded to the Lords of Trade (*C.S.P. Col., A. & W.I.,* 1689–1692, #826).

59. Classis of Amsterdam to Revs. Du Bois, Lydeus, Antonides, and the Consistories of the Province of New York, July, 1710. *Eccl. Records, N.Y.* III:1856–58.

60. Presbyterian Church, New York to John Matthews (n.d., but 1719) and to John Cricton (n.d., but 1719). "New York City Churches, 30, II," NYHS.

61. For Blair see Olson, "Commissaries," in Olson and Brown, eds., *Anglo-American Political Relations,* pp. 110–112.

62. See, for example, the petition of Conrad Weiser of Jan. 10, 1722, to the Board asking them not to recognize one of his rivals among the Palatines (*C.S.P. Co., A. & W.I.,* 1722–23, #8) and Governor Burnet's explanation

of the German divisions in a letter to the Board, Nov. 21, 1722, ibid., #341. Weiser's critics petitioned the Board against him on Nov. 1, 1720. *Eccl. Records N.Y.,* III:2176–77.

63. Marcus, *Colonial American Jew,* I:292–293.

64. See, for example, Charles Weiss, *History of the French Protestant Refugees from the Revocation of the Edict of Nantes to the Present Time* (London, 1854), p. 281.

65. The plight of southern Presbyterian churches is described vividly in Ernest Trice Thompson, *Presbyterians in the South* (Richmond, 1963), I:18, 22, 26–28, 38. For the appeals of New York Presbyterians for help see [?] to John Chricton, 1719. "New York City Churches, 30, II," NYHS.

66. Richard Vann, "Quakerism: Made in America" in Dunn and Dunn, eds., *The World of William Penn,* pp. 157–170.

67. Rev. Lucas to Secretary of S.P.G., June 19, 1720. William Stevens Perry, *Historical Collections Relating to the American Colonial Church* (Hartford, Conn, 1873), III:133.

68. Rev. Samuel Miles' Memorial, Dec. 9, 1713. Ibid., p. 96.

69. Benjamin Coleman to ? [1726], Coleman Mss, MHS. Rev. Samuel Thomas, a South Carolina missionary, wrote, "there are others who are not positively determined as to their choice, who have not actually put themselves under the conduct either of our ministers or those who differe from us" (n.d. but pre–1714). S.P.G. Journals, 1701–1810, Library of Congress.

70. Governor Spottswood wrote the Bishop of London that one Virginia parish had been a long time without a minister, which had "given occasion to a Presbyterian preacher to set up a Meeting house, where a great many begin to resort," but added that "whenever they have had the happiness of an orthodox ministry they have all returned to the Church" (Letters I, 26. Quoted in Leonidas Dodson, *Alexander Spotswood, Governor of Colonial Virginia, 1710–1722* [New York, 1969, reprint of 1932 ed.], pp. 191–192.)

6. The Colonial Governors

1. Kenneth B. Murdock, *Increase Mather, Foremost American Puritan* (Cambridge, 1926), p. 250; Michael G. Hall, *Increase Mather, the Last American Puritan,* (Middletown, Conn., 1988) passim.

2. Everett Kimball, *The Public Life of Joseph Dudley: A Study of the Colonial Policy of the Stuarts in New England, 1660–1715* (London, 1911), p. 75.

3. Representation of the Board, March 12, 1711/12. C.O.5/727 ff312–313.

4. Rev. Vesey to Col. Riggs, Nov. 15, 1715. *NY Col. Docs.* V:467. Vesey wrongly expected a new governor to be appointed.

5. Francis Makemie to Increase Mather, Jan. 17, 1696/8. Boyd S. Schlenther, ed., *The Life and Writings of Francis Makemie* (Philadelphia, 1971), p. 251.

6. Gary B. Warden, *Boston, 1689–1776* (Boston, 1970), p. 34.

7. Gary B. Nash, *Quakers and Politics, Pennsylvania, 1681–1726* (Princeton, 1968), p. 117; Nicholas Wainwright, "John Blackwell," *P.M.H.B.* 74(1950):459–461.

8. See, for example, the Minutes of the New England Yearly Meeting, 17/4 mo., 1715, for reference to an address to Governor Shute.

9. June 21, 1710. Louis B. Wright and Marion Tinling, eds., *The Secret Diary of William Byrd of Westover, 1709–1712* (Richmond, 1941), p. 194.

10. Cornbury to Lords of Trade, May 3, 1702. *NY Col. Docs.* IV:955.

11. Alison Gilbert Olson, "Governor Robert Hunter and the Anglican Church in New York," in Anne Whiteman, J. S. Bromley, and P. G. M. Dickson, eds., *Statesmen, Scholars and Merchants: Essays in Eighteenth Century History* presented to Dame Lucy Sutherland (Oxford, 1973), pp. 44–64.

12. James Blair described Nicholson's methods in a letter to the Bishop of London May (3), 1704. William Stevens Perry, ed., *Historical Collections Relating to the Anglican Colonial Church: Virginia* (Hartford, Conn., 1890) I:132–133.

13. Martha J. Lamb and Mrs. Burton Harrison, *History of the City of New York: Its Origin, Rise, and Progress.* 3 vols. (New York, 1877), I:457.

14. Hunter to Board of Trade, June 3, 1712 (C.O.5/1123 ffll–16) and April 12, 1719 (C.O.5/1124 ff72–76).

15. Dec. 18, 1713. William Stevens Perry, ed., *Historical Collections Relating to the Church in Massachusetts, 1676–1785* (Hartford, 1873) p. 96.

16. William J. Hoffman, "'A Tumult of the Merchants' of New York in 1688," *New York Genealogical and Biographical Records* 74 (July 1943):99.

17. Bellomont wrote Secretary Vernon that "tis said the Bishop of London has writ to Mr. Vesey who's with the angry party that by Easter he and his friends will be rid of their grievances" (Dec. 6, 1700). *NY Col. Docs.* IV:817.

18. John Albert Maynard, *The Huguenot Church of New York: A History of the French Church of Saint Esprit* (New York, 1938), pp. 90–91; D. Bondet to Lord Cornbury, 1702. George F. Daniels, *The Huguenots in the Nipmuck County or, Oxford Prior to 1713* (Boston, 1880), pp. 120–122.

19. As early as Feb. 11, 1698/9, William Blathwayt was warning Bellomont that "Some merchants and others have indeed been very busy and clamorous at the Board with relation to your Lord's proceedings." Blathwayt Papers, Colonial Williamsburg.

    The London merchants' petitions are Feb. 14, 1699/1700, one to the House of Commons and one to the King. C.O.5/1042, ff107–112. The French correspondence is in the Threadneedle Church Letterbook, Huguenot Society, London.

20. Sept. 2, 1710, Diary of Cotton Mather, 1709–1724. MHS *Coll* 7th ser. VIII:15.

21. Robert Beverley, *The History and Present State of Virginia: A Selection* (New York, 1971), p. 134.

22. Sept. 21, 1711, in Wright and Tingling, eds., *Secret Diary of William Byrd,* p. 409; Leonidas Dodson, *Alexander Spotswood, Governor of Colonial Virginia* (New York, 1969, reprint of 1932 ed.) p. 192.

23. Ernest Trice Thompson, *Presbyterianism in the South,* (Richmond, 1963) I:28.

24. Report of the Journey of Frances Louis Michel from Berne, Switzerland to Virginia, Oct. 2, 1701–Dec. 1, 1702, *Virg. Mag.* 24 (Jan. 1916):122ff. See also *Graffenreid's Account of New Bern,* p. 258.

25. Richard L. Morton, *Colonial Virginia* (Chapel Hill, 1960), II:446.

26. Sept. 23, 1710, *William Byrd Diary, 1709–10,* p. 234.

27. Dodson, *Spotswood,* pp. 196–197. See the correspondence in Perry, *Historical Collections: Virginia,* pp. 199–225.

28. May 6, 1716. C.O.5/1364, f444.

29. William Byrd to Philip Ludwell, London, July 3, 1717, Ludwell Papers, VHS Mss. 1 L 51.

30. Spotswood to Board of Trade, Sept. 17, 1718. C.O.5/1365 ff176–177.

31. Ibid., May 26, 1719. R. A. Brock, ed., *The Official Letters of Governor Alexander Spotswood, Collections of the Virginia Historical Society,* 2d ed., (Richmond, 1882–5), II:320.

32. H. L. McIlwaine, ed., *Journals of the House of Burgesses, 1712–26,* (Richmond, 1912) p. 354; Dodson, *Spotswood,* p. 269.

33. Susan Martha Reed, "Church and State in Massachusetts, 1691–1740," *University of Illinois Studies in the Social Sciences,* 3 (Urbana, Ill., 1914):104.

34. Reed, "Church and State," pp. 110–111.

35. Kimball, *Dudley,* p. 45.

36. Warden, *Boston,* p. 62.

37. May de Witt Freeland, *The Records of Oxford, Mass., Including Chapters of Nipmuck, Huguenot, and English History from the Earliest Date, 1630* (Albany, N.Y., 1894), pp. 171, 179.

38. See Charles W. Baird, *History of the Huguenot Emigration to America* (Baltimore, 1966, reprint of 1885 ed.), II:222. *Boston Records, 1701–1715,* pp. 42–43.

39. Feb. 15, 1705–6. C.O.5/912 ff149–150.

40. Bernon paper March 1, 1710, quoted in Baird, *Huguenot Immigration to America,* II:262n.

41. Kimball, *Dudley,* p. 75.

42. Dec. 16, 1708. Perry, *Historical Collections Mass.,* p. 83.

43. October 10, 1706. Ibid., p. 81. Dudley's relations with Anglicans in England are nicely suggested in Richard Johnson's *Adjustment to Empire: The New England Colonies 1675–1715* (New Brunswick, N.J., 1981), pp. 334–347.

44. Dudley to Secretary of S.P.G., May 1, 1714. Perry, *Papers Relating to the History of the Church in Massachusetts,* pp. 97–98.

45. Ibid., p. 108.

46. Arthur J. Worrall, *Quakers in the Colonial Northeast* (London, 1980) p. 68; Board of Trade to Dudley, Feb. 4, 1705–6. C.O.5/912 ff119–120; Dudley to Board, Feb. 28, 1706. C.O.5/912 ff175–176.

47. Reed, "Church and State," p. 112. For Dudley and the Quakers see Worrall, *Quakers in the Colonial Northeast,* p. 120. Dudley to Board, March 1, 1708–9. C.O.5/913 ff113–115; New England Yearly Meeting to London Yearly Meeting, 8–12/4 mo., 1710. Minutes of the New England Yearly Meeting, p. 57 (Microfilm, Haverford College).

48. Hunter was also governor of New Jersey, a colony with its own complicated network of interests. See John Roger McCreary, "Ambition, Interest, and Faction: Politics in New Jersey, 1702–1738" (Ph.D. diss., Nebraska University, 1971), pp. 14–15, 53, 81.

49. Thomas J. Archdeacon, *New York City, 1664–1710: Conquest and Change* (Ithaca, N.Y., 1976), p. 45.

50. John D. Runcie, "The Problem of Anglo-American Politics in Bellomont's New York," *W.M.Q.* 3d ser., 26 (April 1969):204.

51. Edward Porter Alexander, ed., *The Journal of John Fontaine, an Irish Huguenot Son in Spain and Virginia, 1710–1719* (Charlottesville, Va., 1972), p. 19.

52. See Steve J. Stein, "Knickerbockers Who Asserted and Insisted," *New York Historical Society Quarterly* 58 (April 1974):114, 133; Petition of Elders of Dutch Churches in King's County to Gov. Cornbury [1702], *Eccl. Records, N.Y.,* III:1503.

53. Archdeacon, *New York City,* p. 141.

54. Threadneedle Church Letterbook, Huguenot Society, London.

55. Hunter to Board of Trade, 27 August 1715. C.O.5/995 f310.

56. ? to John Chricton, 1719. "New York City Churches, 30, II," NYHS.

57. Jacob R. Marcus, *The Colonial American Jew, 1492–1776* (Detroit, 1970), I:405–406.

58. Alexander, ed., *The Journal of John Fontaine,* pp. 114–117.

59. Hunter to Champante, July 23, 1715. Rawlinson Ms. A 275, Bodleian Library, Oxford.

60. Consistories of Midwout, Breuckelen, and New Amersfoort to Classis of Amsterdam, Jan. 28, 1712. *Eccl. Records, N.Y.* III:1976–8. For a fuller analysis of the Dutch see Randall Balmer, *A Perfect Babel of Confusion; Dutch Religion and English Culture in the Middle Colonies* (New York, 1989), pp. 91–94.

61. Estimated by Caleb Heathcote. Dixon Ryan Fox, *Caleb Heathcote, Gentleman Colonist* (New York, 1926), p. 228.

62. See Sir Edward Midwinter, "The Society for the Propagation of the Gospel and the Church in the American Colonies," *H.M.P.E.C.,* 4 (1935):66–115.

    Lewis Morris spoke of Vesey as the leader of Cornbury's friends in the colony. Morris to the Secretary of S.P.G., Feb. 20, 1711/12. *Eccl. Records, N.Y.* III:1906–09. Hunter complained to the Bishop of London, on March 1, 1712, that Vesey was sending attacks against him to Nicholson and Cornbury. *NY Col. Docs.* V:310–312. Hunter later wrote the Lords of Trade that his enemies were "prompted all along from the other party by a late governor of these Provinces" (March 28, 1715), *NJ Col. Docs.* IV:207. See also *C.S.P. Col., A. & W.I.,* 1711/12, #206, 210, 290; ibid., 1712/14, #293, 404, 665. See also Vesey to S.P.G. of July 26, 1710. Minutes of the S.P.G., II. Library of Congress.

63. See Jerome R. Reich, *Leisler's Rebellion: A Study of Democracy in New York, 1664–1720* (Chicago, 1953), ch. 7; Morgan Dix, *A History of the Parish of Trinity Church in the City of New York* (New York, 1898), pp. 81–96; E. Clowes Chorley, "Outline of Two Hundred and Fifty Years of Trinity Parish in the City of New York," *H.M.P.E.C.* 16 (1947):295; and William Smith, *The History of the Late Province of New York* (New York, 1830), I:128–132.

    For New Jersey see Edgar Legare Pennington, *Apostle of New Jersey, John Talbot, 1645–1727,* (Philadelphia, 1938), and Rev. George Morgan Hills, "John Talbot, the First Bishop in North America," *P.M.H.B.,* 3 (1879):32–55; and Hills's *History of the Church in Burlington, New Jersey,*

2d ed. (Trenton, 1885), pp. 43–44. Edward Vaughan, minister at Elizabeth, New Jersey, later spoke of "the freedom I once took in telling Mr. Vesey . . . that it was inconsistent with the Character of a Minister of Peace to foment divisions, to appear in faction and party opposite to Government." Vaughan to J. Chamberlayne, Nov. 8, 1715. S.P.G., A Mss, XT 292, quoted in John Kindall Nelson, "Anglican Missions in America, 1701–1725: A Study of the Society for the Propagation of the Gospel in Foreign Parts" (Ph.D. diss., Northwestern University, 1962), pp. 281–283. The meetings of the clergy are discussed in Nelson R. Burr, *The Anglican Church in New Jersey* (Philadelphia, 1954), pp. 282–288.

64. Talbot had called Heathcote "the finest Gentleman I have seen in America" and added "I wish the report were true that he were appointed Govr. it would be the best news next to that of the Gospel that ever came over." (Talbot to Secretary of S.P.G., Jan. 10, 1707/8. Pennington, *Talbot,* p. 117). Heathcote had originally recommended Vesey's appointment to Governor Fletcher (Fox, *Heathcote,* p. 10). For Heathcote's letters to the Society on Hunter's behalf see *Eccl. Records, N.Y.* III:1899–1906, and Minutes of the S.P.G., Oct. 10, 1712, #33, 34, 35, and June 1714, #1, Library of Congress.

65. See E. B. Greene, "The Anglican Outlook on the American Colonies in the Early Eighteenth Century," *American Historical Review* 20 (1914–15):75.

66. Revs. Talbot and Haliday to the Clergy met at New York, n.d., Pennington, *Talbot,* p. 126; Poyer to S.P.G., March 7, 1712/13, and Clergy of New York and Pa. to S.P.G., March 30, 1713, in Minutes of the S.P.G., Sept. 4, 1713, #9, 11, S.P.G. Journals II, Library of Congress.

67. Jordan D. Fiore, "Jonathan Swift and the American Episcopate," *W.M.Q.* 11 (1954):425–433 passim.

68. Board of Trade to Queen Nov. 25, 1712, C.O.5/1123 ff60–2. See Dix, *Trinity Church,* pp. 183–184; Smith, *History of New York,* I:170–73; Henry Onderdonk, Jr., *Antiquities of the Parish Church, Jamaica* (Jamaica, 1880), pp. 28–32, gives an interpretation somewhat different from Smith's. The Society's representation to the Queen, the Order in Council authorizing ecclesiastical appeals, and the Additional Instruction are in *Eccl. Records, N.Y.* III: 1971 and 1990. See also Minutes of the S.P.G., July 11, 1712, #4, 7–10; Sept. 4, 1713, #9. S.P.G. Journals II, Library of Congress.

69. Pennington, *Talbot,* pp. 55–57, and Revs. Talbot, Sandel, Phillips, and Humphreys to Gen. Nicholson, May 11, 1714, in ibid., pp. 129–132. The Society petitioned Queen Anne for repeal of the act. Nelson, "Anglican Missions," p. 396n35. The petition from the Church wardens and vestry at Burlington to the S.P.G., March 25, 1714, is in Hills, *History of the Church in Burlington,* pp. 110–113. The Anglicans in Burlington also objected to Hunter's allowing a Quaker schoolmaster to teach there in competition with the Anglican teachers. See, for example, Rowland Ellis to Secretary of S.P.G., May 20, 1714, ibid., pp. 114–116.

70. Minutes of the S.P.G., Oct. 10, 1712, #48, 51; Neau to S.P.G., Nov. 16, 1714, Feb. 3, 1715/16; Abstract of Neau's Complaints, Dec. 6, 1715. S.P.G. Journals III, Library of Congress.

71. Minutes of the S.P.G. Sept. 21, 1716, #2. S.P.G. Journals III, Library of Congress.

72. Hunter to Popple, Nov. 9, 1715. *NJ Col. Docs.* IV:219–220.
73. Hunter to Board of Trade, April 23, 171[8]. C.O.5/1124 ff72–76.
74. Hunter to Popple, April 23, 1718. C.O.5/1124 ff77–8.
75. The merchants' petition was dated April 23, 1718 (C.O.5/1124 f23); their memorial was October 8, 1718 (f57). Their objections to the act for circulating bills of credit are dated April 22, 1719 (f63) and their call on West was on the same day (f64). West's report was also April 22, 1719 (ff64–71).
76. West to Board, April 22, 1719. C.O.5/1124 ff64–71.
77. Board to Lords Justices, June 4, 1719. C.O.5/1124 f93.
78. Hunter to William Popple, Oct. 1, 1718. C.O.5/1124 ff52–54.
79. See Ann Maury, *Memoirs of a Huguenot Family* (Baltimore, 1967, reprint of 1853 ed., pp. 135–139; Robin D. Gwynn, "The Distribution of Refugees in England, London and Its Environs," HSL *Proc*, XXII:523.
80. Conrad von Uffenbach, a well-connected German visiting London in 1710, seems to have been unaware of the masses of Palatine immigrants (*London in 1710. From the Travels of Zacharias Conrad von Uffenbach*, W. H. Quarrell and Margaret Mare, eds. [London, n.d.] passim, but esp. pp. 27–28, 44, 62.)
81. Even the Virginia merchants disagreed from time to time about particular issues. In 1705, for example, Governor Nicholson wrote plaintively about the merchants, "if they can't agree amongst themselves because of their various interests and designs which are sometimes quite opposite, how is it possible for me to please them all?" (Nicholson to Board, May 31, 1705, C.O.5/1361 f346.)

Quakers, of course, are understood to be those who remained in the church and were not affected by the Keithian Schism.

7. The Heyday of London Interests

1. For an excellent discussion of ministerial attitudes toward the colonies in this period see James Henretta, *Salutary Neglect; Colonial Administration under the Duke of Newcastle* (Princeton, 1972), passim.
2. George Rudé, *Hanoverian London, 1714–1808* (Berkeley, 1971), p. 103. Sir Walter Besant, *London in the Eighteenth Century* (London, 1925), App. II. The difficulty of estimating the number of dissenters in England is discussed in Duncan Coomer, *English Dissent under the Early Hanoverians* (London, 1946), pp. 60–61.
3. This is an estimate, based on the number of ministers they were able to support as listed in the Minutes of Three Denominations, I:7–11, 147–154; II:57–61.
4. These figures have been obtained by preparing a separate card for every merchant who signed a petition now in the C.O.5 series (petitions would be addressed to the monarch but handled by the Board of Trade or the Secretary of State), the House of Lords Record Office, or Stock, *Proceedings*, III–V.
5. The signatures were on petitions or memorials to the King referred to the Board of Trade on July 18, 1715 (C.O.5/1264 f301), Sept. 16, 1715, [1716],

March 4, 1716/17 (C.O.5/1265, ff9, 55, 59), Dec. 14, 1732 (C.O.5/392 ff222–223) July 4, 1735 (C.O.5/365, ff38–40) [Nov. 1739], and [1740] (C.O.5/384, ff61a, 81).

6. Mary Dorothy George, *London Life in the Eighteenth Century* (New York, 1964), p. 11.

7. Besant, *London in the Eighteenth Century,* App. II.

8. Ibid. The early churches were the Swedish Lutheran (actually German), the German Lutheran churches in Savoy, and the Court Chapel. W. H. Quarrell and Margaret Mare, eds., *London in 1710: From the Travels of Zacharias Conrad von Uffenbach* (London, n.d.), p. 62; Walter Allen Knittle, *Early Eighteenth Century Palatine Emigration* (Baltimore, 1965), reprint of 1937 ed.), pp. 2–32.

9. Cecil Roth, *A History of the Jews in England* (Oxford, 1964), p. 225.

10. Rudé, *Hanoverian London,* p. 7.

11. It is useful to visualize the interests as pyramids. The new ones were fairly flat and broadly based. The older ones became steeper and more narrowly based.

12. Thomas Cox, *Description of London* (ca. 1725), p. 481, Folger Library.

13. Bryant Lillywhite, *London Coffee Houses* (London, 1963), pp. 908, 878, 623, 774. Notices (incomplete) of meetings are in the Minutes of the Three Denominations; see, for example, Oct. 7, 1735, March 30, 1736, March 6, 1738, March 17, 1741. Unnumbered vol., pp. 22, 23, 24, 26.

14. Lillywhite, *Coffee Houses,* pp. 261–262; Minutes of the Three Denominations, August 29, 1732, II:31.

15. Jan. 29, 1754. George William Pilcher, ed., *The Reverend Samuel Davies Abroad: The Diary of a Journey to England and Scotland* (Urbana, Ill., 1967), p. 65.

16. Lillywhite, *Coffee Houses,* p. 261.

17. Feb. 5, 1754. Pilcher, ed., *Samuel Davies Diary,* p. 69. Peter Manigault to Mother, April 26, 1754, in Mabel L. Webber, ed., "Peter Manigault's Letters," *South Carolina Historical and Genealogical Magazine* 33 (1932):59.

18. Besant, *London,* p. 311.

19. James Knight mentioned a Virginia club in 1725 (Lillian M. Penson, "The London West India Interest in the Eighteenth Century," *English Historical Review* 36 [1931]:377) and the existence of a New York Club about 1731 is suggested by Rodrigo Pacheco's remark that "It fell to my Lott to wait on Coll. Cosby yr governor and gave him an invitation into [polity] in ye name of ye gentlemen traders to yr place" (to James Alexander, Jan. 31, [1731], Alexander Papers, NYHS #5). Other clubs are mentioned in "Proposals for a Merchants' Club," *Gentlemen's Magazine* 4 (Aug. 1734):431–432. See Lillian Penson, *Colonial Agents of the British West Indies: A Study in Colonial Administration, Mainly in the Eighteenth Century* (London, 1971, reprint of 1924 en.), pp. 181–196. In 1727 and 1737 tobacco merchants tried to organize clubs that would run the trade but both attempts came to nothing Arthur Pierce Middleton, *Tobacco Coast: A Maritime History of the Chesapeake Bay in the Colonial Era* (Newport News, Virg., 1953), p. 129, and for the most detailed explanation of their procedures,

see Jacob M. Price, *France and the Chesapeake: A History of the French Tobacco Monopoly, 1674–1791, and of Its Relationship to the British and American Tobacco Trades* (Ann Arbor, Mich., 1973), p. 651.

20. 1772. Minutes of the Three Denominations, unnumbered vol., p. 54.

21. "An Account of News Foreign and Domestic Extracted from the Best Authorities," *West India Monthly Packet*, Jan. 26-Feb. 22, 1745/6.

22. William Baker to Newcastle, January 23, 1746, Add Ms 32, 707 f464.

23. Rev. H. P. Thompson, *Into All Lands: The History of the Society for the Propagation of the Gospel in Foreign Parts, 1701–1950* (London, 1951), pp. 36–37. After 1727 the Secretary had a permanent office in Warwick Court.

24. For example, see London Meeting for Sufferings to Quarterly Meetings of Friends in Chester, Newcastle, Kent, and Sussex Counties 28/12 mo. 1734; Letters to Pennsylvania, Maryland, and South Carolina Yearly Meetings 6/6 mo., 1731, 12/9 mo., 1731, 5/3 mo., 1732; to Virginia Yearly Meeting 19/4 mo., 1741; Epistles Sent, II:495–96, 462, 465, 469; III:45–46; Minutes 18/8 mo., 1734, 20/10 mo., 1734, 25/5 mo., 1737, 17/6 mo., 1739, 3/6 mo., 1744, in Minutes XXV:438, 458; XXVI:324; XXVII:45–45, 450–51.

25. A. T. Gary, "The Political and Economic Relations of English and American Quakers, 1750 to 1785" (D. Phil, St. Hughs, Oxford, 1935), pp. 34–35.

26. *Bevis Marks Records; Being Contributions to the History of the Spanish and Portuguese Congregation of London Pt. 1 The Early History of the Congregation from the Beginning until 1800* (Oxford, 1940) p. 37. Roth, *History of Jews in England*, p. 224.

27. Sept. 25, 1732, Minutes of Three Denominations, I:32.

28. Jan. 11, 1757, ibid., pp. 192–193.

29. Ibid.

30. Carl Bridenbaugh, *Mitre and Sceptre: Transatlantic Ideas, Personalities and Politics, 1689–1785* (New York, 1962), p. 42; Minutes of Diss. Deputies, Nov. 9, 1732. Norman C. Hunt, *Two Early Political Associations: The Quakers and the Dissenting Deputies in the Age of Sir Robert Walpole* (Oxford, 1961), p. 135.

31. There are many Partridge letters in Gertrude Kimball, ed., *The Correspondence of the Colonial Governors of Rhode Island, 1723–1775* (New York, 1969, reprint of 1962 ed.). See Marguerite Appleton, "Richard Partridge, Colonial Agent," *New England Quarterly* 5 (1932):294; unpublished Partridge letters are in the Penn and Pemberton Papers, PHS. See also Mabel Paulene Wolff, *The Colonial Agency of Pennsylvania, 1712–1757* (Philadelphia, 1933), passim.

32. Abercromby's Letterbook is in the Virginia Historical Society and there is a letter from him to the Earl of Halifax, April 7, 1757, in Add Ms 32, 870 f372. There are frequent references to him in Ella Lonn, *The Colonial Agents of the Southern Colonies* (Chapel Hill, 1945), pp. 133–134.

33. Leonard W. Cowie, *Henry Newman: An American in London, 1708–43* (London, 1956); George Fenwick Jones, ed., *Henry Newman's Salzburger Letterbooks* (Athens, Ga., 1966). Some unpublished Newman letters are in the Newman Mss, Rawlinson C 379, Bodleian Library, Oxford.

34. *Chain of Friendship: Selected Letters of Dr. John Fothergill of London,*

1735 to 1780 (Cambridge, Mass, 1971). Gary, "Relations of English and American Quakers," passim. Albert M. Hyamson, *The Sephardim of England* (London, 1951), esp. p. 148. Roth, *History of the Jews in England*, esp. p. 212. Norman Sykes, *Edmund Gibson, Bishop of London, 1669–1748* (Oxford, 1926). D. N. Griffiths, "Huguenot Links with Saint George's Chapel, Windsor," HSL *Proc* 22 (1976):496–508. John R. Weinlick, *Count Zinzendorf* (New York, 1956). William George Addison, *The Renewed Church of the United Brethren, 1722–1930* (London, 1932), esp. pp. 1–89.

35. For example see the minute of April 3, 1734, in Minutes of the Three Denominations, I:46.

36. Pelham attempted with some success to win over the City opposition. See L. S. Sutherland, "Samson Gideon and the Reduction of Interest, 1749–50," *Economic History Review* 16 (1946):23. For a detailed analysis of the City's opposition to Walpole see Nicholas C. T. Rogers, *Whigs and Cities: Popular Politics in the Age of Walpole and Pitt* (Oxford, 1989), pp. 46–86, and Rogers, "Resistance to Oligarchy: The City Opposition to Walpole and His Successors, 1725 to 1747," in John Stephenson, ed. *London in the Age of Reform* (Oxford, 1977), pp. 1–29.

37. Four of the leading merchant lobbyists whose careers also illustrate various patterns of interaction with government and City were John Tomlinson, David Barclay, Edward Athawes, and John Hanbury. Tomlinson and Trecothic went into partnership in 1750. For Tomlinson see the biography of his son in Sir Lewis Namier and John Brooke, *The House of Commons, 1754–1790* (London, 1964), pp. 522–523; reports of his testimony before the House of Commons on March 22, 1730/1, April 1733, April 24, 1749, April 5, 1750, April 19, 1751, March 17, 1755 (Stock, *Proceedings,* IV:958, 323; V:352, 439); R. C. Simmons and P. D. G. Thomas, eds., *Proceedings and Debates of the British Parliaments Respecting North America* (London, 1982), I:60, and his letters in the Tomlinson-Atkinson Papers, MHS. There are frequent references to Barclay in the Minutes of the London Meeting for Sufferings (for example, 18/8 mo., 1734, XXV:438). There are Barclay letters in Richard Kingston Fox, *Dr. John Fothergill and His Friends* (London, 1919), passim, and letters to Barclay in Philip L. White, ed., *The Beekman Mercantile Papers 1746–1799* (New York, 1956), for example, April 28 and Sept. 6, 1757, pp. 299, 304. Some Barclay letters are in possession of Quinton Gurney, Bawdeswell Hall, near Norwich, Norfolk. Very little has been written about Athawes, but a few of his letters survive in the Newcastle Papers, British Library. For Perry see William Purdie Treloar, *A Lord Mayor's Diary* (London, 1920), esp. pp. ix, i; Elizabeth Donnan, "Eighteenth Century Merchants: Micajah Perry," *Journal of Economic and Business History* 4 (1931–32):70–98, and the biography of him in Namier and Brooke, *House of Commons,* II:3341–42. For Hanbury see Amy Audrey Locke, *The Hanbury Family* (London, 1916), II:299; Douglass S. Freeman, *George Washington* (New York, 1948), I:160–169, II:264, 300–302. The advice to Morris was noted by his son, July 29, 1735. Beverly McAnear, ed., "An American in London, 1735–36," *P.M.H.B.* 64 (1940):358. For Hanbury's dominance in the Maryland tobacco market see

The Maryland Gazette, May 17, 1753, and April 18 and May 2, 1754. See also P. M. G. Dickson, *The Financial Revolution in England* (New York, 1967), p. 436; July 13, 1753, Aug. 10, 1753, May 24, 1754, May 14, 1756, June 14, 1754. London Meeting for Sufferings, Minutes, XXIX:274, 282, 355, 512, 373; April 24, 1749, Stock, *Proceedings,* V:353; Board of Trade report to Privy Council on June 25, 1754, C.O. 5/1376 ff39–45; Jas. Buchanan, Wm. Anderson, John Buchanan, Edw. Athawes, and Hanbury to Wm. Pitt, June 6, 1757. Pitt Papers, 30/8/95 ff158–159 Public Record Office, London. Fothergill, *Chain of Friendship,* p. 179; John Dickinson to his father, May 25, 1754, in H. Trevor Colbourne, ed., "A Pennsylvania Farmer at the Court of King George," *P.M.H.B.* 86 (July 1962):272–273; John Shebbeare, *A Letter to the People of England on the Present Situation and Conduct of National Affairs* (London, 1755), p. 33.

38. Baker to Newcastle, Feb. 9, 1755, Add Ms 32, 852 f414.
39. Anthony Take, *A History of Barclay's Bank, Ltd.* (London, 1926), p. 35.
40. See for example, Benjamin Avery's conciliatory letter to the Archbishop of Canterbury, Nov. 9, 1753, Lambeth Palace Mss II, #70; Archbishop of York to Archbishop of Canterbury, Dec. 11, 1762, Lambeth Mss III:287. On Feb. 17, 1755, the Archbishop of Canterbury wrote the Bishop of Oxford "upon the general & benevolent footing in wch all Protestants ought to join of all Denominations." Lambeth Mss II:94. Before his ordination Archbishop Secker had to assure Newcastle that "he is very well with Dr. Avery and Dr. Chandler." Norman Sykes, "Newcastle as Ecclesiastical Minister," *English Historical Review* (Jan. 1942):78.
41. John Hanbury lamented Perry's antiquated business methods in a letter to John Custis on Dec. 20, 1745. Custis himself wrote Perry a letter he never sent: "all mankind belows her[e] much [taken] by your being in so much public business in Parlim't and City; and it is ye opinion of most if not all of your friends yt it had been superlatively more for your interest if you had only minded your Merchandise" (1735; Custis Papers, Library of Congress).
42. *The Journals of Henry Melchior Muhlenberg,* transl. Theodore G. Tappert and John W. Doberstein (Philadelphia, 1942), I:22.
43. Francis Wilkes to Rev. Benj. Colman [Sept. 26, 1735]. Colman Ms, MHS. Hunt, *Two Early Associations,* p. 153.
44. Quoted in Bartholomew Schiavo, "The Dissenter Connection: English Dissenters and Massachusetts Political Culture, 1630–1774" (Ph.D. diss., Brandeis University, 1976), p. 322.
45. William Baker, John Hyde, William Fawkener, and Ezekiel Hall to Newcastle, July 23, 1746. Add Ms 32, 707 f464.
46. April 6, 1736, Minutes of Three Denominations, I:57.
47. Horatio Walpole to Bishop of London, May 29, 1750; Arthur Lyon Cross, *The Anglican Episcopate* (Cambridge, Mass., 1924), pp. 324–330.
48. April 6, 1736, Minutes of Three Denominations, I:57.
49. Hunt, *Two Early Associations,* p. 161. Provincials attended the meeting of April 1740; there is no evidence of how many attended in later years. Manning, *Dissenting Deputies,* p. 46.
50. See, for example, Walter Minchington, *Politics and the Port of Bristol in*

the Eighteenth Century (Bristol, 1963), pp. 70n, 36, 50–51, 54–56, 63, 65, 72, 94, 95. A clear example of cooperative lobbying among some merchants of London, Liverpool, and Bristol was their concerted opposition in 1723 to a Virginia act taxing the import of slaves. They petitioned and appeared at the Board and ultimately succeeded in getting the act repealed. Board of Trade to King, Jan. 29, 1723, C.O. 5/1365 f269, and Board to Gov. Gooch, May 22, 1729, C.O. 5/1366 ff22–27.

51. Jan. 25, 1757, Minutes of Three Denominations, I:208–209.
52. The Quakers' London Meeting for Sufferings appointed a committee "to peruse the Letters rec'd out of the Country; and to write to friends concerning such letters as are deemed unfit to be delivered to the members." Minutes XXVI:121–122.
53. The Yorkshire letter was read 17/1 mo., 1725/6. Ibid., p. 126.
54. Jan. 12, 1732. Hunt, *Two Early Associations,* pp. 195–197.
55. Ibid., chs. 7–9.
56. Benjamin Avery to Newcastle, Nov. 16, 1749 (Add Ms 32, 719 f296), Nov. 15, 1750 (Add Ms 32, 723 f275), Dec. 10, 1751 (Add Ms 32, 725 f480), and Feb. 29, 1752 (Add Ms 32, 726 f195).
57. Jan. 11, Feb. 9, April 12, Jan. 25, Jan. 29, Feb. 1, Feb. 8, Feb. 9, Feb. 15, Feb. 16, March 1, 1757, Minutes of Three Denominations I:143, 197–199, 208–213.
58. Hunt, *Two Early Associations,* pp. 64–92. London Meeting for Sufferings Minutes 26/1, 1735–6, XXVI:130. The London Meeting also advised Quakers in the country about when "to apply to such members of Parliament as our Friends have an interest in" about problems the Quakers were having in the courts. Minutes 27/7 mo. 1734, XXV:426; 26/1 mo., 1735/ 6, 19/2 mo., 1736, 23/2 mo., 1736, 7/3 mo., 1736, 14/3 mo., 1736, XXVI:130, 139, 141, 145, 147.
59. Minchington, *Politics and the Port,* p. 42.

8. The High Point of London and American Cooperation

1. For the Customs Service see Thomas Barrow, *Trade and Empire, the British Customs Service in Colonial America, 1660–1775* (Cambridge, Mass., 1967), app. A. The growth of Anglo-American trade is indicated by table 2.1, "Average Annual Value of English Foreign Trade, 1633–1774," in John McCusker and Russell Menard, *The Economy of British America, 1607–1789* (Chapel Hill, 1985), p. 40; "Official Values of Trade with Various Regions" in B. R. Mitchell and Phyllis Deane, *Abstract of British Historical Statistics* (Cambridge, 1962), p. 312; and table 5.1 in R. P. Thomas and D. N. McCloskey, "Overseas Trade and Empire, 1700–1860," in Roderick Floud and Donald McCloskey, eds., *The Economic History of Britain Since 1700* (Cambridge, 1981), I:91.
2. Charles McLean Andrews, *The Boston Merchants and the Non-Importation Movement* (New York, 1958, reprint of 1916/17 ed.), pp. 2–5. The agreement to form the later committee is in an undated paper in the Storke/ Champion/Savage Correspondence in the MHS. For the development of a

sense of common interest among the merchants of New Hampshire (Portsmouth) see Peter Ralph Barry, "The New Hampshire Merchant Interest, 1609–1725" (Ph.D. diss., Wisconsin, University of 1971), pp. 193–194.

3. Virginia Harrington, *The New York Merchant on the Eve of the Revolution* (Gloucester, Mass., 1964, reprint of 1935 ed.), p. 73.

4. Richard Waterhouse, "South Carolina's Colonial Elite: A Study in the Social Structure and Political Culture of a Southern Colony, 1670–1760" (Ph.D. diss., Johns Hopkins University, 1973), p. 134.

5. Philadelphia had 120 licensed taverns in 1752. Carl and Jessica Bridenbaugh, *Rebels and Gentlemen: Philadelphia in the Age of Franklin* (New York, 1962 reprint of 1942 ed.), pp. 21–22. In 1746 the outgoing mayor gave £150 for building an Exchange, but there is no record of the building being erected (Oct. 7, 1746, *Minutes of the Common Council of the City of Philadelphia, 1704 to 1776* [Philadelphia, 1841], p. 463).

6. Jacob R. Marcus, *The Colonial American Jew, 1492–1776* (Detroit, 1970), pp. 346, 314; Albert M. Hyamson, *The Sephardim of England* (London, 1951), pp. 148, 159.

7. See, for example, George C. Rogers, Jr., *Charleston in the Age of the Pinckneys* (Norman, Okla., 1969), pp. 93–94; Bridenbaugh, *Rebels and Gentlemen*, p. 17. For a general interpretation of the churches' growth, see Patricia Bonomi, *Under the Cope of Heaven* (Oxford, 1986), pp. 87–92.

8. Arthur J. Worrall, *Quakers in the Colonial Northeast* (Hanover, N.H., 1989), p. 74.

9. "Letter from Agricola," Jan. 1, 1752, *South Carolina Gazette.*

10. Bridenbaugh, *Mitre and Sceptre*, pp. 125–128. Records of the Synod are in *Presb. Records.*

11. Worrall, *Quakers in Northeast*, p. 80.

12. William G. McLoughlin, *New England Dissent, 1630–1883; The Baptists and the Separation of Church and State* (Cambridge, Mass., 1971) I:130, 281, 502–503, 508.

13. Note on cover of Minutes of the New England Yearly Meeting, 1683–1849, Haverford College; Worrall, *Quakers in Northeast*, pp. 75–77.

14. Colman to Gov. Holden, [1732]; to Mr. Williams, Aug 19, 1735; to "Rev. Sir," Dec. 29, 1735; to Mr. Cooper, Dec. 30, 1735. Colman Papers, MHS.

15. See for example, minutes of May 26, 1737, May 27, 1738, May 24, 1739, May 29, 1740. *Presb. Records*, pp. 131–140, 144, 150.

16. William Summer Jenkins, comp., Records of the States of the United States of America: South Carolina, Legislative Records, Lower House 1751 sess. Microfilm.

17. "Votes and Proceedings of the House of Representatives of the Province of Pennsylvania," in *Pennsylvania Archives*, Gertrude MacKinney, ed. (Philadelphia, 1931). 8th ser., IV.

18. Hans Jacob Reimerspurgher petition, n.d., Lambeth-Fulham Mss, #45.

19. See, for example, Board of Trade to King, July 23, 1730, C.O. 5/400 ff378–381; Board to Privy Council, May 26, 1732, C.O. 5/401 ff32–40 (concerning the settlement of Swiss in South Carolina); and the Board's representations to the Council, May 5, 1737, and April 21, 1738 (C.O. 5/401,

ff209–216, 221–222, 255–258), concerning the settlement of Germans in the same colony. The Board's report to the Duke of Bedford, June 2, 1749, to the Privy Council, June 5, 1749, and to Governor Glen, Dec. 23, 1749 (C.O. 5/402 ff190–195, 195–206, 222–226), concerning the settlement of Wurtemburgers in South Carolina. *The Colonial Records of the State of Georgia*, Allen D. Candler, comp. (Atlanta), Oct. 2, 1749, Nov. 8 and 15, 1750, VI:291, 351, 353. References to instructions to the governors to grant particular benefits to colonists are scattered throughout the *C.S.P. Col. A. & W.I.* For 1737, for example, see *C.S.P. Col., A. & W.I.* pp. 256, 536, 562, 268.

20. June 4, 1735. *Minutes of the Common Council of the City of Philadelphia, 1704 to 1776* (Philadelphia, 1847), pp. 338–339.
21. January 25, 1770. *J.B.T. 1768–1775*, 13:165.
22. Robert Pringle to Andrew Pringle, May 30, 1742, *Letterbook of Robert Pringle*, (Columbia, S.C., 1972) II:70. James Soltow describes the meetings of Virginia merchants in Williamsburg, which served mainly as a financial clearing house and a central market. (*The Economic Role of Williamsburg* [Charlottesville, Va., 1965], pp. 44–48).
23. Board of Trade to Privy Council, July 1, 1755. C.O.5/918 f312.
24. Hunter to Board of Trade, April 23, 1719. C.O.5/1124 ff72–76.
25. Robert Carter to Micajah Perry, May 25, 1728. Robert Carter Letterbook, VHS.
26. March 14, 1749/50, Oct. 1750, Minutes of the Diss. Deputies, I:324, 328.
27. See the reference to the frequency of communication in comments in Minutes of the S.P.G. for July 20, 1750, Lambeth Palace Ms, #47.
28. The New England Yearly Meeting, for example, had to make considerable efforts to meet Richard Partridge's expenses. Minutes, 10/4 mo., 1726, 8–9/4 mo., 1727, 13–14/4 mo., 1728, Haverford College.
29. For example, see Alan Tully, "Ethnicity, Religion and Politics in Early America" (revised version of a paper presented at a Conference entitled "The Founding of Pennsylvania, 1682–1800," at Philadelphia, Oct. 16, 1982), esp. pp. 5, 46–49; Patricia U. Bonomi, *A Factious People: Politics and Society in Colonial New York* (New York, 1971), esp. ch. 3.
30. I am grateful to Dr. John Hemphill for this observation.
31. For the lack of concerted action see McLoughlin, *New England Dissent*, passim; Jacob C. Meyer, *Church and State in Massachusetts from 1740 to 1883* (New York, 1968, reprint of 1930 ed.), pp. 47–49.
32. John Taylor petitioned the Virginia Burgesses for £100 back pay for his efforts to get royal approval of a Virginia Act for Relief of Certain Creditors. Robert Johnson, "Government and Business Enterprise in Virginia, 1750 to 1820" (Ph.D. diss., University of Minnesota, 1958), p. 73. Discussions of the procedure of particular assemblies are in Robert Zemsky's *Merchants, Farmers, and River Gods: An Essay on Eighteenth Century American Politics* (Boston, 1971), passim; Stanley M. Pargellis, "The Procedure of the Virginia House of Burgesses," *W.M.Q.* (1927):73–91, 143–157; Sister Joan de Lourdes Leonard, "Organization and Procedure of the Pennsylvania Assembly, 1682–1776," *P.M.H.B.* 72 (1948):215–239, 376–412; and

George Edward Frakes, *Laboratory for Liberty: The South Carolina Legislative Committee System, 1719–1776* (Lexington, Ky., 1910). I am also grateful to Harry Ward for letting me see his discussion of the Virginia Burgesses' Committee on Propositions and Grievances in his unpublished paper "Freedom and Dissent in Colonial Virginia."

The other conclusions regarding the procedure of the assemblies are derived from *Pennsylvania Archives,* ser. 8, vols. 2–5, MacKinney, ed.; *Public Records of the Colony of Connecticut,* vols. 10–12, Charles J. Hoadley, ed. (Hartford, Connecticut, 1877–1881); *Journals of the House of Representatives of Massachusetts,* vols. 1, 10, 11, 32–42, (Boston, 1919–1972); *The Colonial Records of South Carolina:* J. H. Easterby, ed., *The Journal of the Commons House of Assembly,* 1739–41, 1742–44, 1749–50 (Columbia, S.C., 1951–1962); *Archives of Maryland, Proceedings and Acts of the General Assembly of Maryland,* vols. 12–28, William Hand Browne, C. C. Hall, Bernard Steiner, and J. Hall Pleasant, eds. (Baltimore, 1910–1942); *Provincial Papers: Documents and Records Relating to the Province of New Hampshire,* vols. 3–6, Nathaniel Bouton, ed. (Manchester, N.H., 1872); H. R. McIlwaine, ed., *Journals of the House of Burgesses of Virginia* 1712–26, 1727–40, 1752–55, 1758–61, 1761–65 (Richmond, 1907–1912); John Russell Bartlett, ed., *Records of the Colony of Rhode Island and Providence Plantations,* vols. 4–6 (Providence, 1856–1865); William L. Saunders, ed., *Colonial Records of North Carolina,* vols. 4–6 (1886–1890). These have been supplemented by and checked against Jenkins, *Early State Records.*

33. See, for example, Alan F. Day, "Lawyers in Colonial Maryland," *American Journal of Legal History* 17 (1973), esp. pp. 151–160. The Pennsylvania assembly hired an outsider, Charles Brockden, to draft their legislation. Clair Wayne Keller, "Pennsylvania Government, 1701–40: A Study in the Operation of Colonial Government" (Ph.D. diss., University of Washington, 1967), p. 26. Elsewhere outsiders took it upon themselves to rewrite unworkable laws. Rollo G. Silver, "Government Printing in Massachusetts Bay, 1700–1750," *Proceedings of the American Antiquarian Society* 67 (1958):149.

Only one in five courthouses surveyed in Virginia had copies. James Kimbrough Owen, "The Virginia Vestry: A Study in the Decline of a Ruling Class" (Ph.D. diss., Princeton University, 1947), p. 184; A. O. Porter, "County Government in Virginia: A Legislative History," *Columbia University Studies in History, Economics, and Public Law* #526 (New York, 1947). A committee of the New Hampshire legislature surveying the enforcement of New Hampshire laws as late as 1759 reported that not a single town in the colony had copies of the laws (*Provincial Papers, New Hampshire,* VI:598). Governor Johnson of North Carolina wrote that "upon the strictest inquiry I can't find there is one complete copy of the laws in any one place." George Washington Paschall, *A History of Printing in North Carolina* (Raleigh, 1946), p. 4. See also William Smith's *Laws of New York from the Year 1691 to 1757* (New York, 1952), p. iii.

The Connecticut assembly passed a law exempting Anglicans from supporting Congregational churches, but local authorities interpreted the law very narrowly. Rev. Henry Caner to Bishop Gibson, March 25, 1727/8, Fulham Ms, 229–230, Lambeth Palace. In Amesbury, Mass., the Lieutenant Governor's order not to rate Anglicans for support of the Congregational Church was disregarded by the selectmen. Rev. Matthias Plant to Bishop Gibson, Dec. 20, 1726, Fulham Papers, IV:206–297, Lambeth Palace. The same thing happened in Marblehead: Rev. David Mossom to Gibson April 28, 1729, ibid., 99–100.

34. Nov. 18, 1754. George William Pilcher, ed., *The Reverend Samuel Davies Abroad: The Diary of a Journey to England and Scotland* (Urbana, Ill., 1967), p. 134.

35. Jonathan Law to Benj. Avery, Nov. 1743. Minutes of Diss. Deputies, pp. 266–268.

36. Diss. Deputies Committee to Jonathan Law, Sept. 26, 1744, ibid., pp. 269–270.

37. These figures are tallied from the C.O.5 ser., vols. 752, 866, 1051, 1124, 400, 914, 995 for the period 1715 to 1720, and 866, 868, 874, 875, 1125, 365, 401–402, 915–917, for the decades after 1720.

38. Alison G. Olson, "The Dissenters' Lobby and Eighteenth Century British Colonial Administration," *Journal of American Studies* (forthcoming).

39. Alison G. Olson, "The London Quakers' Lobbying for Pennsylvania Friends," *P.M.H.B.* (forthcoming, 1992).

40. May 5, 1749, Minutes of Diss. Deputies, I:315. For a general discussion of the issue see Arthur Lyon Cross, *The Anglican Episcopate and the American Colonies* (Cambridge, Mass., 1924), ch. 4.

41. The Board's letter to Governor Clinton, June 28, 1745, is in C.O.5/1126 ff285–286.

42. Lewis Cecil Gray, *History of Agriculture in the Southern United States to 1850* (Washington, 1933), pp. 284–285; Stumpf, "Merchants," pp. 110–112. "Some reasons lately received from Mr. Boon, for the taking off the enumeration of rice from Carolina," Nov 24, 1721, *Journal of the Commissioners for Trade and Plantations from November 1718 to December 1722* (Lichtenstein, 1969, reprint of 1925 ed.), p. 330. The Board prepared a letter to the Treasury Lords, Oct. 3, 17, and 31, 1722. *J.B.T.* 1718–1721, pp. 385–388. A petition to the House of Commons presented Nov. 26, 1722. On March 23, 1724/5, the Commons appointed a committee to draw up a bill on the subject, but it never reported (Stock, *Proceedings,* III:456, 480 and n).

For the 1722 petition to the House of Commons see Stock, *Proceedings,* III:476. In 1725 the Board of Trade recommended that merchants be allowed to ship directly to southern Europe (ibid., p. 480). When the allowance came up for renewal five years after its initial passage, the South Carolina merchants also got the support of the Georgia trustees. Note also that London interests also worked to block or at least delay economic legislation their colonial correspondents would not have liked. We have already seen that some merchants were able to delay paper money legislation for more than ten years. A combination of merchants and, somewhat surprisingly, dissenters with New England connections delayed the Sugar Act (an act levying heavy duties on molasses imported into the American Colonies) from 1731 to 1733; the same combination of merchants and dissenters helped to keep out of Parliament a bill levying additional custom duties on Massachusetts to support government there when the colony's assembly refused to vote the governor a permanent salary. At least four times London merchants helped defeat attempts to limit colonial production of wrought iron before an act to that effect finally passed in 1751.

43. The Virginians' efforts are explained in Robert Carter to Micajah Perry, May 25, 1728, Carter Letterbook, VHS. The repeal is described on Feb. 21, 1728, Stock, *Proceedings,* pp. 12–14. For the London merchants' efforts to develop more formal organization at this time, see Jacob M. Price, *France and the Chesapeake* (Ann Arbor, 1973), pp. 651–655.

44. Benjamin Franklin to Joseph Galloway, June 13, 1767, *Papers of Benjamin Franklin* (New Haven, 1970) XIV:183.

45. Thomas Penn to Gov. Morris, Feb. 26, 1755, Penn Letterbook 1754–1756. PHS. When the Bishop of London submitted a representation (favoring the appointment of an American Bishop) to the Privy Council without getting Cabinet approval the matter was postponed without consideration. Cross, *The Anglican Episcopate* p. 118.

46. Baker to Newcastle, Feb 9, 1755. Add Ms 32, 853 ff414.

47. 26/1 mo., 1735 f6, 19/2 mos., 1736, 23/2 mo., 1736. London Meeting for Sufferings, Minutes, XXVI:130, 139, 141.

48. William Bollan to the Speaker of the Massachusetts General Court, May 12, 1753. Misc. bound Mss, MHS.

49. Romney Sedgwick, *The House of Commons, 1715–1754* (New York, 1970), I:139, 148–150.

50. Partridge to Gov. Greene, Nov [24–30], 1748, *Correspondence of Colonial Governors of Rhode Island,* Gertrude S. Kimball, ed. (Boston, 1903), II:83.

51. Richard Partridge to Gov. Greene, Mar 7, 1754, ibid., p. 10.

52. Paul Langford, *The Excise Crisis: Society and Politics in the Age of Walpole* (Oxford, 1975), p. 58; John Mickle Hemphill II, "Virginia and the English Commercial System, 1689–1733: Studies in the Development and Fluctuations of a Colonial Economy under Imperial Control" (Ph.D. diss., Princeton University, 1964), p. 153.

53. The petitions of Feb. 23, 1728/9 and Feb. 1742 were to the House of Lords. They are in bad condition and many of the names are now illegible. House of Lords Mss, Library of Congress.

54. The opposition had ordinarily to wait until a key issue like the tobacco excise crisis or the events leading up to the wars against France and Spain in 1739 and the mid-1750s temporarily aroused public opinion, embarrassed ministers in Parliament, and undermined the government's ability to keep relevant interest groups happy. On these occasions opposition leaders could block a policy, as they did with Walpole's excise plan in 1733, or effect a change in the ministry, as they did in 1742 and 1756. But these crises occurred rarely, and the English opposition in this period was so weak that interest groups could gain nothing by joining them. Sir Lewis Namier,

"Country Gentlemen in Parliament," in *Personalities and Powers* (London, 1955), pp. 59–77. For the country ideology and the difficulty in developing a country idea of party, see J. G. A. Pocock, *The Machiavellian Moment* (Princeton, N.J., 1975), esp. pp. 483–484. Richard Pares, *King George III and the Politicians* (Oxford, 1954), pp. 4–5.

55. Benjamin Avery to Newcastle, Sept. 5, 1756. Add Ms 32, 867 f244. In a number of cases drawing public attention to an issue might limit the favors the government could give. Thus London Quakers advised Philadelphia Quakers regarding an address sent over from the Pennsylvania assembly "to suspend their application for the present" because the address looked like an attack on the proprietors' conduct. 3/10 mo., 1755, London Meeting for Sufferings, Epistles Sent, 1738–1756, III:ff441–445.

56. To Bristol, Liverpool, and Exeter, Jan. 3, 1733. Norman C. Hunt, *Two Early Political Associations: The Quakers and the Dissenting Deputies in the Age of Sir Robert Walpole* (Oxford, 1961), p. 193. When London merchants threatened that they would lend no money to a government that included Henry Fox because Fox would not pay much attention to American defense, their measures were regarded as "unjustifiable," "violent," and "indecent." James Abercromby to the Earl of Halifax [April 7, 1737], Add Ms 32, 870 f327.

57. Charles Wilson, "Government Policy and Private Interest in Modern English History," in his *Economic History and the Historian: Collected Essays* (London, 1969), pp. 140–155.

58. April 4, 1733, Stock, *Proceedings*, IV:205.

59. Secker to Dr. Johnson, July 13, 1760 in Cross, *Anglican Episcopate*, pp. 248–249. William Bollan was even told that one of his parliamentary petitions could not be accepted because it would be "speaking out to the people of America." Bollan to Josiah Willard, March 5, 1755. Misc. bound Mss, MHS. The S.P.C.K. wrote an account of the Salzburgers' expulsion from their homeland. Some S.P.C.K. members wanted to put copies in the coffee house, but it was decided "only to put them into the hands of discreet persons to be dispersed occasionally in religious families." Leonard W. Cowie, *Henry Newman, An American in London, 1708–1743* (London, 1956), p. 228.

60. John Dickinson to Father, April 22, 1754, in Trevor Colbourn, "A Pennsylvania Farmer at the Court of King George: John Dickinson's London Letters, 1754–1756," *P.M.H.B.* 86 (1962):272–273.

61. Letter to Friends in the Country, 27/7 mo., 1734 London Meeting for Sufferings Minutes, XXV:426.

62. March 23, 1749/50, *Journals of the Board of Trade 1749–53* (London, 1932), pp. 46–47.

63. July 3, 1735, ibid., 1734–41 (London, 1930), p. 35.

64. Feb. 9, 1748–49, Stock, *Proceedings*, V:293.

65. Feb. 26, 1729–30, ibid., IV:57.

66. Horatio Walpole to Bishop of London, May 29, 1750, in Cross, *Anglican Episcopate*, p. 326.

67. Jos. Stennett to Newcastle, Nov. 7, 1757, Add. Ms 5044 f454.

68. William Baker to Newcastle, Dec. 3, 1754, ibid., 32, 737 f403.
69. Rodrigo Pacheco to James Alexander, Jan. 14, 1737/8, Alexander Papers, NYHS.
70. John Hodge, *A Sermon Preached at Little St. Helens* (London, 1751), quoted in *Barlow, Citizenship and Conscience,* p. 112.

9. The Governors and the Interests

1. For several of Belcher's nastiest comments see Robert Zemsky, *Merchants, Farmers, and River Gods: An Essay on Eighteenth Century American Politics* (Boston, 1971), pp. 108–109.
2. Board to Belcher, Sept. 23, 1736. C.O.5/917 ff167–71.
3. For Belcher's other chief patrons during his Massachusetts administration see Thomas Hutchinson, *The History of the Colony and Province of Massachusetts Bay,* Laurence S. Mayo, ed. (Cambridge, Mass., 1936.)
4. David Alan Williams, "Political Alignments in Colonial Virginia Politics, 1698–1750" (Ph.D. diss., Northwestern University, 1959), pp. 280, 319; see also Wesley M. Gewehr, *The Great Awakening in Virginia* (Durham, N.C., 1930), p. 40.
5. Andrew Karl Prinz, "Sir William Gooch in Virginia: The King's Good Servant" (Ph.D. diss., Northwestern University, 1963), p. 92.
6. Gooch's estrangement from the Virginia merchants was the result of the excise crisis. Paul Langford, *The Excise Crisis: Society and Politics in the Age of Walpole* (Oxford, 1975), pp. 31–32, and Jacob Price, "The Excise Affair Revisited: The Administrative and Colonial Dimensions of a Parliamentary Crisis," in Stephen Baxter, ed., *England's Rise to Greatness, 1660–1763* (Berkeley, 1983), pp. 272–307. For the subsequent inactivity of the Virginia merchants see Alison G. Olson, "The Virginia Merchants of London: A Study in Eighteenth Century Interest-Group Politics," *W.M.Q.* 3d. ser. 40 (July 1983):363–388.
7. Gooch to Bp. Norwich, March 27, 1728, Quoted in Prinz, "Sir William Gooch," p. 91.
8. Blair to Bishop of London, October 28, 1727. William Stevens Perry, ed., *Papers Relating to the History of the Church in Virginia, A.D. 1650–1776* (n.p., 1870), pp. 352–353. In 1745 Gooch was elected a member of the S.P.G., further evidence of the respect in which he was held by the Anglican Church.
9. Virginia Yearly Meeting to London Yearly Meeting, 19–20/7 mo., 1735. London Yearly Meeting, Epistles Recd., II:500–501, 21–23/7 mo., 1739, III:26–27. Although Quakers were taxed to support King George's War, the earlier concessions were enough to keep the London Meeting for Sufferings from offering any opposition to Gooch.
10. Katherine L. Brown, "The Role of Presbyterian Dissent in Colonial and Revolutionary Virginia, 1740–1785" (Ph.D. diss., Johns Hopkins University, 1969), pp. 43–44. Minutes of Philadelphia Synod, Sept. 22, 1733, *Presb. Records,* p. 100.

11. A letter from the Philadelphia Synod to Gooch was published in the *Virginia Gazette,* Nov. 21, 1745.

12. Samuel Davies, *State of Religion among the Protestant Dissenters in Virginia* (Boston, 1751), p. 16.

13. George William Pilcher, *Samuel Davies, Apostle of Dissent in Colonial Virginia* (Knoxville, Tenn., 1971), pp. 27–32. See also Brown, "Presbyterian Dissent," pp. 80, 89; Prinz, "Gooch," pp. 95–96.

14. Davies, *State of Religion,* p. 21. Belcher mentions other names in his letter to his son. Nov. 1, 1731, Belcher Corr., Library of Congress. Belcher's acquaintance with the King is mentioned in his letter to Colman, Feb. 27, 1729/30, Colman Mss, MHS.

15. Michael Clement Batinski, "Jonathan Belcher of Massachusetts, 1682–1742" (Ph.D. diss., Northwestern University, 1969), p. 193.

16. Bartholomew Schiavo, "The Dissenter Connection: English Dissenters and Massachusetts Political Culture, 1630–1774" (Ph.D. diss., Brandeis University, 1976), p. 319. Batinski, "Belcher," p. 191. Percival Merritt, "The King's Gift to Christ Church," CS *Publ.,* Transactions, 1916–17, XIX:299–308.

17. Belcher to Bishop of Lincoln, Nov. 18, 1731, Belcher Corr., Microfilm, Library of Congress.

18. Schiavo, "The Dissenter Connection," p. 321.

19. Belcher to [Holden, 1734], Colman Ms, MHS.

20. For example, Belcher to J. B. Jr., Nov. 11, 1731, Belcher Corr.

21. John Schutz, "Succession Politics in Massachusetts, 1730–1741," *W.M.Q.,* 3d ser., 15 (October 1958):517.

22. Colman to ? March 7, 1735/6, Colman Ms.

23. W. Harris to Colman, April 29, 1731, Belcher Corr. After Holden's death Belcher looked to Benjamin Avery, his successor as chairman of the Dissenting Deputies, for help at court. Belcher to Avery, Jan. 15, 1741/2. MHS *Coll* (Boston, 1894), p. 551. Belcher to J. B., Jr., Jan. 27, 1741, ibid., p. 367. Schiavo, "The Dissenter Connection," p. 323.

24. See Belcher to Holden, Oct. 29, 1731, Belcher Ms.

25. Colman to "Honored Sir," [1734], Colman Corr.

26. Batinski, "Belcher," p. 267; "Some Ministers" to Gov. Holden [Nov. 1737 draft], Colman Ms.

27. Colman to "Honored Sir" [Holden, 1734], Colman Ms. Massachusetts Congregationalists objected to exempting Baptists as well as Quakers and Anglicans from church rates. In London Baptists joined Congregationalists and Presbyterians in the same lobbies; in Massachusetts they were political and ecclesiastical outcasts.

28. Draft of letter to Isaac Watts, Daniel Neal, and John Guise, Nov. 1737, Colman Ms. "Some Ministers" to Holden, n.d. but on the same subject, ibid.

29. It is hard to judge exactly the breadth and depth of Belcher's support among English Quakers. Belcher himself remarked that they (?) appointed a committee to "write letters up and down the Kingdom in behalf of the governor" but there may have been more than a little wishful thinking in this descrip-

tion (Belcher to "Quakers," Nov. 10, 1737, quoted in Batinski, "Belcher," p. 269).

30. 20/12 mo., 1729, London Meeting for Sufferings Minutes, XXIV:354.
31. William G. McLoughlin, *New England Dissent, 1630–1833* (Cambridge, Mass., 1971) I:234–235. Susan Martha Reed, "Church and State in Massachusetts, 1691–1740," *University of Illinois Studies in the Social Sciences* 3, #4 (Urbana, Ill., 1914), ch. 5. Five years later Belcher got the act renewed.
32. McLoughlin, *New England Dissent*, I:236.
33. Belcher to R. Partridge, Jan. 26, 1740/1, MHS *Coll*, p. 365.
34. Feb. [ ] 1739/40. Copy of a letter signed by York Quakers to Cholmley Turner, M. P., in *Calendar of Treasury Books and Papers, 1739–41*, William A. Shaw, ed. (London, 1901), pp. 224, 232.
35. Belcher to Bishop of Lincoln, Nov. 18, 1731, Belcher Corr.
36. Henry Newman to Bishop of London, May 20, 1731, Lambeth-Fulham Papers.
37. Commissary Price remained a determined and formidable enemy of Belcher's throughout the governor's administration, repeatedly trying to bring him down. See for example Price's letters to the Bishop of Oxford and the Archbishop of Canterbury, Feb. 3 and May 9, 1740 in Perry, ed., *Papers Relating to the Church in Massachusetts*, pp. 336–337, 339–340.
38. Belcher to Henry Newman, Nov. 20, 1731, MHS *Coll*, (1893), pp. 57–60; Belcher to Bp. Gibson, Dec. 9, 1734, MHS *Colls* (1894), pp. 175–177. Merritt, "King's Gift to Christ Church," pp. 299–308.
39. Harwood to Bishop of London, July 19, 1731, in Perry, ed., *Papers Relating to the Church in Massachusetts, A.D. 1676–1785* (1893), pp. 266–269.
40. McLoughlin, *New England Dissent*, I:238.
41. John A. Schutz, "Succession Politics in Massachusetts," *W.M.Q.*, (October 1958):509. Belcher's friends were associated with the attempts to create a moderate circulating currency in the 1730s. Andrew McFarland Davis, "The Merchant's Notes of 1733," MHS *Proc*, XVII:187.
42. For the sendoff see *Daily Journal* (London), March 5, 1730. I am grateful to Ian Steele for this reference. Belcher's expectation that Governor Holden of the Dissenting Deputies would pull in support from the New England merchants is reflected in his letter to J. B., Jr., June 1, 1734, MHS *Coll*, VII:74.
43. G. B. Warden, *Boston, 1689–1776* (Boston, 1970), pp. 108–109, 117.
44. The petition was considered by the Board in November 1740. See Board of Trade to Committee of Council, Nov. 13, 1740, C.O.5/1917 ff329–331. The petition is C.O.5/882 ff89–92. See also Leslie V. Brock, *The Currency of the American Colonies, 1700–1764* (New York, 1975), ch. 2.
45. For a good discussion of the English politics behind Belcher's dismissal see James Henretta, *"Salutary Neglect": Colonial Administration under the Duke of Newcastle* (Princeton, 1972), pp. 212–213.

10. The Coming of the Revolution: The English

1. May 5, 1749, Minutes of Diss. Deputies, 315, 325, 326.

2. Quoted in J. M. Sosin, *Agents and Merchants: British Colonial Policy and the Origins of the American Revolution* (Lincoln, Neb., 1965), p. 176.

3. Leading English Quakers supported the Seven Years' War, for example, while many American Quakers felt morally unable to participate and hence suffered civil penalties. English dissenters did not have a Great Awakening, hence the Dissenting Deputies were not concerned about discrimination against revivalists in a number of colonies. "They can only espouse it [a defense of revivalism] as the Cause of Liberty but Zeal for it in this View is not so vigorous a principle as the other," wrote one disappointed minister to whom the Deputies did not give very much help. English merchants became concerned that the use of paper money as legal tender (outside New England) meant that their loans to colonists would not be repaid at full value; colonists, convinced that paper money was absolutely essential to the colonial economy, attacked the merchants' "unjust and unreasonable clamor." A. T. Gary, "The Political and Economic Relations of English and American Quakers, 1750–1785" (D. Phil., St. Hugh's, Oxford, 1935), p. 64; Jack D. Marietta, "Conscience, the Quaker Community and the French and Indian War," *P.M.H.B.* 95 (1971), pp. 3–31. Entry of Nov. 18, 1754, *The Reverend Samuel Davies Abroad: The Diary of a Journey to England and Scotland,* George William Pilcher, ed. (Urbana, Ill., 1967), p. 134. Notes of June 16, 1963, "Proceedings of the Virginia Committee of Correspondence, 1759–67: Letters to the Agent," *Virg. Mag.* (1903–4):347.

4. James Henretta and Gregory Nobles, *Evolution and Revolution: American Society, 1600–1820* (Lexington, Mass., 1987), p. 128. Alison Gilbert Olson, "Parliament, Empire, and Parliamentary Law, 1776" in *Three British Revolutions: 1641, 1688, 1776,* J. G. A. Pocock, ed. (Princeton, 1980), pp. 291–293; John L. Bullion, *A Great and Necessary Measure: George Grenville and the Genesis of the Stamp Act, 1763–1765* (Columbia, Mo., 1982).

5. Richard Johnson, "Parliamentary Egotisms: The Clash of Legislatures in the Making of the American Revolution," *Journal of American History* 74 (Sept. 1987):358–359.

6. There was in fact a numerical decline in the membership of various London interests. The number of London merchants who signed petitions relating to America dropped from 300 to 275. The dissenting churches represented in the Three Denominations fell from 91 in 1749 to 83 in 1765 (Minutes of the Three Denominations, I:147–154 and II:57–61). Only six Anglican churches were built or rebuilt in the 1750s, 60s, and 70s compared with twenty between 1715 and 1745 (George Rudé, *Hanoverian London, 1714–1808* [Berkeley, 1971], p. 103). In part also the apparent decline in group activity may have reflected the prominence of certain leading individuals— the Quaker John Fothergill, the Baptist Samuel Stennett, or the Virginia merchant Samuel Athawes, for example—who did not need the formal backing of an organization to work effectively with ministers.

7. May 3, 1755, Add Ms 32, 854 f379; Newcastle to Holderness, Aug. 26, 1755, ibid., 858 f289.

8. Newcastle to Barnard, Aug. 23, 1755, ibid., f266.

9. Stennett to Newcastle, Sept. 5, 1756 and Nov. 7, 1757, ibid., 867 f244 and 50, 447 ff424–5.

10. Avery to Newcastle, Nov. 29, 1759 and Sept. 19, 1760, ibid., 899 f67 and 32, 911 f420.

11. Edw. Athawes, Jas. Buchanan, John Buchanan, Wm. Anderson, and John Hanbury to Pitt, Jan. 6, 1757, P.R.O. 30/8/95 ff158–59. For the insurance see Abercromby to Halifax, April 6, 1757, Add. Ms 32, 870 f370.

12. Report of Committee, Feb. 1, 1757, Minutes of the Three Denominations, I:210–211.

13. Feb. 14, 1757, ibid., p. 212.

14. March 1, 1757, ibid., p. 213.

15. Fothergill to I. Pemberton, April 3, 1756, *Chain of Friendship: Selected Letters of Dr. John Fothergill of London, 1735 to 1780* (Cambridge, Mass., 1971), p. 179. For an interpretation less sympathetic to both Granville and the Quakers see Gary, "English and American Quakers," pp. 92–100.

16. Abercromby to Halifax [April 6, 1757] Add. Ms 32, 870 f372.

17. Arthur Herbert Basye, *The Lords Commissioners of Trade and Plantations, Commonly Known as the Board of Trade 1748–1782* (New Haven, 1925), pp. 84, 93–94, 102–104, 111.

18. Entry of Feb. 6, 1754, *Davies Diary*, p. 10. Dupplin's friendship with Halifax is revealed in Dupplin's accounts of the death of Halifax's wife (Dupplin to Newcastle, Oct. 18, 21, and 24, 1753, Add. Ms 32, 733 ff95, 116, 125).

19. Abercromby to Gov. Fauquier, Dec. 28, 1758, Abercromby Letterbook, 1746–1773, VHS. Halifax to Newcastle, Aug. 15, 1753, Add. Ms 33,029 ff96–101; John Hanbury to Newcastle, June 14, 1754, Add. Ms 32, 735 f462; Halifax to Newcastle, Sept. 7, 1754, ibid., 736 f436.

20. Feb. 23, 1757, Minutes of Diss. Deputies, p. 407.

21. For Halifax's hostility to Quakers see Mabel P. Wolff, *The Colonial Agency of Pennsylvania 1712 to 1757* (Philadelphia, 1933), p. 146n2.

22. Thomas Toller to Newcastle, July 23, 1765, Add. Ms 32, 968 f206, and Samuel Stennett's account of moneys distributed, June 10, 1772, ibid., f209; Stennett and Toller's account for July 23, 1765 is ibid., f208.

23. L. S. Sutherland, "Edmund Burke and the First Rockingham Ministry," *English Historical Review* 47 (1932):46–72.

24. Langford, *The Rockingham Ministry*, p. 39.

25. Oct. 6, 1762, Minutes of Diss. Deputies, p. 398. Archbishop of Canterbury to Bishop of London, Oct. 5, 1762, and Bishop of London to Archbishop of Canterbury, Oct. 11, 1762, Lambeth Palace Ms III, #276, 279. The New England Company also supported the Massachusetts Society. William Kellaway, *The New England Company, 1649–1776: Missionary Society to the American Indians* (Westport, Conn., 1975, reprint of 1961 ed.), pp. 195–196.

26. On April 27, 1763, Hollis wrote Dr. Mayhew that the Archbishop was trying to block the Society. On Nov. 21 and Dec. 6 he wrote offering to help New England against the imposition of a Bishop, but only in secret. *Memoirs of Thomas Hollis, Esq.*, Francis Blackburne, ed. (London, 1780), pp. 212–213. See also Jasper Mauduit to Harrison Gray, Oct. 27, 1762, in "Jasper Mauduit, Agent in London for the Province of Massachusetts Bay, 1762–1765," MHS *Coll* 74 (1918):74–75.

27. Basye, *Lords Commissioners of Trade,* p. 107.
28. Ibid., pp. 158–160.
29. Ibid., p. 171.
30. Board of Trade to Privy Council, July 10, 1967, C.O.5/1130 ff200–1. Portents of the new "legalistic" approach had appeared as early as 1749.
31. The lumber bounty appearances were April 1–2, 15, and 27, 1765; one other appearance concerned an unidentified reference from the Earl of Shelburne, Oct. 27, 1767. The Bishop of London appeared on July 7, 1767, *Journal of the Commissioners for Trade and Plantations from January 1764 to Dec. 1767,* 13 (Liechtenstein, 1970, reprint of 1936 ed.):164, 167, 429, 399–400. For paper money see Board of Trade to King, July 6, 1763, C.O.5/1386 ff234–241; Board Minutes, Feb. 1, Feb. 4, Dec. 8, 1763, *Journal of the Commissioners 1759 to 1763,* p. 330, 333, 418; Joseph Albert Ernst, *Money and Politics in America, 1755–1775: A Study in the Currency Act of 1754 and the Political Economy of Revolution* (Chapel Hill, 1973), p. 80.
32. Board of Trade to King, May 31, 1771, C.O.5/920 ff409–410.
33. Board of Trade to Privy Council, June 13, 1766, C.O.5/1296 ff121–131.
34. Ibid., June 26, 1767, C.O.5/920 ff223–230.
35. Ibid., June 13, 1766, C.O.5/1296 ff121–131. Jas. Abercromby to Gov. Fauquier, Abercromby Letterbook, 1746–1773, VHS.
36. 5/2 mo., 1773, Minutes of the London Meeting for Sufferings, 33 (1771–1775):218.
37. "Naturalization of Foreign Protestants in the American and West Indian Colonies," M. S. Guiseppi, ed., HSL *Publ* 24 (London, 1921):xvii to xix includes Richard Jackson's legal opinion of Feb. 9, 1773; Edward A. Hoyt, "Naturalization under the American Colonies: Signs of a New Community," *Political Science Quarterly* 67 (1952):265; A. H. Carpenter, "Naturalization in England and the American Colonies," *American Historical Review* 9 (1903–4):294.
38. This can be seen by comparing the committee of 1766 with the committee of 1775. See "Letters of John Hancock," MHS *Proc* 55 (Feb. 1922):217–223; *American Archives,* 6 vols., Peter Force, ed. (Washington, 1837–1846), I:1086.
39. Capel Hanbury and Osgood Hanbury to George Washington, March 27, 1766, Custis Papers.
40. Petitions, n.d., Add. Mss 38, 340, f102 Hardwicke Papers.
41. Aytoun Ellis, *The Penny Universities: A History of the Coffee Houses* (London, 1956), pp. 108–117.
42. Robert E. Toohey, *Liberty and Empire: British Radical Solutions to the American Problem, 1774–1776* (Lexington, Ky., 1978), p. 10: John A. Sainsbury, *Disaffected Patriots: London Supporters of Revolutionary America, 1769–1782* (Montreal, 1987), pp. 36. 60; *Public Advertiser (London),* May 24, 1769, p. 199.
43. John Brewer, *Party Ideology and Popular Politics at the Accession of George III* (Cambridge, 1976), 201–216.
44. *The Annual Register for 1770* (London, 1771), 113.

45. Toohey, *Liberty and Empire,* 10.
46. *London Chronicle,* Feb. 28–March 2, 1769, pp. 201–208.
47. For a general discussion of merchant divisions, see James E. Bradley, *Popular Politics and the American Revolution in England* (Macon, Ga., 1986) esp. pp. 33–36. For the fate of the merchant lobby, see Katherine A. Kellock, "London Merchants and the pre–1776 American Debts," *Guildhall Studies in London History* (Oct. 1974), I:109–149; John Adams Letterbooks, 1785–1788, Adams Family Papers, MHS; Nutt and Molleson to Henry Dundas, Aug. 31, Nov. 30, 1791, Aug. 18, Aug. 30, 1792, Melville Papers, Clements Library; "Brief Statement of the Claims of the British Merchants," n.d., ibid.; Charles R. Ritcheson, *Aftermath of Revolution: British Policy toward the United States, 1783–1795* (Dallas, 1969), pp. 41, 57–58, 80, 125, 148, 150, 319; T. M. Devine, *The Tobacco Lords: A Study of the Tobacco Merchants of Glasgow and Their Trading Activities, 1740–1790* (Edinburgh, 1975), pp. 153–158; Edward Papenfuse, *In Pursuit of Profit: The Annapolis Merchants in the Era of the American Revolution 1763–1805* (Baltimore, 1975), pp. 108, 184–185, 207–209, 216, 218, 223; *The Papers of Thomas Jefferson,* ed. Julian P. Boyd, ed. (Princeton, 1950–1974), 9:403–405; *Parliamentary History of England,* Cobbett, ed., 28:177–180, 243–255, 481–483, 662–695, 738.
48. Colin Bonwick, *English Radicals and the American Revolution* (Chapel Hill, 1977), pp. 56–57.
49. Carl Bridenbaugh, *Mitre and Sceptre: Trans atlantic Faiths, Ideas, Personalities, and Politics, 1689–1775* (New York, 1962), p. 287.
50. Richard Burgess Barlow, *Citizenship and Conscience: A Study in the Theory and Practice of Religious Toleration in England During the Eighteenth Century* (Philadelphia, 1963), p. 148.
51. Exact copy of the clergy's petition to the House of Commons against subscription, *London Chronicle,* Feb. 6–8, 1772, p. 129.
52. Barlow, *Citizenship and Conscience,* p. 150.
53. Background note, Jan. 31, 1772, Cobbett, ed., *The Parliamentary History of England,* XVII:247.
54. Barlow, *Citizenship and Conscience,* p. 156.
55. It is impossible to know whether the majority of Anglicans fragmented similarly or favored the petition in the first place: the latitudinarian London ministers who rejected the Articles as too Calvinistic certainly did not have the support of the more Calvinistic clergy in the provinces. But even among those who did object to the Articles some had doubts about the methods of the association. The fact that the petitioners collected only 250 signatures suggests early doubts about the propriety of the informal meetings at which the petition was drawn up. So does the fact that Anglican opponents of the petition enclosed copies of hostile sermons in letters they circulated to all Members of Parliament in the winter of 1772–73. When North objected to the petition, cautious members argued that it would "be more proper to address the Bishops than to bring the matter directly before Parliament" even though the bishops represented an established group known to be government supporters. After the failure of the petition some ministers,

John Jebb and Theophilus Lindsay, for instance, left the church, and most of the others became Unitarian. Some stayed in but were openly critical of the government. Both groups tended to sympathize with the Americans, while the more Calvinistic provincials did not. By the eve of the American Revolution Anglicans, like the merchants, lined up on a continuum from firm support of the Americans to outright hostility. "To the Author of a Letter of the Members of the House of Commons, by a Christian Whig," _London Chronicle,_ Feb. 6–8, 1772, p. 132. "A short appeal to serious and candid professors of Christianity" in support of the petition was sent to members of both houses. H. Venn to the printer of the _London Chronicle,_ March 14–17, 1772, p. 261. Barlow, _Citizenship and Conscience,_ pp. 150–151 n46. After the parliamentary defeat they did in fact address the bishops but got nowhere.

56. Ibid., pp. 171–172.
57. Ibid., p. 178.
58. March 4, 1772. Minutes of Three Denominations, II:109.
59. Barlow, _Citizenship and Conscience,_ p. 184.
60. Anthony Lincoln, _Some Political and Social Ideas of English Dissent, 1763–1800_ (New York, 1971, reprint of 1938 ed.), p. 27.
61. _London Chronicle,_ April 4–7, 1772, p. 336.
62. Barlow, _Citizenship and Conscience,_ p. 177.
63. June 10, 1772. Minutes of Three Denominations, II:116.
64. Israel Mauduit, _The Case of the Dissenting Ministers, Addressed to the Lords Spiritual and Temporal,_ 4th ed. (Boston, 1773), p. 46.
65. Dec. 23, 1772. Minutes of Three Denominations, II:122–125.
66. Lincoln, _English Dissent,_ p. 230. David Doubtful to Rev. Mr. Picard, _London Chronicle,_ Feb. 16–18, 1773, p. 164. The quote is in Letter II to Dr. J-bb, ibid., Feb. 9–11, 1773, p. 141.
67. Joseph Priestly appealed to dissenters: "You have hitherto preferred your prayer as Christians; stand forth now in the character of men." _A Letter of Advice to Those Dissenters Who Conduct the Application to Parliament for Relief from Certain Penal Laws_ (London, 1773), p. 3. See H. T. Dickinson, _Liberty and Property: Political Ideology in Eighteenth Century Britain_ (New York, 1977), pp. 195, 202–203.
68. Francis Blackburne noted that when Parliament debated the issue there were people in the galleries who had "no other conception of the nature of the controversy than what they had picked up from coffee house declamations." _Reflections on the Fate of a Petition for Relief in the Matter of Subscription,_ 2nd ed. (London, 1774), p. 2.
69. Minutes of Three Denominations, Dec. 23, 1772, and Jan. 27, 1773, II:122–125, 126–128; Barlow, _Citizenship and Conscience,_ p. 185.
70. April 21, 1761. Minutes of Three Denominations I:253. On May 19, 1772, the Bishop of London argued, from the example of one meeting, that dissenters were indifferent to the application.
71. March 18, 1779, April 26, 1779, June 2, 1779. Minutes of Three Denominations, II:195–199, 209, 210–217; Ursula Henriques, _Religious Toleration in England, 1787–1833_ (London, 1961), p. 56; Barlow, _Citizenship and Conscience,_ pp. 202–207.

72. Report of May 22, 1772, Lords' debate on the Bill for Relief of Dissenters. *London Chronicle*, May 21–23, 1772, p. 490.

73. Priestly, "Works," 22:482–487, 496, quoted in Bonwick, *English Radicals and the American Revolution*, pp. 120–121. See also Priestly's *Letter of Advice*, p. 29, and Richard Price's *Additional Observations on the Nature and Value of Civil Liberty and the War in America* (London, 1777).

74. Hollis to [Simeon Howard], Jan. 4, 1775, quoted in Bonwick, *English Radicals and the American Revolution*, p. 121.

75. Sir Lewis Namier and John Brooke, *The House of Commons 1754–1790* (London, 1964), I:17.

76. Lincoln, *Ideas of English Dissent*, p. 26.

77. Rippon to James Manning, May 1, 1784. Reuben Aldridge Guild, *Life, Times and Correspondence of James Manning and the Early History of Brown University* (Boston, 1864), p. 324.

78. "The Address and Petition of the People called Quakers," (n.d. 1774 or 1775), Dartmouth Mss, Staffordshire D(W) 1778/II/1237. Fothergill to Dartmouth, Jan 12? and Feb. 6?, 1775, *Chain of Friendship*, pp. 435–437, 442–443.

79. On 17/3 mo., 1769, the London Meeting for Sufferings advised "Friends in the Several Provinces of North America" to keep out of all tumults (Minutes, XXXII:247–249).

80. Gary, "English and American Quakers," (Oxford, 1935), p. 353.

11. The Coming of the Revolution: American

1. For a description of the "shock" Massachusetts experienced over the new parliamentary regulations see Richard L. Bushman, *King and People in Provincial Massachusetts* (Chapel Hill, 1985), pp. 179–182. Marc Egnal divides the colonists into "expansionists" and nonexpansionists in the pre-revolutionary period and suggests that "religion and national origin also helped determine the composition of the parties." *A Mighty Empire: The Origins of the American Revolution* (Ithaca, 1988) pp. 7, 18.

2. William Lee to Richard Henry Lee, Sept. 10, 1774. Lee Papers, University of Virginia Library, Charlottesville.

3. Thomas Fisher to James Russell, Aug. 27, 1774. Russell Papers, Messrs. Coutts & Co., London. William Nelson wrote John Norton that complaints about Norton's political activities "proceed from the Representation or rather misrepresentation of a Gentn now in London to whom I believe you are no stranger." Nov. 18, 1769, William and Thomas Nelson Letterbook, 1766 to 1775, VHS.

4. William Beverley to John Morton Jordan, March 3 [1762], William Beverley Letterbook, 1761–1765, Library of Congress.

5. *Daily Advertiser*, Sept. 30, 1775.

6. Philip Fendall to James Russell, Nov. 15, 1774, Russell Papers.

7. Thomas Nelson to T. and R. Hunt, May 20, 1773. William and Thomas Nelson Letterbook, 1766–1775. Nelson, however, was talking about the Hunts' unwillingness to send goods before reimbursement.

8. Nelson to Samuel Athawes, Aug. 7, 1774. Ibid.

9. Philip Fendall to James Russell, Nov. 15, 1774, Russell Papers.

10. *London Gazette,* Oct. 10–14, 1775.

11. Alison G. Olson, "The 'Rise' of the Colonial Assemblies in the Eighteenth Century: Myth or Reality?" Paper presented at the American Historical Association Meetings, Dec. 1974.

12. R.C. Simmons and P. D. G. Thomas, eds., *Proceedings and Debates of the British Parliaments Respecting North America,* vols. I and II (London, 1982), passim.

13. March 18, 1766, *Eccl. Records, N.Y.,* VI:4046–48. They initially appealed to the governor. Richard W. Pointer, *Protestant Pluralism and the New York Experience* (Bloomington, 1988), pp. 61–62. In March 1775 Philip Shrene and John Vardill wrote Lord Dartmouth urging the incorporation [letter undated: March 1775 written by archivist] D(W) 1778/11/1200 Dartmouth Mss, Staffordshire.

14. In 1767 Boston merchants sent a petition directly to Dennys DeBerdt, the colonial agent. Charles McLean Andrews, "The Boston Merchants and the Non-Importation Movement," CS *Publ.,* XIX:16–17.

15. Philip Davidson, *Propaganda and the American Revolution, 1763–83* (Chapel Hill, 1941), p. 66, discusses the use of workingmen's associations to fight British legislation.

16. For a protest against the Sugar Act see *The Memorial of the Merchants of the City of New York . . . to the Honourable The Knights, Citizens, and Burgesses in Parliament Assembled* (New York, 1764).

17. Dennys DeBerdt to ?, March 1, 1768, "Letters of Dennys DeBerdt, 1757–1770," CS *Publ.,* Transactions for 1910–11, II:331–332.

18. Carl Bridenbaugh, *Mitre and Sceptre: Transatlantic Faiths, Ideas, Personalities, and Politics, 1689–1775* (Oxford, 1962), p. 282.

19. Benjamin Franklin's letter to Thomas Cushing, April 2, 1774, and summaries of the petition against the first coercive act and against the second two acts are in William B. Willcox, ed., *The Papers of Benjamin Franklin* (New Haven, 1978), XXI:155.

20. John Brooke, *The House of Commons, 1754–1790: Introductory Survey* (Oxford, 1964), p. 234.

21. Nicholas Varga, "The New York Restraining Act," *New York History* 37(1956):239.

22. William Williams to Rev. Samuel Peters. 10 Oct. 1774. Kenneth Walter Cameron, ed., *The Church of England in Pre-Revolutionary Connecticut* (Hartford, Conn., 1976), p. 192. A pamphleteer described "the insidious whispers, which the General at London of the American Clergy to the disgrace of his elevated station is ever dropping into the ears of the King's ministers."

23. Nov. 30, 1774. Franklin Bowditch Dexter, ed., *The Literary Diary of Ezra Stiles, D.D.L.* (New York, 1901), I:491.

24. This is discussed much more fully in Alison G. Olson, "The 'Rise' of Three Colonial Legislatures in the Eighteenth Century: Virginia, Massachusetts and Pennsylvania." Paper presented at the Philadelphia Center for Early American Studies, Oct. 5, 1990.

The Massachusetts General Court continued to "direct" cases in other courts and actually increased the amount of time committees spent on petitions from executors of estates. The Maryland assembly also ceased hearing cases, though in one extraordinary session it approved (over the vocal opposition of assembly members who opposed the propriety of even considering the case) a marriage settlement. J. Hall Pleasants, ed., *Archives of Maryland*. Vol. LXI: *Proceedings and Acts of the General Assembly of Maryland 1766–68* (Baltimore, 1944), p. xcvii.

The New York assembly intervened in court proceedings as late as 1772 to acquit a defendant and charge a grand jury with perjury, but this was so unusual as to be widely noticed in the press. See, for example, *Speech of Mr. Justice Livingston Made on Friday the 25th of January in Support of His Claim to a Seat in the House of the General Assembly* (New York, 1771), and *The Sentiments of a Free and Independent Elector on the Resolution of the House of Assembly, for Excluding Judges of the Supreme Court* (New York, 1771).

When the New Jersey assembly interfered with court proceedings in 1756, they felt it necessary to explain that the interference occurred only because riots had prevented the normal functioning of those courts. See the 1756 New Jersey act for the trial of Benjamin Springer. Mary Patterson Clarke, *Parliamentary Privilege in the American Colonies* (New Haven, 1943), discusses the "tumultuous manner" in which mobs rescued prisoners during the land riots in 1747 (p. 124 n93).

The South Carolina assembly increased the number of its standing committees from ten in 1737 to fifteen in 1772, adding among others a standing committee on the colony's poor. Virginia doubled the number of its standing committees from three to six between 1732 and 1765, adding a committee on trade and one on religion. Maryland added one to possibly two to four existing at mid-century. Pennsylvania, which had no standing committees at all in 1720, had two by 1744 and added a third that year. In 1743 New York had a select committee on privileges and elections and grand committees on grievances, courts of justice, and trade. New Jersey established a committee on grievances in 1771. This information is taken from the journals themselves, but see also George Edward Frakes, *Laboratory for Liberty: The South Carolina Legislative Committee System, 1719–1776* (Lexington, Kentucky, 1970), p. 87; Robert Zemsky, *Merchants, Farmers, and River Gods: An Essay on Eighteenth-Century American Politics* (Boston, 1971), pp. 25–27; Sister Joan deLeonard, "The Organization and Procedure of the Pennsylvania Assembly, 1682–1776, *P.M.H.B.* 72 (1948):215–239, 376–412; S. M. Pargellis, "Procedure of Virginia House of Burgesses," *W.M.Q.* 7 (1927):153.

25. Frakes, *Laboratory for Liberty*, p. 37. Zemsky, *Farmers, Merchants, and River Gods*, p. 248. See "professional" politicians in Massachusetts.

26. By 1749, for example, 51.7 percent of all committee assignments went to the twelve most active representatives in the Massachusetts General Court. Zemsky, *River Gods*, p. 288. Ten of the eighteen Virginia Burgesses who served eight or more terms in the top rank of leadership achieved that rank

between 1746 and 1760. Jack P. Greene, "Political Power in the House of Burgesses," *W.M.Q.*, ser. III 16 (1959):485–506. This conclusion is derived from Greene's list of Burgesses.

27. Patricia U. Bonomi, *A Factious People* (New York, 1971), p. 174; *South Carolina Gazette*, Nov. 13, 1749; *The Speech of Joseph Galloway, Esq. Delivered in the House of Representatives, Is Published by Their Order . . . An Act for Granting Compensation to the Sufferers and . . . Indemnity and Oblivion to the Offenders in the Late Times* (Boston, 1767); *The Following Bill Is Printed by Order of the Two Houses . . . An Act for incorporating a Society for Relieving the Widows and Orphans* (Boston, 1767); *Votes and Proceedings of the Lower House of Assembly for September, 1765* (Annapolis, 1765). The inhabitants of Boston met in 1763 to consider a Provincial Tax Bill: *Notice of a Town Meeting in Faneuil Hall on Sept. 21, 1763* (Boston, 1763). *A Dialogue between Two Gentlemen in New York* (Philadelphia, 1744), p. 4.

28. In the period 1750 to 1755, for example, the Virginia House of Burgesses received a petition from tobacco planters seeking a limit on the number of tobacco plants grown, one from merchants opposing the system of tobacco inspection stations, and one from a land company. Between 1760 and 1765 they received petitions from attorneys seeking regulation of their practice, from leather manufacturers seeking encouragement, from innkeepers on the regulation of prices, and a total of thirteen petitions from various groups of merchants on various subjects from peddlers to pilots to collection of debts. In Pennsylvania, where interest groups early began working with the legislature, the number and variety increased only slightly. To the petitions from United Brethren, bakers, merchants and lawyers combined, Chester farmers, coopers, and two from merchants in the period 1750 to 1755, (seven different petitions) we add those from insurance dealers, bakers, merchants, tradesmen, shopkeepers, the Friendly Association, the Ephrata Society, the Seventh Day Dunkers, and two from the Philadelphia Germans in 1760–1765. But in New York the change was striking. Between 1750 and 1755 only the coopers and one church petitioned; between 1760 and 1765 ironworks owners, the Dutch Church, cordwainers, wharf owners, New York City merchants, Ulster linen manufactures, and spinsters all petitioned the legislature. For Virginia see H. R. McIlwaine, ed., *Journals of the House of Burgesses of Virginia* (Richmond, Virginia, 1907–1912), for Pennsylvania petitions see Gertrude McKinney, ed., *Pennsylvania Archives*, ser. 8, vols. II-V (Philadelphia, 1931). For New York see William Sumner Jenkins, comp., Records of the States of the United States [New York]. Microfilm.

29. Arthur Meier Schlesinger, *The Colonial Merchants and the American Revolution, 1763–1776* (New York, 1917), p. 61.

30. Andrews, "The Boston Merchants and the Non-Importation Movement," pp. 3–7.

31. Schlesinger, *Colonial Merchants*, pp. 60–61, 116; Virginia D. Harrington, *The New York Merchant on the Eve of the Revolution* (Gloucester, Mass., 1964), p. 74; Philip Davidson, *Propaganda and the American Revolution*

1763–83 (Chapel Hill, 1941), pp. 63–64. For further political activities of the New York merchants see also John Austin Stevens, ed., *Colonial Records of the New York Chamber Of Commerce, 1768–1784* (New York, 1971, reprint of 1867 ed.), Nov. 1, 1768; June 6, Oct. 3, Nov. 7, 1769; Feb. 15, March 24, 1770, pp. 21, 46, 58–59, 63, 76–77, 87–88. See also "The Meeting of the Merchants, Held in Williamsburg, in 1770," *Virginia Historical Register* 3 (1850):79–81.

32. Germans organized the German Society of Pennsylvania in 1764 and the German Friendly Society in Charles Town in 1766. A. G. Roeber, "The Origin of Whatever is Not English Among Us: The Dutch-Speaking and the German-Speaking Peoples of Colonial British America," in Bernard Bailyn and Philip D. Morgan, eds., *Strangers Within the Realm: Cultural Margins of the First British Empire* (Chapel Hill, 1991) pp. 260–275.

33. Patricia Bonomi has highlighted this in her admirable work, *Under the Cope of Heaven: Religion, Society, and Politics in Colonial America* (Oxford, 1986), ch. 5. The fastest-growing churches in the period were Baptists, Presbyterians, and Congregationalists.

	1750	*1760*	*1770*	*1780*
Baptists	175	240	325	457
Presbyterians	275	310	375	495
Congregationalists	525	625	675	750

The number of Anglican churches grew from 246 in 1740 to 406 in 1780. Edwin Scott Gaustad, *Historical Atlas of Religion in America,* rev. ed. (New York, 1976), pp. 5, 9, 12, 15, 18, 21, 28, 33.

34. For a suggestion of this see the report of the Methodist Conference March 25–7, 1774, to John Wesley. John Telford, ed., *The Letters of the Rev. John Wesley, A.M.* (London, 1960, reprint of 1931 ed.), VI:102–103.

35. Richard Bauman, *For the Reputation of Truth: Politics, Religion, and Conflicts Among the Pennsylvania Quakers, 1750–1800* (Baltimore, 1971) p. 73.

36. In 1759 and 1766 Ezra Stiles proposed a Union of New England Churches and the Presbyterian Synods in the middle colonies. Edmund Morgan, *The Gentle Puritan: A Life of Ezra Stiles, 1727–1795* (New York, 1962) pp. 203–204. In 1776 New England Baptists proposed a Continental Congress of Baptists. William G. McLoughlin, *New England Dissent, 1630–1833: The Baptists and the Separation of Church and State* (Cambridge, Mass., 1971), I:567.

37. Katherine L. Brown, "The Role of Presbyterian Dissent in Colonial and Revolutionary Virginia, 1740 to 1785" (Ph.D. diss., Johns Hopkins University, 1969), p. 354.

38. May 28, 1767 and May 20, 1768. *Presb. Records,* pp. 374, 381.

39. McLoughlin, *New England Dissent,* I:510.

40. Bridenbaugh, *Mitre and Sceptre,* p. 179; Jeremiah Leaming to Bishop of

London, June 5, 1765, Cameron, ed., *The Church of England in Pre-Revolutionary Connecticut*, p. 133.

41. Bridenbaugh, *Mitre and Sceptre*, pp. 260–261. Religious coalitions had developed earlier in Pennsylvania. See Alan Tully's "Ethnicity, Religion, and Politics in Early America," esp. p. 12.

42. For New York, see Richard Wayne Pointer, *Protestant Pluralism and the New York Experience: A Study of Eighteenth Century Religious Diversity* (Bloomington, Ind., 1985), p. 65. For South Carolina, see Richard Walsh, *Charleston's Sons of Liberty: A Study of the Artisans, 1763–89* (Columbia, S.C., 1959), pp. 31, 50.

43. New York, 1769.

44. *Truth Triumphant; or, A Defence of the Church of England Against the Second Solemn League and Covenant, Published under the Title of the Glorious Combination, etc.* (New York, 1969).

45. *The Sincere Friends to the Trade and Prosperity of the City of New York . . .* (New York, 1968).

46. *An Epistle from the Meeting for Sufferings, Held in Philadelphia for Pennsylvania and New Jersey, the 5th Day of the First Month, 1775* (Philadelphia, 1775).

47. May 20, 1775. *Presb. Records,* p. 466–67.

48. Convention of ye Clergy of the Chh of England in Connecticut, Sept. 20, 1774. Cameron, ed., *Church of England,* p. 190.

49. See, for example, Roger William Moss, "Master Builders: A History of the Colonial Philadelphia Building Trades" (Ph.D. diss., Delaware, 1972), pp. 23, 86. See also Samuel D. McKee, *Labor in Colonial New York* (Long Island, 1965), p. 42; Leonard Bernstein, "The Working People of Philadelphia from Colonial Times to the General Strike of 1835," *P.M.H.B.* 74 (1950):323; John Duffy, *A History of Public Health in New York City, 1625–1866* (New York, 1968), p. 65; Jonathan Harris, "The Rise of Medical Science in New York, 1720–1820" (Ph.D. diss., New York University, 1971), p. 25; Erna Risch, "Immigrant Aid Societies before 1820," *P.M.H.B.* 60 (1936):15–33; Richard Harrison Shryock, *Medical Licensing in America, 1650–1965* (Baltimore, 1967), p. 15.

50. *An Historical Catalogue of the St. Andrew's Society of Philadelphia, 1759–1881* (Philadelphia, 1881), p. 16.

51. January 25, 1770. *J.B.T.* 1768–1775, XII:165.

52. The Charleston St. Andrew's Society, for example, included James Crokatt, Alex Skene, James Abercromby, and John Cleland. J. H. Esterby, *History of the St. Andrew's Society of Charleston, South Carolina, 1729–1929* (Charleston, 1929), p. 31. See also John Rowe's references to participating in charitable groups, in Anne Rowe Cunningham, ed., *Letters and Diary of John Rowe, Boston Merchant, 1759–62, 1764–79* (Boston, 1903), esp. pp. 65, 71, 75, 80.

53. This analysis is based largely, though not exclusively, on the following sources: Risch, "Immigrant Aid Societies before 1820," pp. 15–33; George Congouale, comp., *The History of the German Friendly Society of Charleston, South Carolina, 1766–1916* (Richmond, 1935); *An Historical Cata-*

logue of the St. Andrews Society of Philadelphia, 1749–1881 (1881); *Historical Sketch of the Saint Andrew's Society of the State of New York* (New York, 1856); *Rules, etc., of the St. Andrew's Society at New York . . . 1764* (New York, 1915); John H. Campbell, *History of the Friendly Sons of St. Patrick and of the Hibernian Society for the Relief of Emigrants from Ireland, March 17, 1771–March 17, 1892* (Philadelphia, 1892); George Austin Morrison, *History of the Saint Andrew's Society of the State of New York, 1756–1906* (New York, 1906); Louis Hennighausen, *History of the German Society of Maryland* (Baltimore, 1909); Richard C. Murphy and Lawrence Mannion, *The History of the Society of the Friendly Sons of Saint Patrick, in the City of New York, 1784 to 1955* (New York, 1962). Minutes of the Society of the Sons of St. George, PHS. Rules, Minutes, etc. of the Society of the Friendly Sons of St. Patrick, PHS; Remarks of the Society for the Benefit and Relief of Poor Decay'd Masters of Ships, Their Widows and Children, PHS; Burton Alva Konkle, A History of the Presbyterian Ministers' Fund, 1717–1928, PHS; Whitfield J. Bell, Jr., "Social History of Pennsylvania, 1760–1790," *P.M.H.B.* 62 (1938):281–308; Nicholas Wainwright, *The Philadelphia Contributionship* (Philadelphia, 1952), p. 21; James Dow McCallum, *Eleazer Wheelock* (New York, 1969), pp. 141–165; Raymond A. Mohl, "Poverty in Early America, a Reappraisal: The Case of Eighteenth Century New York City" *New York History* 50 (1969):5–28.

For samples of material on labor organizations, see Charles S. Olton, "Philadelphia's Mechanics and the First Decade of Revolution 1765 to 1775," *Journal of American History* 59 (1972):311–326; McKee, *Labor in Colonial New York,* esp. pp. 42–44; James Hutson, "An Investigation of the Inarticulate: Philadelphia's White Oaks," *W.M.Q.,* 3rd ser., 28 (Jan. 1971):3–22.; Bernstein, "The Working People of Philadelphia from Colonial Times to the General Strike of 1835," *P.M.H.B.* 74:322–339; Minutes of the Transactions of the Taylor's Company of Philadelphia, Aug. 20, 1771, PHS.

For professional societies see Milton Martin Klein, "The American Whig: William Livingston of New York" (Ph.D. diss., Columbia University, 1954); Harold B. Gill, Jr., *The Apothecary in Colonial Virginia* (Charlottesville, 1972) esp. pp. 24–28; Duffy, *Public Health in New York City,* esp. p. 65; Jonathan Harris, "The Rise of Medical Science in New York, 1720 to 1820" (Ph.D. diss., New York University, 1979), esp. pp. 25–26; Charles Robert McKirdy, "Lawyers in Crisis: The Massachusetts Legal Profession, 1760 to 1790" (Ph.D. diss., Northwestern University, 1969) esp. pp. 22 to 33; Gerard Wilfred Gawalt, "Massachusetts Lawyers: A Historical Analysis of the Process of Professionalization, 1760 to 1840" (Ph.D. diss., Clark University, 1969); John Robert Aiken, "Utopianism and the Emergence of the Colonial Legal Profession: New York 1664 to 1710, a Test Case" (Ph.D. diss., Rochester University, 1967).

For land companies see Shaw Livermore, *Early American Land Companies: Their Influence on Corporate Development* (New York, 1969), pp. 5 to 626; Kenneth Bailey, *The Ohio Company of Virginia and the Westward Movement, 1748 to 1792* (Glendale, Calif., 1939).

For useful social histories see Carl and Jessica Bridenbaugh, *Rebels and Gentlemen: Philadelphia in the Age of Franklin* (New York, 1962), esp. pp. 229–243, 260; Gary Warden, *Boston, 1689–1776* (Boston, 1970), p. 217; Gary Nash, *The Urban Crucible: Social Change, Political Consciousness, and the Origins of the American Revolution* (Cambridge, Mass., 1979); James Duncan Phillips, *Salem in the Eighteenth Century* (New York, 1937), chs. 15 and 16.

54. Carl Romaneck, "John Reynell, Quaker Merchant of Colonial Philadelphia" (Ph.D. diss., Pennsylvania State University, 1969), p. 145. But note Thomas Doerflinger's reference to a letter from James and Drinker to David Barclay and Sons, Oct. 14, 1765, saying Friends were not involved in political disturbances in 1765. *A Vigorous Spirit of Enterprise: Merchants and Economic Development in Revolutionary Pennsylvania* (Chapel Hill, 1986), p. 189 n76.

55. May 30, 1766. *Presb. Records*, p. 362.

56. May 1766. Cameron, *Church of England*, p. 140.

57. C. and O. Hanbury to George Washington, March 27, 1766, Custis Papers, VHS. See Arthur Jensen, *The Maritime Commerce of Colonial Pennsylvania* (Madison, 1963), p. 161.

58. William Nelson to John Norton, July 25, 1766. William and Thomas Nelson Letterbook, VHS.

59. Eighteen merchants to David Barclay, Jr., Daniel Mildred, Thomas Powell, Dennys De Berdt, Christopher Chambers, Frederick Pigou, Jr., and Richard Neave. *P.M.H.B.* 27 (1903):84–87.

60. Morgan, *The Gentle Puritan*, p. 244; Bonomi, *Under the Cope of Heaven*, p. 207.

61. John W. Tyler, *Smugglers and Patriots: Boston Merchants and the Advent of the American Revolution* (Boston, 1986), ch. 3.

62. Pauline Maier, *From Resistance to Revolution* (New York, 1972), p. 121.

63. For a general discussion of the way larger meetings played on the support of older, more conventional interests in Boston see Warden, *Boston*, p. 217.

64. William Reynolds to George F. Norton, June 3, 1774. Reynolds Letterbook, Library of Congress. Ironically, the Tea Act had provided some London merchants with their best chance to obtain patronage, in the form of commissions to handle tea, for their American correspondents. Frances Drake, *Tea Leaves* (Detroit, 1970 reprint of 1884 ed.), pp. 202–233.

65. James Weems to Russell, Dec. 7, 1774, Russell Papers, Messrs. Coutts and Co., London.

66. Philip Davidson, *Propaganda and the American Revolution* (Chapel Hill, 1941), p. 93.

67. Quoted in Bauman, *For the Reputation of Truth*, p. 143.

68. Ibid., p. 147.

69. Biddle to Jonathan Potts [Feb. 25, 1775]. Paul H. Smith, ed., *Letters of Delegates to Congress, August 1774–August 1775* (Washington, D.C., 1976), p. 315.

70. Quoted in Bauman, *For the Reputation of Truth*, p. 148.

71. Christopher Marshall to J—N P—C (John Peirse?) April 9, 1775, quoted in Oaks, "Philadelphia Merchants," p. 193.
72. Ibid., p. 173.
73. Quoted in Bauman, *For the Reputation of Truth*, p. 148. The statistics are on p. 157. *An Epistle from the Meeting for Sufferings . . . for Pennsylvania and New Jersey . . .* [Philadelphia, 1775] exhorted "gentle admonition to those members drawn into defense of liberty" for using measures not compatible with Quaker beliefs.
74. Wesley to American preachers, March 1, 1775. Telford, *Letters of the Rev. John Wesley,* VI:142–143.
75. Pastoral letter, May 20, 1775. *Presb. Records,* p. 468.
76. John to Abigail Adams. June 11, 1775. Smith, ed., *Letters of Delegates,* p. 478.
77. *Pastoral Letter from the Synod of New York and Philadelphia, May 22, 1775* (New York, 1775).
78. Isaac Backus, *A History of New England with Particular Reference to the Baptists* (New York, 1969), pp. 160, 176–179, 196; McLoughlin, *New England Dissent,* I:580.
79. James Manning to Benjamin Wallen [ ], 1774. Quoted in McLoughlin, *New England Dissent,* I:580; Backus, *History of New England,* pp. 200–204.
80. Rev. Weeks to S.P.G. Committee, Sept. 7, 1775, S.P.G. Minutes. Journals, vol. 20, pt. 2, Library of Congress.
81. Rev. Thomas Barton to Dr. Hind, June 10, 1775. S.P.G. Letters from Pennsylvania, 21.
82. Richard Peters, William Smith, Jacob Duché, Thomas Coombe, William Stringer, William White, to Bishop of London, June 30, 1775. William Stevens Perry, ed., *Papers Relating to the History of the Church in Pennsylvania, A.D. 1680 to 1778* (n.p., 1871), pp. 470–472.
83. General Meeting of New York and New Jersey to Classis of Amsterdam, Oct. 8, 1778. *Eccl. Records, N.Y.,* VI.
84. Rev. J. Weeks to Dr. Hind, Sept. 7, 1775. S.P.G. Inbound Letters from Massachusetts, 1757 to 1784, vol. 22.
85. June 15, 1774, *Letters and Diary of John Rowe,* Cunningham, ed., p 275; *New York Journal,* June 30, 1774.
86. *New York Gazette and the Weekly Mercury,* June 27, 1774.
87. James and Drinker to Benjamin Booth, Sept. 24, 1774. Oaks, "Philadelphia Merchants," p. 159.
88. *New York Gazette,* July 19, 1774.
89. Davidson, *Propaganda and Revolution,* pp. 65–66.
90. Benjamin Labaree, *Patriots and Partisans: The Merchants of Newburyport, 1764 to 1816* (Cambridge, Mass., 1962), pp. 66–67, 84. See also Richard Henry Rudolph, "The Merchants of Newport, Rhode Island, 1763–1786" (Ph.D. diss., University of Connecticut, 1975), p. 232.
91. Robert Michael Director; "The New York Commercial Community: The Revolutionary Experience" (Ph.D. diss., Pittsburg University, 1975), p. 110.
92. June 28, 1774, *Rowe Diary,* p. 276.

93. Tyler, *Smugglers and Patriots,* pp. 258, 272.
94. Bauman, *For the Reputation of Truth,* p. 146; Thomas Wharton to T. Walpole, Aug. 20, 1774. Thomas Wharton Letterbook, PHS.
95. Byles to Dr. Hind, April 29, 1775. S.P.G. Inbound Letters from Massachusetts, 1757 to 1784, vol. 22.
96. Scotch Irish were sharply divided over the Revolution. Maldwyn A. Jones, "The Scotch Irish in British America," in Bailyn and Morgan, eds., *Strangers Within the Realm,* pp. 309–310. For the ambivalence of one group of merchants see Thomas Doerflinger, *A Vigorous Spirit of Enterprise: Merchants and Economic Development in Revolutionary Philadelphia* (Chapel Hill, 1986), pp. 167–168. The divided sympathies of Dutch clergy in New York in 1776 are indicated clearly by the list of clergy in Randall Balmer's *A Perfect Babel of Confusion: Dutch Religion and English Culture in the Middle Colonies* (Oxford, 1989), p. 150. For efforts of church goers and merchants in Newport, Rhode Island to "hedge their bets" see Elaine Forman Crane, *A Dependent People; Newport, Rhode Island in the Revolutionary Era* (New York, 1985), pp. 129–140.

12. After the Revolution

1. Jon Butler, *Awash in a Sea of Faith: Christianizing the American People* (Cambridge, Mass., 1990), p. 223; B. R. Mitchell and Phyllis Deane, *Abstract of British Historical Statistics* (Cambridge, 1962), p. 312.
2. Edward Papenfuse, *In Pursuit of Profit* (Baltimore, 1978), p. 184.
3. Blackburn to [Gerardus Beekman, April 8, 1784]. Philip L. White, ed., *The Beekman Mercantile Papers, 1746–1799* (New York, 1956), III:983–984. Blackburn also quickly renewed his trade with John Van Schaak of Albany. Thomas C. Cochran, *New York in the Confederation, an Economic Study* (Philadelphia, 1932), p. 166.
4. Mary Hayley to Christopher Champlin, Feb. 1, 1783. *Commerce of Rhode Island, 1776–1880* (Boston, 1915), II:170.
5. James B. Hedges, *The Browns of Providence Plantations* (Cambridge, Mass., 1952), p. 288.
6. A third partner, Muir, was added. Papenfuse, *In Pursuit of Profit,* p. 108.
7. This is suggested in Wakelyn Welch's letter to Jefferson, Sept. 17, 1784. Julian Boyd, ed., *The Papers of Thomas Jefferson* (Princeton, 1953), VII:422–423.
8. Beverley to Athawes, March 9, 1780. Robert Beverley Letterbook, VHS.
9. Three came in 1785, two more in 1789. James Bowden, *The History of the Society of Friends in America* (London, 1850), p. 374.
10. Bowden, *Society of Friends,* p. 362. London Yearly Meeting, Epistles Sent, V:282–305, 308–311, 320–333, 342–357.
11. W. T. Whitley, ed., *Minutes of the General Assembly of the General Baptist Churches in England* (London, 1909), II:214.
12. Manning to Rev. John Rippon, Aug. 3, 1784. Reuben Aldridge Guild, *Life, Times, and Correspondence of James Manning and the Early History of Brown University* (Boston, 1864), p. 330.

13. Oct. 3, 1783. John Tilford, ed., *The Letters of the Rev. John Wesley* VII (London, 1931), VII:237–239.
14. [John Carroll?] "The Establishment of the Catholic Religion in the United States" (1790), in Thomas O'Brien Hanley, S.J., ed., *The John Carroll Papers,* (Notre Dame, Indiana, 1976), I:407.
15. Manning to Rippon, Aug. 3, 1784. Guild, *Life of Manning,* p. 327.
16. Rush to John King, April 2, 1783. L. H. Butterfield, ed., *Letters of Benjamin Rush, 1761–1792* (Princeton, 1951), I:300.
17. John Maclean, *History of the College of New Jersey* (New York, 1969), I:340.
18. See also Patricia Hollis, ed., *Pressure from without in Early Victorian England* (London, 1974), pp. 27–31.
19. The question of glebes was most heated in Virginia, where the assembly did not end it until 1802; then it began taking glebe lands away from parishes as their ministers died. Rev. Abraham Beach wrote to the Secretary of the S.P.G. on Feb. 8, 1785, complaining that lands given the S.P.G. missionaries by Gov. Wentworth of New Hampshire were being taken over by unauthorized individuals. S.P.G. Journals 24:97–101.

    See also the petition of Loyalist Anglican Clergy in America to the House of Commons. P.R.O. 30/8/220 ff109, 111. For legacies see Revs. Jeremiah Leaming, Charles Inglis, and Benjamin Moore to Archbishop York, May 24, 1783. Francis L. Hawks and William Stevens Perry, eds., *Documentary History of the Protestant Episcopal Church in the United States of America . . . Connecticut* (New York, 1864), pp. 217–219. See also the petition of the Loyal American Clergy of the Church of England (Md., 1787) to the House of Commons, seeking relief since they had lost their freeholds in America. P.R.O. 30/8/220 ff109, 111.
20. Connecticut clergy to S.P.G., July 18, 1783. S.P.G. Journals 27:ff141–144.
21. April 15, 1785. S.P.G. Journals 24:79.
22. James Barr to John Gray and Thomas Blount and Co., Aug. 4, 1783. Alice Barnwell Keith, ed., *The John Gray Blount Papers, 1764–1789* (Raleigh, N.C., 1952), I:74.
23. Beverley to Samuel Gist. Nov. 25, 1784. Beverley Letterbook, VHS.
24. Henry Bromfield to his father, July 23, 1784. Bromfield Letterbook, MHS.
25. Jonathan Jackson to Stephen Higginson, Aug. 10, 1784. Kenneth Wiggins Porter, *The Jacksons and the Lees* (Cambridge, Mass., 1937), I:357.
26. Jefferson to John Adams, Nov. 19, 1785. Julian Boyd, ed., *The Papers of Thomas Jefferson* (Princeton, 1954), IX:41–47.
27. June 5, 1784. Bromfield Letterbook.
28. Higginson to [John Adams?] April 1784, in "Letters of Stephen Higginson," J. Franklin Jameson et al., *Report of the Historical Manuscripts Commission of the American Historical Association* (Washington, 1897), p. 714.
29. Nov. 8, 1783. Printed in Guild, *Life,* pp. 308–310.
30. Hubbard to Rev. S. Peters, March 19, 1784, in Kenneth Walter Cameron, *The Church of England in Pre-Revolutionary Connecticut* (Hartford, Conn., 1976), p. 275.
31. The term is taken from Robert A. East, "The Massachusetts Conservatives

in the Critical Period," in Richard Morris, ed., *The Era of the American Revolution* (New York, 1965), p. 350.

32. Robert Michael Director, "The New York Commercial Community: The Revolutionary Experience" (Ph.D. diss., Pittsburgh University, 1975), pp. 110, 259–261.
33. East, "Massachusetts Conservatives," in Morris, ed., *Era of American Revolution*, p. 350.
34. Thomas M. Doerflinger, *A Vigorous Spirit of Enterprise: Merchants and Economic Development in Revolutionary Philadelphia* (Chapel Hill, 1986), p. 244.
35. Papenfuse, *In Pursuit of Profit*, p. 46. Gary Lawson Browne, *Baltimore in the Nation, 1789–1861* (Chapel Hill, 1980), p. 12, gives the names of a large number of new and dominant families churned up by the war.
36. Benjamin Labaree, *Patriots and Partisans: The Merchants of Newburyport, 1764–1815* (Cambridge, Mass., 1962), p. 84.
37. Mary Badger to Mary Harrod, March 15, 1784, in Robert E. Moody, ed., *The Saltonstall Papers, 1607–1815*, I (1607–1789) (Boston, 1972).
38. Blackburn to Beekman, April 8, 1784; Beekman to Fludger, Hudson, and Streatfield, May 6, 1783; Beekman to Cooke and Ralph, March 6, 1783; Fludger, Maitland and Co. to Beekman, April 6, 1784; Sandeford Streatfield to Beekman, July 3, 1784. White, ed., *Beekman Mercantile Papers*, III:983–984, 1017, 993, 1019, 1020.
39. Katherine A. Kellock, "London Merchants and the pre-1776 American Debts," *Guildhall Studies in London History* (Oct. 1974), I:134.
40. Ibid., pp. 121–122.
41. Memorial of the Merchants Trading to and Interested in the Commerce of the Province of Quebec, March 15, 1791. P.R.O. 30/8/221 ff9–11.
42. Printed circular, n.d. P.R.O. 30/8/344 ff56–57.
43. Wakelyn Welch to Thomas Jefferson, Sept. 17, 1784. Boyd, ed., *The Papers of Thomas Jefferson*, pp. 422–423.
44. Frances Norton Mason, ed., *John Norton and Sons, Merchants of London and Virginia* (Richmond, 1937), p. xv.
45. Petition of London Merchants to Lord Carmarthen, Sept. 23, 1786. P.R.O. 30/8/220 ff134–135.
46. Molleson to Pitt, Nov. 11, 1791 and Dec. 20, 1793. P.R.O. 30/8/160 ff136–137, 140. Kellock, "London Merchants," pp. 119–120, 134–135, 137–139.
47. For the efforts of one state's church to function during the war see Richard W. Pointer, *Protestant Pluralism and the New York Experience; A Study of Eighteenth-Century Religious Diversity* (Bloomington, Ind. 1988), pp. 90–102.
48. Diblee to Rev. S. Peters, May 3, 1785. Cameron, *Church of England*, p. 225. Another missionary wrote the Secretary that he was losing some members to Presbyterian ideas, and "I have, moreover, had to encounter for three years past with the enthusiastic notions of Ignorant Methodists and Anabaptists." Rev. Tingley to Secretary, March 5, 1782. William Stevens Perry, ed., *Historical Collections Relating to the American Colonial Church* (Delaware, 1878), V:134–135.

49. The subject was mentioned in his letters to the Society, Oct. 7, 1785 and April 4, 1786. S.P.G. Journals 24:ff337–341.

50. April 15, 1785, S.P.G. Journals 24:f82. For Anglicans the chief issue raised by the Revolution was whether they could omit the King from their prayers, as required by Congress, and still maintain the ceremony of the Church of England. The clerical conventions that were able to meet in the first year of the Revolution took different stands in different colonies, but wherever a majority advocated taking a firm position for or against the omision, the minority disagreed, and when conventions decided to allow individual ministers to use their own discretion, the choices went different ways. A majority of Virginia clergy voted to omit the King from prayers while continuing the rest of the service, but a quarter of the members disagreed and ultimately shut down their churches rather than comply. In Connecticut, however, the overwhelming majority of Anglican ministers voted that after the Declaration of Independence they could not "go on as usual in the performance of Divine Service in our churches." (Rev. Abraham Beach of Hartford continued to do so anyway.) In Massachusetts, where it was impossible to hold a meeting because so many ministers were cut off or forced out, Rev. William Clark stayed comfortably in Dedham throughout the war. Rev. Edward Basse of Newburyport stayed on as a Patriot and in 1781 could cheerfully write that "our church increases much in credit and reputation." Elsewhere, recognizing the variety of circumstances and sentiments of individual members, Anglican conventions agreed to allow ministers to act "agreeably to their consciences." Some then fled, some omitted prayers for the royal family, some continued to pray for the King and counted on the support of local "gentlemen of influence and authority" or the British army, if it was present.

Philip Reading to Dr. Hind, Aug. 25, 1776. William Stevens Perry, ed. *Papers Relating to the History of the Church in Pennsylvania, A.D. 1680–1778* (n.p., 1871), p. 486; Rev. Charles Inglis, "State of the Anglo-American Church" Oct. 31, 1776. *Eccl. Records, N.Y.,* VI:293; Convention of the Clergy, July 23, 1776, Cameron, *Church of England,* p. 200; Rev. Clark to Dr. Hind, Jan. 5, 1778; Edw. Bass to Dr. Hind, Oct. 30, 1781; S.P.G. Letters from Massachusetts, 1757 to 1784, 22:84, 308; Rev. Henry Caner wrote from Boston on July 15, 1775, for example, that "Mr. Sargent is concealed in some back Town in New Hampshire and Mr. Weeks is escaped with his family to Kennebec River . . . Mr. Wiswall remains in this town . . . but all his effects are seized by the rebels . . . Mr. Bass has complied perhaps too far, with the Orders of the Rebels," ibid., p. 262. In Philadelphia, where the British Army was present from 1777 to 1779, three-fifths of the clergy were loyalist. Deborah M. Gough, "Pluralism, Politics and Power Struggles: The Church of England in Colonial Philadelphia, 1695 to 1789" (Ph.D. diss., University of Pennsylvania, 1978).

51. Quakers were 20 percent of the New Jersey population but 36.4 percent of the Loyalists. See Dennis Patrick Ryan, "Six Towns: Continuity and Change in Revolutionary New Jersey" (Ph.D. diss., New York University, 1974), pp. 106, 165, 194, 242, 302. The Quaker plight in Pennsylvania and the government's attitude are indicated in John Hancock to William Livingston,

Aug. 30, 1777, and Richard Henry Lee to Patrick Henry, Oct. 8, 1777, in Paul H. Smith, ed., *Letters of Members of the Continental Congress* (Washington, D.C., 1981) VII:572–574, 637. In fact, while Quakers had constituted 40 percent of the participants in Philadelphia nonimportation associations of the 1760s before the yearly meeting had recommended against participation in the protest movements, they still constituted 26 percent of the Patriots even after the yearly meeting had taken its stand against participating in the Revolution. In 1781 a number of the patriot Quakers, particularly those who had been disowned, formed the Free Quaker Society, so at war's end the Quakers were divided not only in sentiment but also in organization. Richard Bauman, *For the Reputation of Truth: Politics, Religion, and Conflict Among the Pennsylvania Quakers, 1750–1800* (Baltimore, 1971), pp. 165–166; Oaks, "Philadelphia Merchants," p. 207.

52. Hubbard to Rev. S. Peters, Jan. 21, 1784. Cameron, *Church of England,* p. 275. See also Bauman, *For the Reputation of Truth,* pp. 166–167; William G. McLoughlin, *New England Dissent, 1630–1873; The Baptists and the Separation of Church and State* (Cambridge, Mass. 1971), I:578. July 16, 1776, Franklin Bowditch Dexter, ed., *The Literary Diary of Ezra Stiles, D.D., L.L.D, President of Yate College* (New York, 1901), II:23; "The State of the Anglo-American Church," Oct. 31, 1776, in *Eccl. Records, N.Y.,* VI:293. See also North Carolina Delegates to the Presbyterian Ministers of Philadelphia [July 3–8] 1775. *Letters of Delegates to Congress,* p. 575, esp. n 1, and Joseph Hives to Samuel Johnston, July 8, 1775, p. 613.

53. Oct. 14, 1783 and Jan. 20 and 25, 1785. *Diary of Ezra Stiles,* III:96, 147, 148. In this case the figures are not as startling as they are for other churches because the Congregationalists usually averaged about one-fourth of their pulpits vacant.

54. Minutes of [Philadelphia ?] Synod, May 21, 1785. *Presb. Records,* p. 511. See also Barbara C. Wingo, "Politics, Society, and Religion: The Presbyterian Clergy of Pennsylvania, New Jersey, and New York and the Formation of the Nation" (Ph.D. diss., Tulane University, 1976), pp. 299–300.

55. *Minutes and Letters of the Coetus of the German Reformed Congregations, in Pennsylvania, 1747–1792* (Philadelphia, 1903); pp. 372–373. Pointer, *Protestant Pluralism,* p. 107.

56. James Barr to John Gray and Thomas Blount and Co., Aug 4, 1783. Alice Barnwell Keith, ed., *The John Gray Blount Papers, 1764–1789* (Raleigh, 1952), I:74.

57. Edmund Pendleton to James Madison, June 9, 1783. David John Mays, ed., *The Letters and Papers of Edmund Pendleton, 1734–1803* (Charlottesville, 1967), II:50.

58. For a general discussion of the new merchants in Virginia see Myra Lakoff Rich, "The Experimental Years: Virginia, 1781–1789" (Ph.D. diss., Yale University, 1966), p. 57.

59. Edward Papenfuse, "Mercantile Opportunity and Urban Development in a Planting Society: A Case Study of Annapolis, Maryland, 1763–1805" (Ph.D. diss., Johns Hopkins University, 1973), p. 214–216.

60. Mary Hayley to Christopher Champlin, May 22, 1783, *Commerce of Rhode*

Island, II:177. Thomas Doerflinger has referred to the "temporary inter-penetration of the British and American commercial communities," *Vigorous Spirit of Enterprise,* p. 245.

61. *The Boston Gazette,* April 18, 1785.

62. J. Beekman to John Ralph, Nov. 29, 1785. *Beekman Mercantile Papers,* III:1000.

63. George W. Corner, ed., *The Autobiography of Benjamin Rush* (Princeton, 1948), p. 160. For a discussion of the movement of English merchants to Philadelphia, see Thomas Doerflinger, "Philadelphia Merchants and the Logic of Moderation, 1760–1775," *W.M.Q.,* 3rd ser. 40 (April 1983):199–200.

64. Burnett, ed., *Letters of Members of the Continental Congress,* VIII:107–108, n4.

65. Circular letter enclosed in Henry Martin's letter to Jefferson, Nov. 15, 1784. *Jefferson Papers* VII:525–527.

66. Thomas Blount to John Gray Blount and Thomas Blount, Sr., Sept. 26, 1785. *John Gray Blount Papers,* p. 219.

67. Pendleton to Richard Henry Lee, June 13, 1785. *The Letters and Papers of Edmund Pendleton,* II:480.

68. Justin Windsor, ed., *The Memorial History of Boston* (Boston, 1881), IV:200.

69. Herbert and Potts to John Hatley Norton, Dec. 17, 1784. *John Norton and Sons,* p. 469.

70. Thomas Blount to John Gray Blount, Oct. 18, 1785 *John Gray Blount Papers,* p. 260.

71. Beverley to Athawes, March 9, 1780; to Samuel Gist, August 8, Sept. 19, 1783, April 14, 1784; to William Anderson and Co., July 8, 1790, May 12, 1791; Beverley and Ralph Wormley to Nathanial Anderson, Sept. 24, 1791; Beverley to James Dunlap [Oct. 16–26, 1791]; to Thomas Hepburn, Jan. 16, 1792; to Anderson and Co., Feb. 20 and May 19, 1792. Robert Beverley Letterbook, VHS.

72. Synod of New York and New Jersey to Classis of Amsterdam, Oct. 8, 1784. *Eccl. Records, N.Y.,* VI:4323–24.

73. As early as March 1783 eighteen Anglican ministers had met in New York City to frame an appeal to the Anglican hierarchy in England for a bishop. Wallace N. Jameson, *Religion in New Jersey: A Brief History* (Princeton, 1964), p. 71. William Warren Sweet, *Religion in the Development of American Culture, 1765–1840* (New York, 1952), pp. 68–75, gives a succinct discussion of the early Episcopal organizations. The address from the Deputies to the archbishops and bishops of England, Oct. 5, 1785, is in P.R.O. 30/8/343 ff84–85. The archbishops and bishops were hesitant at first, partly because the Americans had made some liturgical changes and partly because they were not sure they could convince the Prime Minister that American opposition to bishops had vanished. When the American convention revised the liturgy and American statesmen (led by John Adams) convinced the Prime Minister that once bishops were dissociated from imperial authority they would be acceptable to the American people, Parliament authorized

the ordination and the two American priests became bishops in February 1787. Archbishop and Bishops to Deputies Feb. 24, 1786, ibid., ff90–1; Archbishop of Canterbury to John Adams, Feb. 27, 1786, Adams Family Papers, Library of Congress. *Journals of the General Conventions of the Protestant Episcopal Church*, I:51–62; *Eccl. Records, N.Y.*, VI:4326.

74. Sweet, *Religion in American Culture*, p. 66. Wesley later (Sept. 20, 1788) wrote Francis Asbury, the first Methodist Bishop, "How can you, how dare you suffer yourself to be called Bishop? I shudder at the very thought." Elmer T. Clark, ed., *The Journal and Letters of Francis Asbury*, (London, 1958), III:65.

75. John Carroll to Ferdinand Farmer [Dec. 1784], in Thomas O'Brien Hanley, S.J., ed., *The John Carroll Papers* (Notre Dame, 1967), I:155–158.

76. "An Address from the Roman Catholics of America to George Washington" [London, 1790], in *Carroll Papers*, I:409. Donald Jackson and Dorothy Twohig, eds., *The Diaries of George Washington* (Charlottesville, 1979) VI:537–538; John C. Fitzpatrick, ed., *The Writings of George Washington from the Virginia Manuscript Sources, 1745–1799* (Washington, D.C. 1939), XXX:239, 321, 336, 339, 347, 383, 416, 432.

77. "Address . . . to George Washington," *John Carroll Letters*, p. 409.

78. See Jameson, *Religion in New Jersey*, pp. 82–83. Preliminary organizational efforts are reflected in Synod minutes of May 19, 1786 and May 29, 1788. *Presb. Records*, pp. 518–21, 547.

79. James Thayer Addison. *The Episcopal Church in the United States, 1789–1931* (New York, 1969, reprint of 1951 ed.), pp. 60–61. The conventions corresponded with the church in England until 1892.

80. Sweet, *Religion in American Culture*, p. 81.

81. In 1786 the general committee of the Virginia Baptist Association received letters from Baptist ministers in Massachusetts proposing a correspondence. The Virginia Committee welcomed the proposal, hoping it would lead to the creation of a national meeting, but this never occurred. Robert B. Semple, *A History of the Rise and Progress of the Baptists in Virginia* (Richmond, 1894), p. 103.

82. Sweet, *Religion in American Culture*, p. 80.

83. The background to Livingston's remarks is in ibid., p. 80.

84. Rush's advice is mentioned in Varnum Lansing Collins, *President Witherspoon* (New York, 1969, reprint of 1925 ed.) p. 140.

85. Collins, *President Witherspoon*, pp. 140–142. John Maclean, *History of the College of New Jersey, 1746–1854* (New York, 1969), I:340.

86. Caleb Evans to Pres. Manning, Jan. 26, 1788. Guild, *Life of Manning*, pp. 340–2.

87. Dr. Thomas Bradbury Chandler to Society, July 30, 1786. S.P.G. Journals, 24:322–323. The Society's decision was made April 15, 1785 (ibid., p. 82). On April 25, 1786, the New England Company also decided it could not support missionaries anywhere outside British dominion. Kellaway, *New England Company*, pp. 279–280. The last record of communication between the General Convention of the American Episcopal Church and the

Convocation of English Bishops and Archbishops was Sept. 19, 1792. Perry, ed. *Journals of the General Convention of the Protestant Episcopal Church*, I:167.

88. Bowden, *Society of Friends in America*, I:374–375.

Index

Abercromby, James, 101
Acts, English: against tumultuous petition-
ing, 36; restraining N.E. trade, 147;
uniformity, 21. *See also* Bubble Act,
Clarendon Code, Coercive Acts, Gin
Act, Hat Act, Townshend Duties, White
Pines Act
Adams, John, 169
Admiralty, 68
Agents, N.E., 47
Albany, N.Y., merchants, 73
Alison, Frances, 113
American bishops, proposal, 134, 158
Amory, John, 173
Amsterdam Coffee House, 97
Anabaptists, 42
Anderson, Mr., 183
Andros, Gov. Edmund, 48
Annapolis merchants, 173, 179
Annual Register, 147
Anti-American petition, 157
Anti-immigration riots, 5
Antillon, 160
Archbishops of Canterbury: American
connections, 71, 88, 116; influence, 29,
99, 139–41; Secker, 123; Sheldon, 30,
34
Archbishop of York, 88
Asbury, Rev. Francis, 186
Ascriptive interests, 2; proprietary rela-
tives, 13
Ashurst, Sir Henry, 49, 65, 83
Ashurst, William, 54

Assemblies, colonial, 13, 117, 155, 160–
62
Associational interests, 2
Avery, Dr. Benjamin, 101, 137, 139

Backus, Rev. Isaac, 113
Baker, Samuel, 78
Baker, William, 103, 119, 137, 140–41;
William or Samuel, 90
Bakers, 41
Baptists, English, 3, 7, 96–97, 176; gen-
eral, 22, 31, 52; particular, 22, 31;
West County, 38
Baptists, American, 111–12, 121, 169–70,
186; Massachusetts, 41–42, 63, 117,
159, 169; New England (Warren Asso-
ciation), 163, 169, 176; New York, 43
Barclay, David, 101, 152
Barnard, John, 137
Barr, James, 177
Barrington, Lord, 54
Baxter, Richard, 23–24
Bayard, Nicholas, 71, 79
Bickford, William, 137
Beekman, Gerardus, 179
Belcher, Jonathan, 126, 130
Belcher, Jonathan Jr., 132
Bellomont, Gov., 72, 77–79
Berkeley, Gov. William, 20
Beverley, Robert, 80, 175, 177, 183–84
Biddle, Edward, 168
Bill of Rights Society, 136, 146, 155, 165
Bishop of Bangor, 128